ALSO BY VICTOR DAVIS HANSON

Warfare and Agriculture in Classical Greece

The Western Way of War: Infantry Battle in Classical Greece

Hoplites: The Ancient Greek Battle Experience (*editor*)

The Other Greeks: The Agrarian Roots of Western Civilization

Fields Without Dreams: Defending the Agrarian Idea

Who Killed Homer? The Demise of Classical Education
and the Recovery of Greek Wisdom (*with John Heath*)

The Wars of the Ancient Greeks

The Soul of Battle: From Ancient Times to the Present Day—
How Three Great Liberators Vanquished Tyranny

The Land Was Everything: Letters from an American Farmer

Bonfire of the Humanities (*with John Heath and Bruce Thornton*)

Carnage and Culture:
Landmark Battles in the Rise of Western Power

An Autumn of War

Mexifornia: A State of Becoming

Between War and Peace

Ripples of Battle: How Wars of the Past Still Determine
How We Fight, How We Live, and How We Think

A WAR LIKE NO OTHER

A WAR LIKE NO OTHER

HOW THE ATHENIANS AND SPARTANS
FOUGHT THE PELOPONNESIAN WAR

VICTOR DAVIS HANSON

RANDOM HOUSE
New York

Published in the United States by Random House, an imprint of
The Random House Publishing Group, a division of
Random House, Inc., New York.

RANDOM HOUSE and colophon are registered trademarks of
Random House, Inc.

LIBRARY OF CONGRESS CATALOGING-IN-PUBLICATION DATA

Hanson, Victor Davis.
A war like no other: how the Athenians and Spartans
fought the Peloponnesian War / Victor Davis Hanson.
p.   cm.
Includes index.
ISBN 1-4000-6095-8
1. Greece—History—Peloponnesian War, 431–404 B.C. I. Title.
DF229.H36 2005   938'.05—dc22   2004062892

www.atrandom.com

Printed in the United States of America on acid-free paper

1 2 3 4 5 6 7 8 9

First Edition

Book design by Simon M. Sullivan

Professors John Heath and Bruce Thornton—
friends and classicists of a quarter century

CONTENTS

List of Maps · xi

Prologue · xiii

CHAPTER 1. FEAR
Why Sparta Fought Athens (480–431) · 3

CHAPTER 2. FIRE
The War Against the Land (431–425) · 35

CHAPTER 3. DISEASE
The Ravages of the Plague at Athens (430–426) · 65

CHAPTER 4. TERROR
War in the Shadows (431–421) · 89

CHAPTER 5. ARMOR
Hoplite Pitched Battles (424–418) · 123

CHAPTER 6. WALLS
Sieges (431–415) · 163

CHAPTER 7. HORSES
The Disaster at Sicily (415–413) · 201

CHAPTER 8. SHIPS
The War at Sea (431–404) · 235

CHAPTER 9. CLIMAX
Trireme Fighting in the Aegean (411–405) · 271

CHAPTER 10. RUIN?
Winners and Losers (404–403) · 289

Appendix I: Glossary of Terms and Places · 315

Appendix II: Key People · 319

Notes · 323

Works Cited · 381

Index · 387

LIST OF MAPS

The Spartan and Athenian Empires
The Peloponnesian League and Other Spartan Allies · 21

The Spartan and Athenian Empires
The Athenian Subject States and Allies · 28

Invading Attica · 51

Athens and Environs · 69

The Coast of the Peloponnese · 95

Battles and Sieges of the Peloponnesian War · 181

The Athenians Attack Syracuse, 414 · 215

Final Military Operations, Winter of 415–414 · 222

Naval Battles in the Aegean · 279

PROLOGUE

IN APRIL 404 B.C. the Spartan admiral Lysander finally led his vast armada of ships, crammed with some 30,000 jubilant seamen, into the hated port of Athens at the Piraeus to finish the Peloponnesian War. After the destruction of its imperial fleet at the battle of Aegospotami ("Goat Rivers") in the waters off Asia Minor the prior September, the once splendid city of Athens was now utterly defenseless. Worse still was to come. It was soon surrounded, broke, jammed with refugees, starving, and near revolution. Such an end would have seemed utterly inconceivable just three decades earlier when a defiant Pericles promised his democracy victory. But then neither had 80,000 Athenians fallen to plague nor 500 ships been sunk at Sicily and on the Aegean.

Two Spartan kings, Agis and Pausanias, had encamped outside the walls of the city in command of thousands of tough infantrymen of the Peloponnese, the large peninsula south of the Isthmus at Corinth that makes up the southern part of Greece. The people of Athens were still for a time safe behind massive walls, but tens of thousands of refugees inside were cut off from both homegrown and imported food—and waiting for the end. Gone was the old lifeline of imperial tribute by land and sea. To end this growing general famine, Athens finally gave up, agreeing to dismantle most of what little was left of its once renowned fleet, famed fortifications, and vaunted democracy. Thousands of citizens were thus entirely at the mercy of Spartan clemency; perhaps 100,000 residents congregated in the streets, terrified that they might suffer the same fate they had once meted out to so many other Greeks throughout the Aegean.

The conquering Lysander wasted little time in carrying out the terms of the capitulation, most poignantly destroying most of the Long Walls—two parallel fortified lines extending over four miles from Athens to its port at the Piraeus, and symbolizing Athenian democracy's commitment to seapower and a maritime empire: "The Peloponnesians with great zeal pulled down the Long Walls to the music of flute-girls, thinking that this day was the beginning of freedom for the Greeks."* Liberation was what the Spartans had once promised the Greeks, when so long ago at the outbreak of war they had warned the Athenians, as Thucydides put it, "to give the Greeks their autonomy." And now these parochial warriors seemed to have proved good on their word. The Spartan occupation thus ended over twenty-seven years of conflict with the utter defeat and humiliation of Periclean Athens. How did such an unbelievable thing come to pass?[1]

This book does not answer that question through a strategic account of the conflict's various campaigns. Much less is it a political study of the reasons that caused the Spartans to fight against Athens. Fine narratives in English by George Grote, George Grundy, B. W. Henderson, Donald Kagan, John Lazenby, Anton Powell, Geoffrey de Ste. Croix, and others cover those topics. So there is no need for another traditional history of the Peloponnesian War.

Instead, *how* did the Athenians battle the Spartans on land, in the cities, at sea, and out in the Greek countryside? What was it like for those who killed and died in this horrific war, this nightmare about which there has been little written of how many Greeks fought, how many perished, or even how all of it was conducted? My aim, therefore, after a brief introduction to the general events of the Peloponnesian War, is to flesh out this three-decade fight of some twenty-four hundred years past as something very human and thus to allow the war to become more than a far-off struggle of a distant age.

From the strange label "Peloponnesian War," who imagines bloody civil strife? Most envision instead something akin to the "Persian Wars," "Macedonian Wars," or "Dacian Wars," all tough ancient conflicts that were waged against foreign peoples. But the vast majority of lives lost between 431 and 404 were Greek. The money consumed, the towns sacked, the fields ravaged—these disasters were also mostly Greek. This ancient civil conflict today is called the "Peloponnesian War" since Westerners are in some respects Athenocentric. Everyone equates Athens with Greece. And while moderns are familiar with Sparta, they hear almost nothing of states such as Corinth, Syracuse, or Thebes, Athens' other formidable enemies, who collectively knew the three-decade-long fight quite differently, as the "Athenian War" to destroy the democracy and its empire.

Most later writers, both ancient and modern, have adopted Pericles' view of

---

*All unattributed quotes in the text are from Thucydides' *The Peloponnesian War*.

a "war against the Peloponnesians," its history most famously written by the Athenian Thucydides. Yet in regard to the actual nature of the fighting, the Peloponnesian "War" was not really directed just against the Peloponnesians in open conflict but involved almost everyone in the Greek-speaking world—and many beyond it from Thrace to Persia. The struggle much more resembles the seemingly endless killing in Northern Ireland, the French and American quagmires in Vietnam, the endless chaos of the Middle East, or the Balkan crises of the 1990s rather than the more conventional battles of World War II with clear-cut enemies, theaters, fronts, and outcomes.

A better name for our subject, perhaps, would be something like "the Great Ancient Greek Civil War." Athens and Sparta and their respective allies were, except for the final entrance of Persian financiers, all Greek speakers who worshipped the same gods and farmed and fought in the same manner. Although there was never a successful Panhellenic nation, Greeks of the city-states still felt themselves to be a single people. Their twenty-seven-year strife, in terms of the percentages of the population who fought and died, was one of the most horrific civil wars in early recorded history—conventional battles, terrorism, revolutions, assassinations, and mass murder all unfolding at once among a baffling array of shifting allies and enemies.

In this focus on the battle experience, there is a Thucydidean pedigree to be found. Far from his history being a yearly and comprehensive account of all the events of the war, as he seems to purport, Thucydides (c. 460–395), our chief source of knowledge about the Peloponnesian War, instead offers up exemplary snapshots that ground his entire narrative in the human experience of killing.

For instance, his detailed account of the siege of the tiny town of Plataea allows it to become a template of *all* sieges in the history, which subsequently warrant only passing mention. In a similar manner Pericles' first funeral oration is recorded in full—a Lincolnesque occasion to summarize the essence of Athens. But the other twenty-something Athenian eulogies are never mentioned. The madcap killing on the island of Corcyra is emblematic of ubiquitous later civil strife; the details of the battle of Mantinea serve as a guide to the infantry engagements earlier at Delium and later on Sicily. There were five mass evacuations from Attica between 431 and 425; only the first is described in any detail.

Thucydides offers dozens of poignant illustrative scenes of desperate men and women on ramparts, spear thrusting, and warship ramming at sea. So he was certainly not the dry realist and compiler of exhaustive detail as is sometimes believed but, rather, a humanist and a storyteller who never forgot that people, not inanimate political and economic forces, were the real stuff of his history. This story of how thousands of Greeks fought and died, then, is mostly distilled from and in the spirit of his own history.

Nevertheless, by describing this war in such a different manner, I have less opportunity for chronological continuity or even to reflect larger ongoing political and strategic thinking behind the war. The Spartans cut down olive trees in the first and last years of the war; Athens was conducting seaborne raids both in 431 and in 405. A siege started the war, and Athens quit under a Spartan blockade. Or as Thucydides put it, sieges, ethnic cleansing, mass killing, battles, droughts, famines, and plague "all fell upon the people simultaneously with this war."[2]

This book's chapters are for the most part organized not by annual events but by the experience of battle: "fire" (the ravaging of the land), "disease" (plague), "terror" (coups and irregular fighting), "armor" (hoplite warfare), "walls" (sieges), "horses" (the Sicilian expedition), and "ships" (trireme fighting). These chapter themes are also interwoven with a loose ongoing narrative of the war, again with the understanding that each chapter draws on illustrations taken from the entire twenty-seven-year conflict.

No other struggle can provide such military lessons for the present as the Peloponnesian War. Of course, it was a Balkans-type mess—but also a conflict involving two great superpowers, as well as a war of terror, of dirty fighting in a Hellenic Third World, of forcing democracy down the throats of sometimes unwilling states, and of domestic and cultural upheavals at home brought on by frustrations of fighting abroad. Former secretary of state George Marshall, critics of Vietnam, and contemporary opponents and supporters alike of the so-called war on terror have all looked back to find their own Thucydides and learn from the people who fought that most awful war so long ago.

At times I have drawn on personal experience both with farming and with the modern Greek landscape, offering as well comparisons with battles of other times and ages, including those from our own era. Such straying from the strict protocols of classical scholarship may bother professional historians, but readers will appreciate these often-brutal reminders that men and women of the past were not so different from us after all. There is a commonality to war, it being entirely human, that transcends time and space. Sometimes we can learn about the distant past by evoking subsequent wars in which soldiers were often confronted with the same fears and motivations, their officers struggling likewise with age-old dilemmas of strategy, logistics, and tactics.

All dates are understood as B.C. unless otherwise identified. To avoid confusion, common Latinized forms of well-known Greek names and places are used whenever possible. Some other terms are transliterated directly from the Greek when such spellings better reflect how those words were probably pronounced and are now more commonly known to modern English readers.

References to the history of Thucydides are cited by his book and section number only; ancient historians (such as Diodorus, Herodotus, or Polybius) are referred to by name alone, if they are the authors of only one titled work. Translations from Greek and Latin are my own, though in cases of difficult passages I am also in debt to the work of others. Works listed in the endnotes are found in the Works Cited section as a guide to further studies, and to acknowledge ideas and thoughts drawn from others from over a century of classical scholarship. Glossaries of notable people and terms are provided at the back of the book for easy reference to the baffling array of Greek names and usage. A time line of events of the war concludes the first chapter. Some of the description of the battle of Delium in chapter 5 is adapted from an earlier article I published in the *Military History Quarterly*.

Robert Loomis of Random House, along with my literary agents, Glen Hartley and Lynn Chu, strongly supported my proposal for a new account of the fighting between Sparta and Athens, and likewise believed that modern readers would still be interested in learning how wars of the distant past were won or lost. I thank all three for the genesis of this book—and again Robert Loomis for a great deal of editing after the manuscript was submitted. My wife, Cara, who read the entire manuscript, and our daughter Pauli helped with the preparation of the text. Cara also compiled a number of statistics about losses in the Ionian War that proved invaluable. Along with William and Susannah, our two other children, they aided with chores on our farm that allowed me to write this book.

As always, my two close friends Professors John Heath and Bruce Thornton read the manuscript and saved me from a number of errors. Donald Kagan's various books on ancient war and its influence in the modern world have been a great source of inspiration. I owe gratitude also to Barry Strauss and Paul Cartledge, whose work on the early fourth century remains a foundation for all attempts at assessing postwar Athens. Honora Chapman, my other former colleague in classics at California State University, Fresno, also read a draft in manuscript form and offered additional valuable ideas. Evan Pivonka, a classics graduate of Santa Clara University, helped with cross-checking ancient Greek and Roman citations. Sabina Robinson, a graduate student in classics at Princeton University and the University of Copenhagen, compiled figures on Peloponnesian War battle fatalities from ancient texts. Cynthia Oliphant offered assistance in researching the maps.

The Hoover Institution at Stanford University, where I am now a senior fellow, provided a grant to help with preparation of the manuscript. I thank its director, John Raisian, for his continued kindness—and especially Martin and Illie Anderson, the Field Foundation, and the Stuart Family Foundation for support that made my appointment at the institution possible. In addition, Larry Arnn, president of Hillsdale College, kindly extended to me a month's teaching tenure in September 2004, as an annual fellow of the school, and it was in those pleasant circumstances at Hillsdale College where the last page of the book was written.

VDH
September 25, 2004

A WAR LIKE NO OTHER

CHAPTER 1

FEAR

WHY SPARTA FOUGHT ATHENS (480–431)

Our Peloponnesian War

THE PELOPONNESIAN WAR is now 2,436 years in the past. Yet Athens and Sparta are still on our minds and will not go away. Their permanence seems odd. After all, ancient Greek warring parties were mere city-states, most of them smaller in population and size than Dayton, Ohio, or Trenton, New Jersey. Mainland Greece itself is no larger than Alabama, and in antiquity was bordered by empires like the Persian, which encompassed nearly one million square miles with perhaps 70 million subjects. Napoleon's army alone had more men under arms by 1800 than the entire male population of all the Greek city-states combined. In our own age, more people died in Rwanda or Cambodia in a few days than were lost in twenty-seven years of civil war in fifth-century B.C. Greece.

Nor were Greeks themselves especially lethal warriors, at least by later historical standards. Rudimentary wood and iron of the preindustrial age, not gunpowder and steel, were their shared weapons of destruction. Even the soldiers themselves who fought the war were not much more than five foot five and 130 pounds. They were often unimpressive middle-aged men who would appear as mere children next to contemporary towering two-hundred-pound GIs.

Yet for ancient folk so few, small, and distant, their struggle during the Peloponnesian War seems not so old even in this new millennium. During the weeks after September 11, 2001, for example, Americans suddenly worried about the wartime outbreak of disease in their cities. In October and November 2001, five died and some twenty-four others were infected from the apparently deliberate introduction of anthrax spores by unknown terrorists. During the spring of 2003 a mysterious infectious respiratory ailment in China threatened to spread worldwide, given the ubiquity of low-cost transcontinental airfare. The panic that ensued in Washington and Peking during a time of global tension evoked ancient wartime plagues, such as the mysterious scourge that wiped out thousands at Athens between 430 and 426. Similarly, at about the same time, Sicily, Melos, and Mycalessus were all cited in contemporary media, as millennia later the world once again watched military armadas head out to faraway places, saw democracy imposed by force, and read of schoolchildren killed by terrorist bands.

But even before September 11 the Peloponnesian War was not really ancient history. Scholarly books regularly appeared with titles like *War and Democracy: A Comparative Study of the Korean War and the Peloponnesian War*, or *Hegemonic Rivalry: From Thucydides to the Nuclear Age*. Thucydides had long been assigned reading at the U.S. Army War College. And an array of statesmen such as Woodrow Wilson, Georges Clemenceau, and Eleuthérios Venizélos either taught or wrote about Greek history, in which the use of Thucydides' war loomed large. More recently, controversial thinkers known as neoconservatives ("the new conservatives") were for a time influential in American strategic thinking, and the text that they purportedly consulted frequently was once more Thucydides'.[1]

What is it about this particular ancient clash that causes it to be called to mind during our present wars? Why were the conflict's supposed lessons both astutely and clumsily applied to most of our own struggles of the last century? Russia—or was it really Hitler's Germany?—supposedly resembled oligarchic Sparta in its efforts to destroy a democratic, seafaring America. Did not the Cold War, after all, similarly divide up the world into two armed leagues, led by superpowers who had united for a time against the common enemy only later to face off for decades of bipolar hostilities? Was the Sicilian expedition a precursor to Gallipoli, Vietnam, or any proposed great democratic or imperial crusade abroad? Or does the disaster at Syracuse show, as Thucydides oddly concluded, what happens when folks at home do not support the troops abroad? Because Thucydides first framed the important issues that haunt us still, we naturally return to his original and seemingly unimpeachable conclusions.

The Sorrows of War

WHY EXACTLY IS this rather obscure ancient war between minuscule Athens and Sparta still so alive, and used and abused in ways that other ancient conflicts, such as the Persian Wars (490, 480–79) and Alexander the Great's conquests (334–323), are not? Many intriguing reasons come to mind.

First, it was a brutal and very long struggle. King Xerxes and his enormous Persian military were routed from Greece in about two years. Alexander destroyed the later Persian Empire in a third of the time it took Sparta to defeat Athens. Lasting twenty-seven years, or almost a third of the fabled fifth century of classical Greece, the Peloponnesian War, like the Second Punic War, the Thirty Years War, or the Hundred Years War, was a mess that eerily crossed generations. Those born after the first years of the war often fought and died in the fighting before it was over.

So the catastrophe devoured entire families across generations. The carnage reminds us of imperial Britain tottering after the First World War, the end of empire, aristocracy, and unquestioned patriotism all inextricably tied to trenches that gobbled up the British elite. The Peloponnesian War spared few Greeks, regardless of wealth or family connections. The "great houses" of Athens, or so the postbellum lament went, were almost wiped out.[2]

Take the most famous branch of the exalted Alcmaeonid family. Pericles, the spiritual and political leader of Athens, died of the plague at Athens in 429 in only the third season of the war. His sister, also in her sixties, had perished a year before from the same epidemic, along with his sons Paralus and Xanthippus. Neither of those young men reached thirty.

Later, a much younger bastard son, Pericles the Younger, was elected an Athenian general. He was in part responsible for the great sea victory at Arginusae, some twenty-three years after his father's death. Yet the younger Pericles was subsequently executed by an Athenian jury in an infamous scapegoating frenzy during the battle's aftermath. And Pericles' nephew, the thirty-two-year-old bright and upcoming Hippocrates, fell at the forefront of the battle of Delium (424). Thirty years' worth of plague, political intrigue, general hysteria, and enemy spears more or less wiped out the family of the most powerful man at Athens.

The war also started at the high-water mark of Greece's great Golden Age (479–404). Yet the attendant calamity ended for good such great promise that started with the defeat of the Persians (479). The capitulation of Athens (404) and the end of the fifth-century Golden Age remain symbolically interconnected events to this day. They are also loosely associated as well with the near-contemporaneous trial and execution of Socrates (399), the last and greatest casualty of a once wonderful world seemingly gone mad in a few decades. Contemporaries, among them the comic poet Aristophanes, believed that with the end of the Peloponnesian War, Attic tragedy as emblemized by Aeschylus, Sophocles, and Euripides had lost its splendor.

Indeed, players in and observers of the war were the greats of Hellenic civilization—Alcibiades, Aristophanes, Euripides, Pericles, Socrates, Sophocles, Thucydides, and others—many of whom flourished, were discredited, or perished because of their involvement in the fighting. Much of the greatest classical literature, such as Aristophanes' *Acharnians,* Euripides' *The Trojan Women,* Plato's *Symposium,* and Sophocles' *Oedipus the King,* either deals with issues of the war or employs the conflict as dramatic landscape, leaving with us the depressing possibility that war, not peace, prompted the greatest explosion in the Greek creative genius, a frenzied outburst before a weary collapse. Most Greeks saw the bloody struggle through the eyes of Athens, whose writers enjoyed a near monopoly on reporting, praising, and condemning the war—shocked that in just three decades the entire dream of a cultural renaissance was brought to an end. So north of the Isthmus of Corinth the fight was soon known universally as the "Peloponnesian War," the conflict against those awful supermen who inhabited the southern peninsula of Greece—not, as the parochial Peloponnesians saw it, as a Spartan-led struggle against imperialists in an "Athenian War."

The Peloponnesian War pitted against each other two Greek states that were antithetical in nearly every respect. Athens had 300 warships, a population of over 300,000 residents, a fortified port, a vast countryside, some 200 tribute-paying subject states abroad, and plenty of coined money. Sparta was landlocked. About 160 miles to the south, it relied on an army of only 10,000 infantrymen—less than half of them full citizens—to enforce rule over 250,000 inferiors and serfs, and a hegemony of neighboring communities, without any tradition of either seapower or cosmopolitan culture.

Rightly or wrongly, the fighting was assumed to be a final arbitrator of the contrasting values of each. Which would prove to be the more viable ideology: cultural and political liberalism or a tough, insular conservatism? Does an open society reap military advantages from its liberality or succumb to a license unknown in a regimented and militaristic oligarchy? And who is the most resourceful in an asymmetrical war when both sides either cannot or will not face each other in conventional battle: the ships of a "whale" like imperial Athens or the ponderous armies of the "elephant" Sparta?

Thucydides

THEN THERE IS the matter of Thucydides himself. Greece's preeminent historian was not merely an analytical and systematic writer of a great extant military history of Sparta and Athens. He was also a brilliant philosopher who tried to impart to the often obscure events of the war a value that transcended his age. In his own boast, his narrative would prove to be "a possession for all time," far more important than the actual war itself.[3]

Precisely because of this didactic nature of Thucydides' lengthy narrative—predicated on the belief that human nature is unchanging across time and space and thus predictable—the conflict of Athens and Sparta is supposed to serve as a lesson for what can happen to any people in any war in any age. A central theme is the use and abuse of power, and how it lurks behind men's professions of idealism and purported ideology. What men say, the speeches diplomats give, the reasons states go to war, all this "in word" (*logos*) is as likely to cloak rather than to elucidate what they will do "in deed" (*ergon*). Thucydides teaches us to embrace skepticism, expecting us to look to national self-interest, not publicized grievances, when wars of our own age inevitably break out.

Still, Thucydides was not an abstract theorist but a chief player in the war he wrote about. He nearly died of the plague and was cooped up in the city with tens of thousands of other Athenians who sought refuge there from the invading Peloponnesians. He fought and lost to the cagey Spartan commander Brasidas as an Athenian general in the struggle over the northern allied city of Amphipolis. For that setback he was unfairly exiled in his late thirties by an angry people back home (423), whose leaders are later prominent in his own history. Like Caesar's and Napoleon's, Thucydides' writing is inextricably mixed up with his past life as a man of action—and he too sometimes refers to himself in the third person as a character in his own history.

In response to that injustice of expulsion, the historian traversed the Greek world for twenty-some years of the war as an embedded reporter of sorts. Thucydides was eager to hear from veterans the Peloponnesian and Boeotian sides of the story as well, and his subsequent balanced treatment is riveting. The history is also full of bizarre examples of how ingenious Greeks diverted their singular energy and talent to find horrific ways of killing and maiming one another, from crafting a fire cannon to torch trapped soldiers to throwing overboard thousands of captured rowers.

Yet for all his personal autopsy and firsthand graphic detail, Thucydides can also be hard to read for a modern audience: a difficult vocabulary, strange-sounding names and places, often tedious listings of invasions and expeditions—and long, sometimes contorted speeches whose odd grammar and syntax seem almost impossible for even his contemporary audiences to have understood. While it is fashionable lately to suggest that Thucydides was our first "post-modern" historian whose preconceived theories required that he invent "facts" in the interest of constructing "objectivity," he is much too complex a mind for such a simple sham.

Modern readers are instead more struck by Thucydides' attempts at objectivity, by how this historian went to great lengths to interview combatants, consult written treaties, and look at records on stone. Thucydides was an observer who at various times expressed admiration for the democratic imperialist Pericles. But he also clearly liked the Spartan firebrand Brasidas (whose more brilliant career ended his own). He waxed eloquently over the Athenian right-wing coup of 411 and its eccentric godhead Antiphon—even as he praised the wartime resiliency of democracies. And though a commander of sailors, Thucydides was nevertheless still more enamored with infantrymen. Because his history is a classic of literature and philosophy, the war is known to us in a manner not true of subsequent larger and far more bloody conflicts.[4]

Athens as America

CONTEMPORARY AMERICA IS often now seen through the lens of ancient Athens, both as a center of culture and as an unpredictable imperial power that can arbitrarily impose democracy on friends and enemies alike. Thomas Paine long ago spelled this natural affinity out: "What Athens was in miniature, America will be in magnitude." Like ancient Athenians, present-day Americans are often said to believe that "they can be opposed in nothing," and abroad can "equally achieve what was easy and what was hard."[5] Although Americans offer the world a radically egalitarian popular culture and, more recently, in a very Athenian mood, have sought to remove oligarchs and impose democracy— in Grenada, Panama, Serbia, Afghanistan, and Iraq—enemies, allies, and neutrals alike are not so impressed. They understandably fear American power and intentions while our successive governments, in the manner of confident and proud Athenians, assure them of our morality and selflessness. Military power and idealism about bringing perceived civilization to others are a prescription for frequent conflict in any age—and no ancient state made war more often than did fifth-century imperial Athens.

So great were the dividends of envy, fear, and legitimate grievance against the ancient world's first democracy that the victorious Peloponnesians who oversaw the destruction of the Long Walls of Athens—the fortifications to the sea symbolic of the power of the poor and their desire to spread democracy throughout the Aegean—*did so to music and applause.* Again, most Greeks concluded that, as Xenophon wrote, Athens' defeat "marked the beginning of freedom for

Greece"—without a clue that the victorious Sparta would move immediately to create its own overseas empire in the vacuum.[6] Blinkered idealists in America who believe that the world wishes to join our democratic culture might reflect that at the outbreak of the Peloponnesian War, "the general good intentions of people leaned clearly in favor of the Spartans" and that "the majority of Greeks were deeply hostile toward the Athenians."

The wealth and very liberality of Athens also encouraged dissent and hyper-criticism at home and abroad. The Athenians' detractors expected a much higher level of fairness from them than they ever would have from the Spartans. Not until fourth-century Sparta incurred commensurate jealousy and envy as the Hellenic world's only superpower, following its victory in the war, would the Greeks at last cease their distrust of imperial Athens.[7]

This paradox was an exasperating experience for Athenians. And it perhaps presages the dilemma faced by generations of subsequent powerful Western liberal and imperial republics that were singularly chastised to match their idealistic and high utopian rhetoric with deeds. Just as states reprimanded Athens but preferred to visit the Acropolis rather than the unimpressive national Spartan shrine to Menelaus, so too the West's Cold War detractors roundly condemned its realist foreign policy but usually preferred to accept a visiting professorship at Oxford, the Sorbonne, or the University of California, Berkeley, rather than a teaching slot in Moscow, Havana, or Cairo.[8]

Sparta counted on these inconsistencies in its upcoming war with Athens: the rest of the Greek world would subject Athens to a standard of behavior that it would never apply to illiberal Sparta. The privileged citizens of a consensual and affluent Athens would purportedly have a much lower tolerance for a drawn-out war's pain and sacrifice than the militarists at Sparta, whose society was on a constant war footing and reflective of the barracks. And the volatile assembly would vote for and then reject military operations in a way unheard of at oligarchic Sparta.

Consequently, many have carefully read Thucydides in just that historicist context. Our leaders and pundits are eager to learn from the Athenians' mistakes and successes. They are unsure whether the fate of Athens is to be our own, or whether Americans can yet match the Athenians' civilization and influence while avoiding their hubris. Perhaps never has the Peloponnesian War been more relevant to Americans than to us of the present age. We, like the Athenians, are all-powerful, but insecure, professedly pacifist yet nearly always in some sort of conflict, often more desirous of being liked than being respected, and proud of our arts and letters even as we are more adept at war.

Good and Bad Wars

"A WAR LIKE no other" and a conflict "great and more noteworthy than any that had preceded it." So years afterward wrote the battle veteran Thucydides of the long-anticipated breakout of war between Athens and Sparta.[9] The brutal war seemed to have brought down much of everything great men had raised up. It clearly baffled Thucydides that a Hellenic civilization that had once given man so much now began to self-destruct so quickly. For many Greeks, such a fight between Hellenic speakers was not even properly to be called "war" (*polemos*) at all. Instead, it was something far nastier—"strife" (*stasis*), more like plague or famine than a noble conflict of resolute warriors.

In a good "war," noble Greek city-states fought a few dramatic sea and land battles against foreign barbarians over ideas like freedom and autonomy. But "strife" implied no clear-cut end to civil war, terrorism, murder, and executions. Such killing involved a blurring between civilian and combatant. There were elements of the Peloponnesian War that were traditional, but it was still more often an awful novel experience of Greek killing Greek on a scale that dwarfed all civil discord before and most after.[10]

At the outset Thucydides saw that the struggle would be a cataclysmic *stasis*, the equivalent of an ancient Hellenic world war. "The greatest shaking up [*kinesis*] in history," he soberly added in one of his many apocalyptic pronouncements of this horrendous civil war that consumed his own adult life. Americans who fought a terrible Civil War can identify with such an assessment. Even today, when talking of the carnage of the great twentieth-century wars of mass conscription and industrialization—World War I, World War II, Korea, and Vietnam—historians still assess their horrific carnage with the qualifier "except for the Civil War."

Twenty-five hundred years later most agree also with Thucydides' assertions that this "disturbance" sabotaged much of what Greece could have accomplished.[11] Think of it: for the cost of organizing and supplying the two successive armadas that went to Sicily, in aggregate over 40,000 troops, Athens could have built at least four additional Parthenons. For the outlay of putting 100 triremes to sea for a month, 1,000 tragedies could have been staged, three times the number of plays put on by Aeschylus, Sophocles, and Euripides in their entire careers combined. Americans were traumatized by the Civil War as some 600,000 Union and Confederate troops perished in combat and from disease out of a population of 32,000,000, or about 1 in 50 lost. But the fatalities on Sicily alone in a little over two years were even worse (1 lost for every 25 people in the Athenian empire)—in an enterprise in which it was hard to see Athenian national interests at stake.[12]

Most wars do not end as they start. Before the battle of Shiloh (April 6–8, 1862), for example, Ulysses S. Grant thought one great battle would ruin the South. After the two-day slugfest he realized that several years, thousands of lives, and millions of dollars in capital were needed for the Union to ruin a recalcitrant Confederacy rather than merely defeat a southern army. So, too, the cocky Spartans marched into Attica in spring 431 thinking a year or two of old-style ravaging would bring them final victory by prompting a conventional big battle or unleashing starvation upon the Athenians. But after seven years of continual Spartan failure in Attica, and 80,000 Athenians lost to the plague, neither side was closer to victory. And there were another twenty far worse seasons to go.

The Peloponnesian War, if it did not utterly ruin Athens, surely wrecked the idea of imperial Athenian culture. Yet it brought no lasting security or wealth to the victor; Sparta soon failed even more miserably as a would-be imperial power. The conflict left hundreds of other nonaligned Greek city-states sometimes confused and ambivalent, but more often invaded, sacked, and impoverished. The earlier united Greek victory over the Persian king Xerxes (480–479) had marked the inauguration of the triumphant Golden Age. Yet this classical century that started with such great promise, with the alliance of Athens and Sparta against the Persians, finally crashed into the self-inflicted wreckage of their own civil war.

The butchery that King Darius and his son Xerxes once could only hope for at the battles of Marathon (490) and Salamis (480) was brought to fruition a half century later by Greek generals like Pericles, Cleon, Alcibiades, Brasidas, Gylippus, and Lysander (to the delight of contemporary Persian satraps across the Aegean). Now Greeks often killed more of their own people in a year than had the Persians in a decade. In 406, at the single sea battle off the Arginusae Islands and its bloody aftermath, more Greeks lost their lives than *all those killed by the Persians at the famous battles of Marathon, Thermopylae, Salamis, and Plataea combined.* The expedition to Sicily took more Greeks than the combined fatalities from every hoplite battle in the fifth century. In that sense, the Peloponnesian War was a Persian dream come true. At the war's end Greek Ionia, in western Asia Minor, returned to a de facto Persian satrapy. Athenian literature of the next half century is full of references and allusions to the unhealed wounds from plague, slaughter, military defeat, and national capitulation.

The only Hellenic empire powerful enough to challenge the supremacy of the Persian king in the Aegean, Periclean Athens, was left exhausted. On the horizon were a number of thuggish Greek and Macedonian autocrats ready to end Hellenic freedom under the slogan of "uniting" together to "pay back" the Persians, offering a nationalist antidote to the self-inflicted carnage rendered by consensual governments of the past.

The Peloponnesian War was also the first great instance where Western powers turned on each other. Their common commitment to rationalism, civic militarism, and constitutional government resulted not just in high culture but also in lethal militaries that could square off in mutual destruction. So Athens versus Sparta serves as a warning—centuries before the Roman Civil Wars, Cold Harbor, the Somme, and Dresden—of what can happen when the Western way of war is unleashed upon its own. In modern terms, the Peloponnesian War was more like World War I, rather than the Second World War—the issues that divided the two sides likewise more complex, the warring parties themselves not so easily identifiable as good or evil, and the shock of thousands killed similarly grotesquely novel and marking a complete break with past experience.

Root Causes?

THUCYDIDES FELT STRONGLY that the Spartans had invaded the Athenian countryside in the spring of 431 because "they feared the Athenians lest they might grow still more powerful, seeing most of Greece was already subject to them." That assessment—hardly true, because in the strict sense Athens really did not control "most of Greece"—is nevertheless thematic in his history. The Spartans, in other words, started the actual fighting with a preemptive strike into Attica. They, not the Athenians, were unhappy with the fifth-century status quo. At another point Thucydides concedes that such apprehensions of being slowly overwhelmed in peace "forced the Spartans into war."[13]

"Forced"? Of course, there always seemed other, more immediate pretexts for war that made the conflict perhaps unavoidable. There always are. But in the last analysis, Thucydides at least felt in hindsight that there were such great underlying differences between the two powers, albeit perhaps not always perceptible to contemporary Athenians and Spartans themselves, that the more pressing (and minor) disagreements *must* eventually lead to a catastrophic face-off.

Although both sides claimed that they were coerced into the conflict, in Thucydides' way of determinist thinking, if Sparta did not go to war over the pretexts of Corinthian and Megarian grievances against Athens, then the sheer dynamism of Pericles' imperial culture—majestic buildings, drama, intellectual fervor, an immense fleet, radical democratic government, an expanding population, and a growing overseas empire—would eventually spread throughout its area of influence in southern Greece.*

The Spartans might have lived with the existence of Athenian imperialism. They had done just that for much of the earlier fifth century. But once Athens began to combine its lust for power with a radical ideology of support for democracy abroad, Sparta rightly concluded that the threat transcended mere armed rivalry and promised to infect the very hearts and minds of Greeks everywhere. Their worries were legitimate. Athenian democracy, in fact, was not merely proselytizing and expansionary but also remarkably cohesive and stable. Even the brief revolutions during and after the war in 411 and 403 were short-lived, suggesting a level of support for popular government among a wide variety of Athenians well beyond the landless poor.

Spartans had also seen Athenian-inspired democracy spread throughout the Aegean and Asia Minor in the 450s. They bridled at Athenian influence over the supposedly Panhellenic colony of Thurii, in southern Italy. Their leaders were also furious that sympathetic oligarchs on the island of Samos had been crushed in 440. Elites at Sparta seethed that recalcitrant subject states like Potidaea were not merely besieged but faced with perpetual radical democratic government imposed and maintained by Athenian triremes. How threatening these purported demonstrations of Athenian power really were did not matter; Sparta was convinced that they represented a systematic and dangerous new aggression. Innate ethnic and linguistic differences between Ionian Athenians and Doric Spartans might have been mitigated, but democratic imperialism on the move was again another challenge altogether.

This new Athenian global village would offer incentives to Sparta's friends that a parochial town of infantrymen could not hope to match. Similarly, the die-hard wealthier supporters of Sparta throughout the Aegean must have felt that they were losing influence in their own communities to an upstart underclass. The poor, who did not farm, ride horses, or frequent the gymnasia, liked the security offered by the Athenian fleet and did not mind the obligations of tribute, which fell mostly upon their own rich and landed aristocracy. Behind

* Corinth was angry at Athens for not backing its disputes with its former colony, Corcyra (the modern island of Corfu), and fearful that its own fleet would be no match for an envisioned Athenian-Corcyraean alliance. The key city-state of Megara was strategically located about halfway between Corinth and Athens on the main route from the Peloponnese, and subject to a trade embargo by Athens aimed at discouraging its pro-Spartan sympathies.

all the realist calculations, however, was the undeniable fact that Athens just kept growing—King Archidamus believed that at the war's outbreak it was the largest city in the Greek world—while Sparta was shrinking.[14]

"Athenianism" was the Western world's first example of globalization. There was a special word of sorts for Athenian expansionism in the Greek language, *attikizô*, "to Atticize," or to become like or join the Athenians.[15] Contemporaries accepted the reality that Athens sought to promote the common people abroad whenever it could. In contrast, when Athens engaged instead in realpolitik—such as attacking the similar consensual government of Syracuse—without the necessary revolutionary fervor of democracy, it often failed.[16]

Spartans were oligarchic fundamentalists par excellence, hating "people power" and the danger it represented. Their warrior-citizens were quite wary of the appetites for the hustle and bustle of the good life that even among their own stern elite grew faster than they could be repressed.[17] Although they had been the preeminent Greeks earlier in the sixth and fifth centuries, by the time of the Peloponnesian War the Spartans could sense their own influence waning, based as it was almost exclusively on hoplite infantry rather than the ships, population growth, and money of an ever grasping hyperdemocratic rival—one that in Pericles' own words had ruled "over more Greeks than any other Greek state."[18]

To avoid war with Sparta, Athens was asked to cease its imperialist overstretch and essentially disband the empire: stop besieging cities like Potidaea and let nearby states like Aegina and Megara decide their own affairs. In short, "let the Greeks be independent." To do all that, however, would mean that Athens could no longer be Periclean Athens; rather, it would revert back to its agrarian modesty of an earlier century, when it had no ships, no Long Walls, no tribute, no majestic temples, and no lavish dramatic festivals but was a benign commonwealth not much different from other large Greek city-states.[19]

The Burdens of the Past

WAS WAR INEVITABLE as its logic of violence and death overrode what individual Spartan and Athenian leaders might do or not do to manage crises? The very idea bothers us that Sparta's fault in breaking the peace of 431 was not so much that it or Athens was rationally culpable in any given context. Rather, out of fear, a lot of envy, and some hatred, Sparta was mercurial in its actions, prone to all the wild urges that make men do what is not always in either their own or the general interest.[20]

In almost all the various debates that surrounded the outbreak of the conflict, the enemies of Athens cited fundamental grievances that acerbated political and ethnic fault lines—reckless Athenian character, the growth of an unstoppable empire, and innate Athenian arrogance—just as frequently as adducing legitimate and more specific legal transgressions that demanded immediate redress. Perhaps there was something about Athens that sparked a certain hatred by rival city-states like Corinth, Thebes, and Sparta, a loathing that was deductive, antiempirical, and hopelessly embedded with deep-seated feelings of antipathy.*21

Enemies hated Athens as much for what it was as for what it did. As early as 446 Athens had abandoned claims to almost everything sought in the First Peloponnesian War and was careful not to offer any concrete reason for war to the Spartans themselves. Perhaps that paradox is best summarized by Thucydides' fascinating description of the Spartan debate in late 432 over proposals to invade Attica the next spring. After Athenian envoys and the Spartan king Archidamus both offered sober and reasoned explanations of why war at that particular time with Athens was a bad idea, the dense ephor Sthenelaidas stepped forward in response.† He shouted out a few slogans about Spartan pride and power. The Spartan military assembly then immediately voted for war. They seemed to be swayed (as were the Athenians who later voted to invade Sicily) by emotion rather than reason: "The long speeches of the Athenians I do not understand at all. . . . Vote therefore, Lacedaemonians, for war as the honor of Sparta demands and do not allow Athens to become too powerful."22

In turn, at Athens an entire generation had grown up in Periclean splendor. It, too, seemed deathly afraid of inevitable generational decline, a common apprehension among elites in Western societies that are free, affluent, and experiencing social and cultural change.23 Many felt that if contemporary Athenians did not stand up to Spartan bullying, they would betray the legacy of those tougher "Marathon men"—men like Miltiades, Themistocles, and Aristides, who had fought at Marathon (490) and Salamis (480) and bequeathed a secure and prosperous empire. Perhaps even a handful of these larger-than-life 10,000 hoplite infantrymen were still alive and now in their eighties. They are the frequent heroes of Aristophanes' comedies, the embodiment of the "old courage"

---

* The so-called First Peloponnesian War (461–446), during which Athens more often confronted Corinth and Thebes than Sparta, ended in stalemate and an envisioned thirty-year peace treaty between Athens and Sparta.

† An ephor was one of five elected "overseers" at Sparta; their task was to monitor the conduct of other public officials and, most importantly, audit the military and political activities of the two Spartan kings.

to be contrasted with a lesser and softer generation that would not trust in its own hoplite prowess to meet the Spartans in Attica.

Yet while the Athenians could scarcely field an army of 10,000 preeminent hoplites of the caliber that had plowed through the Persians sixty years earlier on the beach at Marathon, their aggregate imperial military strength—ships, financial capital, manpower—was greater even than that of all their potential Greek enemies combined. Athens was stronger precisely because it had evolved beyond placing its national security in the sole hands of doughty hoplite farmers. These living anachronisms, after all, were a one-dimensional force, as irrelevant off a small flat battlefield as it was deadly on it.

Nevertheless, that burden of past glory loomed over Alcibiades' age group just as the accomplishments of the "greatest generation" of World War II do our own, especially when men like his guardian Pericles constantly harangued younger Athenians about their imperial burdens. Spartans also felt similar apprehensions about becoming soft in comparison to their roughneck Lacedaemonian granddads who had died blocking the pass at Thermopylae. Thus, the Corinthians remonstrated with the Peloponnesians on the eve of the battle: "It is not a just thing that all that was won through poverty should be destroyed through prosperity."[24]

Unforeseen Consequences

THE WAR ITSELF would prove to be a colossal absurdity. Neither a Socrates nor a Pericles could have predicted its course or final outcome. Sparta had the most feared infantry in the Greek world, yet its newly created navy finally won the last great battles of the war. Democratic Athens sent almost 40,000 allied soldiers to imprisonment and death trying to capture far-off Syracuse—against the largest democracy in the Greek world. At the same time thousands more of her old enemies in Greece were thereby emboldened to plunder her property with impunity less than thirteen miles outside her walls from the base at Decelea.* Alcibiades at times proved the savior of Athens, Sparta, and Persia—and their collective spoiler as well.

Athens started off the war with money piled high in its majestic Parthenon. There was the staggering amount of some 6,000 talents of coined silver and another 500 in other precious metals, altogether worth about $3 billion in con-

---

* The infamous Spartan fort in Attica, which from 413 to 404 served as a clearinghouse for booty plundered from Attica; see the Glossary of Terms and the time line on pages 31–34.

temporary value. It ended the conflict bankrupt with a city full of orphans, widows, and the disabled—and thousands of names on its ubiquitous stone casualty lists.

The wartime Athenian treasury was unable even to finish fluting the final columns of the Propylaea, the monumental gateway to the still uncompleted temples on the Acropolis. Much less could it find the money to finish an array of other rural temples at Rhamnous and Thorikos in the Attic hinterland. Most of the capital needed to complete Pericles' grand dream of a marble imperial city went down with some 500 triremes lost off Sicily and later in the Aegean.

Sparta fielded the most terrifying army in Greece. Most of its enemies, however, fell not to its Dorian spears but to disease, sieges, or guerrilla-style killing. Its grand strategy of ravaging the crops of Attica proved a colossal failure within a week of its inception. Yet within a year the Peloponnesian sojourn in the enemy countryside inadvertently set the stage for the plague that nearly ruined Athens.

No government was as calculating or sober—or blinkered—as Sparta's *gerousia*, a governing senate of old men who had seen nothing of civilization abroad and thus were loath to sanction rash action beyond the vale of Laconia.* No government was as reckless and dangerous as Athens' assembly, composed of many leaders who had traveled the Aegean. Yet the latter in a minute's fit could call for the execution of a man—or an entire captured city across the seas—on the flimsiest of charges.

The philosopher Socrates had doubts about democratic Athens' hubris and megalomania, especially the later visions of grandeur in Sicily. But those worries were not enough to prevent him from fighting heroically in her cause in his potbellied middle age. As he reminds the whipped-up audience of accusers in the last speech of his life, he battled bravely in three of Athens' most difficult engagements, at Potidaea, Delium, and Amphipolis.[25] Thucydides used the broad message of the war's apparent senselessness to explore his own bleak views about human nature. Yet despite being exiled on trumped-up charges by the demagogues, no Athenian fought more unquestioningly and without cynicism than did Thucydides in service to his country.

Euripides, the maverick playwright, thought his countrymen's brutal execution of the Mytileneans and poor Melians a criminal act and a moral com-

---

* For the various regional and ethnic names associated with Sparta, see "Sparta" in the Glossary.

mentary about the mindless savagery of conflict. But even Euripides hated the Spartans and seems to have wished the enemy to lose as much as he wanted the war simply to end. Traitorous Alcibiades at times helped Athens, Sparta, and Persia win the war, even as the jaded Athenians refused the infamous turncoat's final sound advice at Aegospotami, which might have saved them from defeat in the last great battle of the conflict.

Aristophanes, the brilliant comic dramatist, argued that the nonending war made the farmers broke, the male leaders silly, the generals bloodthirsty, the poor too reckless, and the arms sellers rich—and nevertheless trusted that Athens was more right than wrong. Patriotism, in both its exalted and its debased forms, finally overshadowed Socratic pretensions that all Greeks were citizens of the world. As Socrates himself is made to say in Plato's later *Protagoras*, it is a "noble" thing (*kalon*) to go to war.[26]

Behind the contradictions of politics and philosophy, and the hypocrisies of the Hellenic world's greatest generation, remain the thousands of ordinary Greeks—the subjects of this book—who were slaughtered for nearly three decades for the designs of fickle men, shifting alliances, and contradictory causes. No war of the ancient world—not Xerxes' earlier invasion of Greece, the later grandiose invasions of Alexander the Great, or Hannibal's romp into Italy—is more riveting and yet contradictory than the three decades of intramural fighting between Athens and Sparta.

Just think of it: a land versus a maritime power, the starkness of the Dorians contrasted with Ionian liberality. Oligarchy was pitted against democracy, practiced dearth set against ostentatious wealth. A rural hamlet dethroned a majestic imperial city; and a garrison state professed the cause of Greek autonomy abroad even as a humane imperialism killed the innocent.

No one foresaw such carnage in 431. Who believed that in just two years, the majestic Pericles would end up covered with pustules, grasping an amulet as he coughed out his life in the fevers of the plague? The millionaire Nicias never imagined that twenty years later he would beg for his life before having his throat slit eight hundred miles away on Sicily. Nor did the handsome Alcibiades, the rage of Athens, envision that he of all people would be murdered by assassins in an obscure hamlet in Asia Minor. Everything considered wisdom at the beginning of the war would be proven folly at its end.

Hopes and Dreams

THERE WAS LITTLE surprise that Athens and Sparta fought a final war to the finish in 431. Perhaps the wonder instead was that they had not done so far earlier. Indeed, between 461 and 446 (the First Peloponnesian War), the two great powers had battled on and off, although most of this earlier conflict was waged between their respective surrogates, the Boeotians, Megarians, Corinthians, Argives, and Thessalians. Still, rarely since their brief alliance to repel Persia (480–79) had there been real affinity between the two states. Not more than a handful of Athenian elites and generals had ever visited Sparta. Almost no Spartans other than a few envoys had ever gazed upon the Acropolis. True, both Athens and Sparta were still Greek *poleis.* They shared a common language and were in matters of religion similar; but on core political, social, and cultural issues they remained mostly antithetical to each other.

By 431 each of the two city-states was in its own way militarily powerful precisely because it had bucked the old Hellenic agrarian tradition that had heretofore moderated the normal conditions of warfare: brutal battles of an hour or so defining war between reluctant farmers with harvest responsibilities at home. Astute prewar observers began to understand why there would be neither natural constraints nor easy victory for either side when helot serfs and galleys meant there was little need for the soldiers of either state to stay home and farm.

Pericles himself, for example, on the eve of the fighting said, "War is inevitable."[27] The idea that Persia might reinvade a divided Greece was unlikely after its calamitous defeat a half century earlier. Instead, there was a general uneasiness that this would be a new, unrestricted civil struggle. The Corinthians rightly warned the Spartans to jettison their "old-fashioned" strategies of war —consisting of attacking farms in hopes of prompting battle—and find new ways to destroy a city like Athens.[28]

The conflict between the principal rivals officially started when the Spartans violated the sworn thirty-year peace treaty and invaded Attica in spring 431. They crossed the border a mere eighty days after their ally Thebes, without warning, had also sought preemptive action by attacking the neighboring Boeotian city of Plataea, a protectorate of Athens about fifty miles away.

Both sides claimed detailed grievances. Sparta's ally Corinth, the rich Greek city on the Isthmus, felt that Athens earlier had belligerently intervened on the side of the rival island of Corcyra against it in a series of disputes. The small nearby state of Megara chafed under an Athenian trade embargo and asked for Spartan support. The nearby island of Aegina, which loomed on the horizon within easy sight from the Acropolis—Pericles once dubbed it "the eyesore of the Piraeus"—claimed that Athens interfered in its internal affairs and expected Sparta to preserve its sovereignty. Athenians, in turn, alleged that the Peloponnesians had encouraged their own tributary ally, the northern city of

Potidaea, to revolt. The Boeotians residing to the immediate north of Athens wished to eliminate the outpost city of Plataea, which had brought the old fear of Athenian imperialism to their doorstep—and on and on.[29]

Of course, an Athenian embargo against Megara, past Athenian interference in the nearby island of Aegina, rivalry over the allegiance of a powerful Corcyra with "its very large fleet," and disputed lands on the border of Megara or Boeotia were no small matters.[30] But more frequently it was again the *perception* of grievance, involving matters of fear and honor, that propelled Sparta to act while it could, especially among generations in both Athens and Sparta that "were unfamiliar enough with war to welcome it."[31] Athens apparently thought that over the long duration its culture really could either ignore or, if need be, overwhelm Sparta, even without demonstrating in any real way in the short term how it could make Sparta pay dearly if it dared send thousands of its hoplites into Attica. Pericles' own goal, instead, was "to survive."[32] Yet planning to just not lose was a poor way in the short term to deter Sparta from acting on its fears; all Spartans believed that they could cross the Attic border with near impunity.

Pericles saw less of a need to enter into any direct squabbles that might endanger the empire or the decade-and-a-half peace since its last brush with Sparta, an armistice during which it reached an unprecedented level of wealth and security. The Athenians apparently felt that the Spartans would grasp that they could not win and so would not try, foolishly thinking in terms of long-term deterrence rather than immediately about how to warn their enemies that invasion across the border was synonymous with their destruction. Pericles was determined to take the first blow and so offered no credible counterthreat because he never really had any clear strategy for how to mount an offensive action that might knock Thebes or Sparta out of the war.

He was at heart an admiral. Before the war Pericles had conducted successful sieges of recalcitrant maritime states and fought sea battles. So he had never directed a long infantry campaign or even led a hoplite army into pitched battle. He apparently envisioned Athenian naval superiority as a tool for unfettered raiding rather than the transportation of a large army to the enemy's rear. Sparta and Thebes were singularly unimpressed. Thousands were to die on both sides because their leaders took them to war without a real plan of how to defeat the enemy on the battlefield and destroy its power.

The Mythical Spartan Fleet

THE SPARTANS HAD their own problems as well. A modern comparison can illustrate some sense of their dilemma: it would be as if in a world without nu-

THE SPARTAN AND ATHENIAN EMPIRES:
Peloponnesian League and Other Spartan Allies

0   MILES   100

0   KM   100

Aegean Sea

AMBRACIA

Leucas   ●Anactorium

OPUNTIAN
LOCRIS

PHOCIS   *Euboea*

OZOLIAN
LOCRIS

B O E O T I A

Gulf of Corinth   ●Thebes

ACHAEA   ●Pellene

Sicyon●   Megara●   A
          T
Corinth●   ●Athens   T
         I
         C
         A

ELIS

MANTINEA✗
      ●Argos
ARCADIA
   ●Tegea

P E L O P O N N E S E

MESSENIA   ●Sparta

LACONIA

Mediterranean Sea   *Sea of Crete*

clear weapons the old Soviet Union at some point before the 1990s had presciently accepted that ultimately it could not compete with the freewheeling democratic and capitalist juggernaut of the United States. Thus, the Soviet hard-liners would have felt it necessary to send 300 divisions into Europe before their own allies, and the world at large, shared this pessimistic appraisal of their future and thus abandoned allegiance to their empire.

The Spartans could field hoplite soldiers who were unbeatable in an open fight. Their tough agrarian ally Boeotia could muster even more heavy infantrymen—perhaps 7,000 to 12,000 if need be—who were every bit as formidable as Spartan professionals. And the league of allied states in the Peloponnese under Spartan leadership could for short periods march out an enormous army of 60,000 that could sweep any adversary off the field of battle. The best cavalry in central Greece was Boeotian and on the Spartan side.

For all these reasons, an impressed Thucydides emphasized that Sparta herself "occupies two-fifths of the Peloponnese, exercises control over the whole, and possesses many allies on the outside."[33] Even if Sparta and its allies could not win such a war against a maritime empire, at least they were confident that such "hard power" precluded an Athenian army occupying the Spartan acropolis.

Yet the strength of Sparta and its league was in some ways a chimera. At the war's outbreak the allied Peloponnesian force could not be projected by sea. It was certainly not sustained through real economic power. Sparta started out with no capital, few ships, and almost no cavalry or light-armed troops. Under the regimented totalitarian system founded by the mythical ancestor Lycurgus, civic virtue, not economic efficiency or individualism, mattered.

For example, iron spits, not coinage, served as money precisely because in such a strange moral universe they could not be used with the ease of ordinary (and thus corrupting) currency. Third-party boatbuilders or rowers for hire did not flock to Sparta in hopes of being compensated with a hoard of metal barbecue skewers. The Spartans had been warned on the eve of the war by their allies that their ossified manner of envisioning war as hoplite battle was a formula for suicide. The harping Corinthians continually urged them to strike out to help friends around the Aegean to resist Athenian imperialism.

Pericles was probably right when he claimed, "The Peloponnesians have no money, public or private." There was certainly no imperial tribute pouring into the Spartan acropolis, and there were few Spartan colonies. Should Athens choose not to fight a pitched battle, Sparta possessed neither the capital nor the material reserves to keep an army in the field for any great length of time. Much less did it have either the know-how or the desire to conduct an unconventional low-intensity war of raiding, plundering, and sustained sieges.[34]

A generation before the war the Spartans had swallowed their pride and called in Athenian siege engineers to help them storm insurrectionist helot strongholds. If Spartans had once needed Athenians to control their own subordinated peoples, what would happen when Athens would inevitably use its money and expertise to incite rather than subdue helot rebellion?[35]

The combined fleet of Corinth and a few other Spartan allies counted only a little over 100 ships, less than half the size of the active Athenian imperial fleet. What triremes the Peloponnesians had existed only because of recent breakneck Corinthian efforts at naval construction to match the fleet of its rival Corcyra, but there was little accumulated capital to ensure that even a 100-ship armada could be deployed for very long. Warriors in heavy armor perched on tossing decks and powered by bought rowers were not Sparta's idea of martial virtue.

In desperation, Sparta ludicrously proposed that her allies build a colossal fleet of some 500 triremes—a pipe dream from a state that had no port other than Gythium, some thirty miles away from the city proper. War planners imagined that the hated Persians might provide capital to lay down triremes and allure new allies to box in the Athenians—strategies that would work only if Sparta could first show some success, such as either a hoplite victory or substantive damage to the cohesiveness of the empire.

These were all grand aspirations that were not well suited for a blinkered and landlocked state. At war's outbreak, only the three city-states of Corinth, Corcyra, and Athens had sizable fleets, and two were hostile to the Spartans.[36] So at least some Peloponnesians realized that eventually they would have to embrace a multifaceted strategy: defeat the Athenians at sea and disrupt her empire, while finding a way to cut the city off from its hinterland permanently. To accomplish those goals, they needed more and diverse allies, both Greeks and Persians, as well as innovative thinkers. Until then, they had to accept the bitter fact that in a simple contest between Sparta and the Athenian empire, the money, manpower, variety of military assets, and experience of military leadership were all on the Athenian side. Indeed, two decades later, even after the Athenian disaster at Sicily (413), when the Greek world predicted an imminent Athenian collapse, Sparta still found it hard to organize a Peloponnesian fleet—so reluctant and timid were her allies to challenge long-held Athenian superiority at sea.[37]

Spartan Calculations

WHEN WAR BROKE out in 431, the Spartan generals remained unimaginative. Two hereditary kings were by law leaders of the army and were often annoyed by the board of ephors, many of whom accompanied the royalty on campaign as overseers. Strategy at Sparta merely reflected the thinking of a closed hierarchical society of group messes and the unquestioning assumptions of a brutal indoctrination that began at age seven, when young boys were inducted into military life. Because so few Spartan statesmen had seen mercantile cities in action, they were both naive about interstate relations and the size of enemy populations and unusually prone to corruption and bribery.

The larger and prouder allied states of the Peloponnese, like Mantinea and Elis, resented brutal Spartan leadership and were in the process of liberalizing their constitutions. In the Peloponnesian way of traditional war, harvesttime was the flash point of battle: infantrymen tramped in to burn ripe dry grain or consume it; defenders tried to evacuate it; and farmer-warriors all worried that there were harvests back home to tend that were far more important than campaigning. The Athenians had once (460–446) controlled the routes through Megara to Attica; now, however, they did not. In the Spartan mind, then, marching into Attica was possible in a way that had been difficult during the First Peloponnesian War.

Nearly 250,000 long-suffering indentured servants in the surrounding territories of Laconia and Messenia (the so-called helots) worked farms under coercion to feed the Spartan military messes. Because of the nature of barracks life and the near-constant drilling and policing in occupied Messenia, male Spartiate warriors were seldom at home. Thus, the population of the city continually fell even as the number of oppressed helots grew. If 8,000 true Spartiates had once fought Persia, by the time of the Peloponnesian War, fifty years later, there were fewer than half that number. The result was a garrison state that could scarcely cobble together 8,000 to 10,000 hoplite soldiers of varying status, while it sat atop a volcano of tens of thousands of male serfs ("a disaster waiting to happen") who purportedly wished, by their own admission, "to eat their masters raw."[38]

The helots and their dream of a free Messenia were not the only fault lines in Sparta's complex pyramidal society. In its immediate environs there were also 20,000 to 30,000 Laconian *perioikoi* ("those who live around"), nearby villagers who enjoyed free but subservient political status and were sometimes just as unhappy as the helots with Spartan hegemony.

Even without the worry of controlling a vast Messenia and its quarter million helots on the other side of Mount Taygetus, Sparta, like many contemporary Western societies, was in perpetual demographic crisis, entirely dependent on the menial labor of serfs. On the eve of the war King Archidamus in vain tried to remind his constituents that they were contemplating war against a state that "had a greater population than any other in Greece." What had developed into the finest infantry in Greece was by nature a domestic police force, or perhaps a Waffen-SS if you will, whose original reason for existence was to thwart domestic insurrection and ferret out alleged dissidents.

Finally, the volatility of most helots was not, as in the case of chattel slaves elsewhere, merely their inferior status. Instead, their zeal arose out of a sense of nationalism about their occupied home of Messenia. They were an entire tribe, in their dispossession somewhat akin to the modern-day Kurds, who despite the absence of a homeland understood that they had once been a free people with a territory and population larger than that of their conquerors.[39]

At the beginning of the conflict, Spartan strategy was as simple as it proved to be naive: the old Pavlovian response of when in doubt "invade Attica." King Archidamus would march a massive force of allies into Attica to challenge the Athenians to battle.[40] If the enemy did not venture forth from their walls, Archidamus would then systematically ravage Attic agriculture, causing famine, or at least humiliation, to make the arrogant and sophisticated city come to terms. Throughout his history Thucydides reiterates that the Spartans were flabbergasted that their simplistic reliance on ravaging had not worked. How, after all, could the Athenians call themselves an imperial power when they could not stop enemies from marching in view of the Acropolis?[41]

Sparta saw no reason to alter its strategy after some two hundred years of success, even if Athens had evolved into a city that could survive despite enemies at its gates. Indeed, the Spartans seemed to have had no clear idea of the size or rural defenses of Athens. They knew even less about the maritime economy of Athens and its theoretical ability to import food to replace the third to half of the city's supply lost out in the countryside. Even more naively, the Spartans believed that if they ravaged Attica the overseas subject states of the Athenian empire would take heart and revolt, despite the reality that Sparta had no real means to send any warships to aid them if and when an angry retaliatory Athenian fleet sailed in.

While the actual degree of Athenian self-sufficiency in grains is unknown, it should have been common knowledge that in a crisis, importing sufficient additional food into the city was assured—especially since Athens had the money to pay the increased costs. Later, even when the Spartans were camped right outside the walls at Decelea (413–404) and the Athenians were denied use of their lands for much of the year, King Agis lamented that his raiders could still not bring the city to its knees as long as he could see grain ships continually sail into the Piraeus.[42]

Too many of the Spartans had also forgotten that during the invasion of

Xerxes of 480, well before the construction of the Long Walls, Athens under Themistocles had survived not only the complete evacuation of its farmland but even the very abandonment of its city as well. Of this fact Pericles would later remind his far wealthier and larger citizenry. If a weaker Athens in 480 could have overcome 250,000 Persians arriving by land and sea, and endured the torching of its Acropolis, surely a half century later, with far greater assets, Athens in its maturity could once more survive the temporary loss of its farm-land to a force one-quarter the size of that of its old enemies.[43]

At the eleventh hour, even Archidamus finally seemed to grasp the dilemma of fighting the new war the old way. On the eve of invasion, he warned his fol-lowers in vain that Athens had ample "public and private wealth, ships, cavalry, weaponry," as well as allies, tribute, and a vast population. It could be opposed only when there were sufficient Peloponnesian "money and ships." Athens' hin-terland was no larger than Sparta's. But the key difference was that, unlike the Peloponnesians, Athens had plenty of ways to augment its impressive local har-vests with food imported from as far away as the Aegean Islands, Asia Minor, the Black Sea region, and Egypt.[44]

The Logic of Athens

THE LONG WALLS, built between 461 and 456, and connecting the city to the Piraeus, were the most revolutionary development in the history of Greek strat-egy. At a single stroke the fortifications provided immunity from the age-old tactic of attacking agriculture to prompt pitched battle or induce starvation through the burning of a dry grain crop. With the Long Walls, Pericles had vastly expanded on Themistocles' earlier achievement. He grasped that with the proper fortified lifeline, only the countryside, not the city proper, needed to be evacuated before the onslaught of a superior enemy. This was a brilliant twist perhaps, but also utterly ruthless and divisive in abandoning the property and livelihood of thousands of his citizens to the enemy.

Athens understood that its ramparts not only offered the city a greater range of defensive options but also had the effect of strengthening democratic con-stituencies inside the walls. Thus, it later began promoting the concept of long walls at other Greek states such as Argos and Patras.[45] The deleterious conse-quences were not confined to conservative Athenian rustics, who were left out-side the municipal walls. Sparta and her allies also later complained that the construction of such extensive fortifications had changed the very strategic cal-culus of Greece itself, giving one state an unfair immunity from traditional pitched battle, and thus should have never been allowed to happen. No wonder they hired flute players to mark their destruction at the war's end.[46]

Athenian silver "owls" were the common currency of the Aegean world.* At the beginning of the war, Athens garnered 600 talents of annual tribute, in addition to perhaps some 400 talents of internal income generated through mining, trade, overseas rent, and commerce. By 431 there were some 6,000 talents in reserve in the temple treasuries on the Acropolis. That pile was the equivalent of 36 million man-days of labor, or over 100 drachmas per person among the 300,000 residents in Athens and Attica, enough wherewithal, in theory, to build 6,000 triremes![47] In today's purchasing power, the treasury would be similar to a medium-sized American city of about 300,000 people possessing an endowment of some $3 billion in cash reserves. In this regard, tragedy, comedy, and the Parthenon were not so much expressions of native genius as reflections of lots of money.

After the Persians withdrew in 479, a Hellenic defense league insidiously, over a half century, transmogrified into an Athenian empire of nearly two hundred states run by seven hundred imperial overseers. Due to fifty years of naval construction, tribute, and the integration of subject states, Athens was far more powerful at the outbreak of the war than at any time in its history. To maintain such an empire, in the fifth century Athens had fought three out of every four years, a remarkable record of constant mobilization, unrivaled even in modern times.[48]

The population of Athens grew at over 2 percent per annum for most of the decades preceding the Peloponnesian War. And Athens, unlike Sparta, crafted a more inclusive society, whose critics complained that to the naked eye slaves, metics, and citizens were nearly indistinguishable in such a crass culture—in opposition to the more utopian efforts at Sparta to create a republic of virtue among a smaller and more static number of citizens.[49]

Athenian infantry, nearly 30,000 of both frontline and reserve garrison hoplites, was at its core probably as good a fighting army as any except for the Spartans and Boeotians. Yet like the Victorian British army, which was hardly designed to fight imperial German divisions in the trenches of Europe, the Athenian phalanx was never intended to face anything like Spartan hoplites, but was perfectly capable as a seaborne force for putting down recalcitrant trib-

---

*These Athenian silver coins, worth four drachmas (in terms of modern American currency, over $300), were stamped with the helmeted head of Athena and on the reverse side her iconic owl.

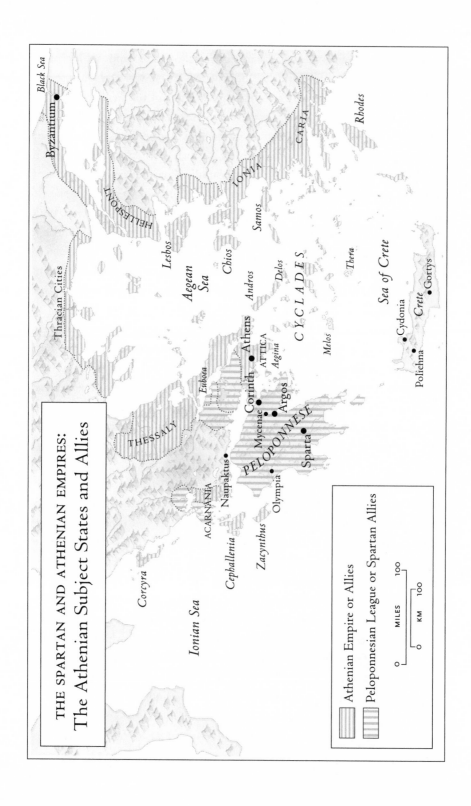

THE SPARTAN AND ATHENIAN EMPIRES:
The Athenian Subject States and Allies

Black Sea

Byzantium

HELLESPONT

Thracian Cities

IONIA

CARIA

Rhodes

Lesbos

Chios

Samos

Aegean
Sea

Andros

Delos

Thera

CYCLADES

Sea of Crete

Athens

ATTICA

Aegina

Melos

Cydonia

Crete

Gortys

Polichna

Euboea

Corinth

Mycenae

Argos

THESSALY

PELOPONNESE

Sparta

ACARNANIA

Naupaktus

Olympia

Cephallenia

Zacynthus

Coryra

Ionian Sea

Athenian Empire or Allies

Peloponnesian League or Spartan Allies

MILES

100

KM

100

0

0

utary allies. In addition, there were reserves of imperial manpower far from Attica that were safe from Spartan ground intrusions—what King Archidamus worried about as the "plenty of the other land" out of his army's reach.[50]

True, the states of the Peloponnese could marshal a large alliance of autonomous Greek militaries, among them real powers like Corinth, Elis, and Thebes. Yet the Athenians retained two real advantages in such coalition warfare. First, Athens had the more ideologically zealous friends. It led not only democratic subjects in the Aegean but also outcasts like the Plataeans in Boeotia, the Messenian expatriates scattered around Greece, and the quarrelsome Corcyraeans, all of whom had real enemies in Thebes, Sparta, and Corinth quite apart from their alliance with Athens.

Second, Athens was a true hegemon, not, like Sparta, the premier state in a coalition of the willing. Thus the Athenians could craft strategy in a unilateral fashion impossible among the Peloponnesians. Another of the ironies of the war was that oligarchic Sparta was far more democratic in its attitudes toward its coalition members than was democratic Athens in relation to its own imperial subjects and allies.[51]

In the eleventh hour before the fighting, Pericles outlined to the Athenian assembly a conservative strategy of attrition. He called for a plan "to overcome" or, better yet, "to survive," counting on the inability of the enemy to kill or starve Athenians. To win, Sparta really needed a fleet. For all its grand talk about creating a vast armada of 500 ships, without foreign money and long training it had little chance of matching the Athenian navy for at least a decade. Instead, faced with unsustainable expenditures of marshaling a huge army to invade Athens, the Spartan oligarchy would soon appreciate the futility of the war. This plan of exhaustion—the enemy would tire itself out without getting inside the Long Walls of Athens or disrupting its empire—counted on time and patience insidiously to do their work.[52]

If Athens' immediate strategy did nothing to prevent a war, its ultimate logic might at least achieve a stalemate that, in turn, would be defined as victory: (1) evacuate the rural population and infantrymen inside the walls for a month or so during the annual Spartan invasions; (2) keep morale high, mitigate losses, and defend the countryside through cavalry patrols and rural garrisons; (3) launch naval patrols in the Aegean to guarantee that the subject states were timely in their dues and grain ships protected; (4) send out triremes with marines to harass and blockade the Peloponnesians far to the rear of their expeditionary army, while besieging rebellious subjects; (5) look to occasional opportunities in nearby Megara or Boeotia to pick off allies friendly to Sparta by either fomenting democratic revolution or even invading places where Spartans could not or would not easily deploy; (6) at all costs, avoid both expensive expeditions abroad and pitched battles against the Spartan phalanx.

Do all that, Pericles implied, and the city's message of Greek equality and the prosperity of an Athenian Aegean might find greater resonance. If one were poor, it might be preferable to be a subject of a democratic Athenian empire than a nonvoting citizen of an autonomous agrarian oligarchy. The trick was to back such idealism with action, since what states would like to do and what they could were two entirely different propositions, always predicated on whether a Spartan phalanx or Athenian trireme was closer at any given moment.[53]

So confident was Pericles of a draw that he apparently envisioned a war of no more than three or four seasons of campaigning. By then Sparta, frustrated in Attica and furious over attacks on its sacred coastal plains, would sue for peace. Perhaps another war of attrition—like the First Peloponnesian War, which had lasted fifteen years (461–446)—would lead to another stalemate that, likewise, would allow another spurt of unimpeded growth of Athenian power.[54]

Relating the War

How, THEN, SHOULD one tell such a complex story? The contemporary historian Thucydides, who sought to provide a military and political framework for the war, chose to narrate events in the annalistic tradition. He recorded the fighting year by year from 431 to 411. But at that point his incomplete history breaks off nearly in midsentence. The last seven and a half years are continued by his successor Xenophon, down to the end of the hostilities in 404–403.

Thucydides is a brilliant narrator. Yet, again, he is not easy to follow in Greek or English. Nor, speeches aside, is he always lively. His greatest moments are when he turns to graphic descriptions of representative horror: the ordeal at Corcyra, the blockade of Plataea, the battle of Mantinea, and the killing spree at Mycalessus. Most of the really gifted modern narrative historians of the Peloponnesian War of the last century—Julius Beloch, Hermann Bengston, Georg Busolt, George Grote, and Donald Kagan—have followed Thucydides' notion of a war told by campaigning seasons. They relate events of the Peloponnesian War in roughly the same chronological order as the great historian narrated them. It is the most logical method for traditional history, but it also presents problems because the Peloponnesian War was fought not merely between Athens and Sparta but rather by a host of other powers as well—Corinth, Thebes, Argos, Syracuse, and Persia—which sometimes conducted operations on their own without coordination with either of the chief belligerents.

But even within his rather neat annual presentation of the events, Thucydides himself sometimes swings widely back and forth from fighting on mainland Greece and in the Aegean to Sicily and Asia Minor, a sentence noting an Argive expedition here, suddenly a paragraph devoted to Sicilian civil strife there. He seldom makes tactical or strategic connections between nearly simultaneous operations. It is not because he is ignorant of the main plot of the war but, rather, because there often was none: Spartans, Athenians, Sicilians, Argives, Corinthians, and others fought in a series of often disjointed and confusing battles, and then seemingly did not fight much at all for months and even years on end. Local rival states, like Argos and Epidaurus, for example, might suddenly battle over disputed pastureland, yet often called such brief and confined struggles part of the larger ideological and ongoing war.

There are other problems in a chronological presentation of events. Indeed, Thucydides' contemporaries were not sure, as he apparently was, that there really was a distinct and continuous "Peloponnesian War" at all that started in 431 and ended with the defeat of Athens in 404. Some Greeks thought the war had begun in 433, when Corinth fought Corcyra at sea, or in March 431, when Plataea was attacked by the Thebans, rather than in May 431, when Spartan soldiers reached Attica. A few ancient historians, such as Theopompus and Cratippus, doubted that the war had even ended in 404 with Lysander's destruction of the Long Walls. Instead, in their views perhaps it did not cease until Athens defeated the Spartan fleet at Cnidus (394) and thus at last the two belligerents put aside their century-long rivalry.

In any case, here is a brief synopsis of the war, one providing a generally accepted outline of events that gives the reader a political and strategic context to the sometimes-confusing experience of battle that follows.[55]

PHASE ONE: THE ARCHIDAMIAN WAR (431–421)
Chapters: Fire, Disease, Terror, Armor, Walls

431 Thebans attack Plataea (March)
Spring evacuation of Attica and first Peloponnesian invasion (May)
Athenian ships raid the Peloponnese (July)
First Athenian invasion of Megara (September)

430 Second invasion of Attica (May–June)
Great plague breaks out at Athens (June)
Besieged Potidaeans surrender city to Athens (winter)

429 Peloponnesians arrive to besiege Plataea (May)
Phormio's Athenian fleet defeats the Peloponnesians in the
  Corinthian Gulf (summer)
Athenian maritime raids against northwestern Greece (summer)
Death of Pericles (September)

428 Third invasion of Attica (May–June)
250 Athenian ships deployed in the Aegean and in the west (summer)
Athenians besiege Mytilene on Lesbos (June)

427 Fourth invasion of Attica (May–June)
Capitulation of Mytileneans and debate over their fate at
  Athens (July)
Surrender of diehards at Plataea and destruction of the city (August)

426 Return of plague at Athens (May–June)
Demosthenes conducts campaigns in Aetolia and Amphilochia (June)
First Athenian expedition to Sicily (winter)

425 Athenian occupation of Pylos (May)
Fifth and last annual Peloponnesian invasion of Attica (May–June)
Spartan surrender on Sphacteria (August)
Athenian raid on the Corinthia and battle of Solygia (September)

424 Boeotians defeat Athenians at Delium (November)
Brasidas captures Amphipolis (December)
Athenians sail home from first expedition against Sicily (winter)

423 Athens moves against Mende, Scione, and Torone (April)
Walls of Thespiae razed by the Boeotians (summer)
Brasidas active in northwestern Greece (summer)

422 Cleon and Brasidas killed at Amphipolis (October)
Peace negotiations between Athens and Sparta (winter)

PHASE TWO: THE PEACE OF NICIAS (421–415)
Chapters: Terror, Armor, Walls

421 Athens evacuates Messenians from Pylos (winter)
Boeotia, Corinth, and Argos discuss various alliances (summer)

420 Alcibiades urges anti-Spartan alliance of Athens, Argos, and
Mantinea (July)
Elis bars Spartans from participation in the Olympic
Games (summer)

419 Alcibiades marches small force into the northern
Peloponnese (summer)
Argos and Epidaurus renew border war (summer)

418 Victory of Sparta at Mantinea (August)
Argos and Mantinea return to Spartan alliance (November)

417 Civil strife at Argos and defeat of the democrats (winter)
Athenian fleet active in northern Greece (summer)

416 Athenian attack on Melos (May)
Debate over sending an armada to Sicily (winter)

PHASE THREE: THE SICILIAN WAR (415–413)
Chapters: Horses, Ships

415 Alcibiades, Nicias, and Lamachus set sail for Syracuse (June)
Recall of Alcibiades, death of Lamachus, and stalemate on
Sicily (September)

414 Arrival of Gylippus with various Peloponnesian relief forces (August)
Second Athenian armada under Demosthenes prepares to
leave (winter)
Spartans arrive at Decelea, on the Athenian plain (winter)

413 Thracian mercenaries attack Mycalessus (spring)
Defeat of Athenians on Epipolae and in the Great
Harbor (July–September)
Execution of Demosthenes and Nicias (September)

PHASE FOUR: THE DECELEAN AND IONIAN WARS (413–404)
Chapters: Ships, Climax

412 Athenians construct a new fleet (spring)
Persian and Spartan military alliance (summer)
Revolts of Athenian allies in the Aegean (June–July)

411 Oligarchic revolution at Athens (June)
Spartan admiral Mindarus sends fleet into Aegean (September)
Dramatic Athenian naval victory at Cynossema (September)

410 Athenian naval victory at Cyzicus (March)
Failure of oligarchic revolution and rehabilitation of
Alcibiades (summer)
Spartans garrison bases in Asia Minor (winter)

408 Athenians seek to regain Byzantium (winter)

407 Cyrus arrives as satrap of Asia Minor and gives greater aid to
Sparta (spring)
Alcibiades dismissed (spring)

406 Spartan admiral Callicratidas defeats Athenians in the Aegean (June)
Athenian victory at Arginusae followed by trial of victorious
generals (August)
Athens rejects Spartan offers of peace (August–September)

405 Athenian defeat at Aegospotami and loss of fleet (September)
Lysander prepares to sail to Athens (November)

404 Ongoing naval blockade of Athens (winter)
Lysander sails into the Piraeus and Athens surrenders (April)
Ascension of the Thirty Tyrants (summer)

CHAPTER 2

FIRE

THE WAR AGAINST THE LAND (431–425)

To Kill a Tree

THE SPARTANS VOTED to fight in autumn 432 but waited to begin hostilities for some six months. During this phony war, their agrarian allies the Thebans first attacked the small town of Plataea even as various envoys shuttled between Athens and Sparta. But once spring came and the favorable conditions for traditional invasion arrived, thousands of Spartans realized that they had to either move or apologize for the reckless preemptive act of their Theban ally.

The Spartan idea was to marshal the Peloponnesian League, invade Attica, destroy farmland, and hope that the Athenians came out to fight. Barring that, the strategy fell back on the hope that food lost at harvesttime would cause costly shortages at Athens and that the humbling presence of Spartans near the walls of the great imperial city would encourage its restless subjects to revolt. And barring that, the Spartans could at least say they were in Attica and the Athenians were not in Laconia.

But the hide of permanent plants is tougher than men's. Orchards and vineyards are more difficult to fell than people, as the Peloponnesians quickly learned when they crossed into Attica in late May 431. Attica possessed more individual olive trees and grapevines than classical Greece did inhabitants. Anywhere from five to ten million olive trees and even more vines dotted the one-thousand-square-mile landscape. The city's thousands of acres of Attic grain fields were augmented by far more farmland throughout the Aegean, southern Russia, and Asia Minor, whose harvests were only a few weeks' sea transport away from Athens. What, then, were the Spartans thinking?

Partly in pursuit of that answer, a few years ago I tried to chop down several old walnut trees on my farm. Even when the ax did not break, it sometimes took me hours to fell an individual tree. Subsequent trials with orange, plum, peach, olive, and apricot trunks were not much easier. Even after I'd chainsawed an entire plum grove during the spring, within a month or so large suckers shot out from the stumps. Had one wished to restore the orchard, new cultivars could have been grafted to the fresh wild shoots. Apricot, peach, almond, and persimmon trees proved as tough. Olives were the hardest of all to uproot. It was even more difficult to try to set them afire. Living fruit trees (like vines) will not easily burn—or at least stay lit long and hot enough to kill the tree. Even when I ignited the surrounding dry brush, the leaves were scorched, the bark blackened, but no lasting damage was done.

Thucydides observes that the Spartans, during their fourth invasion of Attica in 427, needed to recut those trees and vines "that had grown up again" after their first devastations a few years earlier—a phenomenon of regeneration well recorded elsewhere of other such attacks on agriculture. It was difficult enough to bring an army into Attica, but harder still to accept that its destructive work needed redoing within four years. Someone who attempts any of these tasks of destruction—even without enemy horsemen loose on the counterattack—soon understands that when an ancient Greek author formulaically described troops as "ravaging the land" (*dêountes/temnontes tên gên*), he probably really meant something like "they attacked, but could not easily destroy the land."[1]

But wait: did not the Greeks live on bread, not just wine and oil, and thus in fact were not the Spartans easily torching all the city's critical grain that they did not consume on the spot? After all, burning a ripening grain crop for the Spartans in Attica should have been far easier than chopping trees or vines. Gazing out at thousands of acres of swaying dry wheat stalks, one might think that a single ember could make the entire task ridiculously easy. But even igniting grain is not always so easy, for a variety of reasons. If one ignites a dry barley field, in place of the expected sudden inferno, the small fire sometimes burns only a little before the flames quietly go out. The stalks are often greener than they look—and spaced farther apart than what meets the eye.

When and *how* one burned a field seemed to make the difference between conflagration and sporadic fires. Other factors involved atmospheric conditions and the stage of maturity and the moisture content of the grain fields. The same is true of burning permanent crops of trees and vines. Exasperated growers today sometimes rent five-hundred-gallon propane flamethrowers to guarantee that their brush piles will not go out prematurely. And even seemingly dry piles of dead fruit trees are sometimes impossible to ignite.

Even when one is not wearing armor or dodging arrows and javelins, the art of agricultural combustion is a tricky business. Therein lay one of the many paradoxes of traditional Greek land warfare in the decades before the Peloponnesian War: the tactic was just as frequently predicated on anticipated, rather than real, damage. Trees and vines, after all, are permanent crops, whose damage does not entail merely the loss of a yearly crop but rather the investment of a lifetime, with clear psychological implications to touchy farmers in harm's way.

This paranoia of the property-owning—and especially tree- and vine-owning —agrarian is what prompted an anonymous contemporary Athenian reactionary to note, "Those who are farming and the wealthy among the Athenians are more likely to reach out to the enemy, while the commons know that nothing of their own will be burnt or cut down, and so live without fear and don't ingratiate themselves with the enemy."[2] The comic playwright Aristophanes also remarked on the strange patriotic calculus that arose in a fortified Athens: the most prominent stewards of a state's hallowed soil—hoplite infantrymen—were the most likely to avoid conflict, while the shiftless poor were more eager to fight its country's enemies.

In an agricultural landscape, ravaging crops was an affront to the spiritual and religious life of the polis, besides a potential threat to its economic livelihood. Of course, if a state was landlocked and unwalled, if a community was caught napping, and if the enemy came at precisely the right time, an entire grain harvest might be torched with not much effort. Such a loss surely could bring on near and immediate starvation—and on occasion it did. Yet more often in the ancient world that near-perfect scenario would require too many ifs. Thus, neither Spartans in Attica nor Athenians in Sicily ever completely destroyed the agricultural landscape of their adversaries.[3]

Man's creation of cement and steel for roads and factories possesses none of the beauty or the age or the mystique of the olive among Mediterranean peoples. That the olive is an evergreen tree in a hot climate; that it possesses enormous powers of regeneration; that it can grow almost anywhere without constant attention or great amounts of water and fertilizer; that it reaches great age; that its fruits provide everything from fuel to cooking oil to food—all that combines to surround the tree with a nearly religious awe to match its undeniable utility, both now and in the past. That majesty explains why myths surrounded the supposedly indestructible olive growing on the Acropolis and why drama praised the tree as symbolic of Attica itself. The olive tree, in other words, was a fat target, full of symbolic capital.

Land and Soldiers

HOPLITE INFANTRYMEN OUTSIDE Sparta were originally mostly farmers—and, like most other ancient Greek citizens, proud of it; as Aristophanes reminds us, "The farmers do the work, no one else."[4] In a preindustrial world in which it often required nine people to farm to support ten, agriculture was the linchpin of all social, economic, and cultural life. Working the soil defined a man's spiritual existence, from the cultivation of ancestral trees and orchards to the stewardship of revered rural shrines and the preservation of his father's home, which he wished to pass on to his son.

Despite the images of the majestic Parthenon, the sophisticated symposia of Athens, or the crack phalanx of professional Spartan killers, most Greeks were nevertheless food producers. Thus, in multifaceted ways the war was conditioned on precisely that fact. Agriculture is the real landscape of the Peloponnesian War, the source of the food that would fuel the combatants, the home to most of the participants, and indeed often the very locus of the fighting itself.

The rural Greeks were not quite animists who believed that their trees and animals were divine spirits. Yet they accepted that their countryside was alive with lesser deities who protected rivers, springs, trees, and shrines. Such mystical immanence was one reason why agriculture was more than just the art of producing food. The Athenian philosopher, historian, and warrior Xenophon summed up "the best life" as one of farming, which gave man "the greatest degree of strength and beauty." In moral and practical terms, agriculture made "those who work the soil brave, the best citizens, most loyal to the polis." When soldiers evacuated their farms, their anguish arose not merely from the fear of economic losses; rather, the provocation was intended to be as much a matter of wounded pride and generational shame as material damage.[5]

When Aristophanes' characters are portrayed as bottled up in Athens during the Spartan invasions, they sigh that they wish to return to their ancestral farms, see individual trees and vines they have planted, and visit sacred shrines. These scenes were not fantasy creations of a comic poet. During the evacuation Aristophanes had grown familiar with the lives of some of the 20,000 Attic farmers who owned and farmed much of the 200,000 acres that surrounded Athens. They were the doughty rustics who formed the nucleus of the traditional army that in the fifth century alone had beaten the Persians at Marathon, crushed the feared Boeotians at the battle of Oinophyta, and fought shoulder to shoulder alongside the Spartans at Plataea and in Messenia. The best way to prompt these "most loyal" men of an agrarian militia to come out and fight was to assault these symbols of what it meant to be a free landowning citizen—and there were still thousands of these stout farmer-citizens even in 431 in a maritime and imperial Athens.

Whatever the impracticality of the Spartan strategy, King Archidamus and his generals at least realized the spiritual stakes involved. The major Athenian playwrights—Sophocles, Euripides, and Aristophanes—all at one time or another either boasted about the sanctity of Attica or lamented its suffering from enemy devastators.[6] Their anguish during the war reflected a long Greek tradition: during most intramural Greek land warfare between 700 and 450, the sight of a few ancestral olive trees hacked by an ax was enough to draw the angry hoplites who owned them into battle. Wars between property owners can start over perceived rather than real grievances, over a few scarred trunks rather than thousands of acres of obliterated orchards. When a modern visitor examines the scrub and maquis on the rocky borders between Attica and Boeotia or Argos and Sparta, he might wonder why such sophisticated societies started a war over the ownership of such seemingly worthless ground.

The reactionary Spartans were not completely unhinged, then, when on arrival in Attica in late spring 431 they thought that the Athenians would march out in suicidal fashion and form in the phalanx once they experienced fire and sword. True, the Spartan phalanx itself instilled terror and seemingly would have scared off any potential adversaries. But in nearly 75 percent of the cases of hoplite battle, defending Greek armies defeated the invaders and thus were confident in a home-field advantage—so strong was the psychological edge for property owners when defending their own sacred soil.

So accepted a tactic had ravaging become that it was institutionalized in the clauses of farm leases and peace treaties. Devastation of farmland was deeply ingrained in the popular culture, and a general staple of ethical discussion. Catchphrases amplified this almost annual experience of attacking permanent crops, in the form of boasts to make "cicadas sing from the ground" or threats "to turn cropland into a sheep walk" if demands were not met.[7] Much of the logic of war, in other words, had been static for centuries in a rural society of unfortified hamlets. Apparently very few in the Peloponnese realized that all the rules were about to disappear as Greece was on the eve of the first true military revolution in the history of Western civilization.

Only a quasi police state that had no real money, no walls, no lively intellectual life, no notion of upward mobility, and no immigration could naively assume that a parochial tactic that worked with wayward rural neighbors of the

Peloponnese could bring down the greatest state in the history of Hellenic civilization. It was even worse than that: throughout the fifth century Athens had constructed the most massive municipal fortifications in the Greek world precisely to guarantee supplies of imported staples and in part to create immunity from agrarian warfare. In one of the most understated passages in Thucydides' history, the Corinthians remonstrate with their Spartan allies, saying, "Your methods, compared to those of the Athenians', are old-fashioned."[8]

In reality, most of the conservative Greeks also shared the Spartan naïveté— that it would be a win-win situation for the invaders. Surely they would either kill Athenian soldiers or starve out their families. Before the Spartans and their allies actually reached Attica, Thucydides, for example, wrote that they had supposed that they could defeat Athens "in a few years should they ravage its territory." Neutral observers had agreed about the cheery prognosis: "If the Spartans should invade Attica, some thought that the Athenians could hold out for a year; others two; but no one longer than three years." Thucydides does not tell us who those "some" were; they were probably his oligarchic Athenian friends and aristocratic sources in Sparta who—unlike the historian himself— never quite grasped the revolutionary nature and resiliency of a radically democratic Athens. It was only later and after a long decade into the war that the Spartan general Brasidas reflected on how wrong such old and simplistic ideas were. He admitted such to his troops in the field years after the outbreak of the war: "We were wrong in the idea we had of war back then, when we thought that we would be able quickly to destroy the Athenians."[9]

Forgetting the earlier evacuation and abandonment of the Attic countryside before the massive invasion of Xerxes' Persians in September 480, most Spartans instead were wedded to the idea that the Athenians would react as they had a decade earlier to Darius' initial landing at Marathon in 490, some twenty-six miles northeast of the city. During that first Persian invasion of Greece, thousands of Athenian farmers donned their armor and rushed out to protect the soil and prestige of Athens—winning lasting fame as the "Marathon battlers" who had saved the city in a single stroke.

The invaders also drew confidence from a more recent example: fifteen years earlier, when faced with the Spartan invasion of 446 during the First Peloponnesian War, the Athenians had seen a Spartan king and his army turn around right at the border, thus providing an eleventh-hour reprieve for both their troops and their farms.[10] Accordingly, in May 431, older Athenians had good reason to think that the Spartans might once more be cajoled or bought off to make a ceremonial demonstration of force before withdrawing as they had before. On the eve of the war, the edgy Corinthians confidently urged the Spartans to invade "without delay."[11]

The campaign was envisioned by the Spartans themselves as one of a season or two: burn some grain and cut down some vines and trees, wait for 10,000 Attic farmers to pour out to battle, and witness the professional infantrymen of Sparta, supported by thousands of other allies, make short work of them. After all, sixteen years earlier the Boeotians had expelled the Athenians from their homeland and ended their war outright through a single devastating defeat of the Athenian army at the battle of Coronea (447). No one expected the Athenian defenders to fight quite like the Boeotians had at Coronea, but many thought they would at least fight.

Athenian allies in the Aegean would become emboldened by the sheer audacity of Spartan troops near the walls of Athens and quickly revolt. The city would then sue for peace. Sparta would dictate terms: perhaps freedom for Greek subjects to leave the Athenian empire and guarantees of neutrality for "Third World" states. Further Athenian concessions would be made: surrender of border forts, reduction of the fleet, or alliance with Sparta. Everyone could pretty much go back home with the issues of prestige, honor, and status clearly resolved on the battlefield. A few Greeks might have appreciated Spartan past efforts to depose Athenian tyranny and the bravery of the Spartan army fifty years earlier at the battle of Plataea, when it stopped the Persians cold, and thus found its surprising present posture as the liberator of the city-states from Athens somewhat credible.

This inflexible strategy was the first of a chain of tragic miscalculations, as even the commander of the Peloponnesian invading forces at last realized before the march began. "The Athenians have plenty of other land in their empire, and can import what they want by sea," the Spartan king Archidamus warned in a Lord Grey–type "the lamps are going out" speech. He added ominously, "Let us not be caught up in the hope that the war will be over if we just ravage their countryside. I fear instead that we shall leave war as a legacy to our children, so unlikely it is that the Athenians will prove slaves to their land or like amateurs they will become shocked by the war."[12]

The Athenians at the very outset realized, albeit accidentally, that the only way they would lose the war would be when an enemy accomplished what Lysander eventually pulled off twenty-seven years later, when he sailed into the Piraeus and finally sat atop the Acropolis. The Athenians made an arrangement to set aside the enormous sum of 1,000 talents—in today's dollars about $480 million—in an emergency reserve defense fund to draft more troops and build more ships in case the Spartans sent a fleet against the Piraeus. In fact, in 429 the frustrated Spartans attempted just such an incursion, and their daring maritime attackers nearly succeeded in getting close to the harbor before being driven off from Salamis and back to Corinth.[13]

The Shadow of Pericles

As A POPULAR leader of a radically democratic state, Pericles realized that perhaps a quarter of his voters—his core poorer constituents—owned little or no land. Half the citizens of Athens rowed in the fleet or worked in his program of public works to create his majestic imperial city. As the indignant philosophers and elites complained, the poorer thetes would not personally suffer directly from an attack on farmland that they did not own.* Many urban dwellers knew very few Attic farmers. Perhaps they rarely even saw them in town. Instead, they could profit greatly as paid rowers to patrol and to protect the sea-lanes. Out of that domestic self-interested political calculus of sacrificing native agriculture also arose the best way collectively to defend the maritime empire of Athens.

Yet Pericles was not merely cynical or eager in wartime to divide his own people along political lines. He also grasped two other essential shortcomings about Spartan strategy on the eve of the first invasion of 431. First, it was not an easy task for tens of thousands of parochial folk to leave their own harvests, march from over 150 miles distant, live off the land in transit, and systematically destroy in a few days some 200,000 acres—especially when Athenian rural garrisons and cavalry patrols made invaders in small groups and out of formation easy prey. Later the Athenians believed that if they could just knock the Boeotians, who provided cavalry support for the ravagers from the Peloponnese, out of the war, the invasions would cease altogether. Horsemen apparently fought horsemen to keep the Athenian cavalry from riding down vulnerable ravagers.

The Spartans also came in such numbers that their army seemed too formidable to achieve its aim of prompting battle, and likewise almost too large to feed.[14] Just to supply so many thousands while in Attica was a logistical nightmare and was predicated entirely on how quickly they could get to Athenian grain while it was ripe and either unharvested in the field or not yet transported

---

*Thetes (*thetai*) were the poorest of the census classes at Athens and elsewhere—in wartime, mostly landless wage earners who either rowed in the fleet or accompanied the phalanx as skirmishers and light-armed troops.

into Athens. Modern studies have suggested that during the five invasions the Peloponnesians would have consumed in aggregate grain equal to an entire annual Attic wheat and barley harvest. By June 431 there may have been altogether almost 400,000 Peloponnesians and Athenians either out in the Attic countryside or inside the walls of Athens—a vast, mostly nameless mob of desperate folk at war that warrants almost no mention in our ancient sources.[15]

Pericles had warned about the perils of facing the national army of the Peloponnesians: even had the Athenians won a single pitched battle against such enormous numbers of hoplites, such a dramatic victory still would not have decided the war. To meet such an army in pitched battle was a "terrible thing" to contemplate, in which even a miraculous victory might have little strategic effect. It is difficult to know whether Pericles feared the sheer size of the Peloponnesian allied army or the presence of Spartans themselves, who probably made up only 10 percent of the aggregate force, or some 4,000 to 6,000 hoplites. Later, in 406, King Agis brought an army of almost 30,000 troops right to the walls of Athens. But the Spartans marched only on a moonless night, and were not willing to fight a battle within bowshot of the city. In turn, the Athenian phalanx had no desire to meet them distant from the protective support of archers on the ramparts.[16]

As Spartans tried to cut down olive trees in Attica, Athenian marines and light-armed troops, albeit in far fewer numbers, could be ferried to the coastal towns of the Peloponnese to harass through raiding and plundering. Such tactics had been used years before in early battles between Sparta and Athens. In fact, for the first decade of the war, the Athenians conducted raids all over the Peloponnese. They stormed small hamlets where the grain harvests were collected and vulnerable. Pericles' raiders achieved such terror and disruption that a popular tale circulated that the Athenians had done more agricultural damage in the Peloponnese than the Peloponnesians had in Attica.[17] It was just such a ravaging expedition much later against the seaboard of Laconia in summer 414 that outraged the Spartans enough to cause them to renew the war. They claimed that such audacity in attacking their sacred soil at a time of reconciliation was an insult to their pride, thus prompting them formally to annul the provisions of the Peace of Nicias and at last restart full-scale hostilities against Athens.[18]

Very soon the Athenians would exploit the helot paranoia of Sparta. If the Spartans' own Peloponnesian agrarian allies had harvest concerns that limited the amount of time they could be away from their crops, the Spartans worried not about unattended fields but rather about unattended field-workers. They fretted constantly that nearby peoples like the Argives or Arcadians were just waiting to promote helot rebellion to facilitate their own aspirations for independence.[19]

For all these reasons, the Athenian leadership had convinced everybody except the farmers themselves that the Spartans would not seriously damage the heartland of Athens—and most certainly not force the Athenian state to either come out to fight or capitulate. Even the rebellious maritime subjects of Athens, who in the past had believed that invading Attica might allow them to revolt from a distracted Athens, finally came to agree. In seeking Spartan support for their revolt of 427, after four Spartan invasions, the Mytileneans of Lesbos at last shrugged, saying that the "war will not be in Attica" but waged and won on the seas rather than by burning and cutting crops.[20]

Such visions of a naval victory took two decades to evolve at Sparta. In the meantime, the key, Pericles realized, to beating these Dorian reactionaries was to keep everyone inside the walls—no easy task with thousands of hotheaded Attic farmers. He must in addition guarantee that the trade routes were safe and the Athenian triremes vigilant for signs of maritime rebellion. Later, ambivalent states in the Peloponnese like Argos and Mantinea might come over to the Athenian side, and so surround Sparta with nearby enemies. Boeotia, as had happened between 557 and 447, might also be invaded and once more be made a democratic ally.

But all that was in the future. For now, in the spring of 431, Pericles had the more immediate problem of dealing with a 60,000-man enemy army on the horizon. So he reminded his citizens that trees and vines—unlike men—could regenerate when cut down. He announced to his grumbling compatriots, "If I thought I could persuade you, I would have you go out and waste them with your own hands."[21]

But, of course, he could never convince such yeomen of Attica. A few months before Archidamus arrived, the Athenians watched Euripides' *Medea*, a play in which their countryside was praised as "the holy land that is unwasted"—a reflection of how comforting that boast was to most Athenians. Indeed, there is a special word in the Greek language, *aporthêtos* ("unplundered"), that reflects this almost religious pride in land that has been untouched by the enemy due to the courage and strength of its hoplite citizenry. In this context, did the Spartan failure in Attica between 431 and 425 to win the war or concessions prove that the strategy of agricultural devastation was no longer of much value in a conflict as multifaceted and long as the Peloponnesian War?

Not quite. Later in the war, the reactionary practice of ravaging still continued to spark resistance, internal strife, capitulation, or hunger at places like Corcyra, Acanthus, Mende, and Melos. But then, unlike the exceptional case of Athens, none of those places had extensive fortifications connected to a well-protected port, reserve capital, secure supplies of imported food, an empire and fleet, and a relatively united democratic population.[22] In addition, Greeks would come to appreciate devastation as a tactic of economic warfare in its own right, rather than a catalyst to pitched battle.

The Great Gamble

IF KING ARCHIDAMUS and his Peloponnesian army completely underestimated the problems of ravaging Attica and the nature of Athenian countermeasures, Pericles himself also failed to grasp three fatal flaws in his own otherwise cogent strategy of attrition. First, he assumed that a city built for 100,000 urban residents might accommodate—without problems of housing, water, and sanitation in the Mediterranean heat of late spring and summer—an additional population of some 100,000 to 150,000 rural refugees for a month or more. He was in error. Thousands of refugees would be without permanent shelter. They would quickly overtax the fountains, latrines, and sewers of the city. And the evacuees would grow angry at having been forced to leave their homes, and soon become uncomfortable with city folks—most of whom they had never seen before and probably did not like.

Pericles planned to turn the most majestic city of the Greek world into one enormous and squalid refugee camp in an age before knowledge and proper treatment of microbes—a radical policy that had been attempted during neither the Persian nor the First Peloponnesian War. Anyone who has spent summers in modern Athens can appreciate the afternoon heat that descends on the city and the air that grows stagnant—lying as it does in a basin surrounded and cut off by the ranges of Mounts Aigaleos, Parnes, Pentelikos, and Hymettus and without either a major river or the seashore in its immediate environs.[23]

Later a tired Pericles himself confessed to a worn-out and angry assembly, "The plague was the one event that proved greater than our foresight." There is more tragic irony here: the earlier construction of the Long Walls (461–456) was Themistocles' way of ensuring that in the future Athenians could avoid pitched battle, stay in the city, and thus not have to flee en masse to the nearby islands. In fact, that earlier traumatic evacuation of Athens in 480, by dispersing the population among nearby Aegina, Salamis, and Troezen, mitigated the chances of overcrowding and plague. What Pericles needed perhaps was not so much a military strategist as a public health expert. Meanwhile, he appeared as foolish as Archidamus did wise. A chance pestilence proved the strategic insight of the former disastrous—and the banal ideas of the latter inspired.[24]

Second, Pericles gambled that the Athenians—a people that had once marched out to Marathon to beat an army three times its size and had sunk a numerically superior Persian fleet at Salamis in sight of the Acropolis—could now sit idly by without damage to their national psyche while thousands of enemies swaggered in to challenge their martial prowess. Of course, farmers would soon grow irate that their homes were overrun. But the collective population at large would also have to stomach the even more odious idea that none of their men would dare to fight an enemy a few miles from the walls.

War is never merely a struggle over concrete things. Instead, as great generals from the Theban Epaminondas to Napoleon saw, it remains a contest of wills, of mentalities and perceptions that lie at the heart of all military exegeses, explaining, for example, why a Russian army that collapsed in 1917 on its frontier held out in its overrun interior during World War II, or how a completely outnumbered and poorly supplied Israeli army between 1947 and 1967 overwhelmed enemies that enjoyed superior weaponry and a tenfold advantage in military manpower.

So once the Athenians had established the precedent that enemies could occupy their homeland with the near assurance that they would not or could not be forcibly removed, would not an inevitable sense of collective self-doubt and insecurity follow? Again, would other enemies—or Athens' own critical and large Aegean subject states, such as Chios, Mytilene, and Samos—feel that Athens either could not or would not any longer respond to attack? How exactly could a proud empire prevent insurrection on distant island subject states, when it would not even defend its own soil? Most potentially rebellious Greeks were not versed in tactical nuances and thus did the simpler moral arithmetic in terms something like "Did our masters, the Athenians, fight or in fear stay behind the walls?"

Years later, on the eve of the Sicilian expedition, one of the arguments that the sophist Alcibiades used to convince the Athenians—a citizenry that had lost a quarter of its population to the plague and had its land occupied on five occasions—to attack Syracuse was that by nature Athens was suited only to aggressive strategies and would cease to exist if it opted for a passive posture. Perhaps one reason why Alcibiades' often fallacious logic struck a chord was that the hotheads in his audience could recall Archidamus' early invasions— when the Athenians had stayed still, and such passivity had brought them the plague, the death of Pericles, and no clear-cut advantage for ten years.

Ultimately, if Athens entered a conflict against the greatest land power in the Greek world, it had to destroy either the Spartan army or the system—the entire foundations of helotage—that allowed such a professional military to train and march abroad. There is little indication that Pericles, at least at the outset, ever envisioned such bold offensive strokes as organizing a Panhellenic coalition to descend into Laconia, or even a way to pay for the fighting if it went beyond five years. Again, wars do not really end until the conditions that started them—a bellicose government, an aggressive leader, a national policy of brinkmanship—are eliminated. Otherwise there remains a *bellum interruptum*, much like the so-called Peace of Nicias, when Athens and Sparta agreed to a time-out in 421, before going at each other with renewed and deadly fury in 415.

Third, Pericles assumed that a leader of his rhetorical talents, political experience, and moral authority could rein in both conservative farmers and democratic extremists and do so systematically and steadily until the Spartans gave up. His surviving busts in stone, like those of a similar war leader, Lincoln, appear almost serene. His hoplite helmet is pushed to the back of his ample forehead, a visage reflecting concern with monumental issues, while indicating neither arrogance nor insecurity.

For over thirty years, Pericles as an annually elected general had exercised just such Olympian moral clout, and thereby lent a sense of political consistency and continuity unusual for an ancient democracy that functioned without constitutional checks and balances on the majority votes of a fickle assembly. His savvy mix of radically egalitarian sympathies and aristocratic gravitas helped him lead—but not indulge—the volatile mob who could vote to enslave, murder, or forgive rebellious allies as it saw fit on any given day.

True, Pericles in theory was only one of ten annually selected generals—who were elected by a public show of hands in the assembly and could be reelected each year. Yet his age, experience, character, and rhetoric gave him such wide public support that by sheer force of will he was able to persuade his colleagues either to hold or postpone assemblies of the people, and thus to facilitate or stymie outbursts of popular expression.[25]

To an approving Thucydides, "in name a democracy, Athens became a government ruled by its first citizen." Whether such a blanket encomium was entirely an accurate reflection of how politics really worked in Periclean Athens is unclear, especially given Thucydides' propensity to denigrate the Athenian assembly as a "mob" or "crowd" of poorer and less educated people. But a more salient consideration was that Pericles was now about sixty-four years old. There must have been doubts about whether he possessed any longer the physical stamina to meet the greatest challenge in the history of the democracy.[26]

What ultimately would betray the great leader were as much lapses in logic as physical exhaustion and age. Pericles was to be proved wrong on all three of his gambles about the coerced evacuation from Attica. The sudden plague that broke out during the second year of the invasions (430) wiped out thousands of the frontline military infantrymen of Athens. It killed or sickened tens of thousands more, thus taking more lives than could any Spartan phalanx, reminding us that in most wars more usually die from disease than enemy iron. He drove his citizens inside the walls to ensure thousands their salvation, but instead guaranteed destruction to far more. Civic tension broke out among various interests that was never completely resolved, but soon manifested itself in precipitous and poorly thought-out offensive operations, and eventually in the two political coups of 411 and 403. To the conservative historian Thucydides, Pericles' demise was a tragic loss and led to an endless cycle of lesser demagogic figures: Cleon, Alcibiades, Hyperbolus, Cleonymus, and Cleophon, who all played one faction off against the other in cynical pursuit of personal power.

Enemy at the Gates

NONE OF THESE repercussions was anticipated in late May 431. Then a huge allied army of Peloponnesians, consisting of thousands of hoplites, cavalrymen, and light-armed troops—two-thirds of all available troops in the Peloponnesian alliance—mustered at the Isthmus of Corinth. The mass then slogged its way northward on the first of what would turn out to be five late-spring invasions of Attica over the ensuing decade.

The attack was, in fact, somewhat late. Despite hearing a litany of Peloponnesian complaints against the Athenians during the summer of 432, then obtaining a vote that the Athenians were in material breach of the peace, and finally receiving recent word that their allied Boeotians had preempted them by attacking the Athenian protectorate city-state of Plataea in early March 431, the Spartans nevertheless waited months to advance into Attica. Ostensibly, they had to time their arrival with the ripening of the barley and wheat fields, those crops most important to an ancient city and the easiest to destroy by burning.

In such a huge countryside as Attica, replete with different elevations and microclimates, there might be as much as a two-month divergence in ripening times. Thus, finding some combustible dry grain was no guarantee that the crop just a few miles away would also be mature and vulnerable. Ancient armies usually carried three days' rations or so, and thus counted on the harvests of the invaded to supplement what little food they brought along. That Archidamus had actually mobilized such a large army composed from so many small communities was miraculous, given the fact that most rural folk of the Peloponnese had no desire to march away and leave their women and children to care for their own ripening crops. Indeed, even if the huge army marched ten abreast, it stretched out for over fifteen miles, as it slowly wound its way northward into Attica. Its belated advance into Attica formally started the Peloponnesian War. As the Peloponnesians at last crossed the border, a Spartan herald returned from a failed last-minute peace mission to Athens, sighing of the enormous army that crossed into Attica, "This day will be the beginning of great misfortunes to the Hellenes." And so it was.[27]

None of these contingents would have attacked Athens singularly. But now they swarmed in on two guarantees of their safety: the army was huge and thus invincible, and both the red-cloaked Spartans and the feared horsemen of Boeotia were to run loose at the vanguard in Attica. Who knows all the crazy thoughts that raced through the minds of these opportunists: Might Athens surrender and its plush city be left ripe for plunder? Might its chagrined hoplites march out and meet catastrophe in a glorious Peloponnesian victory? Might twenty thousand farms supply enough plunder to enrich an entire generation? Thucydides wrote of the general Hellenic consensus on the eve of the war—of course well before states had much experience with victorious Spartans as overlords—"It was clearly on the side of the Lacedaemonians."[28]

Despite the enemy's hopes that the overseas tributary allies of Athens would revolt on news that Spartans at last ranged freely a few miles from the Athenian Acropolis, or that the Athenians would cease their blockade of Potidaea, not many subjects believed that Athenian power was in any way eroding. And fewer still felt that their own future would necessarily be any better under Spartan hegemony. Even fewer neutral states sent their young men to join the Spartan crusade. In the chaotic world of some fifteen hundred autonomous city-states—where a few stone ramparts were all that sometimes kept invaders on the horizon out of the agora—it always made better sense on rumors of war to pause, take a deep breath, put aside ideological zeal, and carefully size up the respective strengths of potential allies and enemies before committing to battle. The vote of the Peloponnesian League to go to war was taken in August 432; the army didn't reach the borders of Attica until May 431. For eight months—almost exactly the period of the "phony war" on the Franco-German border between the invasion of Poland and the attack through the Ardennes (September 1939 to May 1940)—Sparta not only prepared to muster an allied army but, more importantly, hoped for a final resolution that might bring concessions from Athens.[29]

The Peloponnesians' trek northward to Athens from Sparta followed much the same route as the modern highway. It is a scenic way that, after leaving the Isthmus at Corinth, traverses the Megarid to the high cliffs above Salamis. Then the route passes the sanctuary of Eleusis, before crossing over the slopes of Mount Aigaleos at the modern suburb of Daphni and finally descending into the plain of Athens. The road is not an easy, level march, and it is made worse by the heat of late spring and the scarcity of water along much of the way. What did tens of thousands of Peloponnesians think of as they hiked along the cliffs that tower over the straits of Salamis, where a half century earlier the grandfathers of both sides had united to preserve Greek liberty?

The mob that advanced was itself larger than all but a handful of Greek city-states, carrying along tons of iron, bronze, and wooden arms and armor, unsure whether the cliffs above would be patrolled by Athenian rangers. However, in this initial invasion before reaching the formal border of Attica, King Archidamus first turned to the northeast. He sought to enter Attica instead by a circuitous route near the northwestern garrison at the tiny hamlet of Oenoë and then to descend into the outlying demes on the lower slopes of Mount Parnes.

There the invaders were immediately confronted with a myriad of more mundane problems, from cavalry patrols and rural Athenian garrison troops to confusion about delegating the tasks of agricultural devastation. Thucydides reports that Archidamus had been slow in mustering in the Peloponnese, slow in collecting the final army at Corinth, and was now slow—or perhaps bogged down—in Attica itself. In the leader's defense, no Spartan king had ever been put in charge of such a massive coalition army, a force far larger than any commanded later by either Philip or Alexander, both masters of sophisticated logistics. Second, Sparta had never been known for audacity beyond the borders of Laconia; every Spartan commander, with the exception of the rare Brasidas, Gylippus, or Lysander, was at one time or another dilatory in bringing troops to battle, fearful that helots were free rather than farming.

Despite an array of siege engines, the invaders failed to take the Athenian base at Oenoë, which was well fortified, stoutly defended, and a nexus for frequent Athenian patrolling. Soon a frustrated Archidamus moved on, slowly descending to the Eleusinian and Thriasian plains. There he settled in near Acharnae. This was the largest rural deme of Attica, less than ten miles from the walls of the city proper, and its occupation meant a brazen challenge for Athenians to put up or shut up.

The Acharnians, crusty growers who provide the eponymous title of an Aristophanic comedy criticizing the war, may have normally contributed as many as 3,000 hoplite soldiers to the Athenian army. So they were influential

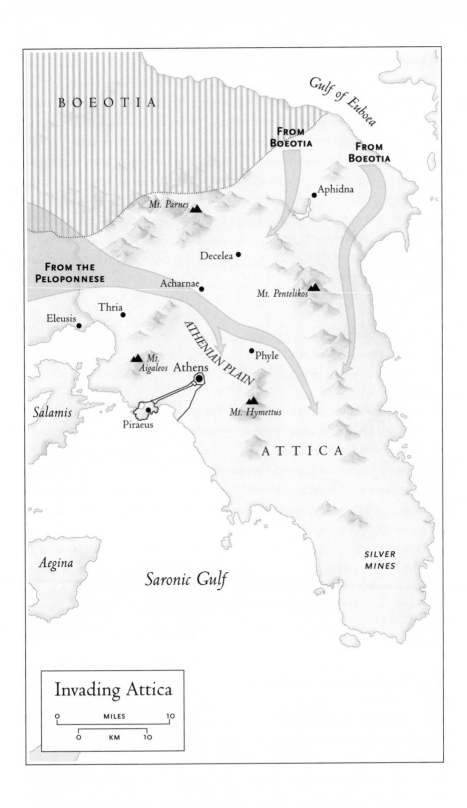

BOEOTIA

Gulf of Euboea

FROM
BOEOTIA

FROM
BOEOTIA

Aphidna

Mt. Parnes ▲

Decelea ●

FROM THE
PELOPONNESE

Acharnae ●

Mt. Pentelikos ▲

Thria ●

Eleusis ●

Phyle ●

ATHENIAN PLAIN

▲ Mt.
Aigaleos   Athens ●

Salamis

Piraeus

Mt. Hymettus ▲

ATTICA

Aegina

Saronic Gulf

SILVER
MINES

Invading Attica

0   MILES   10

0   KM   10

folk, farming a large and fertile district of Attica near the slopes of Mount Pentelikos, not far from the city proper. Many made their living by burning charcoal and knew something about fire in the countryside. In Archidamus' mind, the property of these touchy farmers should be the first Athenian soil targeted, a test case of sorts: the furious Acharnians would either force the others to fight or cause so much dissension inside the walls as to undermine civic support altogether for Pericles' strategy. In Plutarch's words, they surely would march out to battle if for nothing other than "angry pride."[30]

Despite the cynical Spartan attempt to reveal the fragility of democracy in time of war, Pericles held firm and reined in the Acharnians. In desperation Archidamus ravaged their vineyards and orchards and, when no enemy phalanx marched out, moved out of Acharnae. Pericles had kept sending out offensive cavalry patrols; he may have anticipated the present need, because he'd beefed up the cavalry to 1,000 mounts on the eve of the war. He also made sure not to convene any meetings of the assembly where rival demagogues—the fiery Cleon especially—might excite the mob in these times of stress. In Plutarch's words, he "shut the city up tight" and "gave little thought to the slanderers and malcontents."[31]

For all the supposed political turmoil, the Spartans had, ironically, created a weird, novel political cohesion inside the walls. The poor were busy manning the fleet to attack the seaboard of the Peloponnese to pay them back for their ravaging of Attica. The middling hoplite farmers were angry, but safe inside the walls without the need to confront crack Spartan infantrymen. The wealthy every day were bravely riding out to harass enemy ravagers and did a superb job in curtailing the despoiling of the countryside.[32]

Frustrated by this repeated inability either to ruin the countryside or to prompt a battle, after a few days Archidamus moved farther on, to the region between Mount Pentelikos and Mount Parnes. From there the Spartans exited Attica through the northern borderland of Oropus. The army ended up in neighboring and friendly Boeotia before trudging back home a few weeks after it mustered.

In prewar discussions it was little remarked upon that Athens, in fact, had a two-front war on its hands: Peloponnesians to the south, Boeotians on the north. Already, in the first days of the fighting, the Athenians were learning that not only could opportunistic Boeotian raiders plunder with near impunity from the nearby border but also that the Spartans could not really be bottled up in Attica and denied safe exit. They needed only to march on through to Boeotia, rest, replenish their supplies, and then if need be take a circuitous route home that bypassed Attica altogether.[33]

Theory Versus Practice

FOR ALL THE size of the first attacking army, at least two-thirds of Attica was nevertheless left unravaged. In contrast, even if all 1,000 Athenian horsemen had scoured the countryside at once, in theory the cavalry offered a pitiful deterrent. There was only a single defender for every 200 acres of cultivated land. Yet, because the Spartans concentrated on particular hot-button targets in Attica, such as the deme of Acharnae, large bands of cavalry could keep the enemy from fanning out too far from the main body. On this first inroad it seems that Archidamus' dilatory progress and his decision to concentrate mostly on those rich demes within sight of the walls of Athens were designed to provoke rather than ruin the Athenians.

Again, what is striking about both ancient and modern Attica is its vast size, over one thousand square miles, making it one of the larger rural territories of any polis of the ancient Greek world. If half the arable land of Attica was cultivated in olive orchards (e.g., about 100,000 acres, with 50 to 100 trees per acre), there might have been planted anywhere from 5 to 10 million trees! Ravaging all these groves was an impossible task of complete destruction, especially after the initial invasion of a purported 60,000 Peloponnesians, when the enemy probably mustered only about 30,000 in four subsequent inroads. In a few weeks' time, a single hoplite or even a light-armed ravager could hardly hope to cut down, on average, 250 trees, especially when the countryside was still alive with horsemen and a few angry recalcitrant farmers.

Because Attica was so large, an entire corpus of Greek literature attests that even in peacetime many Athenian rustics had *never* ventured into the city at all. This parochialism was not surprising, since some farms were fifty miles distant from the Acropolis and a long hike away.[34] Athenian strength cannot be calibrated only through its silver mines, fleet, and income from overseas tributary allies. Like Sparta and Thebes, much of Athens' financial power accrued from its large rural territory and population. For all the attention paid to gold, silver, and manpower, the real players in the ancient Greek world—Sparta, Athens, Thebes, and Corinth—were precisely those states that controlled the largest or most fertile tracts of farmland, the ultimate source of all wealth in early, preindustrial societies. Even today, despite the unchecked urban spread of Athens, its new sprawling rural airport, and thousands of impressive country homes, there are still tens of thousands of acres in small valleys and plains that are hard to reach and often quite isolated, from the foothills of Mount Parnes to the interior plains and vales of Laurium, some fifty miles to the south.

Earlier, before the campaign had even begun, King Archidamus—in Thucydides' history a tragic Hamlet-like character who hesitates before striking—had outlined to the Spartan assembly his doubts about systematically ravaging the entire Athenian plain and his belief that Greek farmers would still negotiate rather than see smoke arising from their farms. So he voiced his concerns on mostly strategic, if not psychological, grounds: "Do not consider their land anything other than a hostage to hold, and it is a better hostage the better it continues to be cultivated."[35]

Later a popular theme of historians was cataloging those areas of Attica—Decelea, the plain of Marathon, the Academy (the future site of Plato's school), and various private estates with the so-called sacred olive trees—that despite five annual invasions were never attacked and thus perhaps never evacuated. Rumors had it that the Spartans might also skip rural property of some elites who might thus come under suspicion of philo-Laconism or sympathy with right-wing Spartan oligarchy. And if farms like those of wealthy Pericles were spared, it would only inflame public opinion and divide the citizenry over issues of comparative sacrifices under such an unpopular tactic of forced withdrawal. Something besides mere destruction of crops was going on in the mind of Archidamus.[36]

At news of their coming—the Athenians had several days' notice from spies and scouts—the reaction was immediate for those in the path of the ravagers. From public documents on stone, it seems that even before the war the Athenians had made some arrangements to evacuate property from rural shrines, as if they anticipated just such an eventual Spartan invasion. Thucydides, who was sympathetic to the landowning class and may have witnessed firsthand the evacuation, wrote in graphic detail that many rural Athenians carted their belongings inside the walls of Athens. There they hunkered down and counted on cavalry patrols to pick off isolated parties of ravagers.

Urban crowds gathered to argue and fight over the wisdom of withdrawal, something unheard of for almost a half century, since the legendary general Themistocles had organized the flight to the adjoining islands and the nearby Argolid in consequence of the southward advance of Xerxes from Thermopylae. Thucydides' description of this heartbreaking trek into the city is one of the most moving in his history:

> After listening to Pericles' exhortations, the Athenians were won over and so brought in from their fields their children, wives, and all their household furniture, even stripping the very woodwork from the homes themselves. They sent their sheep and draft animals to Euboea and the nearby islands. But the

evacuation was a difficult thing for them to endure because for most they had always been accustomed to live in the country.

Later he adds, "They did not find it very easy to evacuate their homes, especially because it was not that long ago since they had reestablished their estates after the Persian Wars. So they were depressed and took it hard to have to abandon their homes and shrines." This sudden entry of thousands of rural folk into the walls of Athens between 431 and 425—the catalysts of the plague of 430—caused a radical shift in Athenian society itself. Heretofore most farmers and rustics had kept away from the city. Now they were everywhere. Literature of the war, especially Aristophanes' comedies, for the first time in the history of Athenian letters began to see things from the mostly forgotten view of the other Greeks outside the walls.[37]

"I Really Hate the Lacedaemonians"

THE SHEER WORK involved in ruining grain fields might explain stories from later Greek history that sometimes armies brought along special wooden tools, so ravagers might more easily beat and break down the still-green grain shoots. Buildings required even more work, making us wonder whether the laments of lavish estates lost always ring true. Houses, as was true in much of Greece until the mid-twentieth century, were built of mud brick with tile roofs. It was not so simple to knock these nonflammable structures down. The only sure method was to torch their interior wooden support beams and hope for collapse. That, too, was a time-consuming challenge, especially when most of the accessible woodwork and doors that could be used for fuel had already been stripped and evacuated. The paltry remains of the foundations of some prominent classical Athenian farmhouses have been excavated in vulnerable places on the spurs of Mount Pentelikos, the coast at Vari, and near a strategic pass on Mount Parnes. None of them seem to reveal damage or destruction from the later fifth century, suggesting that they either were not seriously attacked or were skipped altogether.[38]

As Spartan infantrymen in small patrols tried to protect the ravagers from Athenian cavalry, the mob of destroyers sought to plunder all that they could carry and eat as they burned and cut. But soldiers, ancient and modern, are trained to fight, and thus infantrymen make less effective looters, engineers, or peacekeepers. The war had surely started, but the initial theater of operations involved no pitched battles, clashes at sea, great sieges, or even terrorist raids, and thus for many Greeks this was already a strange sort of fight, especially given the huge army of Archidamus and the even larger numbers of Attic residents who retreated into the walls.

In the comedies *Acharnians* (425) and *Peace* (421), Aristophanes presented smart-alecky Athenian farmers as wiser than their leadership and slowly radicalized in their anger at the enemy, their own political leadership, and the war in general. These unsung stalwarts were furious that beloved estates were allowed to be overrun by enemy vandals. "I really hate the Lacedaemonians," the hero-farmer Dicaeopolis ("Just City") laments in *Acharnians*, "for in my case too there have been vines cut down." There are plenty more admissions in contemporary literature that the Spartans did not do too much damage, at least in these brief initial annual invasions. Thucydides describes the agony of the losses and yet alludes to areas of Attica that were either not touched at all or not systematically destroyed. In the seventh book of his history, he flatly declares that "the invasions had been short" and had not stopped the Athenians from "making full use of their land during the rest of the year." But how, then, could he later conclude that Athenians made "full use" of Attica before and after a huge Peloponnesian army arrived to ruin it?

As is his wont, Thucydides' generalizing conclusions (e.g., little damage) are often at odds with the gripping description of ravaging presented in his narrative (e.g., apparently lots of ruin). And his contemporary observations are sometimes reemphasized, modified, or even contradicted later in his text, as in the later revision he did not always change his working draft to reflect his final conclusions at war's end.

An anonymous fourth-century historian agreed. The author—his work is known only as the *Hellenica Oxyrhynchia*, named after a chance papyrus find at Oxyrhynchus, Egypt—declared that Attica "was the most lavishly furnished area in Greece." The reason was that "it had suffered but slight injury from the Lacedaemonians" during the invasions of the Archidamian War.[39] The phrase "slight injury" perhaps implies that 60,000 ravagers in 431 could do little amid 200,000 acres of farmland.

For all the comic poet Aristophanes' emotional and wrenching descriptions of ruined vines and trees, remember that his first extant play was not produced until the year of the *last* invasion, 425. Was he a realist observer or a fictive playwright playing on the anger of the recent past? Moreover, an equal number of his passages suggest that much of the Attic countryside did not suffer serious damage. In Sophocles' famous *Oedipus at Colonus*, a tragedy produced after both the agriculture devastation of the Archidamian War and the occupation of

Decelea by the Spartans in 413, the playwright could call the Attic olive "a terror to its enemies" that "flourished most greatly in this land." The Sophoclean olive of Attica was a tree that no young or old man could "destroy or bring to nothing." Audiences in the theater would have found such an ode a cruel joke *if* they had gazed out at millions of stumps in the countryside.[40]

All this skepticism makes sense. The first decadelong phase of the conflict, referred to as the Archidamian War, actually saw little real fighting inside Attica. The Peloponnesian invasions were fast becoming a phony theater. Tempers flared, but few died in actual combat. After the first invasion of 431, the enemy came only four more times. Perhaps they stayed no more than 150 cumulative days during the entire decade between 431 and 421! None of these subsequent ravaging expeditions were as large as the infamous inaugural attack of 431, although the first two invasions were considered the most massive and together delivered a one-two punch that inflicted deep psychological wounds on the rural people of Athens. To put it another way, between 431 and 425 the marvelous Spartan army was used against the Athenians in Attica only three of the first eighty-four months of the war.[41]

Perhaps Pericles' war of attrition, funded by capital reserves, really would wear down the Peloponnesians after all, causing faction among such a loosely connected alliance that lacked the money and unity of the Athenian empire.[42]

Habits Die Hard

AN EXASPERATED KING Archidamus came back a year after the first inroad and tried to be more systematic in his second attempt at destruction. In 430 he remained about ten days longer, perhaps because his army was about half the size of the massive force of the year before and far easier to feed. He now set out beyond the Attic plain, moving into the coastal regions as far south as the mines at Laurium. Thucydides believed that the longer stay, coming after an initial inroad, and the more area that was devastated at this time, made the Athenians later feel that it was the worst of the five invasions, prompting them to prepare to send envoys down to Sparta to talk about a possible armistice.

Perhaps Archidamus reckoned that in some strange way his show of force might precipitate a revolt of Athens' island subjects who saw their master tied down in Attica. Thucydides says little more of this second invasion of late May 430 or even of the next two subsequent attacks of 428 and 427, other than that the enemy now tried to destroy crops that had been bypassed or had grown out again, presumably vineyards and orchards that had sent out new shoots. Apparently King Cleomenes, not Archidamus, led the fourth invasion of 427. He made a systematic effort to cover Attica, as well as retracing Archidamus' earlier trail, aiming to hit farms that were in the midst of recovery.[43]

Fear of the plague had scared the Spartans off from a planned third annual invasion in 429. They instead abruptly headed to Boeotia to besiege the Plataeans. In 426 they also kept away, purportedly because of an earthquake. The real reason was probably apprehension of a recent renewed outbreak of the pestilence. If the key to agricultural devastation was repeated ravaging to wear out a rural population and prevent repair and renewal in the hinterland, then the Spartans' crusade—eventually conducted under the tenure of three different kings, Archidamus, Cleomenes, and Agis, son of Archidamus—was proving to be an utter failure. No Spartan commander was ever able to regroup and mount a second attack in the same year. That persistence might have at least shown that they were serious about either ruining the countryside or making it impossible for farmers to return during the growing season. Why the Spartans kept coming into Attica without altering their tactics is one of the great mysteries of the Peloponnesian War; after 430 they apparently felt that Athenian evacuation was exacerbating the effects of the plague and ruining the city, inasmuch as it was clear that they were neither destroying the food supplies of the city nor cutting off access to the countryside.

The fifth inroad of 425, led by the young Agis, was a disaster. It lasted only two weeks. The grain was too green to be either consumed or burned. But, more importantly, the invaders were hysterical at news that 292 Lacedaemonians—among them 120 elite Spartiates—had been captured off the coast of the Peloponnese at Sphacteria and held as hostages in Athens.

In none of these invasions did the Peloponnesian grand army disrupt the mining operation at Laurium and thus cut off the source of Athenian silver coinage. After 425 the Spartans would not reenter Attica for the rest of the Archidamian War in fear of Athenian threats that their prisoners would be executed if an army ever again crossed into Attica. The Attic war was now for all practical purposes over.

Like most campaigns, it was one thing to talk grandly of a walkover of the enemy's homeland, and quite another to see it through. No one in May 431 could have dreamed that in a mere six years hostage taking—brought about by the surrender of crack Spartan hoplites no less!—could prevent an army of thousands from even crossing the border of Attica. Even before the capture of the Spartan hostages, the reluctant Peloponnesian allies complained to their Spartan leaders that they were busy with their own crops and, despite witnessing almost no combat, were in "no mood for campaigning."[44]

If what had once been a parochial tool to incite hoplite battle was now to be an integral tactic in causing general economic dislocation, there is no sign that armies discovered any new technologies to destroy cropland more effectively with special fuels, arms, or troops. True, in some cases like the seaside town of Acanthus in northern Greece, which was dependent on the export of its wine, fear of the loss of its vintage by armies arriving shortly before the harvest could bring concessions. But with the rise of walled cities in the fifth century, a town that had brought in its grain often ignored enemy provocations and worried more about siege troops than ravagers.[45]

A good example was Pericles' retaliatory plan of semiannual invasions of the nearby farmland of Megara, to the south. After the departure of the Peloponnesians, when it was clear no sizable army was around to face his Athenians in battle, he mobilized his hoplites. Ten thousand ravagers in vengeance devastated the nearby Megarid, a plain centrally located on the Peloponnesians' route into Athens. Although the grain harvest was already in, such a large and unmolested force must have done some short-term damage to local farms on the borders of Attica; the area is remarkable in modern times for its large olive groves. But, again, the real purpose was psychosocial and political. Pericles' bullying army wished to vent its rage at an enemy who weeks earlier had helped to attack Attic farms, to humiliate the Megarians for aiding the transit of enemy invaders, and to cause civic dissension that might lead to a democratic and thus friendly change of government curtailing the Spartans' ability to march freely into Attica.

Yet for all the ceremony of Pericles' massive force of ravagers ("the greatest army of the Athenians ever brought together"), Megarians kept inside their walls and stayed allied to Sparta. Thucydides adds that by 424 the Athenians had invaded Megara twice every year. If he is right, that means an incredible fourteen invasions with an infantry force that might on some occasions have numbered 10,000 soldiers in the field, ironically a testament to the difficulty of even large forces over time to starve a people out or obtain concessions.[46]

Contemporaries remark frequently about the five Peloponnesian forays into Attica, but almost never about the fourteen Athenian invasions of Megara during the same period. In terms of simple manpower, the Athenians may have sent collectively 140,000 ravagers into the narrow Megarid (fourteen invasions of 10,000 troops each), about the same as the number of Peloponnesians who cumulatively ravaged Attica (five invasions of about 30,000 troops), but unleashed on a smaller geographical area. Yet neither strategy brought the enemy to its knees, much less resulted in a decisive pitched battle.

New Strategies

THE SPARTANS LEARNED that they needed to stay in Attica year-round in a fortified garrison—the dreaded strategy in the second phase of the war that would come to be known as *epiteichismos* ("forward fortification")—where the aim was to loot, keep farmers away from their fields, and create a clearinghouse for plunder and booty. Consequently, the Spartan garrison at the fort of Decelea, thirteen miles from the walls of Athens, fortified in 413, caused more material harm to Athens by disrupting commerce, interrupting communications with the supply depots on nearby Euboea, encouraging the flight of slaves, and keeping farmers from their fields, than *all* the futile earlier efforts at chopping and burning trees, vines, and grain during the Archidamian War.

The young King Agis, who had led the last failed Spartan invasion of 425, came back over a decade later to Decelea as a mature commander who now had the resources, insight, and the firsthand experience to craft a tactic that avoided the pitfalls of his prior failed invasion. The fortification of Decelea—urged throughout the war by an array of Spartans and allies—proved one of the brilliant strategies of the entire conflict. It made the Spartans' effort at rural plundering immune from the cycles of the agricultural year and offered a permanent redoubt and refuge from counterattacks and cavalry patrols. With a year-round base, the invaders could arrive well before the harvest and stay after it was over, depending on constant plunder, theft, and stout walls for their sustenance and protection.[47]

But Decelea was a decade in the future, after the Spartans at last vacated Athens in 425. In some ways the idea was a fluke, growing only out of the reaction to the earlier flawed strategy of annual invasions, recent promises of Persian money, and the depletion of Athenian manpower brought on by the disaster at Sicily. Usually the Spartans abhorred forward basing, and thus entrusted such risky operations to expendable lesser-bred mavericks like a Brasidas or Gylippus, who might better lead ex-helots and mercenaries than precious Spartiate hoplites.

For the German military historian Hans Delbrück, such total war evolved into a more complex strategy of attrition waged against the moral and economic capital of a state rather than the more straightforward idea of annihilation in which an army seeks to destroy through hammer blows its counterpart in the field. Why waste lives battering away at like forces when softer and more important resources could be targeted over a longer period and at much less cost? Could a Greek polis really win a war by ignoring the main infantry forces of its adversary in the field? Pericles thought so. The morality of waging exhaustive war was a new and unsettling enterprise for Athens and Sparta, as both sides lacked accessible hard targets and thus soon sought to prevail through ruining civilian resources and attacking third parties.

Yet by not coming out to fight, did Pericles guarantee the death and ruin of the civilians of Athens, both inside and outside the walls, in a vain hope of wearing down his adversaries in a new total war? It was Periclean strategy, after all, that defined the new war as battle not between hoplites or even sailors but rather soldiers against the property of everyday folks. This moral quandary also remains with us today, and it has been raised in connection with the controversial careers of William Tecumseh Sherman, Lord Kitchener, and Curtis LeMay, who all argued that battle is ultimately powered by civilians and thus only extinguished when they cannot or will not pledge their labor and capital to those on the battlefield.

Was it a more moral and effective strategy to burn the slave estates and ruin the property of the plantation class of Georgia, which had fueled secession, or to have Ulysses Grant kill thousands of largely young and non-slave-owning youth in northern Virginia in open battle? Far worse still, was Curtis LeMay a war criminal who burned down the cities of Japan, killing tens of thousands of civilians with his napalm-fed infernos? Or, in effect, did he shorten the war and punish those in Tokyo's household factories whose labor produced the planes, shells, and guns without which the Japanese imperial army could never have murdered thousands of innocent Koreans, Chinese, and Filipinos and killed so many American servicemen?

Hans Delbrück was not interested in such abstract moral questions. It was the efficacy of the respective strategies that mattered to him. Delbrück wrote in a defeated Germany not long after the horrors of the trenches of World War I and was searching for a less costly strategy of battle mixed with more comprehensive economic, cultural, and psychological tactics that might still achieve Germany's strategic aims. He concluded that Pericles had hit upon a formula of success, a strategy that defined deadlock as victory—without ruining armies of young men in the process. *Had* Pericles lived, *had* the plague not broken out, and *had* the Athenians not jettisoned their strategy, Athens could not have been defeated militarily and might have obtained far earlier roughly the peace it found in 421—without thousands of its citizens dead, its army humiliated in Boeotia, and its strategic possessions in the north in enemy hands. For Delbrück such a stalemate, in the manner of Frederick the Great's lengthy campaigns, would have eventually won the war for Athens, since its greater capital reserves gave it a resiliency unknown at Sparta. That latter polis, as Thucydides repeatedly stated, had gone to war precisely "in fear" of the growth of Athenian power.[48]

What, then, had the blinkered Spartans accomplished in Attica during the initial phase of the war? Nothing and everything. Although they had been at war with Athens for nearly seven years, their army had spent an aggregate of less than five months in Attica, and the Spartans' chief strategy of annual agricultural devastation had achieved none of its objectives. It was not cheap to send thousands of farmers into distant Attica. If the Peloponnesians paid their army at the going rate for military service—150 aggregate days for about 30,000 men at a drachma per day per soldier—the total cost of Archidamus' five invasions was about 750 talents (about $360 million in modern purchasing power), more even than the yearly tribute income of the Athenian empire, or about the cost to put 250 ships at sea for three months. The outlay was bearable for a rich state like Athens. (It spent almost 4,500 talents on sieges and seaborne operations in the first seven years of the war alone!)

Yet for the rural Peloponnesians, who had little capital at the outbreak of the war and were used to brief campaigns settled by hoplite collisions, going into Attica for the first years of the war was an exorbitantly high price to pay. When the Corinthians clamored for the Spartans to start the war, the chief method that they outlined to pay for military expenses was to tap the rich reserves at the Panhellenic sanctuaries of Olympia and Delphi. How else, after all, could a state that used iron spits for money ever purchase ships, hire crews, or buy food in an open market? For a Greek world that put a high premium on honor and status, the Spartans had demonstrated that they were walking about freely on the sacred soil of Attica while their hosts were huddled inside their walls.[49]

A Most Remarkable Athenian

THIS WAR IN the fields was more than grand strategy and most certainly was not fought by anonymous thousands. During these annual devastations of Attica a young Athenian noble—acclaimed the most handsome youth in Athens —was slowly emerging from the chaos of war and plague. Alcibiades was just about nineteen when the Peloponnesian War broke out. Months earlier he may have served as a mere teenager with the cavalry at Potidaea during the antebellum siege of that recalcitrant Athenian subject state. By 429 he had returned home to cavalry service and was no doubt in Attica at twenty-one—a hero since he had been wounded at Potidaea and honored with the award of valor despite being saved with his armor by his mentor, Socrates.

Alcibiades' lineage was Kennedyesque. He would be emblematic of the entire glory and tragedy of the fifth-century Athenian imperial state, which started the war with such high hopes among a generation that inherited the pride but not the sobriety of their fathers. Pericles, after all, had been credited with achieving nine battle victories when the war broke out, and knew well that his majestic temples and the brilliance of Athenian drama conducted below the south slope of the Acropolis were the dividends of decades of hard-fought wars. Alcibiades, in contrast, grew up in the latter 440s and 430s, when the earlier conflicts with Boeotia, Sparta, and the rebellious allies were for the most part over—and the largess of empire already manifest in a bustling port, rampant construction, and a vibrant city full of the likes of Sophocles, Socrates, and Euripides.

From his mother, Deinomache ("Terrible in Battle"), Alcibiades claimed membership in the Alcmaeonids, the most powerful and controversial of the centuries-old Athenian aristocratic clans. His father, Cleinias, had died during the earlier Athenian hoplite catastrophe at Boeotian Coronea (446), after being prominent in establishing the fiscal architecture of the entire system of Athenian imperialism in the Aegean. Three-year-old Alcibiades was entrusted to his distant cousins, the brothers Ariphron and Pericles, who taught him something of the manifest destiny of an ascendant democratic Athens.

Little is known about Alcibiades during his twenty-first through twenty-sixth years, when he may have been constantly on patrol in the Attic countryside as a member of the Athenian cavalry. No account exists about how he avoided the plague that killed his guardian Pericles. Only his early personal life was of much interest; after his return from the siege at Potidaea in the second year of the war, a number of salacious stories immediately spread about his raucous carousing. In between his summers of rural mounted service he drank and argued with Socrates, often became the subject of sexual gossip, and apparently embraced a long family tradition of combining his own aristocratic background with opportunistic democratic politics.

Alcibiades' sizable family estate in the Athenian plain was probably ravaged by the Spartans, even as he remained true to the Periclean policy of abandonment of Attica while he rode down enemy ravagers on patrol. After the Spartans ceased their annual incursions, Alcibiades nevertheless reminded the Athenians of their duty to protect the sacred soil of Athens. They were to adhere, he stressed, to the old annual oath that the ephebes took on behalf of their alma mater, swearing "to regard wheat, barley, vines, and olives as the natural boundaries of Athens."*

Later in the war Alcibiades would exhibit a strong desire for the offensive, perhaps as a reaction to the senseless war of attrition in Attica that marked his first years of service. Some eighteen years after the Spartans first marched out to cut down the trees of Attica, a much older and by then treasonous thirty-seven-year-old Alcibiades, ensconced in Sparta, would advise his former enemies that such annual incursions were no way to wreck his homeland. Better, he told his new hosts, to create a permanent fort, thirteen miles from the walls of Athens at Decelea, and thus destroy Alcibiades' own native soil year-round.[50]

But all that was well into the future. For now, the teenager rode into battle against ravagers full of zeal and hope, confident after the first year's assault that Attica had taken the best punch Sparta could offer—scarcely aware that both his country's and his own greatest tragedies lay just months ahead.

* At Athens, and perhaps elsewhere in the Greek world, ephebes of the upper classes, between the ages of eighteen and twenty, entered a period of mandatory training, often on the frontier and in transition to full-fledged infantry or cavalry service.

CHAPTER 3

DISEASE

The Ravages of the Plague at Athens (430–426)

Anatomy of an Epidemic

By the second season of the war, the struggle was not to be decided between spearmen or even ravagers and horsemen. It now seemed to hinge on how well, psychologically as well as materially, refugees could ride out a few weeks of enemy occupation. Thanks to Pericles' strategy, for a second spring much of the population—perhaps well over 200,000—was crammed inside Athens for more than a month. The city of the Parthenon and theater of Dionysus was again to be a fetid refugee camp.

The prior inaugural year of fighting had proved that such massive evacuation and relocation were practicable. Yet in this second season the city's luck quite literally ran out. The combination of Mediterranean heat, overcrowding, lack of plentiful clean water, shelter, and proper sanitation, and the stress of war and invasion provided a suitable landscape for a mysterious and terribly destructive disease. When the epidemic passed, Thucydides would make an astounding summation of conditions in Greece as a whole during the three decades of the war: "What caused the greatest suffering and killed a considerable part of the population was the terrible plague."[1]

None of the other Greek city-states had ever experienced anything quite like the Athenian pestilence. Nearby hostile Thebes, the capital of the Boeotian Confederacy, had doubled its population since the outbreak of the war, due to the influx of refugees from the surrounding unwalled hamlets of Boeotia, many of which lay along the porous border and feared an Athenian invasion.[2] Yet even if it was now twice its antebellum population, Thebes proper still probably had fewer than 50,000 residents, hardly enough population density to guarantee the easy contagion of an infectious disease. In any case, its smaller numbers of refugees were much more easily housed than the tens of thousands who camped out in Athens. Moreover, the refugees in Thebes did not dwell in a port that was a hub to the thousands of possible disease carriers in the eastern Mediterranean. Neither was it besieged and lacking open access to the countryside nor was it even much visited by travelers or traders. Overcrowding was the catalyst for the plague, but Athens was also a magnet for a wide diversity of peoples who might be disease carriers in a way not true of other hard-pressed landlocked states during the war.

Modern militaries have concocted devilish brews of supergerms as would-be weapons of mass destruction against their enemies because they are lethal, cheap, of small weight and size, and can nullify the effect of conventional weaponry or superior manpower. Diseases also instill terror beyond their proven ability to kill, inasmuch as the agents of death are far more indiscriminate, invisible, and, as the poet Hesiod says, silent.

Disaster was not supposed to strike Athens, at least at the moment. This was a city, after all, that had trumped adversity repeatedly. Athens had twice survived incineration by the Persians a half century earlier, during the invasion and occupation of 480–479, only in the war's aftermath to evolve from ruins into the cultural center of Greece. In the postbellum tensions with Sparta, the citizenry had turned out en masse to build the Long Walls in a fevered state of anxiety, thus completing a vast circuit around Athens and Piraeus of over seventeen miles, four miles greater in circumference even than the famous ramparts that protected Constantinople.

For twenty years Pericles had mobilized 20,000 laborers to create his architectural masterpieces on the Acropolis, the Parthenon and Propylaea, as well as massive public buildings and fortifications in the agora and the Piraeus. Despite all the worries about the supposedly terrible grand army of the Peloponnese, Athens had ridden out the first invasion of 431 well enough, and had watched the enemy trudge back home without a sense of accomplishment.[3]

The contrast of previous Periclean grandness with the human depravity induced by the plague drew Thucydides' interest in the disease and prompted his riveting account of the effects of the contagion in the second book of his history.

> Some perished in neglect, others despite plentiful attention. No particular treatment was discovered that worked, for what brought improvement in one case, made things worse in another. Both strong and weak constitutions alike

proved unable to resist, all alike being taken away, although they were careful to seek treatment with strict attention. By far the worst part of the epidemic was the depression that followed when a victim realized that he was sick. The despair that came with the illness right away destroyed the power of resistance, and it left the sick even more likely to succumb. In addition, there was a terrible scene of citizens dying like sheep after they become ill from trying to help one another. This resulted in the greatest morbidity.[4]

Himself a survivor of the infection, Thucydides juxtaposed a graphic narrative of the outbreak with Pericles' solemn funeral oration over the first year's dead soldiers, an encomium that had reminded Athenians of their city's eminence. Apparently, the historian wished to emphasize the capriciousness of fate and the unpredictability of war—and so impress upon his readers the brutal nature of man when stripped of his precious culture and civilization, so vaunted in Pericles' funeral speech, which had been delivered shortly before the plague's outbreak. Thucydides believed that deleterious effects from the plague rippled out for years, sharply reducing the war-making potential of the Athenian military:

> Men did whatever they wished. They easily now dared to try what in the past they had done in private, inasmuch as they were seeing the rapid change that happened to those who were once well off suddenly dying while those formerly poor taking over their possessions. So the citizens felt it better to spend quickly and to live for pleasure, deeming both their bodies and their possessions as things of a day. Careful adherence to what was known as honor was popular with no one, inasmuch as it was doubtful whether anyone would be spared to attain it; instead it was generally felt that enjoying things in the here and now, and all that profited that, was both honorable and useful. Reverence of the gods or respect for man's law there was neither to restrain anyone.

After reading Thucydides' macabre account of the social consequences of the plague, it is unclear, as the historian perhaps intended, whether the Athenians remained the Renaissance men just praised by Pericles in his famous funeral oration or were utter savages who fought with one another over funeral pyres to burn their dead. Clearly the few hundred men who fell during the first year of the war in patrolling the countryside and during sea duty off the Peloponnese earned praise and public funerals, while the next year thousands of men, women, and children died miserably in anonymous droves in the street, often rotting without burial or cremation.

Thucydides had earlier described the miserable conditions inside the city that were prompted by the monthlong evacuation of 431. Agrarian families had probably then reoccupied their farms for a year, only to trek back into the city during the next spring in about the same numbers. Most arrivals had no permanent shelter but camped out in open spaces and sanctuaries. Shacks dotted the base of the Acropolis. Some refugees lived in towers atop the city's lengthy fortifications. Conditions were probably worse during these initial first two invasions, at least before the city made arrangements to construct more permanent shelters in the four-mile corridor between the city proper and the fortifications at the Piraeus. Athens, like Los Angeles, lies in a basin surrounded by three large mountain ranges. The sea lies almost five miles away, and there are only small rivers that flow near the metropolitan area—all of these conditions making it difficult to dump sewage in any nearby moving body of water that could wash effluent out to sea.

Shanties offered no real relief from the summer heat and stood in stark contrast to the abandoned spacious country homes of the more affluent refugees. Later Plato would argue that Greeks should have two residences, urban and rural, to reinforce the social fabric of the polis. But he was reacting against the turmoil of wartime Attica, when estate owners were reduced to refugee status under Periclean strategy, and the urban poor scarcely knew what life in the long-suffering countryside was like. By the time the war broke out, over 20,000 Athenians had almost nothing to do with farming.[5]

Those who once had the nicest estates in Attica within a few days occupied the worst, which explains the particularly hostile opposition to Pericles' policies from refugee landowners. Aristophanes remarked often on the ridiculous scene in wartime Athens, a city brimming with exasperated rural folk at every juncture who resorted to squatting in birds' nests and casks. Much of the turmoil resulted from this radical change in fortune: the wealthy were now on the bottom rail and veritable visitors in their own city—guests of the radical poor, who wanted the war, were losing little in it, and might see profit accrue from nonstop naval service.[6]

The outbreak of the mystifying disease occurred sometime in late May 430. Athenians started to die mysteriously in droves during the forty days the Spartans ravaged, the longest of all the Peloponnesian invasions, which might have put even greater stress on the cramped refugees in the city. Thucydides' description is somewhat vague about the chronology of the outbreak. He says only that the plague (called a *nosos*) descended upon the city while the Spartans were ravaging in Attica.

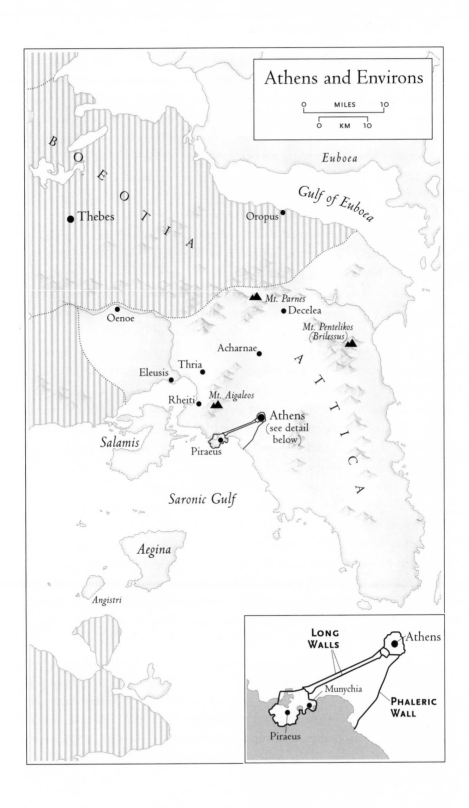

Athens and Environs

MILES
0 — 10

KM
0 — 10

Euboea

Gulf of Euboea

B
O
E
O
T
I
A

● Thebes

Oropus ●

Oenoe ●

▲ *Mt. Parnes*
● Decelea

Mt. Pentelikos
(Brilessus)
▲

Acharnae ●

Thria ●

Eleusis ●

Rheiti ●

▲ *Mt. Aigaleos*

A
T
T
I
C
A

Athens
(see detail
below)

Piraeus

Salamis

Saronic Gulf

Aegina

Angistri

**LONG
WALLS**

● Athens

Munychia

**PHALERIC
WALL**

Piraeus

The disease probably prompted them to cut short their devastation; they heard frightening rumors of the havoc inside the walls and from the country-side could see clouds of funeral smoke in the city. Still, the second invasion turned out to be the longest of all the Spartan inroads—forty days in all, in which they covered the most ground in Attica and sought to do thoroughly what they had not completed the year before. Most likely fear of approaching the rich Athenian plain near the disease-ridden city induced the Spartans to roam far to the south to devastate the seaside districts of southern Attica and the hinterland around the mines at Laurium.

The Spartans had learned that the invasion of 431 had done nothing to weaken Athens or its empire, and had figured on a much longer campaign the next year. This sojourn of tens of thousands of rural folk inside the city also in-directly helped to spread the disease, which in turn had the paradoxical effect of cutting short what must have been planned as the most devastating and comprehensive ravaging campaign of the Archidamian War.[7]

The fact that the disease broke out "not many days after" the Spartans neared the plain and was raging by the time they left suggests that less than a month after the disease first touched Athens, it had reached epidemic propor-tions. Indeed, it swept the city, and even inadvertently infected the Athenian fleet. Disease-carrying but symptom-silent fighters set sail from the Piraeus to raid the Peloponnese and to press home the siege at Potidaea in the north, in part to be away from the misery of the infected city. When they attacked the Peloponnese town of Epidaurus in reprisal for the Spartan-led invasion, local inhabitants were said to have been sickened from proximity to the soldiers.[8]

Many contemporary Athenians believed that the plague was *no accident.* Surely, they thought, it was a direct result of deliberate Spartan efforts to infect them in a time of war. There was something to their paranoid logic: plagues of such virulence were almost unknown in classical Greece, which prompted Athenians to consider almost any explanation to account for such a terrible and rare oc-currence. Some Athenians may have remembered folktales of their hero Solon, who a century earlier had easily stormed the nearby city of Cirrha after putting a powerful purgative into the town's stream water, thereby sickening enough of the defenders to cause capitulation. The Athenians themselves may have pol-luted the city's water supply when they departed ahead of Xerxes' occupying troops in late summer 480. In a hot Mediterranean climate, where water was al-ways scarce, enemy pollution of fountains, cisterns, and rivers was a nearly con-stant fear during times of war. Military handbooks would later recommend such contamination of water supplies as an effective way of stymieing hostile forces by bringing on either illness or thirst. In Sicily the Athenians themselves later sought to ruin the terra-cotta pipes that conveyed water to the besieged city of Syracuse.[9]

So the outbreak of 430 seemed to coincide roughly with the arrival of enemy troops in Attica. Odd timing, was it not? The conspiracists had even more ammunition. The disease first attacked those who drew water from cisterns in the port at Piraeus that were rumored to be poisoned by the enemy. The outbreak never infected the cities of the Peloponnese, instead following both Athenian troops up north besieging Potidaea and sailors off the Peloponnese. The crowds did not bother to ponder the obvious criteria of overcrowding at Athens and its singular congestion; rather, in despair, they must have thought something along the lines of "We are sick, they are not; therefore, they must be responsible."

After news of the outbreak, some communities in the Peloponnese apparently began to build impressive temples to their gods precisely because they had been spared this awful nightmare. Wisely, the Peloponnesians deliberately stayed away the next year and instead spent the spring of 429 besieging Plataea, on the other side of Mount Kithairon, keeping a mountain range between them and the infectious disease.

In prophecies, the epidemic was connected with the fulfillment of an old, hotly debated warning that "a Dorian war will come and with it a plague." In his denial of these theories, Thucydides nevertheless has an understandable propensity to record the popular myth of Spartan culpability, the idea of water contamination, the resurrection of old prophecies, and the general de facto immunity of the Spartans from the disease, almost as if he is not quite sure himself whether such a natural event that was so obviously militarily efficacious could be entirely accidental.[10]

The Limitations of Medicine

WHAT, THEN, EXACTLY was the disease? Today the generic word "plague" conjures up bubonic plague, especially the terrifying epidemics of the Black Death in Medieval Europe and Renaissance Italy, and the images of fleas, rats, and horrific pustules. In fact, the use of the English term is inexact inasmuch as the Athenian epidemic was most likely *not* bubonic plague, despite disagreements about its etiology.

Classical scholars and physicians who collate Thucydides' account with other plague narratives and contemporary symptomatology, have spent over a century in bitter disputes about the nature of the epidemic. At various times they have postulated a mass outbreak of typhus, typhoid fever, measles, influenza, smallpox, scarlet fever, or—somewhat more fancifully—various hemorrhagic fevers, including Ebola, leptospirosis, tularemia, anthrax, dengue fever, and ergotism.[11]

The arguments are complex. Often analysis hinges on the esoteric. Few can agree whether the plague-bearing species of rat (there seems to be no word in Greek for *Rattus rattus*) even existed in ancient Greece or whether the ancient word for "heart" (*kardia*) sometimes really meant the mouth of the stomach or, reaching even farther, whether surviving stone busts of Thucydides himself reveal the telltale pockmarks of smallpox infection. Although Thucydides provides detailed descriptions of an array of terrible symptoms—fever, inflammation, eye problems, sore and bloody throat, sneezing, hoarseness, chest pain, cough, intestinal pain, vomiting, diarrhea, skin eruptions and ulcers, thirst and dehydration, general weakness and fatigue, gangrene in the extremities, permanent brain damage—it is not easy for modern medical sleuths to connect the precise meaning of his Greek vocabulary with either a formal ancient or a contemporary medical lexicon.

Since ancient medicine was empirically based—it could offer diagnoses and prognoses based on past careful clinical observation of symptoms, rather than through scientific identification of microbes at the cellular level—there was no formal ancient catalog of diseases anything like our own clinical classifications of viruses and bacteria. Perhaps the most likely explanation of the plague, if it was not a form of malignant confluent smallpox, is that it was caused by an organism now extinct, or at least one that has evolved over two millennia in ways that make it no longer deadly.

Any infectious disease that achieves about a 30 percent lethality rate among a pristine population probably provides immunity to survivors. If it depends on frequent person-to-person contact, it needs a fresh supply of thousands of urban hosts to spread and survive. Thus the plague may well have burned itself out in the singular conditions of wartime Athens. As Thucydides notes, it returned only sporadically after its initial deadly appearance, even when the conditions inside Athens once again became as bleak as those of 430, especially after the Spartan occupation of Decelea (413).

In 404, for example, after the debacle of Aegospotami and the destruction of the Athenian fleet, which brought the war to a close, Lysander's enormous 200-ship fleet scoured the Aegean, sending tens of thousands of expatriate Athenians back home to a city shut in by the continual presence of the Spartan king Agis at the nearby fort of Decelea and another army marching northward from the Peloponnese. Contemporary sources report fears of widespread famine and starvation at Athens at war's end, but *not* another outbreak of the plague.

A quarter century later, the lack of a similar outbreak among the hungry, cooped-up Athenians at war's end might suggest either that there were enough plague survivors in the city with immunity to prevent an easy flare-up or that after years of evacuation the Athenians were more adept at accommodating sudden demands on housing, garbage removal, water, and sewage treatment. In any case, it was probably the vain hope of the victorious admiral Lysander that a cramped and besieged Athens in 404 might re-create the horrific nightmare of 430, which a quarter century earlier had proved to Spartan advantage.[12]

The outbreak seems to have originated in Africa. Then the plague made its way northward from Ethiopia into Egypt and Libya. From there it settled into various parts of the Persian Empire before arriving at the Piraeus. Greece and the surrounding eastern Mediterranean were just days away by sea from the millions in Africa and Asia, and a natural nexus for tropical disease. Most plagues in Greek and Roman times arose in the south and usually broke out during the summer, presumably when microbial life best survived outdoors amid stagnant water, foul sewage, active insects, and rotting food. Still, the Athenians had never seen an epidemic of this magnitude, even though less virulent forms of similar maladies had apparently swept the Aegean Islands, especially Lemnos, in the immediately prior decades.

The Infected

ALTHOUGH THUCYDIDES OBVIOUSLY drew on his own clinical experience, and recognized that the disease affected individuals in different ways, he sought to provide a generic description of the infection. Typically, the dreaded signs started with a violent heat in the head, the eyes quickly burning and turning red. Both the throat and tongue appeared bloody and became malodorous.

After these initial symptoms, those infected soon began sneezing and became hoarse, maladies shortly accompanied by severe coughing. Once the stomach was affected, the sick began vomiting bile of all sorts. At the same time they experienced dry heaves and violent spasms. These convulsions sometimes immediately followed the initial symptoms, but on other occasions they became manifest only much later. In some patients the infection seemed to attack both the respiratory and intestinal tracts almost simultaneously, which explains in part the terror of a disease that could strike so comprehensively. In an age when vaccination has rid us of the worst infectious diseases of our past, it is hard to imagine a worse sort of malady, as if a modern patient experienced the flu, dysentery, measles, and pneumonia all at once.

The ill appeared neither warm to the touch nor especially pale in appearance. Instead, the body was flush and livid, with an outbreak of small blisters and sores. The unfortunate afflicted soon felt so hot that they could not endure even the slightest touch of clothing or linens. Many often found it preferable to remain naked. In their last stages, the more aggrieved patients often wanted to throw themselves into cold water. Some jumped into cisterns in vain hopes of quenching a terrible thirst, a fact prompting some nineteenth-century scholars to wrongly identify the plague with rabies.

Still, if most people believed that tainted water had caused the outbreak, in their death throes they felt no compunction about plunging into it for immediate relief. Whatever the actual etiology of the disease, common medicine of this time did not grasp the danger of passing microbes from person to person by contaminating common drinking water.

Worse still, there was no respite through sleep. The victims were restless and suffered constant insomnia. Yet even at the apex of the affliction, most sufferers did not immediately perish; many endured until the seventh to ninth day, when they succumbed to fever and exhaustion. Even when the more hearty passed that point of crisis, many subsequently experienced both ulceration and watery diarrhea, which, for these survivors, ultimately resulted in exhaustion, dehydration, and death.

For the remainder who held out even after the intestinal attacks, the infection descended into the extremities. Once there it sometimes rendered the genitals, fingertips, and toes deformed and useless. Others were left blind or with brain damage. Thucydides suggests that the deformed and maimed limped around Athens for decades after the initial outbreak of 430. They were perhaps still visible, like ghosts after the war, when he returned to finish his history after his twenty-year exile—prompting us also to wonder exactly how the historian himself struggled with the residual effects of his own bout with the malady while composing his work. Although the mortality rate stymied Athenian military operations for a decade, there is no real evidence of a similar toll on Athens' war-making ability from so many weakened and maimed survivors.

Careful nursing or simple neglect—it seemed not to matter much to the sick, since so many died anyway. In such a miserable climate, the first symptoms of the plague usually sent the afflicted into a profound depression. Only those who had survived the disease and acquired resistance showed any real pity for the suffering—because of both their trust in their newfound immunity and a shared empathy acquired from their own ordeal.

We moderns must put the infection in even a wider context of suffering to comprehend fully the dire predicament of ancient Athens in 430. Most of us when sick with a fever go to bed, and feel pangs of real worry with the onset of secondary symptoms such as vomiting or diarrhea. Despite familial care, a doctor's visit, patient caregivers, and plentiful medications, postillness fatigue can affect us for days or even weeks. But imagine such sickness in a time of war. While enemies at the gates were trying to kill the infected's family, he clung to life in delirium. Medicine, clean water, toilets, bedding—all the appurtenances of modern convalescent care—were not available to ailing Athenians. To the terror of enemy soldiers, add the daily trauma from the deaths of children, siblings, and spouses, attributable to a disease of unknown cause, duration, cure, or prophylaxis. Amid such calamity, someone must provide food, tend the ill, take away the bodies, and keep the ramparts manned and the sorties sent out.

In such a chaotic climate, had the Spartans themselves not feared infection during the second invasion of 430 and assaulted the walls, or had they returned the next year rather than gone to Plataea, they might well have taken the city, given the skeleton garrisons and the general despair at Athens. On the contrary, Spartan worries over manpower—especially the sense of how precious and few were the state's hoplite class of elite, full-citizen infantrymen—made the army go home earlier and not return until its soldiers were sure the chance of catching the malady was over.[13]

Even the half dead soon fell prostrate in the streets and fountains. Their last visions were the moldering remains of friends and family and the realization that they too would soon experience such a grisly fate. How could a city under siege dispose of thousands of corpses within its walls? Recent excavations of a proposed Athenian subway station near the ancient Kerameikos cemetery revealed one such mass grave and over a thousand tombs quite near the surface. In some cases dozens of skeletons were found thrown helter-skelter into large shafts, apparently without the normal care and usual offerings accorded the dead. The evidence of hasty group interment suggested to the excavators that the subway engineers had stumbled upon one of the many mass burials necessitated by the epidemic of 430, something apparently not repeated in the subsequent twenty-five-hundred-year history of the city.[14]

A similar nightmare of mass burials on a far larger scale in the ancient world occurred during the bubonic plague at Constantinople a millennium later, during the reign of Justinian, in the sixth century A.D. There the cemeteries soon filled, causing rotting bodies to pile up in the streets and along the seashore. Even huge pits that were dug with the intention of holding 70,000 corpses soon overflowed, causing the dead to be thrown into towers on the walls.[15]

At Athens, within days the responsible officials were unable to cart away, much less bury or burn, the mounting piles of corpses. Individuals lacked the resources to care for their fallen family members. Sometimes they stole fuel or entire pyres—or heaped their own lost ones onto the biers of others. Dissension broke out. Many of the longtime residents of the city blamed the newcomers from the countryside, whose numbers and rustic habits purportedly might explain the sudden onset of a novel pestilence. Such tension may well have simmered for decades, laying the foundation for political upheaval some twenty years later.[16]

The scene of rotting corpses and bodies unburied throughout the city made an indelible impression on the Athenians. Just six years later, in the aftermath of the battle of Delium (424), the victorious Thebans allowed the Athenian dead from the battle to rot while haggling over concessions, an outrage that encouraged Euripides to condemn it a year later in his *Suppliant Women* (423). In similar fashion, the hysteria that swept the city after reports that the bodies of Athenian seamen were not picked up after the victory at Arginusae (406) prompted trials of the triumphant generals. That suicidal act seems an inexplicable madness until one remembers that the Athenians never really recovered from the horrific images and memories ingrained in that most disastrous year of 430. And on Sicily, corpses were often left to decompose in the fields, the bones of the dead picked up only months later, when hostilities ceased.[17]

Culture and Mass Death

WHY DID THUCYDIDES devote such a prominent place in a supposedly military history to discussion of the disease, careful to chart in detail the descent into barbarism on the part of the Athenians? Besides his own recovery from the malady, he had both wider historical and philosophical interests. First, as a product of the Athenian enlightenment of the mid-fifth century that sought to explain natural phenomena through scientific rather than religious or folk exegesis, Thucydides, the didactic historian, wanted to demonstrate to his readers his own faith in the rationalist method of identifying symptoms. Careful clinical observation might lead to a diagnosis of some previously known illness. Only that way could the rationalist in turn provide a prognosis for the patient. So he wished "to set out its symptoms by which it might be known should it ever break out once more."[18]

Thucydides often takes special pains to dismiss false knowledge, such as the preposterous idea that recovery for the lucky ensured their future immunity from all other illnesses. He also rejects a supernatural cause for the epidemic. And he ridicules those who sought to explain the outbreak by associating it with the old prophecy about a Dorian invasion. Again, overcrowding, not the gods, caused the disease. Human activity, not divine dispensation, was the culprit.

Like his later famous descriptions of the civil war on Corcyra, the murder at Mycalessus of Boeotian schoolboys by Thracian mercenaries, and the final destruction of the Athenian army on Sicily, the Thucydidean discourse on the plague becomes a reminder of how close humans always are to savagery—and how precious is their salvation won through law, religion, science, and custom. This thin veneer of civilization is a universal constant, one immune to the arrogance of modernism that professes that technology has at last nullified the age-old pathologies of human nature. The historian's skill at dissecting the etiology of the disease serves also as a reminder that his larger history is equally empirical and didactic, lacking the romance and folklore of Herodotus or the epic poets.

The plague infected Athens with utter lawlessness, what Thucydides called *anomia*. Men, convinced that the end was near anyway, "showed a more careless daring." When death hovered over all, most lost the old self-control and instead "turned themselves over to the pleasures of the moment." They forgot fear of both law and the gods, Thucydides adds, because no one could determine whether righteous conduct provided a defense against the disease. But since a horrible death came indiscriminately and without warning, people lived for the day and thus often acted criminally in order to obtain some "pleasure" from life.[19]

The plague reflected a theme found throughout the history: a horrific liberating effect is likewise brought on by the conundrum of wars, making men resort to things that they would otherwise never consider during their rational calculations in peace and tranquillity, when they have so much to lose. And because Athens was Greece's intellectual center and entertained pretensions of singular humanity and a self-proclaimed elevated culture, the pandemonium that followed from the plague reminds us that civilization can be lost anywhere and at any time.

Furthermore, because the outbreak occurred in the second year of the twenty-seven-year-long war, a threshold had been crossed: once the Athenians had been reduced to such straits, it was nearly impossible to recover their moral bearings in subsequent years. Criminality and savagery become accustomed, or rather institutionalized, behaviors, almost as if the Athenians, once freed from decades of civilizing influences, could not shake off the newfound habits of brutality. The death of Pericles during the epidemic is emblematic of the Athenian descent, the perishing of the last singular statesman who might have had the intellect and moral authority to steady the Athenians amid the savagery. To Thucydides, the wages of the plague are not just misery, death, and disability. They are the lawless precursors to more deliberate policies that follow in a variety of brutal Athenian actions taken against rebellious allies and neutral states.

Thus, in a key passage Thucydides says the plague "first" introduced into the city a greater lawlessness. He suggests that many of the awful things that Athens did in the later years of the war were inculcated between 430 and 426, when the citizenry was in peril of being wiped out. If this analysis is true, then the disease also had a profound effect on the tactics and methods by which Athens conducted the Peloponnesian War—a fact perhaps lost on those military historians who underappreciate the cultural ripples of disease that were felt across the empire, from Mytilene to Melos.[20]

The Most Deadly Enemy

NEVERTHELESS, THUCYDIDES' ULTIMATE concerns remain military: the incredible losses to the plague almost immediately altered the tenuous balance of power and, with it, the entire course and strategy of the war. After another, though less virulent, return of the disease in 427–426, the historian flat out concludes, "Nothing did more damage to Athenian power than the plague"— a sweeping retrospective assessment that would seem to include battle defeats at Delium (424) and Mantinea, the disaster at Syracuse (413), the depredations from the permanent Spartan fort at Decelea (413–404), and a number of key Athenian setbacks at sea (411–404). While Thucydides states that there were two severe onsets of the disease, he also says, "At no time did it completely leave," suggesting that for nearly four years Athenians were dying from the mysterious outbreak.[21]

Still, one of the great mysteries of the war remains the precise effect of the plague on the war-making capability of Athens. Thucydides does not exaggerate the calamity that befell Athens, but it is not clear how the epidemic altered Athenian tactics, other than by diverting Spartan ravagers in 429 from the Attic hinterland to nearby Plataea and depleting Athenian manpower over the next few years. Yet if nothing else, the plague raises a number of what-ifs about what Athens might have done without the sudden loss of tens of thousands of its citizens.

The historian follows his general summation of the epidemic's ill effects with the explicit statement that 4,400 Athenian hoplite infantry "in the ranks" perished, and another "300 cavalrymen," as well as "an indeterminable number" of the common people.[22] What do these vast numbers tell us about the ultimate harm to the Athenians' ability to wage war?

At the outbreak of the fighting Athens probably had a male citizenry of somewhere between 30,000 and 40,000, about half of which in theory qualified for service as hoplite heavy infantrymen. These roughly 15,000 to 20,000 hoplites were augmented by noncitizen resident aliens; they mostly served on garrison duty and could be pressed into the phalanx in emergencies. Thus the entire army was also broken down in terms of the frontline (13,000) and reserve (16,000) hoplites. If 4,400 hoplite fatalities "in the ranks" refers only to losses from the 13,000 citizens who were prepared to go into battle, then over a third of all such infantrymen were felled within four years—or a 34 percent loss among the best troops the city could muster. In relative terms, the plague turned out to be the Athenians' ancient equivalent of a Somme or Stalingrad.

In addition, the 300 lost horsemen meant that 30 percent of Athens' precious 1,000-man cavalry was now also gone. There is no information on the effect of the disease upon horses stabled in the city or whether sorties could continue against Peloponnesian ravagers who had headed south, past the Athenian plain. The only defense against enemy patrols in Attica was the Athenian cavalry, which in a single year lost more horsemen than its aggregate casualties over three decades. Even nine years after the plague departed, the Athenians still found themselves critically short of cavalry in Sicily, at just the moment when mounted patrols were to become even more crucial back in Attica.

Thucydides adds that the expeditionary force besieging the northern city of Potidaea likewise became infected. Even though the Athenians would eventually take the city, they lost 1,050 hoplites out of 4,000 in a mere 40 days (26 percent). The percentage of fatalities and the rapid six-week spread of the infection at Potidaea were eerily similar to the effects of the disease at Athens proper.

Whatever the causative organism, the epidemic was an especially lethal one to have resulted in such high rates of mortality among healthy adult men. Infected Athenians probably died in greater proportions of the population than did residents of medieval London during the worst years of the Black Death. Sickness always has a certain affinity for war, a time when food is short, stress is widespread, and soldiers—like Hagnon's Athenian besiegers at Potidaea (432–430)—are forced to bivouac in outdoors tents and barracks. Some of the great plagues of the ancient world—the Antonine epidemic that killed as many as one-third of the population in certain places in Greece, Italy, Asia Minor, and imperial Egypt, as well as others during the reigns of the emperors Decius (A.D. 249–251) and Gallus (A.D. 251–253)—started first in military camps and before they had finished nearly ruined Roman armies.

Besides these explicit figures of an aggregate 5,750 crack Athenian troops lost, one can extrapolate from the remarkably consistent percentages of fatalities (around 30 percent) to reach some type of figure for the reserve hoplites (about 4,800 dead of the 16,000?) and the "indeterminable number" of thetes, metics, women, children, and slaves. The latter combined group of Attic residents might have totaled at least 200,000. (In 1920, before the arrival of the great exodus from Asia Minor, the Greek census reported that Attica's total population was 501,615, excluding the metropolitan and industrial heart of Athens and the Piraeus.)

If the people of ancient Attica suffered deaths in numbers commensurate to the percentages of males in the cavalry and army—perhaps well over 10,000— then at least 60,000 additional civilians also perished. In terms of annual wages lost that would have been otherwise garnered by these stricken soldiers and laborers, the death of somewhere between 20,000 and 30,000 adult males of all statuses meant an immediate shortfall of well over 1,000 talents to their families—or the yearly equivalent of the entire reserve fund that was set aside for the protection of the city from an Athenian fleet, a sum in contemporary American dollars approximating $500 million in lost economic activity. Athens' financial troubles in the ensuing decades of the war were due not just to skyrocketing military expenditures and rebellious allies but also to the loss or disablement of thousands of workers in Attica at the very start of the war.

The deaths of another 40,000 to 50,000 women, slaves, and children proved catastrophic. Aside from their essential role in the Athenian economy, even during wartime such "noncombatants" often played a pivotal role. At sieges, for example, women cooks were invaluable in keeping the defending garrison alive and healthy. The loss of such caregivers no doubt explains the high numbers of deaths of those who otherwise might have been fed and nursed through the illness. The Athenian phalanx could not march in full force into Megara or Boeotia without servile baggage carriers, while thousands of slaves were beginning to row in the Athenian imperial fleet, whose triremes required somewhere between 40,000 and 60,000 sailors.

The plague probably killed at least five times more frontline hoplites than were lost at the bloody battle of Delium. Its aggregate cost even exceeded the number of those who perished in the notorious catastrophe at Sicily. None of these fatality figures includes the thousands who were maimed and crippled by the disease—or, even more catastrophically, the effects on Athenian demography for years to come when so many of child-bearing age were swept away. Pausanias, for example, wrote that over thirty years later the postwar Athenians begged off from joining the Panhellenic expedition to Asia Minor on the pretext that they were still suffering from the vast manpower losses of the war and plague.[23]

The sudden death of so many hoplites also had more immediate repercussions in the following years. Athens would field only 7,000 hoplites at the battle of Delium in 424. They sent fewer than 1,000 to the even more critical battle of Mantinea in 418—thousands fewer hoplites than the 10,000 Athenians who fought at Marathon in 490. Both defeats were close-run battles. Three or four thousand more Athenian infantrymen might have made the difference between victory and rout. Had the Athenian alliance won at either critical engagement, the entire war might have ended on terms favorable to Athens with the departure of Boeotia from the enemy alliance, and a new democratic Peloponnesian axis encircling an emasculated Spartan state.

So the death of some 10,000 frontline and reserve hoplites, coupled with 300 horsemen, along with ongoing sieges and naval patrols, suggests that Athens was unable to commit to any serious land efforts for years. The disaster might also explain why there was no hoplite campaign such as even the halfhearted Athenian efforts at Delium or Mantinea initiated during the five years immediately after 429. Instead, the Athenians were paranoid about revolts among the subjects of the empire, in part due to losses from the plague and the impression that the city was too beleaguered to enforce its overseas rule.[24]

Something had gone drastically wrong in just a few years. The army that had once put 16,000 hoplites in the field to ravage the Megarid at the beginning of the war, seven years later at Delium was less than half that size. For Athens to defeat either of the qualitatively better Theban or Peloponnesian armies, numerical superiority, not parity, was essential. If the thetic class who manned the fleet perished from disease at aggregate percentages commensurate to the hoplites and cavalrymen (i.e., about 30 percent), then of some 20,000 citizen rowers, perhaps 6,000 to 7,000 also died over the course of the epidemic—or enough sailors to man 30 to 35 triremes outright. That is more than the total of all the Athenian dead at the naval victory of Salamis fifty years earlier, an event that had kicked off the great Athenian half century.

It was not until 415, nearly fifteen years after the initial outbreak, that the

Athenian military was restored to even tolerable strength. For example, in a discussion of the preparations to invade Sicily in 416, Thucydides explains that the population was confident in their preparations since "the city had just recovered from the plague and the long war," adding that financial capital had been restored during the Peace of Nicias "and a number of young men had grown up."[25]

Tally up all the cavalrymen, hoplites, and thetes who perished, add in the adult male metics, and assume that a like percentage of women and children, as well as slaves of all ages and both sexes, died: somewhere around 70,000 to 80,000 residents of Attica suddenly were gone. Most probably succumbed within a few months after the initial outbreak of 430. Thus a quarter to a third of the entire resident population vanished before the war really started in earnest. Yet because the plague was a natural, rather than human-induced catastrophe, the historian Thucydides devoted only a fraction of his attention to the epidemic in comparison to the later Sicilian fiasco, even though twice as many Athenians died in the streets of Athens as perished later in Sicily.

Crisis in Confidence

IF MODERN SCHOLARS do not always factor the plague's losses into discussions of the military history of the Archidamian War, the Athenians, at least, knew that their city had been irreparably damaged. They certainly saw their army and naval strength in terms of "before" and "after" the epidemic. Thucydides remarked that the invasion of the Megarid during the first autumn of the war was the greatest display of Athenian infantry strength in its history, inasmuch as it "had not yet been stricken with the plague." Pericles concluded of the first year of outbreak that it had done more than any other calamity to ruin the spirit of Athens. He implies that his initial policy would have been far more successful had not the pestilence confounded his carefully wrought strategy. Even during the outbreak Athenians were concluding that there had never been anything quite like it, and that the disease had radically altered the course of the war.

Similarly, the leaders of the revolt on Mytilene begged for Spartan help, with the argument that just two years after the outbreak "Athens had been ruined by the plague and the costs of the war." For Thucydides, who survived the disease, the ripples of the plague were to be felt everywhere: decreased military capability, political unrest, imperial revolt, changed strategy, and, worst of all, death of the only Athenian leader who seemed to be able to keep the factious citizenry together during the dark hours of war.[26]

Pericles, worn out by age and the loss of two of his sons, Xanthippus and Paralus, to the disease, himself at last crumbled. The disaster hit him hard. Pericles lost a sister as well as "the greatest number of his relatives and friends." He died two and a half years into the war, after a drawn-out and debilitating bout with the illness, a detail omitted in Thucydides' famous obituary of the great leader. His loss at the outset of the conflict—inasmuch as he had more or less guided Athens as an annually elected official for nearly thirty years—left the city leaderless. Athens was unsure whether Pericles' strategic view was flawed and had led to the disaster of the plague or, in fact, was still viable and after the city's recovery would eventually lead to victory.[27]

If Thucydides acknowledged that the second generation of Spartan leaders, including Brasidas, Gylippus, and Lysander, were more skilled and audacious than old Archidamus, he seemed to think that Pericles' successors, such as Cleon and Alcibiades, were only more reckless and amoral. Moderns sometimes bristle at the "great man" theory of history, the nineteenth-century notion that events can be shaped by the peculiar careers of individuals rather than long-term and more insidious demographic, social, and cultural processes. But few would argue with the idea that had Churchill, Roosevelt, Stalin, or Hitler succumbed to smallpox in early 1939, World War II might have had a far different course, if not outcome, altogether. Throughout the Peloponnesian War and its aftermath, the death of prominent individuals seems to have had a profound effect on the course of events: the speech of old Pagondas alone convincing the Boeotians to head for Delium; the end of both Brasidas and Cleon at Amphipolis leading to the Peace of Nicias; Lamachus' unfortunate demise above Syracuse, which helped doom the expedition; the appearance of Lysander, which galvanized the Spartan fleet; and, in the immediate aftermath of the war, Cyrus the Younger's death at Cunaxa, which left the victorious 10,000 in the position of the defeated, despite their having prevailed on the battlefield.[28]

Thucydides recovered after his bout with the disease. But it is unclear whether the ordeal helped shape his largely pessimistic view of human events or left him with permanent physical handicaps that hampered his generalship and thus led to his exile. Surely his ideas about the importance of culture in harnessing nature had something to do with his brush with death amid a sea of stricken thousands who randomly perished about him. In some sense, his dark impressions of the war formed in the second year of the fighting, when the plague quite literally determined the tone and theme of its own subsequent chronicler.

To make good the losses of the plague, Athens looked to a number of desperate measures, which had incalculable effects in eroding the cultural cohesion of the city. Later, popular myth circulated the idea that casual polygamy was de facto allowed for the first time. Luminaries like Socrates and Euripides, out of patriotic fervor, purportedly had additional children with second wives.[29] Changes in nationality laws now allowed citizens' rights to those born in Attica to one Athenian parent, whereas the previous law had required two. Pericles had once reminded the Athenians that, as in the past, their citizenship was a rare honor and a privilege. Yet in postplague Athens it was the quantity, not necessarily the pedigree, of people that now mattered if the city was to survive the war. With the death of his two legitimate sons, Pericles immediately sought legislation to extend citizenship to his surviving illegitimate son, Pericles the Younger.[30]

An ancient community that professes faith in an adolescent science—like an enlightened fifth-century Athens—has real trouble in accounting for naturally occurring calamity when its own novel god Reason fails. Later stories told of visits to plague-ridden Athens by the legendary father of medicine, Hippocrates himself. Some ancient accounts reflect scientific theories that weather conditions were the causative agents, or perhaps polluted grain brought on by unseasonably moist conditions. Even though so-called miasmatic conjectures—the air of 430 was contaminated by mysterious gases, dead bodies, or stagnant water—were apparently common explanations for the outbreak, Thucydides did not think them worthy of discussion in any detail. But many others did. The historian Diodorus, for example, argued that the crowding had produced "polluted" air that sickened the citizenry.[31]

Yet while "air" has little clinical connection with infectious disease, the ancients were not entirely wrong in their empirical suppositions. Many viruses and bacteria circulate through tiny airborne droplets expelled through coughing. In addition, stagnant water can explain outbreaks of ill health, inasmuch as pools are ideal breeding grounds for mosquitoes that breed malaria ("bad air").

Still, if Hippocratic science could not adequately explain, much less ameliorate, the effects of the plague, if Greek cosmologists and natural philosophers offered not a clue about the true etiology of the epidemic, and if Socratic ethics failed to explain why for the good of the city one should be civic-minded amid such calamity, then even a sophisticated people like the classical Athenians—Pericles included—could turn to cult and superstition in preference to both science and traditional Olympian religion. What had Zeus, Apollo, or Athena done to stop the plague? No more than had Hippocrates and the doctors. Thus, in both Thucydides' history and Aristophanes' contemporary comedies, offbeat prophets and soothsayers fill the vacuum and find a renaissance during the plague years among a disillusioned populace.

The biographer Plutarch thought the spiritual odyssey of Pericles himself offered an object lesson about the descent from science to false knowledge. Traditionalists had parodied the Athenian leader for much of his earlier career for being a rationalist, a student of the natural philosophers Anaxagoras and Protagoras. Silly stories circulated about him idling his time away in dialectics with Protagoras, attempting to discover whether a javelin or its thrower was morally responsible for the accidental death of its target. Yet in his last days, even Pericles, Athens' wartime leader, was reduced to pathetic false notions, and so wore an amulet around his neck to save him from the enfeebling disease. Before this terrible war was over, the Athenians would see things even worse than their great rationalist general reduced to embracing superstition on his deathbed.[32]

In the aftermath of the disease, the cult of Asclepius, along with that of Hygieia ("Health"), was introduced from Epidaurus in the Peloponnese to Athens sometime around 420, as if worshipping these newer gods of medical cures on a regular basis might save the city from further cycles of epidemics. The so-called Asclepion ("House of Asclepius") was constructed directly to the west of the great theater of Dionysus, beneath the Acropolis, a bitter reminder that in addition to public drama Athens now needed divine medical relief. Meanwhile, on the border between Boeotia and Attica at the Oropus, the legendary hero Amphiaraos soon also won his own cult sanctuary, in hopes that such a healing deity might provide prophylaxis from further infection.

There was more worry that the gods were angry. Just four years after the outbreak, and shortly after a return of the disease in 426, the Athenians took the drastic step of purifying the island of Delos—the legendary center of the old Greek Delian League—in hopes of regaining the favor of Apollo, who traditionally warded off disease. Under the leadership of Nicias they removed all the graves from the island and set up annual games in the god's honor.[33]

More untraditional cults from the East—the Phrygian mountain goddess, Cybele, Sabazius, the Thracian Dionysus, and Asiatic Bacchus—would soon be imported by the beleaguered Athenians, hedging their bets in case the traditional Olympians, like Apollo, Athena, and Zeus, could bring no relief in the future. Yet for all the rise in supernatural explanations and their collective hysteria, even in their worse moments the Athenians never resorted to human sacrifice to mollify the gods or engaged in witch trials or ritual scapegoating in hopes of alleviating their misery. Nevertheless, just as Athens was reeling from outside enemies, inside the walls of the city began the greatest spiritual transformation and period of religious uncertainty in the history of the city. All subsequent campaigning at Mytilene, Melos, Scione, and Sicily must be seen in light of the cultural chaos unleashed on the democracy at home.

The Survivors

DIFFICULT TIMES CALL for different men. Pericles was dead. Yet his orphaned young ward Alcibiades was emerging to prove indestructible—and, later, shameless. He had survived four years of exposure to the plague, both in the hot zones at Athens and earlier, when the disease had killed every fourth soldier at Potidaea. Through the first five years of the war at home and abroad, the veteran cavalryman had kept intact his hard-won honor. With the death of the old guard to disease, Alcibiades, in his mere twenties, was on the verge of emerging as one of the new leaders of an Athens now so chronically short of healthy men. Plutarch relates how amid the misery of plague-ridden Athens, the resolute and robust Alcibiades visited the dejected Pericles and persuaded him to ignore his recent censure and resume public life. In normal reckoning, age and sobriety might ensure accession to political leadership; in these dark years of plague, however, youth, robust health, and even recklessness were the better criteria for the times.[34]

War had earlier killed Alcibiades' father and now made him a hero at Potidaea and a respected stalwart among the Athenian cavalry who kept the Spartans away from the precincts near the city. It had taught him that no one was immune from fate, as he watched his patron die of disease, and the city of Sophocles and the Parthenon descend into the miasma of death. Time now waited for no one in Athens, and it was far better to seize the day than to die ignominiously alone, crusted with disease.

When the plague quieted in 426, Alcibiades was only twenty-four. Yet in the five-year-long war he had seen cannibalism, disease, and slaughter at Potidaea, women and children dying in the streets at Athens, and the estates of his wealthy friends abandoned and sometimes torched in the once beautiful Attic countryside, where his own family had owned for generations at least two large farms of about eighty acres.[35] The lessons the young man took away from all of this were Thucydidean: war really was "a tough schoolmaster," and only a few astute, callous men could see it through. Alcibiades almost alone of his generation would; but he also would take his city down with him. Thucydides points out that those who survived the plague wrongly believed that they would never again be susceptible to other illnesses. It is likely that Alcibiades likewise felt that his survival and that of his mentor, Socrates, were somehow part of his unusual luck and proof of an exceptional destiny to come.[36]

Athenian soldiers went into battle for the next twenty-three years, from 426 through 404, with the knowledge that their parents, themselves, their children, or their friends had suffered from the disease, which might return to kill thousands without warning at any given time. The dread of epidemic must have hung over the combatants for much of the war. When the Spartans and Argives considered a peace treaty in 420, they wrote a codicil stating that either side might be exempt from some of the agreed requirements if they were at the time suffering from a plague.[37]

The ripples of the plague also lapped over into both contemporary and later classical literature. The playwright Sophocles, who purportedly became involved in the cult of the healing god Asclepius when it arrived in Athens in 420, had presented his magisterial *Oedipus Rex* perhaps just five years after the outbreak to an audience that had recently lost tens of thousands. The play begins with the city of Thebes beleaguered by a sudden epidemic that accompanies crop disease, stock losses, and general infertility. All such calamities the Athenians in the audience would have recognized as recent burdens brought on by either the plague or the invasions of Spartan ravagers—and feared that they could return at any minute. Whereas Thucydides focuses on scientific descriptions of the epidemic and either ignores or ridicules folk stories, the religious background to the plague is central to the plot of Sophocles' drama: the Thebans must suffer collective punishment for the unknown incest and unacknowledged parricide within its royal family.

In the play, traditional religion—the wisdom of Apollo and the seer craft of Teiresias—provides the proper way to discover both the etiology of and the cure for the disease. Athens, in Sophocles' mind at least, may have lost over a fourth of its population not from overcrowding or poor hygienic practices but because of an absence of traditional piety. He seems to suggest that it is hubristic to assume that logic alone—perhaps the contemporary city's sophistic elite or Pericles himself were to be equated to his all-too-proud Oedipus—can simply cut through the disease and thus find rational causes and answers for what ultimately must remain divinely inspired problems. Oedipus is rational, imperious, and—like Pericles—in way over his head against a foe that is beyond the calculation of hoplites and triremes.

Such later writers as Lucretius, Virgil, Ovid, and Josephus also wove vivid descriptions of plagues and natural disasters into their work, often with striking echoes of the Athenian epidemic: an African origin, rural flight into cities, mysterious causation, no cure, and social chaos as the dividends of mass dying. In a more historical context, the Byzantine chronicler Procopius used Thucydides to provide an equally striking description of the social calamity that followed an epidemic (most likely the bubonic plague) that struck Constantinople in spring 542 and for a time killed perhaps as many as 10,000 people a day. The Athenian disaster proved to be the locus classicus to later Western historiography that chronicled such disastrous outbreaks, as if any subsequent description must entail a Thucydidean account of the social chaos that inevitably followed such mass death.[38]

Still, for the first years of the war, the Spartan invasions neither achieved economic ruin nor prompted the hoped for decisive battle, even as thousands of Athenians perished from disease. Because neither the traditional arenas of agricultural devastation and hoplite battle nor the plague led to decisive victory, each side prepared to redefine its strategy. Athenians would no longer stay within their walls and die. Sparta could not merely send out its massive armies in a vain search for enemy hoplites. Instead, new men in fresh theaters turned up to conduct a dirty war never quite seen before in Greece.

This novel way of waging the Peloponnesian War would suit audacious leaders like Alcibiades quite well.

CHAPTER 4

TERROR

AFTER A ONE-YEAR hiatus arising from fear of the plague, the Spartan alliance resumed invading Attica in 427, even as its Boeotian partners pressed on with the siege of Plataea begun during the epidemic at Attica. Yet in these first years of the conflict, not all Athenians were dying from the pestilence or patrolling the Attic countryside in futile efforts to repel Peloponnesian ravagers. Thousands in the imperial fleet, infected or not, were determined to make Sparta and its friends pay for their attacks and to experience something of the humiliation that they had inflicted on others both out in Attica and inside Athens.

In Plutarch's words, as a result of these raids against Spartan territory there was for the Athenians some "consolation to be had from what their enemies were suffering." If prewar observers had worried that the internecine conflict between Athens and Sparta might be far different—far more lengthy—than past Greek wars, they were soon to be proven prescient.[1]

The first years of hostilities (431–423) more or less bore this gloomy antebellum prognosis out: the Athenians avoided battling Spartan infantrymen, while Peloponnesian ships were usually not willing to meet the Athenian navy in any major engagement. The stage was set for "asymmetrical," "fourth-dimensional," or "postmodern" war—conflict in which an array of political, social, and cultural factors, rather than conventional military doctrine or traditional combatants, determines how one side chooses to harm its adversary. Some pretty uncouth killers would now step out of the shadows of the Greek world to do what traditional generals and admirals could not. Both sides would employ fear in unconventional ways, reminding us that terror is a method, not an enemy, a manifestation of how a particular belligerent chooses to wage war rather than some sort of independent entity that exists apart from men, money, and places.

Peter Krentz has made the point that hoplite battle was not the primary means of fighting by counting up all the examples of deception and surprise attacks, often by night and fought by nonhoplites.* His thirty-seven instances in the Peloponnesian War dwarf the two large, set-piece hoplite encounters at Delium and Mantinea, and the smaller clashes of phalanxes at Solygia and Syracuse. Similarly, W. K. Pritchett collated forty-three examples of night attacks during the Peloponnesian War, engagements that were antithetical to the old idea of drawing up armies in broad daylight to settle the issue through infantry clashes.[2]

Such nontraditional hostilities broke out immediately in spring 431. Predictably, they intensified once the stalemated conventional war turned to distant theaters beyond the annual invasions of the Attic countryside, involving a host of surrogate forces that were not evenly matched. The tragedy here was that rarely was the fighting symmetrical or the outcome in these localized engagements in doubt. It was lamentable because only evenly matched and conventional combatants were likely to adhere to the old Hellenic idea of rules and protocols that tended to preclude gratuitous killing, given the uncertainty on both sides of victory and thus the shared need to worry about their own treatment after defeat. But in the backwaters and hinterlands of Greece, away from public duels in the plains, the Athenians and Spartans, and an array of their odious henchmen, usually did not meet the main forces of the enemy but instead found in particular locales and for brief moments unquestioned superiority in numbers. In those cases, the lives of the weak and innocent depended entirely on the particular attitude of a particular commander on a particular day, the likelihood of mercy diminishing as the war escalated ever more.

The New Killers

FOR THIS TYPE of war there was no need for either the cumbersome personal armor of the hoplite infantryman—breastplate, greaves, shield, helmet, spear, and sword—or the costly state investment in triremes (170 to 200 seamen in an

---

* "Hoplite battle" is meant to denote heavily armed spearmen fighting in the close-ordered formation of the phalanx against a similar formation, most often at daytime and by some sort of arrangement.

expensive galley). True, hoplites were used on ships, for raiding, and at sieges, but they increasingly often lightened their panoplies and questioned their traditional training as misguided for such a new theater of warfare. Instead, novel types of combatants were emerging—the light-armed warriors, known variously to Greeks as the "light-guys" (psiloi), the "peltasts" (because they carried the small crescent-shaped shield known as the peltê), or simply the "naked" (gymnoi) and "unarmored" (aoploi or anoploi). Traditionally, light-armed corps contingents were only loosely organized and used primarily in pursuit and ravaging. These were less frequent arenas where hoplite formations were either absent or already in shreds, and thus lighter, more nimble warriors could outmaneuver armored combatants, who were vulnerable outside of rank.

Before 431, Athens, for example, whether due to its enormous fleet, which required the full service of the poorer and landless population, or because it trusted in naval engagements abroad and hoplite and cavalry defense at home, never organized an official body of light-armed troops. Instead, its older and younger citizens might tag along on expeditions to nearby Megara or Boeotia in hopes of plundering or ravaging under the aegis of heavy infantry. The Peloponnesian War would change all that. By the last decade of the war, even Athens was regularly hiring and deploying its own light-armed forces, with enormous implications for the future of Greek warfare.[3]

Originally, light-armed troops were identified as the "other" in the sense of both geography and expertise and thus were often concretely and metaphysically outside the Greek city-state. In Greece proper they were the poorer without land who could not afford body armor, much less a horse, and usually brandished a spear or javelin and only a cheap wooden or leather shield. Outside of the mainland, on the periphery of the Greek world, the light-armed were more specialized and often tribal warriors adept at fighting in rough terrain with little or no experience in, or need of, facing down phalanxes.

Peltasts were originally a Thracian specialty, quick tribal fighters without much body armor other than their crescent-shaped shields, often leather caps, and long thrusting spears or throwing javelins. Early in the war both Athens and Sparta hired such Thracian mercenaries, and they played key roles in the Athenian victory over the Spartans at the island of Sphacteria (425) and Brasidas' success against Athenian subject states in the Chalcidice (423). Yet by the end of the war Greek troops that had copied the Thracian equipment and tactics were deployed far more frequently than hoplites.[4]

Slingers were a specialty from the island of Rhodes, while the best archers were imported from Scythia and Crete. In the same manner that superior cavalry roamed the plains of Thessaly and Macedonia, so too areas of the Greek-speaking world that had never fully embraced the agrarian protocols of the polis saw no reason to deploy heavy infantry to dispute their extensive plains. Rather, they found it cheaper and more effective to fight in the hills or to hit, run, and raid, a fact well illustrated by the multifaceted force that Thucydides says the Athenians sent to Sicily in its first wave. Besides hoplites and sailors, there were 700 poor Athenians equipped as marines, 480 archers (including 80 Cretan experts), 700 slingers, and another 120 light-armed Megarians—in other words, 2,000 light-armed troops, or about 40 percent of the 5,100-man hoplite force itself. And of the total manpower sent on the 134 ships of the first armada to Sicily, hoplites made up less than 20 percent of the roughly 26,800 sailors and combatants. Even earlier, the Athenians had deployed slingers in Acarnania in hopes of matching the irregular troops of their unconventional enemies there. Similarly, the Boeotians called them in before finishing off the trapped Athenian garrison at Delium in 424. Light-armed warriors—not hoplites in phalanxes—turned up everywhere in the Peloponnesian War.[5]

What was the attraction of such missile fighters? In a word, they could kill from afar. Through long training and expertise, they achieved lethality without the expense of either heavy armor or ships. When slingers, for example, had access to aerodynamic small lead projectiles of between twenty and thirty grams, rather than rougher clay pellets or stones, they could easily outdistance archers and hit targets at some 350 yards. Heavily armored men in rank with shields raised would be largely invulnerable to a rain of pellets, but how often did that occur in the Peloponnesian War, when most infantry fighting was outside the phalanx?

As the war progressed, the use of these nonconventional troops only increased. Even the reactionary Spartans drafted a corps of both bowmen and cavalry by 424. Their sudden turn to these forces only came after the disaster on Sphacteria, and the Athenian use of Pylos and Cythera as forward bases in Peloponnesian territory. After the failures in Attica, and the inability to match Athens at sea, the Spartan leadership at last grasped that their own crack hoplites were not the answer. This recognition sent shock waves throughout Sparta, a state dependent on a homogenous hoplite elite now revealed to be unable to win the war it had started.[6]

Radical social and cultural effects followed widespread use of the light-armed killers in their new unconventional war. Because Greek military service had for so long been predicated on class—the nature and size of land owned rather than military efficacy per se determining how citizens fought—the turn to the poor and the skirmisher called into question all the existing protocols of centuries past. This military revolution risked overturning the very social accords of the Greek city-state, and is best appreciated in retrospect from the fourth century when nostalgic elite Greek thinkers deplored the legacy of the Peloponnesian War, especially the importation of foreign killers who were as deadly, but not nearly as respected or honored, as hoplites.[7]

It is a truism of most Western militaries that their peacetime bureaucracies are centered around heavy conventional infantry forces that are designed to fight their counterparts of a similar nation-state. In contrast, reliance on irregulars and special forces not only calls such assumptions into question but temporarily elevates a type of warrior who is himself uncomfortable with any protocols and thus the logical target of social and class disdain.

The dichotomy is as old as Homer himself, whose *Iliad* of the late eighth century B.C. relegates the archer and the irregular to a decidedly inferior social caste. Achilles or Ajax, spearing in the melee, seems the more resolute, honest fighter than the cowardly (although lethal) archer Paris. Contemporary hostility to the terrorist, guerrilla, and insurgent—who, armed with rocket-propelled grenades, land mines, and suicide bombs, can raise havoc with the billion-dollar armored divisions of the nation—is not unlike ancient lamentations over the newfound power of the bowmen, catapult, or light-armed skirmisher who lacked the respectability of the hoplite infantryman. Unlike hoplites, ancient skirmishers, again like modern insurgents, were more likely to target civilians, whether on Corcyra or in the small Boeotian hamlet of Mycalessus. There is no record in earlier Greek history of a hoplite phalanx murdering civilians, and little evidence that hoplites killed many combatants who ran away from battle.

Tit for Tat

PERICLEAN STRATEGY WOULD prove enormously expensive and far-reaching—and, ironically, far more intricate than the much simpler "offensive" plan of meeting the Spartans in pitched battle. Almost immediately on news of the first Spartan invasion of Attica, the Athenians sailed southward to plunder the coast of the Peloponnese. Perhaps they remembered that a quarter century earlier, during the First Peloponnesian War, their legendary general Tolmides had been so brash as to burn the Spartan dockyards at Gythium and ravage the Peloponnesian coastal plains. Now they at least sensed that the muster of the Spartan allied army and its subsequent march into Attica made it likely that back home there was little territorial defense of the seaboard of the Peloponnese. The modus operandi of the allied Athenian armada of some 100 ships was simple, requiring only ships, bases to supply food and water for the fleet, and circumspect commanders who would select the most vulnerable hamlets and villages and not tarry too long, blood drunk on easy killing and plunder.[8]

What was the ultimate Athenian purpose behind such operations, strategies that had, in fact, been tried numerous times earlier during previous conflicts with the Peloponnesians in past decades? It was obvious: disrupt commerce on land and sea, destroy war matériel, demoralize the enemy home front, and demonstrate that the Spartans either would not or could not protect their friends. All the while they were to assure a long-suffering Athenian public back home that despite the avoidance of pitched battle their military was not as inactive or cowardly as it seemed.

Over the course of the long war there were somewhere around fifty-five clear-cut naval engagements, land battles, and sieges—instances of conventional fighting, in other words, with an identifiable beginning and an end aimed at tactical objectives. In contrast, the sheer instances of towns, states, and regions attacked by the Athenians in the first few years of the conflict were in the many hundreds, and represented almost constant engagement, as their fleet sailed around the Peloponnese, throughout the Corinthian Gulf, along both the northwestern and the northeastern coasts of Greece, and freely in the southern Aegean. This was raiding and killing, not formal war as previously defined by the Greeks.

There is no accurate record of how many were killed or lost in such operations. A partial chronological tally of the targets from 431 to 421 burdens the reader: Sollium, Astacus, Thronion, Acte, Methone, several towns in Elis, Aegina, Epidaurus, Troezen, Halieis, Hermione, Prasiae, Aetolia, Amphilochia, Acarnania, Oeniadae, Leucas, Corcyra, Anactorium, Melos, Cythera, and Crommyon. Thucydides points out that the second seaborne punitive expedition of 430, led by Pericles himself, was in some respects as large as the first armada that set sail for Sicily.

Indeed, 150 imperial triremes, 4,000 hoplites, and 300 horsemen gave the Athenians immediate—if transitory—numerical superiority at almost any Peloponnesian territory they chose to attack. The raids were not merely symbolic reprisals (even though attackers rarely ventured more than five miles inland from their ships). Instead, the incursions were deliberately timed to be simultaneous with the Peloponnesian assaults, and thus effective in getting the enemy to leave Attica early—and provide a retaliatory deterrence for the future. Yet the constant deployment of Athenian troops abroad between 431 and

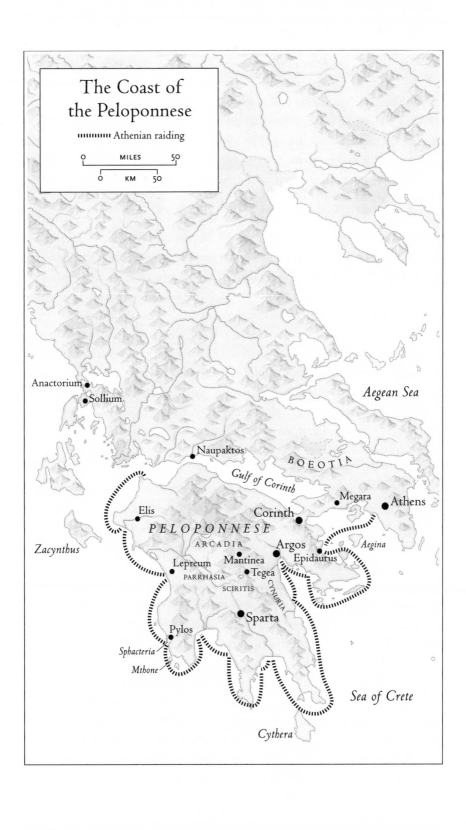

The Coast of the Peloponnese

|||||||||| Athenian raiding

0 —— MILES —— 50

0 —— KM —— 50

Anactorium
Sollium

Aegean Sea

Naupaktos

BOEOTIA

Gulf of Corinth

Megara
Athens

Elis

Corinth

PELOPONNESE

Zacynthus

ARCADIA

Argos

Aegina

Lepreum
Mantinea
Tegea
Epidaurus

PARRHASIA

SCIRITIS

CYNURIA

Sparta

Pylos

Sphacteria

Mthone

Sea of Crete

Cythera

426—at Potidaea, in Thrace, around the Peloponnese, in the Corinthian Gulf, at Mytilene, at Sicily, and in the wilds of northwestern Greece—altogether cost the state nearly 5,000 talents and nearly led to state insolvency.[9]

What transpired in these brief incursions? The fighting primarily involved low-level killing and plundering. The aim was to hurt the enemy and yet find some way in the process to pay the cost of deploying such a large fleet and forces of marines on a round-trip cruise of some eight hundred miles. For example, along the coast of the Peloponnese and the southwestern mainland, hostages were taken at Thronion, Prasiae pillaged, the Amphilochian Argives enslaved, Ambracia plundered, and Cytherans held for ransom. Sometimes permanent bases were established at places like Cythera or Naupaktos, where the Athenian fleet could regularly find supplies for subsequent expeditions as well as provide a base for local resistance. The more frequently the Peloponnesians entered Attica in the first seven years of the war, the more likely the Athenians were to raid the farms and towns of their allies to the rear—likewise achieving very little material advantage, but in the process by trial and error fashioning the foundations of a radical new strategy that would soon become devastating to the Spartan cause.

Some 30,000 Athenians and their allies combined to cruise the coast. Rarely did ravagers meet resistance, such as the Spartan Brasidas' heroic defense of the poorly defended hamlet of Methone on the southwestern Messenian coast. Instead, as the fleet made its way slowly around Laconia and up the northwestern coast of the Peloponnese, they found less conflict the farther they sailed on past Sparta, stopping for two days of ravaging in the rich countryside of Elis. Before the Eleans could muster an army, the Athenians were back at sea and heading for the critical mouth of the Corinthian Gulf, where they captured the Corinthian port at Sollium.

Meanwhile, as they traveled even farther northward, past the Corinthian Gulf, storming enemy allied cities in Acarnania, yet another fleet of 30 more Athenian ships raided Locris and Phocis, off the northeast coast of the mainland. While these twin armadas of Athenians and their allies—now totaling 36,000 combatants!—hit Spartan interests, yet still another Athenian maritime force set out from the Piraeus, and promptly attacked the nearby island of Aegina. Perhaps the rage over the Spartan ravaging explains why the Athenians felt no hesitation in expelling thousands of Aeginetan men, women, and children, and then cleansed the island of all its inhabitants within a few days.

The original fleet of 100 Athenian ships had broken off operations, left the Corcyraeans in turmoil, and set sail for home, but not before stopping in the

Megarid to join a land force of 10,000 Athenian hoplites who were raiding that hated Peloponnesian corridor of access to Attica. At the same time, 3,000 hoplites were still busy besieging Potidaea and expending 2,000 talents in the process—the price of constructing two Parthenons, or enough capital to build and launch an armada of 2,000 triremes and keep them busy for half a year. By the start of the third year of the war, the single siege of Potidaea had cost Athens 40 percent of its prewar capital reserves, an enormous sum that should have warned all the city-states of the financial catastrophe that might accrue from a drawn-out siege.[10]

No Rules

ALMOST IMMEDIATELY AFTER 431 there arose two Peloponnesian Wars. Historians more or less concentrate on the well-known land battles at places like Mantinea and Delium, the famous sieges of Mytilene, Syracuse, and Melos, and the climactic naval showdowns such as Arginusae and Aegospotami. But an even more atrocious combat in the shadows, in out-of-the-way places like the Aeolian Islands, off Italy, and Sollium and Cythera, went on simultaneously. The repetitious language of Thucydides' descriptions of these raids—"they plundered," "they attacked," "they killed"—by needs is matter-of-fact, given the frequency of indiscriminate slaughter that quickly became part of this low-intensity plundering.

Both Spartans and Athenians began to augment their major theater operations with smaller incursions for the next twenty-six years. Before the war was over, almost every sector of the Greek-speaking world had suffered a sudden attack from marauding Spartan or Athenian commandos. At one time or another, the Spartans hit Salamis, Hysiae, Argos, Iasos, Clazomenae, Kos, and Lesbos, while the Athenians continued during and after the Peace of Nicias (421–415) in their reign of terror, landing and plundering Melos, dozens of Sicilian villages, Lampsacus, Miletus, Lydia, Bithynia, Caria, and Andros.

Thucydides himself was often repulsed by the sheer barbarity of these raids. Both attacker and attacked gave no quarter, and battle often turned into little more than chasing down desperate men and killing them from the rear. A particularly graphic example was the Athenian disaster in northwestern Greece during the sixth year of the war, in summer 426. After the Athenian attackers became confused and were ambushed in the unfamiliar hills of Aetolia, General Demosthenes lost control of his panicked army. And once the arrows of the surviving Athenian archers were exhausted—the last bastion of the army's safety—the light-armed tribal skirmishers of the Aetolians rushed in from every quarter. It was a ghastly scene where the Athenians fell into "pathless gullies," many buried by a sea of javelins but even more caught in dense underbrush and woods, where they were torched alive:

> Every type of flight was attempted; but every manner of destruction befell the Athenian force. Only with difficulty could the survivors flee to the sea at Oeneon in Locris, the very place they had started out from. Many of the allies perished and 120 Athenian hoplites as well. So great was the number of such dead, and all of the same age that perished here—literally the best men that the city of Athens lost in the entire war.[11]

"The best men" suggests that the aristocratic Thucydides, like Plato later, particularly abhorred this type of combat, when good infantry found no conventional theater to showcase their training and bravery. An even worse massacre transpired not far away in Amphilochia, a few months later (winter 426) during another large-scale Athenian raid, as part of the ongoing efforts early in the war to secure the shores of the Corinthian Gulf and the gateway westward to Sicily and Italy. After a truce, some Ambraciots tried to flee their captors without being noticed by the Athenian general Demosthenes and his Acarnanian allies. But almost immediately the Acarnanians ran them down and slaughtered about 200. Meanwhile, a relief column of Ambraciots arrived and in ignorance camped nearby for the night. Demosthenes' men fell upon the sleeping Ambraciots and began butchering them as they struggled to rise.

Most Ambraciots making it out of the camp were hunted down by the native Amphilochians. Like the fate of the Athenians the summer before in Aetolia, they were soon chased into ravines and rough country and killed in droves. A few terrified Ambraciots waded out to the sea and jumped into the surf, despite the presence of an Athenian fleet patrolling the shores. So desperate were the Ambraciots to get out of the undergrowth and flee the hated tribes of Amphilochians that they preferred to be killed or captured in the water by Athenian sailors. All of this was a long way from the pomp and protocol of hoplite battle.

The exact number of those who were murdered in flight is unknown. Killed in their sleep, in the woods, or in the water, the dead Ambraciots counted well over 1,000. In an unusual editorial note of disgust, Thucydides remarks that the Ambraciot holocaust was the greatest disaster that befell a Greek city in such a short period of time. He adds that he could not give any precise figure of the dead, since "the multitudes of those said to have perished seem unbelievable given the size of the city."[12]

During this sad spectacle in Amphilochia, the Acarnanian allies of the Athenians slaughtered troops retiring under truce, turned on their own generals who sought to stop such gratuitous violence, and got confused over the exact nationalities of the troops they were supposed to be killing. The archconservative Plato hated such unconventional war in his own time (429–347). He seems to have blamed its fourth-century ubiquity on its odious birth during the Peloponnesian War. Then in his teens and twenties, he had seen imperial Athens lose the war, his aristocratic friends fail in their efforts at oligarchic overthrow, and his mentor, Socrates, executed by radical democrats shortly thereafter. Apparently connecting the dots, he offered a strange rant about the pernicious use of "naval infantrymen." Plato deplored battle in which there were no clear-cut combatants to settle the issue through discipline and courage.

Instead, rabble "jump ashore on frequent stops and then run back as quick as they can to their ships. They think there is no shame at all in not dying courageously in their places." Apparently so disgusted was he at the practice of employing ships to tarnish the reputation of war and the heroic code of good hoplite infantry that he scoffed that in mythical times it would have been better for the Athenians to have given old King Minos all the hostages he wanted rather than to have resisted him by sea, and thus have initiated the successful maritime example that led to the present shame.[13]

The Lebanonization of Greece

A CLIMATE OF lawlessness soon swept Greece, much like the terror and chaos that characterized Beirut between 1975 and 1985, during which 150,000 Lebanese lost their lives. Very quickly after the Spartans crossed the Attic border, almost any Greek in transit became fair game—if he ventured into the wrong place at the wrong time. In 430, for example, some Peloponnesian envoys traveled through Thrace on their way to Persia as part of the initial Spartan plan of obtaining Persian capital. Local Athenian ambassadors, however, convinced the Thracians to have the diplomats arrested and extradited to Athens. Once there they were summarily executed without trial, their bodies thrown unceremoniously into a pit. The kidnapping of diplomats was an abject violation of Greek custom, which both respected the sanctity of heralds and envoys and often provided for proper burial of the dead.

In explanation of this shocking behavior, Thucydides relates that the Athenians were furious because of the recent Spartan practice of intercepting all Athenian or neutral vessels, both warships and merchant transports, found off the shores of the Peloponnese, and then executing the crews. How many civilian sailors and military crews were killed in such a piratical and atrocious manner, as is true of so many bloody incidents in the Peloponnesian War, is not known. Yet the number could well have been in the thousands. These were state-sanctioned operations to harm the enemy, but in many instances personal profit was the primary incentive for the thousands who opportunistically joined in.[14]

Cowardice was a requisite for such butchery, since rarely were troops willing to meet like kind. A good example is the especially cruel Spartan admiral Alcidas, a thug who found his natural calling in the war once it quickly degenerated into no-holds-barred theft and murder. With 40 triremes he was sent from the Peloponnese in 427 to relieve the embattled rebels at Mytilene on the island of Lesbos, who themselves would shortly surrender and face mass execution by the Athenians. While Alcidas was in transit, word reached him that Mytilene had fallen and the revolt from Athens had been crushed. In response, he immediately discarded suggestions either to sail on to Mytilene and confront the victorious Athenian fleet or to raise a general revolt among the Athenian subject communities of Asia Minor. Both were risky propositions that might result in a set-piece fight with the superior Athenian fleet.

Instead, Alcidas looked for easier prey—and then a quick getaway back home to the Peloponnese. Before the Athenian disaster on Sicily and the loss of two-thirds of the imperial fleet (413), it was a dangerous thing for a Spartan fleet to be anywhere in the Aegean for very long. Alcidas ducked into the small Ionian town of Myonnesus, where he summarily executed all the crews that his triremes had intercepted en route from the Peloponnese, in line with the Spartan vow at the beginning of the war to kill any seamen thought to be allied with the Athenian cause. How Alcidas advanced Spartan war aims, and in what manner his fleet of killers fitted into the general calculus of the war is unclear; apparently, though, he wished to send the message to neutrals that his breakout voyage across the Aegean meant that the seas were no longer the sole domain of the Athenian fleet.[15]

Guarantees now meant nothing. The Athenian general Paches, for example, who was chasing Alcidas, gave up the pursuit and wound up landing with a fleet at Notium, in Asia Minor. There he quickly sought to recover the town for the Athenians and put down an incipient rebellion. Rather than being outraged at Alcidas' behavior, the Athenian admiral adopted his tactics. Thus, he offered to parlay with one of the enemy mercenary commanders, the Arcadian Hippias. When Hippias came out of his negotiations, Paches quickly attacked, took his garrison, and then broke his promises of immunity and killed Hippias on the spot.

Next Paches went on to deal with the rebels at Mytilene, rounded up the Spartan instigator Salaethus, and sent him back to Athens, where he was exe-cuted—even as the assembly sent word for Paches to kill en masse the guilty parties at Mytilene.[16] In a metaphor for the entire war, the Athenians sent to hunt down the Spartan butcher proved to be greater butchers themselves, each side now fearful that mercy would be seen as weakness while murder conveyed a salutary warning that the wages of rebellion or even neutrality were death.

There was no general rule—any more than there was in Beirut during the Lebanon crisis—indicating whether captors, either out of concern for eventual ransom money or from transitory feelings of mercy, might keep alive their hostages. Instead, innocent civilians were abducted, whisked away for safekeep-ing, and then brought out to be executed at a more opportune time. Such was the fate of 300 Argive conservatives whom Alcibiades kidnapped in summer 415, on charges that they harbored "pro-Spartan" sympathies and were thus a danger to his efforts to reforge an Argive-Athenian democratic alliance. A year later, when the Argive democrats were worried about a possible coup and foreign in-vasion and Alcibiades himself was under suspicion, the Athenians retrieved the 300 from the islands and sent them home, where they were executed upon arrival.

Such hostage taking was not new. At the very beginning of the war, the Athe-nians had arrested all the Boeotians found in Attica on news that the Theban terrorists and insurrectionists had attacked Plataea. And in 424 the Athenians had captured some Aeginetans at the Argive frontier town of Thyrea—but only after they sacked the town, razed the walls, and enslaved all the inhabitants. They transported the entire cargo of captives to some unnamed but safe islands, and then on order of the Athenian assembly later executed them all—appar-ently an unexceptional event given the hatred between Aegina and Athens.[17]

The historian Xenophon noted, when news arrived at Athens that Lysander was on his way into the Piraeus, that panic broke out among the citizens who thought that they might now suffer some of the barbarity that they had in-flicted on others, running the gamut from planning to cut off the right thumbs or entire hands of captive seamen and throwing captured crews overboard in the high seas, to butchering the Histiaeans, Scionaeans, Toronaeans, Aeginetans, "and many other Greek peoples." In the new Athenian world there was nothing intrinsically at odds with citizens watching a play of Euripides' one day and voting to kill the adult male citizens of Scione the next.[18]

Indeed, in the very midst of the war the Athenians nevertheless pursued art and culture as they always had. Take, for example, a sample period between 411 and 408, when a seemingly exhausted Athens was plagued by internal revolution and the Spartan plundering from Decelea, while fighting for its life in a series of climactic sea battles at Cynossema, Abydos, and Cyzicus. Nevertheless, in the midst of such killing and calamity, Aristophanes staged his masterpiece antiwar comedy *Lysistrata* (411), followed by *Thesmophoriazusae*—fantasy plays in which women take state policy and the courts into their own hands. And while the masons were nearing completion of the Erechtheum, the last and most daring of Pericles' envisioned Acropolis temples, Euripides produced one of his darkest tragedies, *Orestes,* and Sophocles his majestic *Philoctetes*—about the unconquerable will of an unfairly tormented hero who resists the forces of accommodation. Actors, theatergoers, and artisans alike might ride, row, or riot in between plays and stonecutting.

Meanwhile, once these Athenians got into their collective minds to butcher, butcher they did, whether the citizenry of Melos or old Socrates, with impunity. Under the laws of Athenian democracy there was neither an independent judiciary to strike down a popular decree as unconstitutional nor a sovereign and immutable body of constitutional law protecting human rights and proscribing the powers of the assembly. Athens' conduct during and right after the war—whether killing Mytileneans, Melians, or Socrates—was all done according to majority vote, besmirching the reputation of democracy itself for centuries to come. Almost every savage measure taken by generals in the field was either preapproved by the sovereign Athenian assembly or understood by fearful commanders to be in line with the harsh dictates of an unforgiving voting citizenry back home.

The Spartans were often worse—as a horrendous case of mass murder of 2,000 Messenian helots attests. Terrified by the Athenian base at Pylos (425), which raised the specter of wide-scale helot revolt, the Spartans passed a proclamation offering freedom to any of their Messenian serfs whose prior military record on behalf of the state might serve as proof of courage and their past benefaction. Once 2,000 came forward, the Spartans crowned them and paraded them as heroes around temples. Then in secret they executed all of them on the logical fear that such resolute men might someday pose a threat to the Spartan state. How so many serfs were slain in secret—Thucydides says "no one knew how any of them died"—we are not told. The murder of the helots was never acknowledged by the Spartans. It is one of the tragic quirks of history, or perhaps a reflection of the biases of ancient historians themselves, that more is known about how 120 Athenians died in Aetolia than 2,000 murdered serfs in the Peloponnese.[19]

How exactly were so many Greeks, like the 2,000 helots or the 1,000 Mytileneans in 427 or the thousands of Athenians taken after Aegospotami, executed en masse? "Executed" is a euphemism in the age before the guillotine, gas chamber, firing squad, electric chair, or lethal injection. For those who were not run down and stabbed or shot by hostile skirmishers and archers, a variety of macabre methods are recorded, besides the usual lining up of bound captives and slitting of throats. The Spartans, for example, often threw bound prisoners live into a pit not far from town, the feared Kaiadas, where the disabled and wounded slowly starved or bled to death.

Thucydides relates an especially brutal method of killing on Corfu, where in 425 the Athenians stormed Mount Istone in an effort to put an end to the ongoing civil unrest that the oligarchs had precipitated over two years earlier. The Athenians then claimed they would grant leniency to the captured garrison, on the provision that not a single one of the prisoners dared to escape. But after tricking a few to risk flight, they executed the rest on grounds that the accords had been broken. Apparently the remaining captives were roped together in twos and whipped by special executioners equipped with cat-o'-nine-tails as they were forced to run a gauntlet between two long lines of jabbing hoplites. After sixty or so were torn apart, the rest refused to come out of their barracks. They either perished under a hail of arrows and roof tiles or killed themselves by jabbing captured arrows into their throats or hanging themselves with nooses made from their own clothes.[20]

Coups and Ethnic Cleansing

A SYSTEMATIC STUDY of all the major betrayals recorded in literary sources during the Peloponnesian War, for example, revealed fourteen overt instances between 431 and 406 of various factions colluding with the enemy to turn over towns and garrisons. Such tactics brought far more dividends than pitched battle, collaborators being successful in about half the instances recorded. Indeed, both sides were busy undermining the other's civilian base, as agents were about evenly divided in their efforts to intrigue with either Athens or Sparta. For their part, traitors wished personal aggrandizement, political change, revenge on old enemies—or a simple end to the war and its accompanying misery. The use of the fifth column was integral in Nicias' efforts to win over Syracuse through betrayal of the city, and in King Agis' efforts to wear Athens down from Decelea, by appealing to insurrectionists and exiles to join his fortified stronghold right outside the city.[21]

When the war appeared to be stalemated and the eventual victor uncertain, internal revolution was less likely. Yet after a particular setback—the Spartan surrender at Pylos or the Athenian catastrophe on Sicily—one side or the other grew emboldened that change at home might reflect the course of the larger war. If proof were needed that many people lack an ideology but instead prefer to look first to their own self-interests, no better examples exist than the Peloponnesian War; Thucydides repeatedly and drily points out the ebb and flow of popular Greek opinion that followed each particular Spartan or Athenian reverse. War, his "harsh schoolmaster," when combined with political tension, turned what would have otherwise been heated, but mostly restrained, civil disputes into unchecked bloodletting. Like the plague, internal upheavals served as didactic examples in which all of society's careful constructs—language, mercy, reason, and customs, ranging from burial to due process of law—were stripped away by war. Thucydides thought civil unrest and coups were central to his story of the war itself and that soon after hostilities broke out the "entire Hellenic world, so to speak, was so convulsed."[22]

Those Greeks who owned larger farms (i.e., twenty to one hundred acres) and accumulated capital generally favored constitutional oligarchy, or at least government run by property holders with social privileges accorded to those of "good" birth. Despite the peculiar nature of the Spartan state, Greek oligarchs nevertheless looked to Sparta to help ensure their own rule or, if on the outs, to find support for a coup attempt. In contrast, democracies believed that all residents, rich or poor, born to two citizen parents—later, just one sufficed—should be accorded full privileges of citizenship and most office-holding. Accordingly, they often crafted a number of institutions, from forced liturgies to ostracism, to engineer an equality of result rather than of mere opportunity.

For all the coercive tactics of the Athenian empire, most of the Hellenic world's poor by the time of the Peloponnesian War saw that the Athenian fleet could be an instrument of revolutionary change. Once the war broke out, the perennial tension between rich and poor took on new urgency since there were now outside powers willing and able to bring issues to a head—and that occurred frequently, at Corcyra (427), Megara (424), Mende (423), Thessaly (424–423), and Argos (417). The promise of insurrection and outside intervention lay behind the killing all over the Greek world, from the revolt at Lesbos (427) and the entire Pylos episode (425) to the Delium campaign (424) and Brasidas' efforts in the Chalcidice (423–422). Oligarchs usually sought to parade their cause under the misleading rubric of wishing for "a temperate aristocracy" (*aristokratia sôphrôn*). Democrats countered by professing loyalty to the idea of "equality under the law" (*isonomia*). Once the struggle began, the former were rarely temperate and the latter seldom lawful.

Athens' allies had most of the advantages. The poor were always more numerous. In the early years of the war the Athenian fleet could usually arrive more quickly at a crisis spot than the Spartan hoplites, all the more so since the democratic assembly at Athens was far more audacious than its risk-averse counterparts of old men of the Spartan *gerousia*. Moreover, the class of small-property owners that made up almost half the population—sometimes known as the "middle guys" (*mesoi*), the "hoplites" (*hoplitai*), or the "farmers" (*geôrgoi*)—was not all that reactionary. The birth of the Greek city-state was a result of the rise of just this class of arms-carrying farmers, and they often had no desire to hand back government either to tyrants or to a small clique of aristocrats. They frequently stayed out of the contest. Sometimes they even joined the radical landless democrats against the oligarchs. Yeomen farmers in bronze armor were a tough force to be reckoned with when the light-armed poor targeted the aristocrats, who traditionally rode small ponies but were as lightly armed as the landless.[23]

Such strife didn't usually end in stalemate but ceased only when one faction drove out or killed the prominent representatives of the other side. In most cases local oligarchs seemed to have started the unrest in hopes of coming to power during the dissolution of the Athenian empire, especially after strategic catastrophes such as the plague, Sicily, or Aegospotami. But the democrats, with help from a swift Athenian fleet, usually finished it by murdering their richer opponents, who paid for their gambit with their lives or their property or both. In the midst of such political strife, these revolutions often became more than mere proxy wars between Athens and Sparta, unleashing a real fury that transcended the strategic calculus of the war. Wealthy citizens joined the democrats if they saw advantage in taking out powerful rivals. In turn, among the masses (*dêmos*) there were always factions who either welcomed in or resented Athenian succor or cut private deals with the wealthy. Much of the Athenian success in spreading democracy—Plato once remarked that the Athenians had run an empire for seventy years by making key friendships in each of their tributary allied communities—hinged on convincing wealthy people to support a new democratic order. The result was that in the general chaos thousands were killed for reasons that had nothing to do with Athens or Sparta and affected their ultimate struggle not at all.[24]

Mytilene, Corcyra—and Beyond

THUCYDIDES HIMSELF WAS particularly interested in four or five of the bloodiest incidents. For example, in 428 some thousand or so wealthier residents of the capital city of Mytilene, on the island of Lesbos, not far from the coast of Asia Minor, sought to change the makeup of the citizenry by recruiting sympathetic and conservative rural folk into the city. Apparently these out-of-touch idealists thought that they could unite the entire island under nationalistic, oligarchic, and anti-Athenian auspices. And they seem to have been prompted by both Spartan and Theban agents, who, in collusion with the propertied classes, wished to remove Mytilene from the Athenian empire, thereby either making it a neutral or a de facto ally of the Peloponnesians. The degree of popular support among Mytileneans for leaving the Athenian empire is uncertain. Yet as long as the rightists' plan had some chance of succeeding, perhaps even the poorer classes might well have supported the nationalist idea of ending tribute to Athens and increasing the power of Lesbos. An intrigued Sparta apparently thought such a defection might spread and could accomplish what its inferior fleet could not.

Despite the effects of the plague and the presence of thousands of Peloponnesians in Attica, Athens responded—as it always did to revolt—with a rapid naval assault on the rebellious capital. A state could join or remain in the Athenian empire, but one could rarely leave. Thus a systematic blockade of the city soon followed. In typical dilatory fashion, the Spartans neither mounted a sufficiently large second invasion of Attica to draw off Athenian support nor sent a fleet rapidly enough to relieve the city. The result was that soon the revolution collapsed.

The furious Athenians took some 1,000 ringleaders captive. They even rounded up a number of the poorer who for a time had joined the wealthy to contravene the Athenian blockade. In the end, after raucous debate at Athens— the Athenian popular leader Cleon had wished to slaughter thousands on the grounds of collective guilt—about 1,000 were executed. Much of the island was ethnically cleansed and redistributed to Athenian settlers. The number of dead Mytileneans equaled all the hoplites that Athens lost at the battle of Delium and essentially wiped out the aristocracy of Lesbos in one fell swoop. The usually cool Thucydides called the action of his countrymen "savage" (ômon).[25]

The bloodletting at Corcyra (the modern-day island of Corfu) that followed in 427 was even worse. The series of revolutions and counterrevolutions is almost impossible to reconstruct, given the myriad of plots and counterplots. Suffice it to say that the Peloponnesians thought that through subterfuge they could turn Corcyra, which had the second-largest fleet in Greece and was critical in monitoring naval traffic to Italy and Sicily, away from Athens very early on in the war. In lieu of a naval battle, they began by returning some 250 Corcyraean prisoners of war taken earlier from fighting around Epidamnus. These suspicious folk might, as sleeper cells, induce a right-wing coup, ensuring Corcyra's return to neutral status and with it taking some 100 triremes away from the Athenian fleet.

Soon the Corcyraean terrorists murdered the democratic leader Peithias and some 60 of his prominent followers, emboldened to such desperate action by the timely arrival of some Spartan agents. In response, the "people" waged a guerrilla counterwar inside the city. The poor hoped that their greater numbers and the liberation of hundreds of slaves would prevail over the capital of the oligarchs, who in response forthwith hired 800 foreign mercenaries. The hired and unfree, not hoplite militias, were the key to winning Corcyra.

Next the democrats descended from the heights of the city to rout their adversaries, who were terrified in turn by the arrival of an Athenian fleet. Slaves cut down their masters. The women of the city joined the democrats and pelted the rich with roof tiles. In desperation, the oligarchs tried to torch the city, vainly attempting to ward off the popular uprising even as their hired soldiers deserted in droves. After lengthy but confused negotiations with the democrats and their Athenian supporters, about 400 of the oligarchs agreed to leave their sanctuary and to be transferred to a small island off Corcyra for safekeeping. At that critical point—houses burnt, slaves freed, mercenaries hired, key politicians assassinated, and killing in the streets—the *stasis* began in earnest rather than abated. Corcyra was one of the largest states in the Greek world; its combined free and slave population was not that much smaller than Attica's, perhaps almost a quarter of a million residents.

In a strange sequence of events, a Peloponnesian fleet of more than 50 ships under the notorious Alcidas, the Spartan butcher of Myonnesus, now showed up, fresh from his killing spree in the eastern Aegean. He quickly engaged the Corcyraean fleet of some 60 triremes, reinforced by 12 Athenian ships. Several oligarchic sympathizers were on the Corcyraean triremes. These local rightists immediately tried to win their crews over to Alcidas; in the midst of a naval battle, there was additional fighting among the crews of the triremes as well.[26] As was so frequent during the Peloponnesian War, whether at Plataea, Mytilene, or Amphipolis, there were two wars going on at once: the ostensible conventional struggle between Athenians and Peloponnesians, and the internal, nontraditional ideological battle between the richer conservatives and the more radical democrats.

The Peloponnesians won the subsequent fight, not surprising given the open dissension among the Corcyraean crews and the paltry number of Athenian ships. Yet Alcidas chose to ignore the advice of his brilliant subordinate Brasidas to follow up with a general assault on the city. Instead, he withdrew. His retreat was perhaps none too soon: reports circulated that a huge Athenian fleet of some 60 ships was on its way to help the democrats, commanded by the nononsense Eurymedon, a tough admiral who fifteen years later was to have his rendezvous with death as part of the doomed Athenian armada in the Great Harbor of Syracuse.

Immediately the newly confident Corcyraean democrats turned on the 400 imprisoned oligarchs, began murdering them, and then went on a general killing spree against anyone suspected of oligarchic sympathies. Eurymedon looked on. He was apparently convinced that such mass killing could only benefit Athens, which welcomed the continual alliance of a strong maritime and democratic state like Corcyra. The Peloponnesian War had opened with executions in the town of Plataea, and now many Greeks were grasping that murder and insurrection were weapons as lethal as hoplite phalanxes or triremes.

Many of the trapped oligarchs in despair killed themselves. About 500 others escaped to the mainland and for a time renewed guerrilla operations against Corcyra. But months later they surrendered, having been promised legal trials at Athens. Instead, the democrats made some run the gauntlet, executed the rest, and allowed the remainder to commit suicide. How many perished in the revolution at Corcyra in this first round of killing? If one includes the 250 original firebrands sent back by the Corinthians, adds the 400 hostages taken and held offshore, and counts the 500 who fled to the mainland, then well over 1,000 men of oligarchic sympathies and an unknown number of their enemies perished. This tally does not include those who died later fighting on the acropolis, in the subsequent fires, in the battle at sea, or in the general roundup of the oligarchs. Thucydides' graphic description implies a holocaust that may well have engulfed thousands more who were targeted on charges of subverting the democracy:

> Some perished also merely as a result of private hatred. Others were murdered by those who owed them money. Every form of death followed. Whatever type of killing is apt to transpire at such times took place—and things even worse. In fact, father murdered son; suppliants were dragged from the temples and executed on the spot; some others were even walled inside the temple of Dionysus and thus perished.[27]

Thucydides went on in another famous aside to show how in the chaos that soon spread throughout Greece language lost its meaning, as the extremists took control of the public debate and libeled the men of moderation. Oaths, the ancient simplicity of fair dealing and lack of guile, and the rule of law were all thought passé and the refuge of the naive and the weak. The historian's aim in such a bleak commentary on human nature is to provide a background for the numerous other revolutions that would break out later on in the war and would thus need far less attention given the detailed blueprint of civil insurrection at Corcyra. Almost one-quarter of the third book of Thucydides' history is devoted to the bloodletting on just Mytilene and Corcyra.

The Third World

DESPITE THE LACK of any clear strategic results from fomenting revolution in the first decade of the war, both the Spartans and the Athenians still realized that at very little cost to themselves—almost no Athenians or Spartans had died on either Mytilene or Corcyra—they could instigate civil unrest that in theory could win over an entire state to their side. The Athenian general Eurymedon, remember, who commanded the second Athenian fleet of 60 ships, watched the killing proceed even though he had some 12,000 seamen and 500 hoplites under his command who could have easily restored order. And Corcyra was to experience more killing and *stasis* for years; in 410 another 1,500 people were killed, fifteen years after the initial outbreak.

Still, not a single important ally of Sparta—Megara, Corinth, Thebes—was permanently taken over by democratic insurrectionists. In contrast, given the nature of the far-flung Athenian empire, Athens would lose, at least for a time, a few of its strongest allies and subjects—Argos, Messana, Chios, and Mantinea—which either became mired in civil strife or had their governments turned over to oligarchs eager to join the state to the anti-Athenian cause. More importantly, when one examines even the fragmentary figures of the dead provided by Thucydides from these dirty wars, the number of killed quickly reaches the many thousands: 1,000 executed at Mytilene (427), another 1,000 on Corcyra (427–426), hundreds slain at Argos (417), as well as those caught in the upheavals at Megara, Boeotia, and in Thrace.[28]

In 411, for example, 200 were murdered on Samos, another 400 exiled, and the lands and houses of the rich confiscated, all to be followed months later by a second round of killing those suspected of fomenting oligarchic revolution. In 412, civil strife returned to Lesbos. A decade and a half after the horrific Athenian executions on the island, the Spartan and Athenian fleets once more vied to support their own local surrogates. And in 412 Chios also revolted and for the next two years was wracked with nonstop civil unrest. The rebellious island was convulsed by executions of its democratic supporters of Athens, then constantly plundered by Athenian forces from their permanent fort at Delphinium, all while massive slave revolts went on in the countryside and the entire population was beset by famine.[29]

Ethnic cleansing on a massive scale was commonplace to "purify" sanctuaries, eliminate suspicious populations, or steal land and redistribute it to friendly peoples. Thus, all the Aeginetans were forcibly removed by the Athenians from their island in the first year of the war. The Athenians also exiled the entire population of the island of Delos in 422. In 415 Melos was ravaged, starved, sacked, conquered, and its population rounded up, all the adult males being killed, women and children enslaved. Little is known of the ultimate fate of the Athenian colonists who were settled in their place, since at war's end Lysander brought back some Melian natives, and these must in turn have completed the cycle of violence by either exiling or killing the Athenian interlopers who had farmed their island for a decade. Such nightmares were repeated at Mytilene, Naupaktos, and Scione.[30]

Finally, there was simply war as the Greeks had always known it, the border disputes that went on throughout the great conflict, now and then heightened by the allegiance of one of the parties to the larger Spartan or Athenian cause. How many were killed, wounded, or enslaved in these mostly forgotten tangential wars on the frontiers does not interest Thucydides much. But now and again in his history he matter-of-factly hints that thousands here, too, were lost in often quite enormous expeditions.

A good example was the massive muster of King Sitacles of Thrace, the erstwhile ally of Athens, who in winter 429 invaded the Chalcidice and Macedon. He may have raised the largest land army of the entire war—some 100,000 infantry accompanied by a huge cavalry force of 50,000 mustered from thousands of miles of Thracian territory—which for a month overran much of northern Greece and threatened states as far south as the pass at Thermopylae.

By the same token, a coalition of Syracusans and Italians in 425 invaded nearby Messana and attacked Rhegium. Much of northern Sicily and southern Italy was subsequently engulfed in an ongoing border conflagration. In summer 419 the Argives mustered a formidable army and marched into Epidaurus, ravaging the countryside and causing enough havoc eventually to draw in the Spartans, prompting in part the battle of Mantinea the next year. Perhaps the largest invasion of the entire period was the Carthaginian attack on Sicily shortly after the Athenian defeat (410–404), a savage war that saw tens of thousands of dead, far more even than the losses incurred during the Athenians' massive and failed efforts. In some sense, the Punic attack on Sicily was predicated on the idea that the island was still reeling from the failed Athenian invasion and thus ripe for attack.[31]

The Indirect Approach

BOTH ATHENS AND Sparta had no thought-out, consistent policy of overthrowing neutral states, much less a general sense of how to thwart each other's war-making potential by attacking to the rear. But a few remarkable men emerged in the first decade of the war to refine these unconventional methods of winning the war. Key to the new strategy was one salient fact: Athens and Sparta alike depended on both servile labor and manpower from dependent subjects.

Athens had thousands of chattel slaves who served as arms carriers for hoplites, rowers in the imperial fleet, miners of silver, and farmhands in Attica, in addition to workers in allied states who provided the grain and timber so critical to the engine of the Athenian empire. Sparta was in an even more vulnerable position. It sat on a volcano of angry helots, perhaps 250,000 indentured servants in both Laconia and Messenia, by whose field work the Spartan state was fed, and its some 10,000 elite warriors freed from the drudgery of farm labor to drill year-round.

Quickly two capable generals, the Athenian Demosthenes and Sparta's Brasidas, grasped that in theory the enemy could be robbed of its wherewithal to make war should the thousands who worked for either empire be induced to revolt or be killed. The problems with such an audacious strategy, however, were multifold. It required expeditions deep into the heart of enemy-held territory—lengthy and often isolated deployment abroad, plus some sort of permanent base or fortification to serve as a clearinghouse for booty and a refuge for runaway slaves. Inciting the slaves also evoked internal opposition from traditional generals who had no confidence in such unconventional strategies and were not sure that servile revolts might not backfire into a Panhellenic notion of radical equality, given the presence of slaves in every military. Yet precisely out of that calculus arose the strategy of *epiteichismos*, or the fortification of forward bases, and the creation of light, mobile armies that could work well with cavalry troops and easily be transported by sea.

For a man like Brasidas or Demosthenes, the world was not, as in the past, divided between slave and master but, rather, between those either pro-Athenian or pro-Spartan. A helot was a better friend to Athens than a free

Spartan was; and the Athenian slaves that later fled to Decelea were seen as Spartan assets, not the free men inside the Long Walls some thirteen miles away. Cleon might have smelled of tanned leather, but he, not Nicias, better understood the weakness of the Spartan empire.

It was a terrifying thought for Athenians to land in a far corner of the Peloponnese and in the heart of darkness, so to speak, two hundred miles from home—and attempt to overturn the very basis of the Spartan state. The Pylos campaign of 425 in some ways is analogous to the long-range patrols of Major General Orde Wingate, whose much-celebrated Chindits in 1943–44 conducted hair-raising raids deep behind Japanese lines in Burma to disrupt supplies and communications, but in the process suffered terrible losses without systematically thwarting the main enemy forces. The Athenian maverick general Demosthenes was an archetypical Wingate himself; in 425 he landed in the southwestern Peloponnese at the small harbor of Pylos. Almost immediately he constructed a small fortification to serve as a base to harass Spartans in Messenia and offer refuge for runaway helots.

Prior to Pylos, Demosthenes had had a checkered record in such unconventional warfare—disaster in Aetolia followed by military success in Ambracia—despite mobilizing indigenous peoples to bring about an Athenian presence in strategically valuable locations. Such operations were fraught with peril. They relied on surprise and good communications in an age when intelligence was rudimentary and generals often had little reckoning of the exact time or distance involved in operations. Even after his stunning success at Pylos, Demosthenes would fail utterly to raise insurrection the next year in Boeotia in the Delium campaign—and then engineer an even more foolhardy night attack on Sicily, before being executed by the Syracusans after the general surrender of the defeated Athenians. But whether due to luck or timely support from Cleon, in 425 his audacious plan of hitting the Spartans in the rear bore stunning results that reversed the course of the war in just a few weeks.

In spring 425 an Athenian fleet of some 40 ships under the command of Eurymedon and Sophocles set out toward western Greece and beyond with two main goals. They sought to restore Athenian prestige in Sicily (eroding after setbacks following its first invasion of 427) and to cut off easy commerce around the Peloponnese, and thus provide support for the democratic factions on Corcyra. Demosthenes accompanied the fleet. He had only a vague mandate from the assembly "to employ the ships, if he wished, around the Peloponnese." That afterthought almost led to the outright defeat of Sparta, as a series of unlikely events unfolded to bring an unforeseen bonanza to the Athenians.[32]

A sudden storm prevented the generals' progress toward Corcyra. Demosthenes was able to persuade the fleet first to dock at Pylos, a small promontory on the southwest Peloponnese. There he apparently had plans to fortify a base and harass Spartan-held Messenia. As the high command waited out the storm, Demosthenes persuaded the idle crews to build a wall around the base, despite the absence of tools and iron. After the weather improved and the fleet departed, Demosthenes was at least left with an ad hoc defensible position and a small fleet of five ships. For one of the few times in Greek history, a permanent Athenian force was now acting independently on Spartan-held territory nearly two hundred miles from home. Demosthenes was apparently counting on the notorious inability of Spartans to take fortified positions, the spontaneous support from helots in the region, and the resolve of the Athenian navy to keep out Spartan ships operating in their own homeland.

"A Most Amazing Thing"

EVEN MORE MIRACULOUS events followed from such daring. The terrified Spartans cut short their invasion of Attica. They proved more afraid of a few hundred Athenians in the Peloponnese than tens of thousands of them in Attica. But instead of immediately storming Pylos, the Spartans landed 420 hoplites on the nearby island of Sphacteria. They hoped that by garrisoning the island and deploying a fleet, they could cut off the tiny base of some 600 enemy sailors at Pylos from land and sea support, and starve its hoplites and light-armed troops into submission.

The Spartans mounted one assault against Pylos, led by none other than the brilliant Brasidas. But they quickly retreated and then found themselves confronting the Athenian fleet that promptly returned from Corcyra with 50 allied ships. The attackers were now the attacked, with little chance for success even in home waters. After defeating the Spartan fleet and driving it off, the Athenians blockaded Sphacteria, prompting hysteria back at Sparta. The elites in the Spartan assembly were now terrified that some of their leading warriors were trapped on a desolate island off the coast of Messenia, surrounded by the Athenian fleet, with a magnet garrison for runaway helots nearby.

Sphacteria was hardly a Stalingrad. The 420 hoplites on the island represented only about 5 percent of the Spartan state's hoplite strength. Besides the fact that many of those on Sphacteria might have been well connected, much of the Spartan mirage rested on the appearance of invulnerability. Thus even a small loss near home—or, worse, the annihilation of a small force in the field

—could send ripples of instability throughout Messenia, where a few thousand patrolled tens of thousands.

After a brief truce, both sides hunkered down. They were still unsure whether in this new war of attrition it would be more difficult for the Athenians to maintain a large blockading fleet and expeditionary force now totaling some 14,000 men in Spartan territory or for the Spartans adequately to supply their hoplites when cut off from their mainland. But soon it was Sparta who sued for a general cessation of hostilities. Athens refused—in a tragic preview of what would happen numerous times later in the war after climactic Spartan reverses. Both sides then pressed on with the struggle that took on cosmic importance in a manner that was not true of even the thousands who had battled earlier at Potidaea, Plataea, and Mytilene.

After recriminations at Athens over the failure to accept the armistice and the ensuing stalemate so far from home, the assembly voted Cleon full powers to join Demosthenes, and thus along with the admirals in the region to take Sphacteria. As Thucydides put it, "The sensible men were delighted: for they figured that they were bound to obtain one of two good results—either they would be rid of Cleon, which they preferred, or if they were disappointed in this matter, he would beat the Spartans for them."[33]

Cleon met up with Demosthenes. In the meantime, the latter had made a probing raid on Sphacteria, accidentally set the island's dense brush afire, and thus inadvertently removed much of the cover that had helped hide the fact of the shockingly small Spartan garrison. Now, upon arrival of Cleon's auxiliaries, the two generals attacked the island. They used their missile troops to good effect in the newly cleared landscape, killed 128 Spartans, and took 292 prisoner, among them 120 of the Spartiate elite. Few Athenians perished. As Thucydides recorded, "The battle was not a hand-to-hand affair." Cleon had boasted that he would solve the problem in twenty days. And that is precisely what happened; "a most amazing thing," Thucydides concluded, more so than any event of the entire war.

Nothing in the conflict—except for the stunning Athenian naval victory at Arginusae (406) two decades later—was so inexplicable as a disreputable Athenian politician boasting about defeating the Spartans in the Peloponnese and then sailing down to accomplish just that in a matter of days. Not much later, the aristocratic Thucydides himself would fail utterly to save Amphipolis, despite knowing far more about the Thraceward region than Cleon did about the southwest Peloponnese.

Suddenly the psychology of the entire war was changed. Spartan hoplites, the mythical heroes who had perished to the man at Thermopylae, did not lose infantry battles. And on the rare occasion they did, at least they never surrendered, especially to Athenians. "Of everything that happened in the war, this came as the greatest surprise to the Greeks. For none believed that the Spartans would ever hand over their arms, either out of hunger or any other necessity, but rather would keep their weapons and fight as long as they were able until they died."[34]

The mystique of Spartan invincibility was now shattered. Worse still, the entire Spartan state was held hostage in fear that their 120 elite Spartiates, in this new style of war, might be executed at Athens should they not meet the terms of a new armistice. The next year Athens would lose 1,000 dead at the battle of Delium and have another 200 taken hostage by the Thebans. Yet the loss of so many men and the knowledge of Athenian captives in Boeotia had little effect on the democracy, which could neither be intimidated nor blackmailed. Athens had far more manpower resources than did Sparta and had never invested in the mythology of hoplite infallibility.

The Spartans now ceased their invasions of Attica out of fear of execution of the prisoners. They did not return until their hostages were recovered and the Athenians were reeling from the disaster in Sicily—for over a decade, between 425 and 413. The tiny fort at Pylos was to remain a thorn in the Spartans' side for some seventeen years, as it was not handed over during the so-called Peace of Nicias, and its Messenian garrison fell only in 409, after a period of Athenian retrenchment following the losses in Sicily and the Aegean.

The Other

THE ROLE OF slaves in the war has until recently often gone unappreciated—odd, considering that both Herodotus and Thucydides pointed out that the richest city-states in the Greek world, such as Athens, Syracuse, Chios, and Naxos, possessed thousands of chattels.[35] But in the Peloponnesian War they began to play at least several critical roles in the fighting, especially during the latter years of the conflict as the manpower reserves of both sides were increasingly depleted.

Given that there may well have been over 100,000 hoplites who took part in the war (the aggregate heavy-infantry strength of Argos, Athens, Corinth, Sparta, Syracuse, Thebes, and the major cities in Asia Minor), at least half that number of slave baggage carriers may have at one time or another gone out on infantry campaigns. Furthermore, by the end of the conflict nearly one in five rowers in the Athenian navy may well have been a slave—perhaps as many as 10,000 or so oarsmen—with even greater numbers serving in the allied and Peloponnesian navies. At the climactic last sea battle of the war at Aegospotami, Athens had over 180 ships, and this was only a decade after losing more than 40,000 imperial sailors and marines on Sicily. Only the drafting of slaves could have ensured rowers for such an enormous deployment in the city's eleventh hour. Naval outlays had nearly ruined Athens; but the expense was not so much in building triremes as in manning them. When it cost as much in one month to row as to build a warship, the recruitment of slaves became the only way of cutting costs.

Thousands of slaves changed sides during the war, markedly affecting the pulse of the war, both by serving in the military forces of their masters' adversaries and robbing their former owners of critical manpower. Thucydides, for example, thought that over 20,000 slaves fled from the Athenian countryside to the Peloponnesian base at Decelea, and implies that such a loss had a terrible effect on the economy and security of Attica in the last decade of the war. How many helots made their way over to Pylos during the seventeen-year Athenian occupation is not known, but the number of runaways must have been in the hundreds, if not thousands. One of the reasons for the rapid deterioration of the fleet and army on Sicily during the last wretched months was the flight of slaves, who were critical for carrying the arms and baggage of the infantry and sailors.[36]

Pylos was a metaphor of just how radically the war had evolved since the Spartans had crossed into Attica six years earlier. The entire infantry campaign involved only 420 Spartan and 800 Athenian hoplites. In contrast, some 8,000 rowers, 800 archers, and 2,000 light-armed Athenian troops had overwhelmed the Spartan elite on Sphacteria—the triumph of soldiers from the lower classes without body armor who were not supposed to beat hoplites, much less Spartan hoplites, even at numerical advantages of 20 to 1. Thucydides remarked that their agility and ability to bombard the clumsy hoplite with missiles made them "most difficult to fight."

Athenian generalship was equally unconventional. Cleon was a radical demagogue, hated by Thucydides (who may well have been exiled through Cleon's machinations) and slurred by Aristophanes as a rabble-rousing tanner. Yet he had accomplished what neither the majestic Pericles nor the aristocratic Nicias could even have envisioned. Everything about the successful campaign was untraditional. Many of Demosthenes' troops were Messenian exiles, that is, former helots who had fled their Spartan overlords. Moreover, the strategy had nothing to do with forcing the Spartan fleet to meet the more formidable

Athenian armada (though they did and lost), much less with staging a pitched battle against Spartan infantry.

Instead, the vision of Demosthenes was predicated on the idea of rebellious serfs: how best to encourage helot desertion and thereby rob the Spartan state of its critical field hands. True, the idea that all 250,000 helots might flee to such a small sanctuary such as Pylos was a fantasy; but Demosthenes apparently thought the mere chance of insurrection would be enough to prompt some wild Spartan response. Pylos helped to expose the absurdity of the Spartan state: it was paranoid about the loss of any of its scarce Spartiates and yet accepted that these very same troops were of little value in keeping sailors, light-armed troops, archers, and helots from doing what they wished in their own backyard.

Right after Pylos and Sphacteria, the Athenians occupied Methana, on the coast of the Argolid, hoping that such a fortified base in the Peloponnese would help raise additional insurrection among allies throughout the Argive peninsula. The next season, Athenian maritime troops grabbed Cythera, in the sea off Sparta. This was a key base for merchant ships heading to northern Africa, and an ideal fort from which to mount continual seaborne raids on the southern Peloponnese. With Athenians ensconced in the Peloponnese by land at Pylos and at sea on Cythera, Thucydides concluded that a stunning change suddenly came over the Spartans, one achieved at very little cost in lives to the Athenians. They had more or less ignored the thousands of crack hoplites stationed at Sparta and instead sought to tear the very political and economic fabric of the Spartan state:

> At the same time the reversals of fortune that had come in such number and in such a short time caused an enormous shock, and the Spartans became afraid lest once more another setback befall them of the type that had transpired on the island. Thus, for this reason they were far less confident in battle, and figured that whatever move they would make would end in failure, inasmuch as they lost all their confidence after having no experience in the past with real adversity.[37]

The Athenians had not beaten Sparta—to do that would require an invasion of the Laconian heartland—but they seemed to have achieved the stalemate that Pericles once envisioned. The Pylos syndrome proved contagious. Within months of its success the tactic of forward basing was breaking out almost everywhere. By 424 almost the entire Peloponnese seemed to be ringed by permanent Athenian forts—at Aegina, Cephallenia, Cythera, Methana, Nisaea,

Naupaktos, Pylos, and Zakynthos—designed to cut off trade to Sparta from Sicily, Italy, Egypt, and Libya, to encourage helot rebellion, and to provoke dissension among the Peloponnesian alliance.

Still, the problem in this conceptually brilliant plan of encirclement that arose after Pylos was threefold. The maintenance of these bases with enough permanent troops to cause harm to the economy of the Spartan state was beyond the resources of Athens. The strategy presumed that the Spartans themselves would not copycat such success and send long-range patrols deep into Athenian territory. And there was still no plan to deal with the 10,000 Spartan hoplites who, in theory, could march anywhere they pleased to put down rebellious states.

After Pylos

IF CLEON AND Demosthenes had turned out to be not quite the regular sort of Athenian generals, then neither was Brasidas. He had started out as a traditional Spartan ephor, or government overseer, and ended up as something altogether different. But even in the first few years of the war Brasidas had proved no mere functionary. In 430, for example, he had rushed to save the Messenian town of Methone from Athenian seaborne raiders. For much of the early 420s he patrolled the Corinthian Gulf and tried to intervene on behalf of the oligarchs in the bloody killing on Corcyra. Brasidas led a spirited attack against the Athenian fort at Pylos in 425, and was almost killed for his efforts. The next year this Spartan fireman rushed to Megara to head off a democratic revolution.

Pylos obviously made a terrible impression on him. Consequently, in the year after the capture of the Spartans at Sphacteria, Brasidas sought to turn the tables on the Athenians, striking deep at their rear, both to disrupt their commercial trade in the Thraceward region of northern Greece and to put such fear in the heart of the Athenian empire that it would think twice about persisting in attacks deep into the Peloponnese. As Thucydides drily put it, "The Lacedaemonians thought that the best way to hurt the Athenians in return would be to send out an army against their allies."[38]

Unlike traditional Spartan generals, Brasidas enrolled a new army of Peloponnesian allies, mercenary soldiers, and, most interestingly, 700 helots—the "Brasideans," a force not unlike many of the enslaved peoples of the Third Reich, who on occasion were conscripted into the Wehrmacht as if it were the better of two bad alternatives. Spartan officials were only too glad to see potentially rebellious helots (and perhaps Brasidas too) sent far from their homes as Spartan shock troops. And thus Brasidas headed hundreds of miles north-ward to free some of the most important states of the Athenian empire.

Once there, in less than two years he "liberated" the key Athenian subject city of Amphipolis—Thucydides himself was exiled by a furious assembly at home for his failure to keep Brasidas from the town—and began raising general insurrection in neighboring communities. These were no marginal cities. Instead, Brasidas' targets were renowned for their rich farmlands, supplies of timber critical for Athenian naval construction, and numerous gold and silver mines—an area where the aristocratic Thucydides had substantial holdings and in vain, with an Athenian fleet, was trying to thwart the Spartan intrusion.

The largest city, Amphipolis, situated on the Strymon River, might offer a good base to raid routes to the Hellespont by land and sea. With a quasi-private army, Brasidas more or less ignored the brief armistice of 423 and kept at his grand plan of raising havoc throughout the entire northern theater of the Athenian empire, before dying—along with his Athenian adversary Cleon—in a desperate clash during the defense of Amphipolis. At the battle some 600 Athenians perished to the Spartans' 7 fatalities; but the death of Brasidas meant that Sparta lost its only gifted leader of the Archidamian War and thus the confidence to continue the conflict.

Brasidas' battles were like none Spartans had ever waged—offering the carrot of autonomy and liberation to key subject cities of the Athenian empire along with the stick of brilliantly unconventional war that ignored the old Hellenic distinction between civilian and combatant. At the grape-growing port city of Acanthus he threatened to destroy the town's vintage, ripe for harvest outside the walls—the sole cash crop of the entire coastal community. Next he set up camp outside nearby Amphipolis and began to plunder the rich farms of the surrounding countryside, while his agents inside the city laid the groundwork for the citizenry to go over to the Spartan cause. Arriving at Torone, he sent assassins into the city by night to open the gates and allow his own light troops to storm the city. After taking Scione, he refused to give it up, even though the newly concluded armistice agreement of 423 had made it clear that the city was to be returned to the Athenians.[39]

When Brasidas was finally killed in the defense of Amphipolis, the locals gave him a hero's funeral, erected a monument to him as the "liberator of Hellas," and instituted yearly games and sacrifices in his honor. Brasidas' preference for irregulars and soldiers of questionable background, coupled with his romantic lectures about the need for freedom from Athenian imperialism, made him a near saint among Third World Greeks—a most un-Spartan Spartan.

Indeed, his dash and magnetism must have been formidable if he could make thousands forget that he was an agent for the most repressive state in the Greek world, which had itself enslaved 250,000 Messenians. In that eerie sense, the 700 Brasideans did more harm to the cause of promoting helot unrest than all the good done by the liberators at Pylos. What is striking about the near-simultaneous careers of Demosthenes and Brasidas is that while the Athenians in the south tried to promote instability by offering freedom to Sparta's underclass, in the north the Spartan used such serfs to advance liberty and autonomy among the subject states of Athens—suggesting that realpolitik rather than consistent idealism was the engine that drove both men and the policies they advanced.

Of all the characters in Thucydides' history Brasidas is the most intriguing, an ancient romantic version of Fidel Castro or Che Guevara who combined ostensible idealism and brutal guerrilla warfare in such a dazzling fashion that most formerly enslaved soldiers forgot the nature of the harsh master they worked for. In the last analysis, Brasidas' efforts counterbalanced Pylos and achieved a rough stalemate, as he proved that the Athenians had just as much to lose to their own rear as did the Spartans. His ragtag mercenaries and few hundred freed helots did more damage to Athens than had King Archidamus' enormous grand army of 60,000, which eight years earlier had trudged into Attica, convinced by its sheer size that it might bring the empire to its knees.

In peace treaties that followed throughout the war, the terms sometimes reflected the new realities. No longer was an armistice a matter of seamen and hoplites ceasing hostilities. There was rarely a call to forgo sieges or a delineation of territory to be returned and alliances to be established. Rather, all sorts of codicils called for specific conduct regarding plagues, slave revolts, hostage taking, plundering, and forward field fortifications, as both sides took formal account of the new, multifaceted warfare.[40]

Where was Alcibiades amid the raiding and terror of the Peloponnesian War? In fact, no mode of war better fit his skills as both an intriguer and a practitioner of diplomatic subversion. Wherever the arts of betrayal, plotting, and execution were needed, Alcibiades could be found. Apart from his presence at the major hoplite battles, naval engagements, and sieges of the war, a simple recitation of his career following the agricultural conflict in Attica and the plague at Athens reveals that throughout his late twenties and early thirties Alcibiades was knee-deep in the new terror. Indeed, he was now in his proper element.

Aside from the fact that he intrigued to establish democratic governments at Argos and Patras, bolted from Sicily, persuaded the Spartans to attack his kinsmen in both Sicily and Attica, triangulated with the Persians, and then rejoined the Athenians after toying with revolutionaries at Samos, Alcibiades was more directly involved with a number of paramilitary operations. He may well have been one of the architects of sending the Athenian fleet to besiege Melos, and then a strong advocate in the assembly of the subsequent execution and enslavement of all the island's inhabitants.

In the same year, 416, Alcibiades arrived at Argos and kidnapped 300 rightists as insurance against an oligarchic coup that might bring in the Spartans. They were all later brought to Athens and executed. He was also probably involved in the assassination of the popular Athenian leader Androcles and some other radical democrats, an act instrumental in facilitating his own return to the Athenian side in 411. A little later Alcibiades was equally responsible for the murder of the rightist Phrynichus. Again, the employment of terror, rather than any sign of ideological consistency, was his trademark.

After his second exile from Athens, at the end of the war he used his skills gained from raiding the coast of Asia Minor to craft a life as a privateer in Thrace with his own hired army. Alcibiades, like few others in the Peloponnesian War, grasped that the conflict was no conventional fight but, rather, a new sort of civil war in which there was no divide between war and politics, external policy and internal intrigue, killing on the battlefield and murder off it.[41]

It is hard to calibrate exactly what effect the unconventional fighting had on the ultimate outcome of the war. Certainly the Pylos campaign and the subsequent Spartan operations in Amphipolis resulted in the eventual temporary peace of 421, in a manner none of the traditional fighting at sea or on land had accomplished for either side. The fort at Decelea irrevocably harmed Athens. The city itself soon suffered irreparable psychological damage as well from a rightist revolution in 411. At the end of the war the city was taken over by oligarchs who concluded the peace with Lysander. Ultimately, however, terror, revolution, and murder were no substitute for the climactic battles of thousands that were to decide entire theaters. Had the Spartans lost the battle of Mantinea, had the Thebans been defeated at Delium, or had the Athenians won Aegospotami—a mere three critical days among some twenty-seven years of conflict—the outcome of the war would have been forever changed, in ways impossible to envision being accomplished by all the daring and machinations of a Brasidas, Demosthenes, Cleon, or Alcibiades. Thus, Athens, of all city-states, finally resolved to organize allied armies to end its wars with Boeotia and Sparta through single days of battle—efforts that were as heroic as they were doomed.

CHAPTER 5

ARMOR

Hoplite Pitched Battles (424–418)

Why No Battle?

AFTER SEVEN YEARS of war, there was still a virtual stalemate in the fighting. Even by 425 no Spartan fleet had emerged to challenge Athenian naval supremacy. The Corinthians had left the seas except for the nearby Gulf. Spartan ships, such as Alcidas' armada, which had headed for Lesbos in 427, were capable only of short voyages akin to the German battleship *Bismarck's* brief breakouts into the North Atlantic during 1941. These short-lived Peloponnesian raids were intended to harass merchants and tributary subjects before Athenian superior triremes could find and hunt them down. In turn, Athens had no desire or ability to force a showdown with the Spartan phalanx. Invasions of the Athenian homeland had ceased in 425, after Spartan prisoners had been captured at Pylos and brought back to Athens with the announcement that they would be killed the moment another Peloponnesian army entered Attica.

Widespread helot revolt had not followed the Athenians' establishment of a series of bases in and around the Peloponnese. Seaborne raids of the Peloponnese had bothered the Spartans but had caused neither massive defection from its alliance nor famine or panic. Perhaps a quarter to a third of the Athenian population alive at the start of the war was dead seven years later, but mostly because of the ravages of the plague rather than Spartan spears. While small bands of killers and innovative commanders murdered and plundered, so far the Athenian empire remained intact. Mytilene was subdued. Corcyra did not become an oligarchic ally of Sparta. Persia was still hesitant to begin subsidizing the construction of a Spartan fleet that might wrest away the eastern Aegean.

A few old-style generals on each side began to see that major changes in the strategic calculus of the war might still come about only through some large-scale, dramatic victory. In Athenian eyes, that meant either knocking Boeotia out of the war or marching into the Peloponnese and crafting a hoplite alliance to defeat Sparta once and for all, on its home turf. If only Athens and Sparta had agreed to face-off in full armor on a summer afternoon—what Herodotus once labeled "a silly and most absurd" way of fighting "on the best and most level ground"—then at least Sparta could have won the war in a few minutes and saved Greece twenty-seven years of misery. Yet for that very reason Pericles in 431 had thought it "a terrible thing" for Athenians all by themselves to join battle with 60,000 Peloponnesian and Boeotian hoplites, to gamble the survival of the city itself on "a pitched battle."[1]

In both 410 and 406, it looked for a moment as though a much smaller Spartan contingent of occupation in Attica might precipitate an old-style battle by marching out from its fortress nearby at Decelea to the very walls of Athens. Yet in the first instance, the Spartan king Agis' smaller force backed away at the last minute. On the second occasion, in 406, his more formidable army of 14,000 hoplites, as many light-armed troops, and 1,200 horsemen moved on the city again. But his nearly 30,000-man force was not willing to meet the Athenian phalanx until the latter ventured beyond the protection of the archers, slingers, and javelin throwers on the walls of Athens. Instead, a three-decade-long war raged between Athens and Sparta in which the chief Hellenic method of re-solving conflict—hoplite pitched battles—never occurred once between the two chief belligerents! Still, there were too many hoplites in too many places elsewhere in the Greek world for some old-style confrontation now and then not to transpire in the span of so many years. Thus, near the small seaside sanc-tuary of Delium, on the border between Athens and Boeotia, one of the tradi-tional battles at last broke out seven years into the war in November 424.[2]

It is hard to walk freely now over the seaside hills overlooking the modern resort town of Dilesi. Vacation homes, wire fences, and access roads are spring-ing up on what just thirty years ago were mostly open grain fields and range-land. Few of the contemporary upscale Athenians who spend their weekends here realize that thousands once battled near their backyards. This was a fight that saw middle-aged Socrates in defeat grimly fighting off pursuers, the corpse of Pericles' nephew moldering in the dirt for over two weeks, brave Alcibiades winning the award for valor as he galloped through these gentle rises, and

Plato's cowardly father-in-law running for his life. Delium was but a two-day hike from the Athenian Acropolis.

The Hope of Delium

WHY DID ATHENS, which purportedly knew it was not wise to fight in such pitched battles with better hoplites, risk a campaign that might involve facing the Boeotians? Again, it was the age-old desire to be free of a two-front war, the specter that later haunted Rome when it faced the Carthaginians and Philip V of Macedon, the traditional German dilemma of being wedged between Russia and France, and the predicament America found itself in during World War II, with both Pacific and European theaters. In his hasty final few words, the surprised Athenian general Hippocrates had stirred his men with the promise that a victory would mean the Spartans could no longer cross Attica at will into the sanctuary of Boeotia, as the northern front would be forever closed. In contrast, he assumed that a defeat would doom Athens to a perpetual two-front war of attrition that it could not win.

So a single bold win at Delium, as was the case after the Athenian triumph at the battle of Oinophyta in 457, might lead to the democratization of Boeotia and the cessation of its open support for Sparta and its near-constant raiding across the border. Brasidas and the Spartans who were operating to the north would be cut off, with hostile territory barring their return to the Peloponnese. In short, the Athenians thought that they might have a chance of knocking out Boeotia in a single blow in a manner they believed impossible with Sparta, whose territory was too distant and invincible by land and its army far too formidable. On the other side, the older Boeotians, like the tough Theban general Pagondas himself, remembered that for a decade before the war (457–447) Athens had turned Boeotia into a friendly democratic federation and once more had similar dangerous ideas. At any rate Alcibiades, whose father, Cleinias, had died during the Athenian defeat at Boeotian Coronea (447), realized that regime change in Boeotia was not an impossible proposition.

The Athenians, encouraged by the recent amazing success at Pylos and Sphacteria, had sought to subvert the government of Boeotia in ways that might have avoided a single pitched battle like Delium. The Athenian general Demosthenes had sailed from home three months earlier, intending to raise democratic insurrection through the southern Boeotian countryside by an unexpected amphibious landing. Then, aided by partisans, he was to march east toward Delium at about the same time that Hippocrates and his Athenian hoplites marched northward to the border. The outnumbered Boeotian army would thus scatter beneath the hammer and anvil. Then the surrounding countryside would rise up in open revolt, in an operation that would take the logic of the Pylos campaign to an even more audacious level. After all, two years earlier, in the summer of 426 Nicias had landed 2,000 Athenian hoplites at the Oropus, met up with an even larger army marching from Athens under the commanders Hipponicus and Eurymedon, and together they had won a skirmish against the Tanagrans and a few Thebans in a small prequel to Delium. Apparently, their subsequent braggadocio had convinced the Athenian board of generals that another, but much larger, combined land-and-sea armada could repeat the petite victory in Boeotia on a massive scale.[3]

Or so it was thought. But triumph was possible only if the superior infantry forces of the Boeotians would face two simultaneously advancing Athenian armies and an aroused countryside eager for more egalitarian government. Unfortunately, Demosthenes' naval assault to the west at the Boeotian town of Siphae was timed too early. Once his insurrectionary plans were betrayed by local oligarchs to the Boeotian authorities, he was of little value in drawing off opposition from the Athenian land troops marching up from the south. Diodorus says that Demosthenes, hardly eager to face an aroused assembly back home, then sailed away "without accomplishing anything."[4]

But it was even worse than that. Demosthenes' failure had ensured that a ragtag Athenian army of reservists by themselves would meet in open battle what may have been the finest infantry force in Greece. After the battle of Plataea (479), all Greeks talked of the "Dorian spear" of the Spartans. But throughout the latter fifth and fourth centuries, it was the Theban farmers who proved "mightier in war"—fighting a series of ferocious battles at Delium, Nemea, Coronea, Haliartus, Tegyra, Leuctra, and Mantinea, where they either crushed their opponents or died trying. In 424, Thebes was relatively unscathed. Its meager contribution heretofore in the war was parasitic and opportunistic: attacking a neutral Plataea, raiding across the Attic border, and joining in the invasion of Attica when the Peloponnesians first arrived in the thousands. In contrast, in the first seven years of the war an exhausted Athens had lost thousands to the plague, emptied its treasury in the nearly constant deployment of over 200 ships, and had its sacred soil violated on five occasions.

Throughout the later fifth century there had rarely been pitched hoplite battles, mostly because of two rarely remarked on reasons: first, the Spartan reputation won fifty years earlier at Plataea against the Persians suggested that it was national suicide to engage such an army; second, the only other formidable land power, the Boeotians, were similarly oligarchic and friendly to Sparta. But at the close of the Peloponnesian War, when the Spartan empire quickly imploded and Boeotia turned more liberal and finally democratic, their shared hoplite monopoly ceased. Old ethnic and new political differences arose; and they subsequently fought each other with a vengeance on at least a half dozen occasions. Hoplite battle, then, returned to its preclassical frequency, albeit settling theater disputes rather than local wars over borders. A mere three years later (421) the Athenians accepted a peace offering from Sparta, on the ostensible grounds that they had been beaten at two battles, at Delium and Amphipolis, and had thus lost "the confidence in their strength."[5]

The Promised Showdown

THE LONG-HOPED-FOR battle was at last fought in late 424. The Athenian phalanx crossed its border to end the northern front against the Boeotian confederation on a late November afternoon, precisely on the assurance that the Spartans were far away and the majority of poorer Boeotians themselves might welcome rather than oppose the invaders on the promise of democratic liberation from landed oligarchy.*

Between 40,000 and 50,000 warriors met at Delium. Besides the 7,000 hoplites in each army, thousands more without armor were present on the Athenian side, outnumbering even the 10,000 or more light-armed troops of the Boeotians. The formal engagement broke out when thousands of demoralized Athenians were caught unawares walking back home after the failed invasion of the general Hippocrates. Most of their Boeotian pursuers were also squabbling among themselves, with no real desire to risk pitched battle with an enemy already in retreat. But then a Boeotian veteran general in his sixties, Pagondas, persuaded his reluctant generals to press home the attack and strike first. They must attack, the old man shouted to his Boeotians, even should the retreating enemy escape into Attica.

Pagondas' pursuing army pulled up out of sight on a knoll across from the Athenians' right on the poorly demarcated Athenian-Boeotian border. Suddenly, without much warning, his spirited hoplites charged downhill. The

---

* "Boeotians" is used to denote the residents of Boeotia, the large region to the north of Attica, which was united under an oligarchic federation led by its largest city, Thebes. Both in ancient and modern usage, "Boeotians" is sometimes used interchangeably with "Thebans," although, strictly speaking, not all Boeotians were citizens of Thebes.

Athenian general Hippocrates was haranguing his own troops and was caught in mid-sentence. The lateness of the hour, the rolling terrain, the autumn dust, and the surprise approach of the Boeotians made Delium a different kind of hoplite battle, in which from the very beginning nothing was quite what it first seemed.

Pagondas had arranged the phalanx by confederate villages, his Thebans on the honored right wing of the allied Boeotian line. The hilly terrain probably explains why until the last minute the Athenians had little idea that the enemy was so near, much less had occupied a superior position. Caught unawares, the Athenians had few choices. This time they were not burning up the fields of nearby Megara without enemies but were pitted against the fiercest hoplites in Greece, who sixty years later would tear apart the Spartan phalanx not far away at the battle of Leuctra (371). The alternatives for the surprised Athenians were to trot uphill into the Theban mass, to retreat, or to stay put and be bowled over. Two large gullies on each side of the battlefield cut off any real chance of an outflanking movement. In fact, the two armies scarcely fit into the plain of little more than eight hundred yards or so. The ravines on each side of the killing ground may explain why Pagondas could pull some of his men off the line and safely stack them twenty-five shields deep on the right flank, three times the normal eight-man depth of a phalanx.

For better or worse, Hippocrates and his elite Athenian right chose to charge bravely ahead uphill. The Athenians may have thought that the hills and ravines offered some advantages in limiting the use of the enemy's horsemen. They probably could not see just how deep the Theban right wing had stacked and so had no idea of the peril to come on their left from the greater enemy weight. The battle that decided the entire northern front of the conflict appears to have lasted not more than a few minutes—giving some credence to the two-century-old agrarian idea that brief hoplite collisions could settle entire theater wars. At first, despite the uphill run, the Athenian right wing broke through Pagondas' weak confederates. From the very beginning it was a classic instance of each army seeking to win the battle on its strong right wing before its own weak left lost it.[6]

The allied villagers of Thespiae took the brunt of the Athenian right's uphill assault. Thucydides called the gruesome fighting there "hand-to-hand," which probably assumes spear jousting, pushing, swordplay, and finally brawling with shields, broken spear shafts, and even bare hands. Soon all 500 Thespians were at the point of obliteration. The allied contingents of another 2,000 hoplites on their immediate right had wisely, but less courageously, fled from the charging Athenians.

The collapse of most of the Boeotian left wing doomed the Thespians. They now would be cut off, detached from the main phalanx, encircled, and then butchered. The degree to which they slowed the Athenian juggernaut was their chief legacy of sacrifice, allowing their right wing under Pagondas time to finish off its own opponents without worry of being swarmed from the rear. Near the trapped Thespians, the other Boeotian allies of the left and center did not all escape. Some in vain tried to flee outright. Others fought. The more resolute hung on until their own right, across the way, scattered the Athenians and came up in support. Nearly all the 500 Boeotian dead infantrymen of the battle were either the surrounded Thespians or their disoriented and stampeding neighbors. The historian Diodorus says at this point the Athenian right wing "slew great numbers" of the enemy. Precisely what "great" means is unclear. But the cursory remark suggests that the fighting was ferocious if hundreds of soldiers protected by massive shields, breastplates, helmets, and greaves were nevertheless stabbed and hacked apart.

Killing a man in full bronze armor—breastplate, helmet, and greaves—was not an easy task, especially when all hoplites' first concerns were to keep close to one another and to have their wooden shields locked in a near wall of defense. The playwright Sophocles once characterized Greek hoplite battle as the "storm of the spear." That image suggests that heavily clad lumbering hoplites were jabbed repeatedly from all directions by a whirlwind of spear tips and hacked by swords in the limbs, groin, and neck—a very different type of warfare than that fought by unarmored men who might kill one another with a blow or two. In any case, compared to the lethality of the mace or the Roman sword, the spear did not easily penetrate armor, and was usually effective in killing a hoplite outright only when wielded with a downward stroke against the neck or groin, relatively small targets.

Too busy hammering the enemy Thespians to keep their bearings, the victorious Athenians on the right, at the cutting edge of the phalanx, soon began to circle completely around in the wrong direction. Then the confused Athenians stumbled head-on against their *own* troops shuffling up from the rear. There the general Hippocrates, a nephew of the dead Pericles, probably along with the philosopher Socrates, Alcibiades, and many of the elite of Athenian society, including Plato's own stepfather, Pyrilampes, and Laches of a later eponymous Platonic dialogue, suddenly found themselves spearing other Athenians. Before these crazed hoplites could be pulled apart, dozens must have been impaled by their own brothers, fathers, or friends.

Thucydides drily notes of this chaos, "Some of the Athenians becoming confused because of the encirclement mistook and killed one another."[7] How such a self-inflicted calamity was possible in hand-to-hand fighting is difficult to imagine. Yet there are other instances in Greek literature of hoplites who became disoriented and attacked the wrong soldiers. Friendly-fire casualties in war are not just a phenomenon of the modern age of high-tech weapons and bombing from great altitudes but a result of the fear, panic, and confusion endemic to the fog of war of all ages. In the ancient world even sailors often grew confused and killed friends in ships of the same fleet. Triremes, like hoplite arms, were weapons uniformly adopted by friends and enemies alike, partly a reflection of a Panhellenic acceptance of the protocols of battle, partly testament to the excellent form and function of such appurtenances themselves.

Next, something even more inexplicable transpired at Delium: at the climax of the battle, this victorious Athenian right wing abruptly disintegrated when it wrongly identified a few squadrons of Boeotian horsemen approaching over the hill as a fresh army. Men in bronze with spears and shields, arrayed in column, were usually able to withstand such wealthy aristocrats perched on stirrupless small horses. But to the victorious and exhausted Athenians under Hippocrates, apparently the idea that cavalry would play a decisive role in phalanx battle was entirely unexpected. Even more unanticipated was the notion that such fresh troops on the horizon were still uncommitted and appeared seemingly out of nowhere. At last elated with the sense that the battle on their wing was won, the mercurial Athenians suddenly imagined that an entirely new army was upon them, replete with horsemen, and thus despaired. Again, rumor and panic were the prime forces in battle when thousands yelled, charged, and collided without clear sight and with impaired hearing. "Nobody," Thucydides once wrote of battle, "knows much of anything that goes on except right around himself."[8]

What was happening far to the right with Pagondas and his selected phalanx of Thebans? "Gradually at first," Thucydides says, they "pushed" the Athenian left downhill, and cleared the battlefield through the advantage of favorable terrain and greater depth. Diodorus adds that their success was due to the superior physical strength of individual Theban hoplites—as if the agrarian lifestyle across the border had created stronger men than most found at more sophisticated Athens. But the momentum was just as likely due to numbers rather than bulging muscles—the force of 25 shields concentrated against 8, and the fact that the most experienced Boeotians were pitted against the less reliable of the Athenians. Greater mass (what the Greek historians called *baros* or *plêthos*) frequently decided battles in any case. The poor Athenian left disintegrated. Soon the entire army was "in panic"—the once victorious and savage right wing now running away from a mythical new army, the left wearied, beaten down, and fragmented by the pressure of the accumulated shields of Pagondas' mass bearing down from higher ground.

Warring Against the Dead

ALL ATHENIANS NOW fled to nearby Mount Parnes, the fortified sanctuary at Delium proper and the safety of Athenian ships, or for the woods in the Oropus along the border in Attica—the ancient equivalent of the disastrous Battle of First Bull Run, where thousands of the panicky defeated headed for the refuge of their own capital. In moments the ordered columns of a neat phalanx were shredded. Shields, helmets, greaves, and breastplates littered the hills; each man calibrated his survival on how quickly he could toss away his heavy equipment and outrun the victors. This was how the Peloponnesian War was supposed to be fought, brutally, quickly, and decisively. But for those unfortunate enough to be caught up in the whirl of spears, nothing quite matched the bloodletting of thousands crammed into a few thousand square yards of a killing field.

Some opportunistic Locrian horsemen, the perennial mounted scavengers of the classical battlefield, arrived for the spoils and joined the Boeotian predators in the open-ended killing spree that went on until darkness. Delium was the first battle in or on the border of Attica since Marathon (490), and it would prove as embarrassing as that earlier victory, paraded as the exemplar of native Attic courage and skill, had been glorious. The retreat was seared into the popular collective memory, the stuff of both Athenian contemporary history and later Platonic dialogues. The question "What did you do at Delium?" seems to have haunted men like the runaways Cleonymus, Laches, and Pyrilampes, and emboldened stalwarts such as Alcibiades and Socrates.

Soon the Boeotians learned that at least a few of the terrified Athenian fugitives had retreated to their seashore garrison at Delium. These holdouts not only continued in defeat to occupy Theban ground but were also ensconced on a Boeotian precinct sacred to Apollo. Why would the Athenians not give up and retreat in shame as the "rules" of hoplite battle usually dictated to the defeated? No doubt the five Peloponnesian invasions of Attica, the 80,000 Athenians lost to the plague, the nearly constant deployment of 60,000 imperial oarsmen and endemic terrorism across Greece had long ago destroyed any notion that the Peloponnesian War would follow the niceties of agrarian warfare, where one side admitted defeat when its manhood was routed in open and decisive fashion.

The Boeotians themselves decided to hold the decomposing Athenian dead "hostage" until the sanctuary at Delium was clear of its garrison. The Athenian sacrilege of occupying a holy place in Boeotia was now to be answered with the greater crime of holding on to the enemy dead, and then letting them rot. After seventeen days in the open autumn air, most of the corpses were probably a putrid mess. The outrage for a people just recovering from the horrors of unburied corpses from the great pestilence probably prompted the playwright Euripides to produce his tragedy *Suppliant Women* the next year. He revived the myth of the "Seven Against Thebes," who in legendary times had attacked Thebes, been killed, and then been left to decay. The play was to convey to an audience of veterans recent moral outrage in denying soldiers a proper burial. The barbarity of the Thebans, so the Athenians in the theater were reminded, remained constant over the centuries. Euripides soon found a new direction in his wartime tragedies—perhaps starting with the horrific bloodletting in his *Medea* (431)—that for nearly three decades would serve as moral commentary on the ongoing and increasingly barbaric war.

After almost three weeks, the Boeotians brought in more reinforcements from their allies and formally besieged the trapped Athenian refugees in Delium. They even crafted an enormous flamethrower of sorts, a hollowed-out beam through which they blasted a pressurized concoction of sulfur, coal, and pitch to send a jellied flame into the Athenian breastworks. Quickly the garrison went up in flames, men and all. The few terrified troops who survived the flames and the noxious fumes boarded ships to evacuate the sanctuary, leaving behind the cinders of 200 of their trapped fellow Athenians.

The sordid finale to the battle was at last over. Again, there is no exact knowledge of how many corpses were finally given back to the Athenians to be burned, the bones collected and buried. The total may well have been over 2,000 if both hoplites and the irregulars are included. The Athenian losses at Delium constituted only a fraction of the fatalities that would follow nine years later, during the debacle on Sicily, and were probably no more than had been lost in any two-week period of the great plague. Yet the strategic consequences were just as calamitous: Boeotia, on the northern border of Attica, would remain an oligarchic and especially powerful ally of Sparta. Its continued hostility meant that Athens would be stuck with a two-front war for the duration of the conflict. Rumors of the entire debacle—unlike the news from Sicily, which took several days to arrive at the Piraeus—spread through the Athenian agora within a few hours, reminding the citizenry that a victorious enemy was a few hours' march away.

Dreadnoughts of the Battlefield

CERTAIN TYPES OF fighting are more memorable than others. The world of the samurai, the chivalry of the ponderous medieval knight, and the colors and pageantry of Napoleonic columns have captured popular imagination in a manner not explicable just by the record of battle or the degree of lethality of the warriors. Hoplite collisions were equally unforgettable. Maybe it was the frightening look of the shiny bronze armor or the formality and grandness of the massed columns. Certainly the shock and sounds of the colliding armies made a lasting impression. Surely such a formulaic way of fighting allowed thousands of combatants to assemble in a relatively small space—in a way impossible during raiding, ravaging, or amphibious assaults. Various phrases in the Greek language—"battles in the plain," "battles by agreement," "just and open battles," and "drawn up"—were used to evoke the formality and morality of traditional hoplite forces squaring off.

From the anachronistic fighting of even the single collision at Delium comes a glimpse into the very cultural foundations of the Greek city-state—the protocols of an earlier age, in which small rural settlements agreed to solve their differences over contested border ground through formal pitched battles of armored militiamen. Although very little of the military history of the *poleis* before classical times is recorded, the Greeks at least preserved a tradition that hoplite warfare between 700 and 500 had been the most common and preferred way of fighting. War had once been heroic, local, and waged over disputed boundaries by like agrarian communities. In Plato's *Republic*, his ideal states would naturally squabble over borderlands, assuming that proud and overbearing people would always covet ("give themselves over to the endless acquisition of material things") the resources of another nearby.[9]

In the later romantic legends of hoplite supremacy, early wars supposedly had been decided honestly by picked contingents who fought at prearranged times and places to avoid larger bloodshed. Formal rules often outlawed the use of missile weapons. In the popular myth, armies were to seek out prearranged flat plains, where each side in similar heavy armor could more easily charge into the other. Battle then was not merely utilitarian but also moral: it was not just against whom or why one fought that mattered, but apparently *how* as well.

For centuries after the Peloponnesian War, later Greeks looked back nostalgically at just those lost hoplite moments, even if in reality they had been rather rare. Reactionaries lamented that militaries of the later fifth through third centuries had no longer sought to "crush the spirit" of an enemy by "fighting in open battle"—and that this avoidance of simple collisions resulted in disasters like the twenty-seven-year war of Sparta against Athens (431–404), the later Theban-Spartan near-constant fighting (378–362), and the rise of Philip of Macedon (358–338).[10]

Thucydides himself, anywhere in his history that he records the death of hoplite soldiers caused by light-armed troops, guerrillas, or archers, makes it a point to lament the loss in poignant terms. Yet this mythical hold of the hoplite on the popular Greek imagination seems to have made no rational sense. For example, throughout the Peloponnesian War, when there were very few occasions at all for phalanx battle, authors continued to talk of war only in terms of heavily armed soldiers. Thus the pacifist characters in Aristophanes' comedies refer to getting rid of breastplates and spears, even as the tragedians describe battle courage as the domain of the hoplite, the favorite martial figure as well of contemporary vase painters and pedimental sculpture on temples. Yet rarely after the classical age would civic governments embrace war as defined largely by heavy infantry, in a manner so ill-suited to the rough terrain, Mediterranean summers, and narrow passes of the southern Balkans.[11]

Archidamus and his Spartans, in their original hope for a hoplite showdown in May 431, did not envision the annihilation of the Athenian people or their property through plague and fire. Instead, by fighting without many tactics and in the open, Spartan reactionaries felt that there would remain no real excuse other than courage and strength for victory or defeat—no reason, then, to repeat the battle again and again until the manhood of one side was wiped out or, worse still, to transfer the conflict to messy third theaters that were as indecisive as they were deadly to good hoplite infantrymen.

Even by the beginning of the Peloponnesian War there was a brutal logic to such simplistic Spartan thinking. After the Athenians experienced defeat at Delium, they *never* again tried to invade Boeotia in force, despite later having available far more troops than those on hand in 424. Similarly, after the Spartan alliance won at the great hoplite battle of Mantinea in 418 (to be discussed at length in this chapter), there was never again talk of a grand democratic alliance to overthrow its Peloponnesian hegemony until the invasion of Epaminondas a half century later. There still remained some mystique to the hoplite code in the late-fifth-century mind from the earlier aura of great battles, making them pivotal in ways that cannot be explained entirely in terms of casualties, tactics, or strategy. After all, for the purposes of killing, hoplite warfare made little sense: fewer than 40 percent of the combatants of the phalanx could even reach the enemy with their spears at any given time, quarter-inch armor kept most thrusts from hitting flesh, and the spear itself was not an especially lethal weapon.

Nevertheless, it was not just that Athens had lost 1,000 of 7,000 hoplites at Delium, a surprising 14 percent fatality rate unmatched in classical phalanx battles, in which 10 percent was more the average. Rather, the real significance was that they had been beaten so badly in an apparently fair fight. The clash and the subsequent mad Athenian flight appeared to offer a clear referendum on the respective courage and skill of both sides. After the dramatic victory at Mantinea six years later, Thucydides relates that the Spartans "had wiped away through this one occasion" all the recent calumnies that arose from their supposed cowardice on Sphacteria.[12]

Alcibiades could later brag that earlier, in 418, he had forced the issue so that "the Spartans had staked their all on one day at Mantinea." Although the defeat had in effect set back terribly the cause of Athens and her allies, Alcibiades claimed the battle as a work of his own genius that at least was able to bring both sides to the battlefield. There his allied coalition, in theory, had a 50 percent chance of winning the war outright. When, after all, were such good odds possible in the Peloponnesian War? "One occasion" and "one day" were used only in association with pitched battles, in a way impossible to use to characterize the Attic devastations, the cycle of revolutions at Corcyra, or the operations at Pylos or Amphipolis.

If there were only two major hoplite battles of the Peloponnesian War, the ubiquitous Alcibiades was involved in some ways with both of them. The fame he had won saving his kindred during the traumatic retreat at Delium, coupled with a succession of deaths of prominent Athenians—Pericles, Hippocrates, and Cleon—and the shame of others like Cleonymus and Laches, meant a meteoric rise in the career of the twenty-two-year-old hero.

Later he engineered the entire Argive-Athenian resistance at the battle of Mantinea, despite the fact that the Athenians had only committed a small number of combatants, and had sacrificed only 200 hoplites for the cause at the battle. Yet Alcibiades himself was not officially an elected general at the time, his oratory far more influential than his actual political clout to match fighting words with actual soldiers. In fact, unlike his ubiquity at Delium, he was nowhere to be seen on the day of the battle of Mantinea.

Churchill recalled of the battle of Jutland in World War I that the commander of the British fleet, Admiral Jellicoe, was the only man who through his failure might have lost England the war in a single day: battleships, like hoplites, were assets rarely used, but their destruction nevertheless left the enemy a deadly freedom of action. Athens may have had fortifications that stopped Spartans from reaching the Acropolis, but the very fact that its army could not prevent enemy hoplites from marching up to the walls took a psychological toll on the great city's reputation.

A Thing of Fear

THAT IS PRECISELY what the Boeotian poet Pindar said of Greek warfare prior to the early fifth century, when hoplite battle was a common way of solving disputes. What was the carnage like for these men of the old phalanx in battles like Delium? Pretty awful by modern sensibilities. Enemy or ally, Pagondas' Boeotians or Hippocrates' Athenian hoplites, all alike donned helmets, breastplates, and greaves that were hammered out of bronze. About a quarter to a half inch thick, this armor provided substantial protection from the blows of most swords, missiles, and spears, but at a terrible cost in weight, discomfort, and heat. That thousands on both sides of the battle line, often from disparate city-states, owned almost identical armor implies an implicit shared understanding of such fighting in the life of the Greek city-states.

The entire ensemble might cost a citizen-soldier well over 100 drachmas. That was the equivalent of about three months' wages. Later in the war, small factories—like the orator Lysias' family shieldworks in Athens—could turn out the standard wooden elements of the panoply en masse. As the war became more desperate, in its second and third decades, the old idea of hanging inherited ancestral arms over the hearth was becoming passé, since the state armed thousands of the poorer regardless of their particular census status. Most fighters now used the panoplies to fight as skirmishers or marines rather than traditional hoplites arrayed in the formal ranks of the phalanx. Sometimes hoplites ditched the breastplate and Corinthian helmet altogether. Instead, many wore conical caps (*piloi*) and leather jerkins for combat that was increasingly often against light-armed troops rather than other hoplites in pitched battle.

Surviving examples of wooden shield cores and the thin bronze veneers that went over the wood—at the Vatican museum, the Athenian agora, and the sanctuary at Olympia—reveal real craftsmanship, reflecting pride in private ownership, as well as the small size and stature of the wearers. Until the Peloponnesian War, most armor was donned by its owners only in times of national muster. The panoply's weight and design made it almost useless for hunting or skirmishing—in fact, for much of anything other than pitched battle. But like modern tanks, which are sometimes caught singly outside an armored division, an individual soldier who put on all the cumbersome hoplite armor and carried a heavy shield was often easily surrounded and ambushed by the quicker and lighter-clad, who in the bargain gained the psychological satisfaction of killing their hoplite betters. Some of the most notable of Athenians—for example, the generals Cleon, Laches, and Lamachus—were killed in heavy armor when fighting in fluid formation or in retreat, most probably by skirmishers or peltasts.

Since the advent of gunpowder, moderns have tended to deprecate the idea of body armor. The fiery offensive arts have for some six centuries overshadowed the much older sway of personal defense, so much so that surviving panoplies in modern museums seem ridiculous to the modern eye. Nevertheless, the age-old tension between attack and defense is not static. Only recently an emphasis on body armor has returned as scientists have at last discovered combinations of synthetic fibers, plastics, ceramics, and metals that can withstand even the onslaught of high-velocity, metal-alloy bullets and shrapnel fragments, which can strike the body instantaneously with incredible force and numbers. Ironically, the catalysts for Kevlar helmets, bulletproof vests, and assorted insertable ceramic plates are somewhat similar to those that led to heavily armored hoplites: first, such protection can save lives; second, the value of each combatant is now prized in a way not true of previous wars of the twentieth century.

The grotesque shield insignias, the incised artwork on the bronze breastplates and greaves, and the masklike appearance of the helmets crested with horsehair all indicate that elements in the drama of hoplite battle were almost eerily ostentatious. Certainly the equipment only heightened the psychological terror of the formal meeting of two phalanxes. Recall that both like-armed armies formed up in similar columns, stared at each other across the battlefield, and lowered spears on command. Pan (whose name led to our word "panic") was considered a fickle deity who could appear on the battlefield to scatter columns before battle even began.

For that very reason, the Spartans polished their bronze shield veneers to a high shine, wore long scarlet cloaks, draped their oiled and braided hair over their shoulders, and painted bright lambdas (for "Lacedaemon") on their shields—to stunning visual effect, if one can believe ancient accounts that enemies sometimes turned tail and ran rather than endure the Spartans' slow measured march to the killing zone, accompanied by the music of pipes. At Mantinea, despite being surprised and confused by the sudden appearance of a large enemy coalition force, the Spartans never lost their nerve. Instead, they quietly walked right into the enemy wall of spears, quite in contrast to the noisy "sound and fury" of their adversaries.[13]

In the actual fighting, the hoplite depended on the man next to him to shield his own unprotected right side and to maintain the cohesion of the entire phalanx, military service now solidifying the valued egalitarianism of the property-owning citizenry. Thucydides makes that point about mutual protection offered by close-ordered ranks throughout his history—implying that rote technique was critical, since men were not freelancing as individual warriors but cognizant that their own spearing must always be done in concert. Later writers stressed the importance of agility that might be formally inculcated by mastering set moves and war dances, but we are still not sure whether such individual skills were advocated for the pursuit or retreat, or simply to help hoplites attack within the confines of ranks and files.

Indeed, it is hard to think of any other form of fighting in which so much rested on the support of the men in the ranks. When the Spartan general Brasidas invaded Illyria in 423, he reminded his hoplites that their discipline and interdependence made them far more formidable warriors than the loud-shouting barbarian rabble they faced. In the eyes of Thucydides' Brasidas, the Greeks differed from the barbarians precisely in the manner in which they preferred to fight, as if their singular group discipline on the battlefield was the dividend of Hellenic civilization itself. The Illyrians, Brasidas scoffed to his men, "are not what they seem" since they "have no regular order" and are no different from "mobs."[14]

Of these supposedly preeminent Greeks, the Spartans themselves were far the best. Their domination was not necessarily due to their bodily strength (here the agrarian Thebans were far more formidable), numbers (Athens could field more hoplites than the aggregate number of Spartiates), or equipment (shields and body armor were almost uniform in size, shape, and construction the Greek world over). Instead, the Spartan mystique was a product of singular discipline and organization, and the ability to stay in rank. And why wouldn't order be a premium when the typical hoplite of the phalanx was subject to tremendous pressures in every direction: men pushing at his back, comrades in line crowding him to the right, rows in front presenting an impenetrable obstacle? As he was buffeted by the force of armored bodies, the hoplite also dodged incoming enemy iron, the sharp bronze spear butts of his friends in front bobbing in his face, and the razor-sharp spear points of the ranks to the rear darting over his neck and shoulders. All the while he trudged over the detritus of fallen wounded and dead hoplites, friend and foe, often both sons and fathers.

Hoplite Logic

IN THIS REGARD of close-order fighting, our present-day notion of Western discipline—marching in time, advancing and retreating on command, preservation of formation, and mutual protection within files and ranks—started with the Greek phalanx, was passed on through the Roman legions, and survived in medieval Swiss, Spanish, and Italian columns and tercios of pikemen to find its way into the gunpowder age with European mastery of drill and volley fire. If that seems a chronological stretch, remember that with the onset of firearms, the Europeans best seemed to have the prerequisite traditions to use guns most effectively in cohesion and mass, with ample attention paid to firing in unison and in accordance with group protocols. That legacy of the Greeks defining courage as staying in rank rather than counting individual kills seems as important for the survival of the Western tradition as the much more heralded ideas of democracy and rationalism, though a heritage for the most part underappreciated today.

Hoplite technology was craftsmanship at its highest. The three-foot in diameter shield, sometimes known as either the *aspis* or *hoplon*, covered half the body. A unique combined arm- and handgrip allowed its oppressive weight to be held by the left arm alone. Draw straps along the inside of the shield's perimeter meant that it could be retained even should the hand be knocked from the primary grip, a common mishap given the shield weight and the constant blows of massed combat. The shield's strange concave shape permitted the rear ranks to rest it on their shoulders. Anyone who has tried to hold up fifteen to twenty pounds with a single arm, even without the weight of other armor amid the rigor of battle, can attest to the exhaustion that sets in after only twenty minutes. Yet the hoplite shield was an engineering marvel: the round shape allowed it to be rotated in almost any direction even as the sloped surface provided more wood protection from the angled trajectory of incoming spear points.

Worse than the weight of such arms and armament was the sight of hundreds of enemy spear points, which ancient authors sometimes compared to the bristles of a hedgehog. That sea of incoming iron explains why such an unusually large shield was necessary, as well as the peculiar compactness and density of the ranks and files to deflect jabs at all angles and directions. Again, the aim was not to rack up kills through individual prowess—the polis Greeks deprecated as "barbarians" those such as the Carthaginians who kept such scores—but to keep the spear level, shield high, body in rank, and then to defend, push, and kill anonymously, as the collective body moved ahead in rank and formation.

At the battle of Mantinea, Thucydides takes great effort to explain the natural tendency of each hoplite to seek protection for his vulnerable right side in the shield of his companion on his right. Here one can appreciate just how pivotal the nature and shape of the shield was to the entire method of hoplite fighting: ranks were almost always referred to by Greek authors as so many "shields" deep—rarely as so many "spears" or "men." Still, for all the genius of concavity and flexibility, there were grave problems with the round shield. Its circular, rather than rectangular, shape ensured that the body was not entirely protected; thus every soldier by instinct needed to lean to his right to find cover in the left part of his neighbor's shield.

Greek generals—except for Spartan monarchs, usually amateur and elective officials—led troops on the right wing to spearhead the attack. In defeat, leaders usually perished: Hippocrates at Delium, the Corinthian general Lycophron at Solygia in 425, and both Athenian commanders at Mantinea (418), a battle in which the small Athenian contingent suffered 20 percent fatalities (200 of the 1,000 Athenian hoplites died). This exposure of leaders was sometimes quite in contrast to the practice of the Greeks' foreign adversaries. No Greek elected official, like Xerxes at Thermopylae or Salamis, sat above his men on a throne, gazing at the fighting below and issuing orders to a throng of court toadies to kill this fainthearted company and reward that resolute one. Thucydides himself was exiled for allowing Brasidas to take Amphipolis, probably through little fault of his own, since his promptness and audacity probably saved nearby Eion. There is also not a single major Greek general from any city-state in classical Greek history—Miltiades, Themistocles, Pausanias, Aristides, Pericles, Cleon, Brasidas, Gylippus, Lysander, or Epaminondas—who was not put on trial, demoted, fined, exiled, executed, or killed in battle.

After the great naval victory at Arginusae (406), the Athenian assembly nevertheless worked itself into one of its murderous moods and executed 6 of the 10 admirals responsible for the victory—among them Pericles' own son—on dubious charges of negligently allowing wounded sailors to drown. Oddly, the chief crime for Greek commanders seems not to have been lost fights per se. Charges were more likely brought against those alleged to have avoided battle or to have failed to recover the dead. Generalship in the field was also in and of itself a deadly business: 22 Athenian elected leaders died in battle during the Peloponnesian War, or about 12 percent of all those who took up some sort of command.

Even more astounding was the Panhellenic custom of accountability and audit of generalship, often right on the field of battle. Some generals in effect apologized on the battlefield to troops for tactical defeat, partly to recover their morale, partly to instruct them about their past mistakes in hopes of better performance in the future. The Spartan general Gylippus, after a small loss of his Syracusan fort, said he was sorry by pointing out that it was his fault for leading a force dependent on light-armed and mounted troops into a confined space against hoplites. Although Nicias was de facto commander of the entire first expedition in Sicily, he nevertheless felt it necessary to explain his plight in detail in a lengthy letter to the Athenian assembly. In the modern world, many successful generals eye a postbellum political career; in the Peloponnesian War, most battle commanders were themselves already politicians.[15]

Killing Hoplites

BECAUSE OF THE limited tactical options open to a phalanx once battle commenced, complex maneuvers and tactics were problematic and so rarely attempted. A phalanx plowed through "like a trireme ram" on the stronger right side before its own inferior left wing collapsed and eroded the cohesion of the entire army. Well apart from a king on a hill, there was not even a grandee on horseback galloping in the rear—issuing complex orders by trumpet and signal flag for particular segments of the phalanx to attack in echelon, backpedal, or be held in reserve. Such articulation of forces would wait a century, for Alexander and his phalangites.

Thucydides goes to great lengths to explain how innovative the Theban decisions were to mass deeply and coordinate cavalry at Delium, as well as the Spartan frantic ad hoc efforts to redirect their attacks in the midst of the melee at Mantinea. In most normal cases, the generals apparently had sent their similarly formed columns out to hit each other head-on, tactical thinking being essentially nonexistent and almost unwelcome.[16]

In the two great battles of the Peloponnesian War, at Delium and Mantinea, one sees the very beginning of the Greek infantry tactics of deep columns, reserves, integrated cavalry units, adaptation to terrain, and secondary maneuvers, which would only accelerate in the fourth century under Epaminondas and come to fruition with Philip and Alexander. Hoplite battle in the Peloponnesian War began a slow transformation, from phalanxes rather artificially deciding wars to hoplites becoming a part of an integrated force of horsemen, light-armed troops, and missile troops that could win theaters of conflict on the basis of military efficacy rather than traditional protocol.

To kill and maim, the hoplite depended on his spear. Should the shaft break, he might turn around what was left of its nine-foot length to employ the reverse end, which was outfitted with a bronze spike, sometimes called a "lizarder" (saurotêr). Some hoplites stumbled and fell, only to be stomped on by oncoming infantry who slammed their upraised spears downward, the butt spike providing the coup de grâce as it smashed through the unfortunate man's backplate into his chest or stomach.

A small iron sword was carried in case the spear was lost altogether. Vase paintings often show broken shafts; reference at Delium to "hand-to-hand" battle probably meant slashing with swords or stabbing with butt spikes. Because of the congested nature of the fighting, hoplites were hit repeatedly from all sides. But to be lethal, strikes had to be aimed at the unprotected groin and neck. Wearing hoplite armor in battle was in some sense the equivalent of placing a bull's-eye over one's unprotected throat and genitalia.

Sometime during the Peloponnesian War, the Greeks first began to explore the dilemma of proper depth versus width. Taking men off the battle line to stack them deeper than the standard eight shields gave the phalanx more penetrating power, even as the shortened front was in consequence left vulnerable to outflanking movements. The green Syracusans, for example, fought their sole hoplite battle against the Athenian invaders sixteen men deep, in hopes that their stacked columns would provide moral reinforcement to their inexperienced troops, while the resulting vulnerable and extended flanks were covered by a huge force of some 1,200 cavalry.

At Delium, Pagondas' spirited hoplites, like Napoleon's columns, thought they could blast apart their adversaries without being flanked, but only with the assurance that cavalry or rough ground protected the margins of the battlefield. This entire modern military dilemma of column or line, depth in contrast to breadth (or power versus maneuver) also first arose in the Greeks' search to find the proper ratio within their phalanxes. The problem remained unsolved well into the nineteenth century, even in the age of gunpowder, until Wellington's thin red line at Waterloo tore apart the massed ranks of the French Old Guard. Those who stacked deep, like the Syracusans and Thebans, in the manner of the later Macedonians, usually had superior cavalry to guard the exposed long files. In the same manner, George S. Patton repeatedly urged his division commanders to plow ahead, without worry about the flanks; but then he was protected by superior air support, the modern equivalent of ancient heavy cavalry.

If the hoplite kept his nerve and formation with his fellow fighters, his seventy pounds of armor and the length of his spear made him invulnerable to cavalry charges and skirmishers alike *on level ground*. Even in the most desperate circumstances his line was impenetrable to any but other hoplites, as long as every man (a *parastatês*, or "one who stands side by side in rank") kept his nerve in battle, did not waver, and held his shield up and his spear out. At Delium the nearly 20,000 unarmed or light-armed auxiliary fighters dared not attack either side's phalanx while in formation. The unusually large contingent of 1,200 horsemen at Syracuse rode into the fray in the flight and pursuit only when both sides found themselves out of formation. When the victorious Athenians on the right ran from the sudden appearance of cavalry behind the hills of Delium, it was largely on the impression that it presaged the arrival of another infantry army altogether.

One of the peculiarities about Greek warfare at the dawn of the Peloponnesian War was the archaic idea of class, not military efficacy, determining the role of the soldiers. In theory, the landless rowed and threw missiles. The propertied served as hoplites. Only the very wealthy rode horses or outfitted and commanded triremes. Thus, the armored ranks of spearmen were not solely a military hedge against cavalry but a social statement as well that the larger property owners of the city-state who could afford ponies were nevertheless not as important as yeomen farmers to the collective defense of their societies. This cherished idea was also a casualty of the Peloponnesian War.

This class element in classical warfare has always struck me as paradoxical. In the ancient Greek world, those with property were the most likely to fight in the deadliest fashion, as if owning a farm earned one the privilege of getting stabbed in the face in a way unlikely for the landless. On occasion wealthy Athenian knights could feel the pressure to go "hoplite." Thus, wealthy horsemen bragged that they had chosen to give up their mounts and fight instead as hoplites, illustrating that the greater military cachet was acquiring real "combat experience" in the melee alongside agrarian infantry rather than patrolling as aristocratic horsemen.[17] In general, like everything in the Peloponnesian War, twenty-seven years of fighting finally eroded the strict correlation between status and military service. By the last years of the war, citizens (as well as aliens and slaves) fought in any manner that the city needed at its moment of crisis, as knights rowed and the poor donned state-supplied armor.

After the meeting of phalanxes, hoplites marched out screaming the war cry *Eleleu!* or *Alala!* Blinded by the dust and their own cumbersome helmets, they stabbed away with their spears, and in unison pushed ahead with their shields, sometimes grabbing, kicking, and biting, desperately hoping to make some inroad into the enemy's phalanx. Usually they had little idea whom, if anyone, they had killed or wounded. Hearing and sight by those in the ranks were difficult, if not sacrificed entirely. Both of Thucydides' descriptions of the two major hoplite battles of the war—Delium and Mantinea—reveal just such rampant confusion and misdirection: the Athenians accidentally killing their own at the former, or the Argives in the latter battle completely being unable to see an entire Spartan army approaching nearby.

The din of clashing metal and screaming men must have been earsplitting, but it went relatively unnoticed by the hoplites, their hearing almost obliterated by the heavy bronze helmet that had no cutouts for the ears. Dust, the crowded conditions of the battlefield, and the crested helmets with small eye slots would have limited their vision severely. Mistaken identity was commonplace, given that distinctive uniforms and national insignia were often absent.[18]

Descriptions of gaping wounds to the unprotected neck and groin, involuntary defecation and urination, and panic abound in Greek literature. This dark and mostly forgotten side of hoplite battle suggests that once the two sides clashed together, the interior of the melee was sheer bedlam. In such a mess, weight and discipline were crucial to hoplite success: the greater cohesion and thrust of the column, the more likely it was for a phalanx to shove itself over and through the enemy. Perhaps all the terrible battle calculus of this type of fighting was what horrified Pericles. Certainly, the very idea of sending his citizens into such an inferno against trained killers like the Spartans must have driven him to craft a strategy to win the war without risking hoplite confrontations.

Usually, within an hour the pushing (ôthismos) ceased, as one side collapsed and then fled the field. The exhausted victors stripped and returned the dead, and erected an ostentatious trophy as testament to their prowess. Often they annexed the disputed territory from the defeated. There are few instances of multi-day pitched battles in the manner of a Shiloh or Gettysburg, much less a weeks- or months-long holocaust like a Somme or Verdun. Instead, at Solygia, Delium, Mantinea, and outside Syracuse, the fight was probably over in a few minutes. During some twenty-seven years of war, Greek hoplites fought in pitched battles probably no more than four or five hours in the aggregate.[19]

Scholars debate endlessly whether the parochial rules of hoplite war stifled tactical and technological innovation or reflected the preexisting backward state of Greek warfare before Alexander. For example, did a characteristically limited chase really reflect the rules of battle, or was it a de facto admission that exhausted winners in armor, without many horsemen, could hardly catch losers who tossed away their equipment and fled once lightened by sixty or seventy pounds of cast-off weight? Quite unlike the bedlam at Delium, at Mantinea the entire defeated left wing of the democratic allies ran to safety without much serious pursuit from the Spartans: "The flight was neither pursued nor did the retreat go on very far; for the Lacedaemonians fight their battles long and stubbornly until they turn back their enemies; but once their enemies flee, their pursuits are both brief and only for a little distance."[20]

Terms of deprecation like *lipostratia,* "leaving the ranks," and *tresas,* "trembler" or "fleers," referred to those who fled the phalanx or showed manifest signs of fright. The classical Greek language in addition had at least two specific terms of aspersion just for jettisoning the hoplite shield (*rhipsaspis*, "shield tosser," or *apobolimaios*, "throw-awayer")—an act that threatened the integrity of the phalanx and revealed the hoplite's worry about his own, rather than the group's, survival. These public slurs were serious stuff and stuck, haunting a man for the rest of his life, given the public nature of both phalanx warfare and civic life within the polis. In his comedies, Aristophanes was merciless to the Athenian popular leader Cleonymus for tossing away his shield to save his life at Delium. His infamy three years after the battle became a stale joke repeated ad nauseam in front of several thousand Athenian theatergoers.

In the same manner, the young Plato was probably ashamed that his stepfather, Pyrilampes, had also run at the first sign of trouble at Delium and was captured by (and later ransomed from) the Boeotians, a battle where his teacher Socrates' fortitude, in contrast, became a subject of table talk at an entire generation of subsequent Athenian dinner parties. Much of the family cachet that propelled the teenager Alcibiades into prominence at Delium derived from the fact that his father, Cleinias, had died bravely at the front ranks not far away, twenty-three years earlier at Coronea.

If Greeks sensed that fright and courage were not so public during sieges, in the midst of civil strife, or at sea, hoplite battle was a different story. It could make or break a man's civic life for decades afterward. The good citizen, in other words, throughout the Peloponnesian War was not the tosser but the *aspidephoros* ("shield carrier"), who always holds his shield steady and right, and stays in rank in the phalanx—even though there was almost no opportunity to do so over some twenty-seven years of war.[21]

Panic and fear were ubiquitous on the battlefield, given the curtailment of sight and hearing, and the ever-present danger of panic among such large mobs. Often in the Peloponnesian War unexpected natural phenomena—sudden thunder and lightning, an eclipse, or an earthquake—would shatter the morale of a Greek human herd in massed rank.

Rampant slaughter could on occasion occur, but careful analysis reveals an economy to pitched fighting, and that the real killing occurred well off the hoplite battlefield. Rarely did more than 10 percent of the men who fought die in a single pitched battle—1,500 total hoplites were killed at Delium, or a little over 10 percent of the 14,000 armored assembled on both sides. Although the Athenians suffered a staggering 14 percent fatality rate among their hoplites, such a number of dead was unusual and made the battle among the most costly in classical Greek history. At Mantinea the combined hoplite dead of 1,400 suggests a similar fatality rate of about 7 or 8 percent—if, in fact, 17,000 to 20,000 hoplites crashed together. Throughout the entire war, Athens lost little more, on average, than 200 hoplites a year. Its aggregate of only 5,470 hoplite battle dead was less than half of those heavy infantrymen who perished during the war from the plague alone—and the vast majority of them fell outside hoplite battle in skirmishes, sieges, and at sea.[22]

Posthoplite Warfare

TWO NEW FACTORS in the fifth century had changed three centuries of past hoplite practice. First, the Persian Wars, particularly the invasion of Xerxes in 480, had shown that even a successful battle like Marathon or Plataea could not guarantee total victory against an enemy that did not share ideas about the primacy of agrarian warfare but sought annihilation of its enemy by land and sea through any means available. In response, that war was largely won through the destruction of the Persian fleet at the sea battles of Artemisium and Salamis, but only after Athens, along with most of northern Greece, had been burned and occupied. Had the Athenian defenders depended solely on their hoplites, the Persian Wars would have been lost. Ten thousand Athenians, even if they were the brave veterans of Marathon who a decade earlier had defeated 30,000 of Darius' invaders, could hardly have withstood 100,000 Persians in a pitched battle in the Athenian plain.

Classical hoplites and later phalangites might defeat Persian infantry—as the Hellenic infantry victories from Marathon and Plataea to Issus and Gaugamela attest—even at a 5 to 3 numerical disadvantage, but *not* at 10 to 1. At the battle of Cunaxa (401) the Greek Ten Thousand routed their Persian adversaries. But after the death of their patron Cyrus the Younger, the vastly outnumbered mercenary force found itself on the Euphrates facing tens of thousands of enemies in what is now southern Iraq, and conducted a fighting retreat rather than invite a pitched battle.

By the time of the Peloponnesian War hoplites enjoyed a role similar to that of the majestic dreadnoughts of the First World War, formidable capital assets that likewise "feared nothing." Highly prized and much touted even in their anachronism, such imposing ships could blast apart in minutes an entire fleet and thus change a war—and yet rarely got the chance to fight one. So it was too with a classical hoplite phalanx. On the eve of the expedition to Syracuse, Alcibiades deprecated the supposed hoplite strength of Sicily by scoffing that throughout the Peloponnesian War states usually bragged of hoplites whom they did not have, even though such highly prestigious forces rarely any longer won wars outright.[23]

Alcibiades seemed to wish to reassure the Athenians that they might win, given the paucity of Syracusan heavy infantry—and then brought far too few cavalry along, only to discover that it was Sicilian horsemen, not hoplites, that most harmed the Athenian army. Such hoplite chauvinism lingered even after the Peloponnesian War. In the fourth century, Plato's Socrates makes the almost treasonous claim that the great naval victory at Salamis was an unhappy occasion because it empowered the landless naval crowd at the expense of proud landowning hoplites. Again, it was *how* you fought, not whether you won or lost, that mattered. War had as many internal ramifications as it did external consequences. The great catastrophe to the founder of Western philosophy was not that the democracy at Athens had lost, but that it had inaugurated a type of fighting in the Peloponnesian War that divorced virtue from military efficacy.

During the discussion about the Peace of Nicias (421), the Argives suggested to the Spartans that they both resolve their disputes "just as once before" by selecting champions to meet at a prearranged time and place. Even the conservative Spartans at first scoffed at such reactionary thinking. "A moronic [*môria*] thing" was their initial reaction to the strange proposal of deciding an entire war by allowing a few hoplites to crash together in phalanxes. After a decade of frustration in Attica and having been stymied by light-armed troops on Sphacteria, the Spartans were no longer under the illusion that ceremonial battles could settle any dispute.[24]

Triremes, along with the poor men who rowed on them, the marines who sailed along as skirmishers, and the public taxes that built them, proved far more critical to the war effort than agrarian militias. Yet at the outbreak of the war Thucydides takes care to note that Athens had at least 13,000 front-rank hoplites and another 16,000 reserve garrison infantrymen made up of old and young citizens and augmented by resident aliens with heavy armor. In other words, the Athenians had enough men to have manned an additional 150 ships. The purpose of these nearly 30,000 Athenian deployable hoplites under a policy that sought to avoid their use in pitched battle is not altogether clear, other than for marching out to Megara to intimidate the smaller city and provide cover while light-armed troops ravaged its agriculture.

By the outbreak of the Peloponnesian War both Athens and Sparta, far more so than other city-states, found themselves immune from the old restrictions on hoplite warfare. Neither needed to be home at harvesttime—triremes or helots, respectively, could supply enough food to exempt thousands from farm chores. Thus, neither learned to predicate short wars on the prestige of winning rather insignificant borderlands. Throughout the Archidamian War (431–421) it was the Peloponnesian agrarian allies, not the Spartans per se, who were reluctant to march northward to Attica. Why? Unlike Sparta, they worked their own fields, and, as Pericles had foreseen at the outbreak of war, such men had no capital to endure a long war.[25]

Athens, through its overseas empire of tribute and imported food that supplied at least two-thirds of the population, had similarly transcended seasonal hoplite warfare. With the port at the Piraeus, a navy of some 300 ships, a large populace of voters who did not farm, and annual commercial income, it too did not confine itself to a few weeks of spring campaigning in hopes of deciding conflict by glorious battle. Moreover, since the Greek victory at Plataea over the Persians, the Spartan phalanx had established a reputation of invincibility that was to last well into the fourth century, the disaster at Sphacteria (425) being considered an aberration and quickly redeemed by the dramatic hoplite victory at Mantinea.

Quasi Hoplites

THUS, ALL DURING the Peloponnesian War the Athenians felt that meeting such hoplites on a flat plain was tantamount to suicide, like sending out cruisers to face battleships when there were carriers available.[26] The victors of Delium and Mantinea—the Boeotians and Spartans—came away from the conflict convinced that their own hoplites were unbeatable, thus explaining why both confident armies were willing to meet each other in the numerous battles to come at Haliartus, Nemea, Coronea, Tegyra, Leuctra, and second Mantinea, which followed the Peloponnesian War. Despite only two major old-style battles, fighting throughout the twenty-seven-year war was nearly constant and took place everywhere—on rough terrain, in mountain passes, and through amphibious operations. Indeed, there are some eighty-three instances in the text of Thucydides of what might legitimately be called a land "engagement" of some sort, illustrating that most soldiers were killed far apart from a typical phalanx battle.

On long marches, cavalry, light-armed troops, and archers were needed to provide reconnaissance, cover, and pursuit against like kind. Light troops, mostly highly mobile javelin throwers unencumbered by body armor, were especially prized once battle moved away from the plains and onto difficult ground. Clumsy hoplites away from the phalanx were often ambushed, their breastplates of quarter-inch bronze not always a sure defense against a storm of arrows and missiles from skirmishers who could target arms, legs, and the neck. Horsemen were no longer mere ancillaries at the peripheries of hoplite battle but were often critical to military success against a mélange of enemies in a variety of locales. Poor men, rich grandees, slaves, foreigners, aliens, even women and children during times of siege—they all got into the fighting, once more disdaining the old idea that rural communities would let farmers adjudicate border disputes by brief collisions.[27]

As the fighting wore on, the nostalgic Thucydides could find ever more poignancy in the destruction of the old hoplite infantry of both sides of the Peloponnesian War, especially when they died outside of pitched battle or at the hands of their social inferiors. He listed the losses of the Athenians to the plague first in terms of dead hoplites. A Spartan who surrendered at Sphacteria after seeing his hoplite comrades suffering from a barrage of arrows was made to sigh, "An arrow would be worth a great deal if it could pick out noble and good men from the rest." When the Athenians lost 120 hoplites in the wilds of Aetolia to hill men, he remarked of the dead that they "were truly the best men whom the city of Athens lost in this war."

Recalling an earlier incident before the war when Corinthian hoplites had been ambushed and slaughtered, he pronounced it a great "tragedy." He also concluded that the dead Thespian hoplites at Delium had been the "flower" of their city-state.[28] In Thucydides' view, hoplites should have fought in pitched battle—not fallen less gloriously to disease, ambush, or missiles. The Greeks themselves were conscious of the military revolution in their midst. In the fourth year of the Peace of Nicias (418), Thucydides grieves that the two sides went after each other through ambushes and raids, precisely because neither side would march out to fight a battle "with formal preparation." Aristophanes ridiculed the youth of his day. They could not even hold their shield chest high—as if that skill would ever be needed in a war without hoplite battles. Both during and after the Peloponnesian War, Greeks agreed that something had gotten out of control and led to slaughters never before anticipated, not unlike the modern repulsion at World War I, which soon proved to be quite unlike the expected short and decisive campaigning a half century earlier during the Franco-Prussian War of 1870.[29]

Besides Delium and Mantinea, there were only a few other occasions when two phalanxes collided. These engagements were usually small affairs and thus decided little. In summer 425, for example, the year before Delium, the Athenians had embarked a small army of some 2,000 hoplites near Corinth, just the sort of nontraditional mixed use of hoplites that Plato would later condemn as impure. At the small village of Solygia, seaborne Athenian hoplites were met by Corinthian heavy infantrymen. The two sides fought a tough, though atypical, hoplite battle in difficult terrain. Thucydides points out that the battle was "entirely hand-to-hand," and apparently brutal. Reserves, a retreat behind fortifications, and the prominent role of the cavalry—as well as confusion, panic, dust clouds, pushing, and the death of the defeated general—proved more pivotal to the Athenian victory than hoplite courage.

The Athenians claimed Solygia as a tactical victory, by virtue of driving the Corinthians off the field, losing little more than 50 dead to the Corinthians' 212, along with their general Lycophron. Still, they were unable to establish a secure base, and so suffered a strategic setback in that they returned to their ships and sailed away. Then the general and old conservative hoplite Nicias belatedly discovered that two Athenian corpses had been left behind, requiring an embarrassing return to ask the defeated for the bodies, thus in formal terms nullifying the psychological dividends of the limited victory.[30]

About a year and a half later, in winter 423, the Mantineans fought the neighboring Tegeans, in a precursor to the great battle of Mantinea that would follow in that same valley five years later and at last involve the great powers of the Peloponnesian War. Of this earlier and similarly minor affair Thucydides notes only that the engagement was hard-fought and mentions some characteristic elements of phalanx battle: each side claimed victory on its right wing and broke off hostilities at darkness. Such backwater and mostly unrecorded fights between hoplites must have been ubiquitous as smaller states over the three decades of the war went on with the normal business of settling border disputes—even as Sparta and Athens simultaneously tried to transport their own larger hoplite armies into peripheral theaters to obtain local advantages against numerically inferior and poorly armed and led militias.[31]

Thus, such "hoplite" battles were not exactly purely hoplite affairs. In most of them there were ambushes, seaborne attacks, and hoplites employed more on garrison duty than in rank. Perhaps the most famous was the engagement at Amphipolis (422), where 600 Athenian hoplites were killed at a cost of a mere 7 on the Spartan side. Both opposing generals, who had agitated for continuation of the decadelong war, the Athenian demagogue Cleon and the maverick Brasidas of Sparta, were killed in action. With their joint demise, peace factions arose to allow the Peace of Nicias the next year, suggesting that most of the war's key figures died with their armor on, and that hoplite battle in a day still had a tendency to alter the course of the war. Of course, Thucydides makes it a point to note that Amphipolis was not quite a "regular battle" (what he calls a *parataxis*) but, rather, a more confused effort by Cleon to approach the Spartan garrison at Amphipolis—only to be surprised by joint sallies of Spartans from the city walls who surrounded the Athenians and quickly routed them.[32]

What did the term "hoplite" then come to mean? Not much more than a heavy infantryman with some sort of bronze armor. He was no longer per se of a particular class. Nor did he necessarily fight in the phalanx—or even observe the age-old protocols about notification and cessation of pitched battle.

The Last Hurrah at Mantinea

AFTER THE SPARTAN failure of annual ravaging (431–425), after the Athenian toll from the plague (430–426), after the Spartans had lost at Sphacteria (425), and some of their best warriors—among them high-ranking officers—had shamefully surrendered and been taken hostage (425–421), after the Spartans became terrified that their helots might revolt en masse, after the defeat of the Athenians in Boeotia (424), and after Cleon and Brasidas both perished at Amphipolis (422), both sides acknowledged that the war had degenerated into a messy calamity that neither could win outright.

A breather was welcomed. After some failed brief truces, the conservative Athenian statesman Nicias negotiated with the Spartans the peace that bears his name and would prove to last about six years (421–415). If Athens was exhausted from the plague and the dislocations of evacuating the Attic countryside, Sparta had been so shattered by the rather light losses at Sphacteria and the Athenian garrisoning of Pylos and Cythera that its citizens "thought they would fail in whatever risk they undertook, because of the loss of self-confidence arising out of not before experiencing such calamity."[33]

So eager were the Spartans to get back their prisoners taken at Sphacteria some four years earlier that they signed on to the agreement over the objections of their allies Thebes, Megara, and Elis, which, in fact, remained nominally at war with Athens. However, rarely do peace agreements last when the original conditions for hostilities have not ended. Both Sparta's purported fear of the power and growth of the Athenian empire and Athens' unwillingness to make painful concessions to assuage Peloponnesian anxieties were not altered. Despite a decade of carnage, by 421 neither side believed it had really been beaten.

Thus, the "cold war" lasted only a few years before it began to heat up again in the Peloponnese, near the small town of Mantinea in 418, as the old Spartan alliance threatened to unravel. Alcibiades and the war party at Athens were the surrogate players. Their grand strategy—once more like the ambitious schemes that had come to naught at Delium in 424—was bold, hinging on creating a democratic revolutionary movement that might turn once-hostile Peloponnesians into friends and thus in one big battle shut down an entire theater of the war in the south.

Under the leadership of Alcibiades, the Athenians intrigued with Argos to fashion an ad hoc coalition of newly democratic Peloponnesian states—Argos, Elis, and Mantinea—that might surround Sparta and dissolve her alliances, especially with Thebes and Corinth still nursing resentments on the sidelines over the recent peace with Athens. The Peloponnesian League itself was rife with tension. Argos had fought Sparta repeatedly in the early fifth century, both in pitched battles and border skirmishes, and always represented a potential nexus of rebellion. Elis was a wealthy unified city-state, home of the Olympic games, site of the magnificent temple to Olympian Zeus (larger than the Parthenon), and itself quasi-democratic as early as 460.

During the peace, the Athenians were at last starting to fathom the rough outlines of a winning approach of fomenting helot rebellion in Messenia—all the while in hopes of liberating the major Peloponnesian allies in the Argolid, Arcadia, and Elis. The occupation and fortification of Pylos, along with the defeat and taking of the Spartan hostages on the island of Sphacteria, were now to be complemented by surrounding Sparta with hostile democratic states. At the hub of this grand plan of anti-Spartanism in the Peloponnese, both figuratively and geographically, was Argos. Its leadership sensed that the Spartan surrender at Sphacteria, coupled with the failure of devastation in Attica, had improved Argos' chances to serve as a democratic and autonomous Peloponnesian rallying point. The post-Pylos leadership in Sparta had done nothing between 420 and 418 to stifle this growing alliance other than to marshal a few troops on the border and then disband them because of "bad omens."

Athens, however, failed to grasp this golden opportunity to undo the Peloponnesian empire. Alcibiades had led the groundwork for this anti-Spartan alliance, but in a foolhardy move the Athenians had rejected his candidacy for general in 418, preferring instead the lethargic Nicias and his associates. This ensured that they would only haphazardly support the resistance when it finally came to real fighting in the Peloponnese.

Alert to the danger in early summer 418, the Spartans under King Agis arrived in the Mantinean plain to put an end to such nonsense and protect Tegea, their first outpost ally that was targeted in the new coalition's grand ambitions.

This insurrection proved to be like none other in Sparta's recent history. The recalcitrant states were the most powerful in the Peloponnese. And they could field good infantrymen. Had they won then, the Peloponnesian War would have been, for all practical purposes, over in an afternoon—as the Spartans could never have marched northward into Attica again, Corinth and Thebes would not have returned to the Spartan coalition, and the state itself would probably have been immediately plagued by massive helot revolts at home.

King Agis brought some 12,000 hoplites into Arcadia to force battle and restore the old reputation that it was not a wise thing to face the Spartans in battle. Thucydides thought his force "was the finest Greek army brought together up to that time"—apparently a suggestion that these elite hoplites were intent not on ravaging the Attic countryside but on killing Argives in pitched battle. After a few false starts, each army—the allies had roughly equivalent forces— maneuvered for position in the plain of Mantinea before squaring off and colliding. The final onslaught probably took place sometime around August 1, 418—the hottest time of the year in one of the hottest and most humid plains in mainland Greece.

At the very outset of the war Pericles, in advising his countrymen to retreat into their walls, had conceded that the Peloponnesians *could* defeat "all the Greeks put together in a single battle." Unfortunately, he would be posthumously proved right, as Mantinea would now confirm the late Athenian leader's worst fears about the prowess of Spartan hoplites. Unlike the Spartans' arrival into Attica in 431, King Agis came to the flatlands of Mantinea with a much smaller force that convinced their adversaries to march out in hopes that a victory was possible after all. Yet so ready were the Argives and the Mantineans to induce battle that their brashness startled the late-arriving and methodical Spartans. Thucydides claimed that few could recall another occasion on which the Spartan army had been so dumbfounded.[34]

Both Delium and Mantinea were in a tactical sense near accidents. The respective armies did not know quite where their adversaries were camped, or even less their exact location seconds before they charged. Take away just two old men—Pagondas at Delium and an anonymous old Spartan hoplite who warned King Agis to back off his initial approach—and the two decisive hoplite engagements of the war either would not have taken place or at least would not have been fought where and when they were.

If one were to pick a place to fight a hoplite battle, Mantinea would be just about right. For killing people out in the open, generals need ample space, lots of food, clean water, level ground, easy accessibility, and nearby protection.

Mantinea, unlike Delium, fits all such requisites. As the nearby modern freeway proves, it is on the strategic route between north and south. Mantinea is also a narrow plain where 20,000 warriors can still easily fit, as they did in August 418—and on several occasions afterward.

The killing fields are surrounded by mountains that provide both defense for the flanks of heavy infantrymen and a refuge after defeat. A few thousand brave men who can span such a narrowing plain can stop whole armies. Thus, Mantinea served as a choke point where the grand routes from southern Greece constrict to a mile or so—before opening up again to flatland and various roads that branch out northward to Argos, Corinth, and Athens. If Sparta had lost this battle, it would not only have gained an entire host of new enemies but found its main artery out of Laconia essentially blocked.

Mantinea is fertile. Then and now the black earth can grow wheat in abundance, and so it ensured food for thousands of men as they milled and jockeyed around for days, seeking preparatory advantage to kill one another. The plain suffers from too much rather than too little water. The runoff from the surrounding steep mountains explains the ubiquity of sinkholes and streams. Greek generals of the ages liked Mantinea. Numerous times in Hellenic history Spartan kings, the Thebans under the great liberator Epaminondas, and the national hero Philopoemen (253–182) all fought in battles here for causes and ideas that are now the stuff of classical scholars, but of little interest to anyone else.

Few tourists, then, visit Mantinea today. The new freeway interchange is about five miles distant; and the ugly modern cement city of Tripolis lies about ten miles away. There is nothing here at the battlefield but a few country homes, a bizarre church that a wild-eyed eccentric spent his life building by scrounging marble and bricks from the countryside, and the traces of a vast lost city that peeks out amid the weeds and wheat fields.

But walk carefully again through this plain. Scan the random blocks of the amphitheater. Climb among the fallen bastions of the once great circuit wall, navigate through the precincts of the ancient sanctuaries of Herakles and Poseidon, and far from being empty, Mantinea is, in fact, full of ghosts. Thousands have died here over the centuries. The voices of Greece's greatest statesmen, generals, and writers once echoed off these hills before they fell in the alluvial mud of the battlefield. Well off to the distance there is the small hillock of Skopê ("Lookout Hill"), where the greatest military man Greece produced, the liberator Epaminondas, died in 362—his retainers pulling out a spear from his guts as he gazed down at his retreating Theban army, which had broken on news that its beloved general had been carried off and was bleeding to death on the hill above them.

Somewhere beneath the present-day barbed-wire fences and cement irrigation ditches are the footprints of the rabble-rouser Alcibiades, who well before the battle traversed the landscape, trying to create an alliance of democratic states to encircle Sparta and crush oligarchy for good—only in typical fashion to miss out on the actual fighting in 418 altogether. His grand machinations to end the Peloponnesian War in an hour also ended in vain here on the battlefield of Mantinea.

Alcibiades was nowhere to be seen. After crafting the alliance, his candidacy for general was rejected, his homeland sending a scant 1,000 Athenian hoplites and 300 horsemen to fight in the climactic battle that it had engineered. Perhaps Athens was worried about inciting the Spartans by arriving en masse at a time of ostensible peace; if so, nothing in war is so dangerous as to be a little aggressive or somewhat provocative.

The Spartan army that lined up on the plain was emblematic of the demographic crisis that would eventually undo the entire military caste system of the state. In short, its hoplite military was no longer an army of elite Spartan Similars. The left of the line was manned by some 600 Scirtae, tough mountain people from the borderlands of Arcadia who enjoyed some limited privileges of Spartan citizenship—and as a token of appreciation usually found themselves in battle facing the enemy's elite right. Next to them were several hundred freed helots. These were equally brave men, but without the training or the élan of the Spartiate class.

The core of the Spartan army manned the center, along with some Arcadian allies; the right was given to local Tegeans and another division of Spartiates. If one adds up the 12,000-some Peloponnesian hoplites, 5,000 light-armed troops, and 1,000 mounted Boeotians, King Agis had roughly 18,000 men with which to break up the Argive bid for a free Peloponnese.

The allied coalition opposite had somehow collected 11,000 to 12,000 hoplites, which was an approximate match of King Agis's heavy forces. About 2,000 skilled Mantineans anchored the right, opposite the Scirtae. Along with 1,000 picked professionals from Argos and some Arcadians, they constituted about as good a force of hoplites as any in the Peloponnese and were determined to be free of the Spartan yoke.

The rest of the Argives, the Eleans, and militias from some smaller cities filled out the center and left of the battle line (about 7,000 men), along with a mere 1,000 Athenians on the extreme left wing. Unfortunately, the center and left stared across no-man's-land at the cream of the Spartan army. Their only hope of salvation was to hang on long enough for the Mantineans and the Argive elite to finish off the Scirtae and immediately come to their aid. Beneath barren Mount Barberi, King Agis marched his Spartan killers right through the enemy left, his right and center wings immediately shattering the men of Argos, along with the trapped Athenians. His professional killers plowed on and lowered their spears, "walked slowly to the music of pipes," and then impaled the few who fled too slowly.

Thucydides wrote that the hoplites of the terrified and collapsing allied phalanx "trampled each other" in their very eagerness to escape the dreaded red-cloaked spearmen. An entire corpus of passages in Greek literature reflects the ancient view that the Spartan army—its look, discipline, skill, organization, and method—terrified any Greek hoplites unfortunate enough to regard it across the battlefield as it slowly walked to the killing zone. Just as it was felt a terrible thing to go against the German army in the twentieth century's two world wars, so too the Greek world recognized that it was deadly to square off against the Spartans.[35]

Like a methodical modern cyborg, the victorious Spartan center and right of the phalanx stopped, turned hard left, allowed most of the frightened and defeated Argive survivors to run away—after killing some 700 of them with their allies—and continued on laterally across the now broken battle line. All the tough talk about teaching the Spartans a lesson like Pylos had vanished in the reality of having to face such unrelenting killers on their terms. Once more silently walking en masse, the Similars sought to rendezvous head-on with the enemy's other wing of Mantineans and allies, over a half mile away.

For a brief moment these Argives and Mantineans were relaxed and ebullient that they had driven off the weaker Scirtae and freed helots before them. Fools! Their transitory sense of victory only further incited the approaching Spartans, who, as if stung by a bothersome pest, now unleashed their remaining fury on these men, planning to cut them apart without mercy. Little did the victorious Argives and Mantineans know that for a few minutes a few thousand men had almost had in their power the ability to reverse the entire course of the Peloponnesian War, a brief window of opportunity to accomplish what all the raiding, siegecraft, and trireme war of the last decade could not. That unforgiving moment was lost almost as quickly as it arose.

The only hitch in the final Spartan battle plan to finish off the coalition had occurred during the initial few minutes. The outmanned Scirtae on the left had been outflanked by the Argives and Mantineans. As Peloponnesian companies from the middle of the line drifted leftward to form a buttress against the surging enemy right, for a moment a dangerous gap opened in the Spartan lines. King Agis ordered two companies on the victorious right to disengage and head over to the hemorrhaging left. Both Spartan officers refused such an unparalleled order—and were later exiled on charges of insubordination arising from alleged cowardice—on the logic that the reckless enemy would not capitalize on their temporary victory and hit the Spartans on their vulnerable left sides, but rather first plunder and chase the defeated. Thus, soon enough the Argives and Mantineans would find themselves vulnerable and targeted by the elite Spartan right, once it polished off the enemy and turned to deal with these unsuspecting allies.

If hoplite battle was a story of each right wing winning as its left lost, then total victory was determined only by a second phase of the battle—by how quickly and effectively the triumphant right could make a hard left and hit its counterpart in the flank. Sometimes such a collision could lead to only more death and stalemate as the two best wings slammed head-on and found their adversaries a different sort of folk from the inferior troops whom they had each just routed. Unfortunately for the allies, that did not happen here, and the second Spartan collision proved almost as deadly for the coalition as the first. At Mantinea, Sparta won the second phase of the battle and with it obtained victory as it blasted apart the Argives and Mantineans before they knew what hit them. For professionals who so rarely had the opportunity to put their long training into practice, the Spartan hoplites at Mantinea killed as if it were second nature.

Most of the once victorious 200 Mantineans who were now caught and killed by the Spartans were buried in the soil where they had been born and had worked. For centuries they remained in obscurity, until a few decades ago American archaeologists found a stone inscription embedded in one of the surrounding abandoned houses. It may well record a partial casualty list of these Mantinean dead of some twenty-four hundred years past. Who were these hoplites with names like Eutelion and Epaines, and where on the battlefield did they die? Modern readers of epigraphy have no idea what Glausidas and Mnasias did in their last minutes. But they and dozens of others at least live on as names in stone because they died in glory rather than perished old and in obscurity—and so were commemorated on heroes' lists that ended up over the ages as thresholds and windowsills for today's similarly struggling farmers in the same plain of Mantinea.[36]

Thucydides himself probably sat in these hills and wrote what he saw, with a bird's-eye view of the killing as it unfolded below. His eyewitness description of the great fight of 418 remains the ancient world's most detailed and informative battle narrative, ending with his dry assessment that here transpired "the greatest battle that had occurred for a very long while among the Hellenes." By "greatest" Thucydides apparently did not mean size. More soldiers were likely present seven years earlier at Delium. Thucydides instead implied that for once the outcome of a single battle might have determined an entire conflict, inasmuch as Sparta at last got her long-hoped-for hoplite clash against most of her enemies.[37]

Yet there is another Mantinea that transcends tactics, strategy, and politics, a story of accidents, brutality, and human fickleness. Alcibiades' intrigue prompted the battle. But other Athenian generals, not he, fought and died here, among them Laches, the eponymous interlocutor of a Platonic dialogue, who was stabbed in the back as he ran away. Years earlier the same Laches had taken off from Delium; this time he was just as nervous but not so lucky. The Spartan king Agis, deemed incompetent or worse, had no belly to fight at Mantinea, and so twice backed his army out of the valley in the week before the battle. But fight he finally did and won the greatest single-day Spartan victory of the Peloponnesian War—ensuring that Sparta would at least not lose its struggle with Athens and that he would conduct a successful war against Athens in the decade to come.

The Anatomy of Battle

WHEN THE SPARTANS invaded the plain of Mantinea to break up the nascent democratic alliance of rebellious Peloponnesian states, they faced a coalition enemy army of radically variant composition. That group of 1,000 elite Argives, who trained at public expense and were mostly oligarchic, were ostensibly to serve as crack troops on the coalition's right. They, along with the Mantineans, had initially broken through the weak Spartan left, where a gap had opened between it and the center. But then the allies had foolishly paused to plunder the baggage train and had not continued spearing the Spartan center from the rear. Had they pressed home their attacks against the backs of King Agis' elite, the Spartans may well have lost the battle and the hundreds of Athenians and Argives would probably have been saved over on the left. Either the chance of plunder or the sheer fear of meeting Spartiates—even from the rear—explains their fatal hesitation. Clearly, allies on the same side of the battle line did not always work in concert.

Such leniency accorded a trapped adversary was soon reciprocated. The

Spartans on the right and center blew apart the regular Argive army and slew hundreds. Then for some reason when they swung over and turned their attention to the victorious Mantineans, they left the retreating 1,000 Argive elite—the real spearhead of the enemy coalition—alone. The suspicion immediately arose that the Spartans were looking past the battle and plotting for a return of a docile oligarchic Argos. Such a reconstituted conservative ally later would need men like the 1,000 elite to keep democratic firebrands at bay. In contrast, the more hoplites killed from Mantinea the better, to teach them the wages of democratizing against fellow Peloponnesians.

What about those equally defeated Athenians on the allied left? The Spartans killed only 200 of them, allowing the other 800 to flee. After all, the two states were officially still at peace. So it made no sense to annihilate Athenians, especially when a moderate board of generals at Athens had already chosen not to send a full force to Mantinea, several thousand additional hoplites that might well have spelled defeat for the Spartans.[38]

In coalition warfare in which several allied city-states fought alongside one another, who and what determined which phalanx fought where, either on the esteemed right, where there was little danger, or the inglorious left, where peril was greatest? Usually the honored right slots were given either to the host poleis—the Tegeans and Mantineans, respectively, in 418—or to the strongest and most numerous force, usually Thebes, Athens, or Sparta. In response, allies usually resented the fact that they had followed the lead of such larger city-states only to end up fighting the strongest adversaries as their supposed betters over on the right wing faced the enemy's weakest troops.

The later tactical breakthrough of the general Epaminondas at the battle of Leuctra in 371 was not merely that he put his best on the left to a depth of 50 shields to ensure a slugfest with the Spartan elite right, but that by doing so he ensured to his own allies—and Sparta's confederates across the battlefield as well—that neither weaker side would have to face their betters and play the roles of sacrificial lambs. The next winter Epaminondas invaded Laconia with a unified army and encountered Peloponnesian states that appreciated his past magnanimity and were now eager to join him. How odd that the basic idea that a leader should bear the greatest risk in battle by putting his men on the left of the phalanx waited until the twilight of the hoplite age.

Normally, however, because such alliances were often shifting and predicated on internal political upheavals—various factions installing democratic government one day, oligarchy the next—there was constant suspicion within a coalition army. Sometimes as much enmity arose along as across the battle line. At Delium, remember, the Boeotian confederation was racked by internal strife among its several member city-states. The Theban hegemons especially distrusted their neighbors the Thespians. It was probably out of enmity that Pagondas and his generals placed the suspect Thespians directly across from the Athenian right wing, perhaps in hopes that they would either fight well and hold off Hippocrates or be annihilated in the attempt.

As the battle unfolded, the Thebans got both their wishes. The Thespians were almost obliterated and yet kept back the Athenian elite until reserves could arrive to stabilize the wing even as Pagondas shattered the Athenian left. The result of such sacrifice was that there were at least 300 Thespians killed at Delium, perhaps out of an original contingent that numbered 600 to 700.

What were the ramifications of the fatalities at Delium: *cui bono?* Almost 50 percent of the Thespians present at the battle were killed in an hour or so. Such catastrophic losses meant that a third of *all* the small farmers at Thespiae were now dead. Of the roughly 7,000 Boeotian hoplites present at the battle, perhaps 60 percent of the dead came from those that made up 10 percent of the army.

There were immediate consequences to such one-sided sacrifices. Thucydides reports that a few months after Delium, in summer 423, "The Thebans destroyed the walls of the Thespians, on the allegation of pro-Athenian sympathies. They had always wished to do this, but now they found an easy opportunity since the flower of the Thespians had been annihilated in the battle against the Athenians." Thespiae, it should be noted, had suffered the same fate when its hoplite army had been wiped out at Thermopylae a half century earlier, and would again lose nearly its entire small army at Nemea (394), thirty years after Delium.[39]

Hoplite Fumes

AFTER THE BATTLE of Mantinea, the allies of Athens never again fought the Spartans in pitched battle. In a mere hour or so, the Spartans and their allies had killed at least 1,100 of the democratic coalition at a cost of only 300 Peloponnesians. Like the battle of Delium, a supposedly anachronistic way of fighting had settled an entire theater of war for the duration of the conflict. For the final fourteen years of fighting, there was only one more traditional hoplite battle—a small skirmish between the Athenians and Syracusans in Sicily. By 413 Sparta began to develop a serious fleet and to build permanent fortifications in Attica, giving up the old pipe dream that any army would meet its own in battle.

The hoplite battle outside the walls of Syracuse (415) did not involve all the combatants of the Sicilian campaign, and the Athenians' victory did nothing to prevent their eventual defeat. The Athenians formed in almost the same way they had three years earlier at Mantinea: Argives and crack Mantineans on the right, Athenians in the center with assorted allies on the left. But this time the Athenians and their allies grew confident because they were facing amateurish Syracusans, not deadly Spartans.

The fight once more revealed the usual chain of events. Confusion was evident at the very beginning. The Syracusans, like the Athenians at Delium, were surprised at the sudden attack. Thunder and rain panicked the less experienced Sicilian defenders. After a fierce struggle, the battle was, as was customary, won on the right, where the Argives and Mantineans scattered the enemy. Cavalry no longer protected just the flanks, but played an integral role both in the pursuit and defense of the defeated.

The small battle was similar to the earlier engagement at Solygia, even down to the number of dead: 260 Sicilians, a little more than 50 Athenian and allied fatalities. But just as earlier the seaborne Athenian hoplites, with 300 horsemen, had won a tactical victory over the Corinthians but been unable to translate such battle success to strategic advantage, so too in 415 the Athenians won a small battle but could not press their advantage. In short, hoplite fighting in such small numbers had little effect on the strategic goal of their campaign: the capitulation of Syracuse.[40]

If during the Peloponnesian War cities were increasingly often protected behind strong stone walls, and if they weighed carefully the wisdom of committing their entire armies to old-style collisions against either numerically superior or more experienced phalanxes, then naturally fighting would be redirected against the entire urban community itself. Moreover, since the two most-feared armies of the age—those of Sparta and Thebes—were allied, what army would be so foolish to fight either and thereby guarantee its own destruction?

Yet if there was a dearth of hoplite battle in the Peloponnesian War, there were instead attacks on cities in a manner unprecedented in earlier Greek history. Each side soon ignored the old idea that courage should determine victory, but instead looked to innovation, capital, and sheer manpower to storm the strongholds of their adversaries. Few, if any, Greeks were executed or enslaved in the aftermath of the hoplite battles at Mantinea or Delium. Tens of thousands most surely would be when war turned to the cities.

CHAPTER 6

WALLS

SIEGES (431–415)

Plataean Nightmare

SOMETIMES THE SIEGES of small towns and cities that have little strategic significance—a Guernica or Sarajevo—become emblematic of both the senselessness and the barbarity of war by the fact of their deliberate destruction and the inability or unwillingness of others to save them. So it was with the neutral hamlet of Plataea, which slowly perished in a series of death throes.

Plataea's eventual capture made very little difference in the larger calculus of the conflict, even though it ostensibly guarded a key pass over the mountains to Attica, and might be an obstacle to any Boeotian army that thought about invading Attica in force from the northwest. As the town died, Athenians fifty miles away and mostly oblivious to its plight died in droves from a mysterious disease, while Spartans sought to cut down olive trees and burn houses in Attica. Yet throughout its four-year ordeal, the on-again, off-again siege to take this small Boeotian hamlet illustrated the multifaceted ways that the classical Greeks assaulted and defended fortified cities. In that sense, the death of Plataea won the attention of Thucydides, who was fascinated by the misplaced scientific genius of both the attackers and the attacked, and saw the strategically unimportant city's fate as emblematic of the savagery of the war at large.

Today the site is little more than a few stone foundations, coupled with the traces of the circuit walls and towers—most likely the remains of the rebuilt fourth-century town that grew up on the ruins of its fifth-century predecessor. A new paved road, in fact, goes right through what remains of ancient Plataea, almost exactly where twenty-five hundred years ago the Thebans and Spartans so desperately tried to break in. The modern visitor to Plataea rarely sees a single tourist. This solitude is true of most of the killing grounds that dot the Boeotian countryside and were once so famous in Greek literature: nearby Delium (vacation homes now encroach on the landscape where Socrates backpedaled out of battle), Leuctra (a quiet grain field and irrigation ditch mark the spot where Epaminondas crushed the Spartan army), and Chaeronea (now a nondescript orchard where Philip and his teenaged son destroyed Greek liberty).

The fortified city's end began in peacetime on a late March night in 431, seven months after the Spartans had officially declared the peace with Athens broken, and yet seventy days before they and their allies crossed the Athenian border. The Peloponnesian War ostensibly pitted Athens against Sparta, but its precursors were Corinthian and Theban attacks against the Corcyraean and Plataean allies of Athens.[1]

About 300 prominent Thebans had secretly made their way to Plataea along the gently rising eight-mile road from Thebes during a rainy cold night. Their oligarchic ringleaders had counted on kindred reactionaries inside the border city to open the gates, since it would have been impossible to storm the walled community by day. Buoyed by the surprise arrival of a foreign force inside the walls, the Plataean zealots could then round up their sleeping democratic opponents, kill their ringleaders, and hand the city over to Thebes. Or so the right-wing conspiracists thought.

Nothing is worse than for a state to have nearby enemies and distant friends —as the lonely experience of Armenia, Cuba, Taiwan, and Tibet attests. Adversaries loom daily on the horizon; far-off allies often pledge support that they cannot really provide, thereby ensuring that their friendship is as costly as it is undependable. The city of Plataea—like poor Poland squeezed between Germany and Russia—had the misfortune of resting on the border of powerful and hostile Thebes while miles away from stronger and friendly Athens.

In fact, for much of the latter fifth century the Plataeans owed their independence from Thebes' Boeotian Confederacy not to tangible Athenian military assistance or its strategic location on the main road into Attica. Instead, the backward state of Greek siegecraft meant that the city's impressive stone walls could still guarantee it autonomy from the entire Boeotian Confederacy—despite the latter's aggregate population of at least 100,000 people and nearly one thousand square miles of territory.

The advantages in the age-old battle between offense and defense lay with the masons and stonecutters, whose stout ashlar courses, towers, and crenellations, and reinforced wooden gates could withstand the ram and the hand-propelled missile. In this age before the torsion catapult and movable artillery —which in the postwar era to come could hurl stones over 150 pounds up to three hundred yards distant—patience, treachery, hunger, and disease were the better assets of the besiegers. The exceptions during the Peloponnesian War when walls were breached are instructive: Torone, Lecythus, and Mycalessus were all stormed precisely because their walls were said to be in a state of disrepair.

Athens was an old enemy of Plataea's immediate neighbors, the Boeotians. It was no accident, for example, that much of the incest, patricide, and civil strife of the classical Athenian stage—involving Oedipus, Antigone, Creon, Teiresias, Pentheus, and the Bacchae—was situated in or near Thebes, Plataea's contemporary adversary and the chief city of Boeotia. Nearly thirty years before Plataea's destruction, Athens had once subdued Boeotia, and for over a decade had reestablished it as a friendly and democratic client state. But when the Athenians in turn were defeated in 447 at the battle of Coronea, and then mostly kept to their own side of Mount Kithairon, Plataea was once more left alone as an isolated vestige of hated Athenian imperialism. Consequently, the Boeotians, during the increasing tensions of 431, preempted the Spartans and sought to win over or finish off Plataea in a cheap victory before the Athenians realized that they were even at war.

Once the Theban advance party got inside and made its way to the public square, everything suddenly went wrong. Their rightist Plataean co-conspirators wanted to kill all the democrats immediately. The more sober Theban invaders instead preferred to awaken the city. By virtue of their unexpected presence they would shock the people into accepting a forceful and peaceful inclusion into the Boeotian Confederacy. Yet it was not a wise thing for right-wing insurrectionists to call for conciliation in the midst of their own nighttime raid on a much larger democratic citizenry—especially when there were no more than 300 of them to bully the opposition.

At first, the "shock and awe" tactics of the small party of invaders seemed to work. The stunned Plataeans were ostensibly pondering the terms. Yet in their ad hoc negotiations the sleepy democrats very quickly awoke to two surprising facts: there were not many Thebans, and there were even fewer of their own traitors who had invited in the foreigners. Within a few minutes they quietly retreated to their homes and plotted a counterassault. Soon dozens began burrowing through the common walls of their dwellings—Greek houses were made of mud brick without reinforcing studs and often had common partitions. Unseen, the resourceful democrats assembled to devise as best they could a sudden counterresponse. In no time they were barricading the streets and charging out en masse to confront the shocked and vastly outnumbered Thebans.

The attackers became the attacked. Everything now turned against this tiny band of Theban interlopers, who, after all, were soaked, tired, and hungry. It was a black night, stormy, without much of a moon: good for sneaking in—terrible for finding a way out. The rain and mud increased the newcomers' sense of disorientation, but then none of the foreigners knew their way back out of the winding streets anyway.

In a frenzied retreat the Thebans got lost searching for the main gate, through which they had originally entered; it was now mysteriously jammed closed. The 300 Thebans immediately broke into scattered parties. Some tried to climb over the walls—and then mostly perished or were disabled in the subsequent fall of some twenty to thirty feet onto the rocky ground. Others got trapped in dead-end streets and were butchered by their pursuers. Still more were captured hiding in buildings. In a war to decide the future of the Greek world, this preemptive strike was a particularly inglorious beginning.

Shared Barbarism

THE GIDDY PLATAEANS quickly sent out heralds to abort another and far larger supporting enemy force that was now arriving as planned in front of the city. After battling the rain and a swollen river, the Theban relief columns were shocked to find the city barred. Worse still, a Plataean envoy appeared from the darkness warning them to retreat without molesting any people and property outside the walls; otherwise the summary execution of all their kindred attackers now captured inside the walls would follow. On the first night of the fighting, the Plataeans—not known as a particularly savage bunch—would threaten, and soon carry out, the execution of captives. When the Plataeans got word to Athens of their plight, the first thing the Athenians did was to round up Boeotians residing in or visiting Attica, purportedly to use them as bargaining chips in the war that would inevitably follow from the night attack on Plataea.

Such immediate resort to hostage taking—six years later the Athenians would threaten a similar immediate execution of 120 elite Spartiates should the Peloponnesian army again invade Attica—suggests that the Peloponnesian War was a scab that was torn off, revealing preexisting and deep festering wounds of a half century prior. Scholars who have catalogued all the major massacres documented in our literary sources during the fifth century note the depressing trend: seven massacres in the long history of fighting before the outbreak of the war and some twenty-four near the beginning and throughout the three-decade-long conflict.[2]

After rounding up Boeotians, the Athenians responded by marching in and leaving a few garrison troops, aiding in the provisioning of the city, and arranging the evacuation of most of the Plataean women, children, and disabled to Attica. Having recovered from their recent nightmarish experience with treachery, murder, and broken oaths, some 480 Plataeans and a few Athenians in the city braced for the inevitable counterassault.

They had a long wait. A surprised Sparta had prior concerns, and instead would soon find itself busy for two seasons of campaigning in Attica before the outbreak of the plague. It is unclear what went on inside Plataea for the next twenty-four months, other than the fact that Thebes apparently could or would not begin a full-fledged siege. Apparently the city was more a ghost town of adult males than a real community, as the tiny skeleton garrison kept watch for an assault that mysteriously did not come. A few rural Plataeans may have drifted back to their farms, making private alliances with the Boeotians who now surrounded the countryside and patrolled the fields. Plataea, in fact, was becoming a matter of prestige for both sides: the Spartans could not afford to allow their Theban allies to fail to polish off a small renegade city, while Athens for the security of its own empire belatedly realized that it was critical to prove that it would pay any price to help save its most proximate loyal ally. That being said, both sides had their hands full a few months later when the real war broke out.

It was not until the beginning of the third year of the war—May 429—that at last the Peloponnesians went into Boeotia to help their Theban allies deal with the festering Plataean sore. Yet even when Archidamus led his massive force up to the walls, he offered two startling last-minute proposals: those Plataeans still holed up in the half-deserted city could either immediately announce their neutrality, let in his garrison, and thereby stay put—and alive. Or, if still distrustful of their Theban neighbors, they might leave the city in safety on the guarantee that their property and land would be looked after under Spartan auspices—with full rent, no less, for a decade or until the war ended.

The Spartans, with a poor reputation for siegecraft, were not exactly eager for a protracted siege, one that even if successful would be costly and beneficial mostly to their mercurial Theban allies, who had acted unilaterally and without prior consultation. Archidamus also remembered the symbolic stakes involved, namely the once gallant role of the Plataeans in the prior Persian Wars (490,

480–479). He was right then encamped near the hallowed battlefield where the Persian army a half century earlier had been crushed by the grandfathers of those now both inside and outside the walls.

The pious Spartan king also had a problem of sorts with ancestral oaths, well known to all the Greeks, that had been pledged to protect the autonomy of Plataea, now by general consent the shared memorial of the Hellenes. The rolling plains around Plataea had, over some fifty years, become enshrined as the Omaha Beach of the Greek world, a hallowed battleground and Panhellenic graveyard where squabbling allies in better times had once fought, died, and been buried together to push back autocracy. It was one of the crimes of the Peloponnesian War that many of the consecrated places of the Persian Wars where Greeks had earlier united to preserve their freedom were slowly to be desecrated by internecine bloodshed: first the battlefield of Plataea; then another evacuation of Attica, but from a Greek rather than a Persian invader; and soon Spartan raiding in the seas off holy Salamis.

The Plataeans asked for, and got from Archidamus, more time, and then immediately once more sent emissaries to Athens to explain their new dilemma. Themselves surrounded by Spartans, the Plataeans also had worries over many of their dependents who for over two years had been residing inside Athens, some as guests, perhaps most like quasi hostages in the plague-infested city. When they received word that real Athenian help was at last on the way to face the latest threat, the Plataeans felt emboldened enough to reject Archidamus' final offer. They may have recalled that the Spartans enjoyed a poor reputation for storming cities and had failed two years earlier to capture even the small Attic garrison at Oenoë. The Plataeans now braced for the siege.

If it had been a terrible error two years earlier for the Plataeans to break sworn oaths and execute the Theban saboteurs, it was even more disastrous to place the city's future under the protection of an ally on the wrong side of Mount Kithairon—one at war, beset by a terrible plague, and no more likely to defend a distant and tiny foreign community than it would protect its own farmers and farmland in front of its own walls. In short, the Plataeans on the ramparts seemed to be trapped inside their circuit by the Spartans, even as their families were residing as detainees among their "friends," the Athenians.

Misplaced Genius

THE SECOND ASSAULT on Plataea that now followed proved to be the most remarkable example of the multifarious arts of Greek siegecraft during the entire

Peloponnesian War. The ferocious attack and spirited defense warranted Thucydides' full attention, in part because of its savagery and the ingenuity of the combatants. Within a day Archidamus had encircled the entire city with a makeshift wooden palisade, piled together from the limbs of fruit trees that his ravagers were only too happy to cut down. The circumference of Plataea's walls was only fifteen hundred yards. The Peloponnesian army that arrived in Boeotia probably averaged somewhere around 30,000 combatants, in addition to various servants and auxiliaries. That meant that there were easily over 20 men responsible for each yard of circumvallation, explaining why they finished their first ad hoc blockading fence in about twenty-four hours. Clearly this was a far easier task than ravaging Attica. Unlike the later Athenians on Syracuse, the Spartans grasped that the key to any successful siege was to throw up some sort of makeshift wall immediately, so that from the outset food and water might be denied the enemy. That way they could start the countdown to starvation well before more elaborate and time-consuming permanent walls of encirclement could follow.

Convinced that the garrison was trapped, an impatient Archidamus now turned to building an earthen ramp that might serve as a road right over the top of the battlement. The work on the sloped mound—so famous in the Old Testament sieges and later at the horrific Roman encirclement of Masada—may have been the only instance of such a technique in the entire Peloponnesian War. Yet the Greeks were not unused to this sort of earthen construction. For centuries they had rolled up the column drums and architraves of their archaic temples by fashioning temporary earthen inclines. But whether in peace or war, such construction remained a time-consuming task that took even Archidamus' huge force some seventy days, or almost double the time he would usually have spent ravaging in Attica.

Immediately the reaction and counterreaction of the combatants reached a fevered pitch, inasmuch as the Plataeans were fighting for their very existence, the Spartans against time itself. Much of King Archidamus' army was made up of Peloponnesian yeomen who needed to get home and attend to their own summer harvests. Moreover, the besiegers would have quickly devoured most of their provisions and soon found the wheat fields of Plataea insufficient to feed such a horde—itself probably now larger than almost any city in Boeotia.

As the ramp grew, the Spartans added reinforcing logs and stones to keep the earth compact and stable. In response, the Plataeans tried to increase the height of their own wall faster than the ramp could reach them, by adding additional courses of mud brick faced with timber. Just in case the more numerous enemy force might win the race for the top, the Plataeans also secretly bored holes through their own lower walls, right into the foundations of the ramp, and began stealthily removing earth—thus insidiously sinking the entire mound nearly as fast as it was rising! The Spartans countered by stopping up the breaches with makeshift clay-and-reed plugs. So it went, back and forth, on and on, as challenge met response, the Greeks from dozens of city-states now using the same energy and genius that had crafted magnificent temples and created classical literature to fight over the tiny wall of a tiny town.

To cover their bets in case the Spartan mound still rose faster than it could be undermined or outwalled, the Plataeans also erected a new inner semicircular fortification not far to the rear of the old circuit. If the mound went over the original fortifications, the Spartans who stormed in now might be surprised by a completely new rampart, and thus would be forced to start the siege over again.

But the Spartans were just as adaptable. For the first few weeks, at least, they had the advantages of steady supplies of food and provisions, and far more men working to break in than those laboring to keep them out. They now began bringing to bear several crudely constructed siege machines—large timber battering rams, most likely on wheels—and not only pushing one of them up the ramp but banging others against the less-well-defended portions of the fortifications.

Not to be outdone, the desperate Plataeans—they had been engaged nonstop in tunneling, mining, and raising an entirely new wall—began to fashion even stranger counterweapons. Someone thought up the idea of a cranelike device of enormous rope nooses that could be lowered to catch the rams; so the besiegers' machines were snagged, raised, and then dropped. In case the ram heads were not shattered from the concussion, the Plataeans also crafted twin poles to which heavy beams were chained. The contraption was then extended over the besiegers, carefully aimed, and the timber dropped down to snap the heads off the rams.

Archidamus was utterly exasperated by such pesky ingenuity. Plataea's skeleton garrison of 600—480 combatants and 120 women cooks—had held off his entire army for weeks. These stubborn defenders showed no signs of either starvation or civil dissension, the usual indications that capitulation was imminent. If ravaging had proved futile in either starving Athenians or prompting battle, siegecraft was proving even more maddening.

He next turned to fire. His engineers sought to burn down the city they could not storm. Brush was dropped from the mound and piled in next to the wall. More was thrown over the ramparts. Pitch and sulfur were mixed, poured on the piles, and then lighted. If the fire did not weaken the mud bricks and their wooden supports, then perhaps the fumes would sicken the garrison. Thucydides believed that much of the city would have been engulfed had the winds been favorable and the weather stayed dry.

Instead, the breezes remained calm and sudden rains came. The fires burned out without damaging the stone walls and their timber braces or the wooden supports of the houses inside. Nor did the smoke from such a sulfurous mixture incapacitate the defenders—if that was also an intent of the conflagration.

With the failure of the fire attack, coupled with the discovery of the Plataeans' new secondary wall, the Spartans felt stymied. It was now late September. They had been stuck at Plataea for over three months with nothing to show for their efforts in a backward hamlet. If anything, Archidamus was proving to neutral Greek city-states that the Spartan reputation for incompetence in taking fortified positions was largely justified—a disastrous development for a state that exercised sometimes tenuous authority over a number of fortified cities in the Peloponnese.

Allied troops were restless. Archidamus finally realized this when he conceded that he could neither take nor afford to abandon the city. So he compromised somewhat, allowing most of his hoplites to trudge back home to the Peloponnese, as he marshaled some others to build a more permanent wall of circumvallation to augment the temporary one of local fruit trees. Now his men set to work digging trenches on both sides of a circuit of twin walls. That way they sought not only to extend the height of the ramparts and create protective moats but also to provide mud bricks for their construction.

In fact, the Peloponnesians were building a curious circumvallation like nothing seen before in the history of Greek siegecraft—albeit on a smaller scale, perhaps as sophisticated as Julius Caesar's twin palisades some four hundred years later at the siege of Gallic Alesia. Two parallel walls rose about sixteen feet apart, roofed in between, and outfitted not only with towers, battlements, and gates but also with interior quarters for the garrison. While the parapets must have been somewhat flimsy—some escaping Plataeans would later knock down a section as they scaled the wall—the besiegers would still have good shelter for the winter, while remaining protected from sorties from both the city and the surrounding countryside.

To take the city, in other words, Archidamus had essentially built an alternative city in the middle of nowhere. His fieldworks were double the circumference of Plataea's own walls and nearly as elaborate. When he finished, he further divided his army and left behind a garrison, splitting the responsibility for the strangulation of Plataea between Peloponnesian forces and local Boeotians. To a neutral outsider, all this labor and capital expended on a mere hamlet was nonsense; but to the Peloponnesians and their Boeotian allies, Plataea had now become a symbol of both their intent and their ability to wage a murderous war against the Athenian empire.

Respite

THE COURAGE AND genius of the Plataeans for a time won out. But they soon realized that with the erection of this curious barrier they could neither leave nor be rescued. Still, the stalemate now persisted for yet another year and a half after Archidamus departed—or about forty-five months since the initial night attack by the Thebans. In the meantime, Pericles had died; Attica had been ravaged twice; the plague had killed over one-quarter of the Athenian population—and 600 defenders of Plataea went about surviving in a ghost town on ever-dwindling stored provisions, long abandoned by most of its inhabitants and mostly forgotten by their beleaguered and disease-ridden Athenian would-be protectors across the mountain.

In 429 the citizens of the northern state of Potidaea had finally given up their city to Athenian besiegers, an ongoing blockade that mirrored the contemporaneous siege far to the south at Plataea. The surviving Potidaeans were starved out, and allowed to leave with the clothes on their backs and a tiny amount of road money to see them on their exodus. At the time, the harsh treatment accorded the Potidaeans—captives after hoplite battle were usually exchanged or ransomed, and nearby civilians left alone—must have outraged the Greek world, the ripples of indignation lapping all the way to the ongoing assault at Plataea. If the fate of Potidaea steeled the Spartans to persevere against the Plataeans, they should have remembered that the Athenians had at least not executed those who surrendered. But in the future, with the fate of the soon-to-be murdered Plataeans also on their mind, the Athenians would rarely show any mercy at all.

The last phase of Plataea's long ordeal came to an end through slow starvation. But first, in December 428, almost four years after the Thebans had burst into the city, the beleaguered garrison voted for breakout. About 220 of the most audacious snuck out of the city—on a night as rainy and moonless as the initial Theban assault years earlier. The fugitives scaled the twin counterwalls with specially measured and constructed ladders, killed some of the occupying garrison, and escaped to Athens. The breakout was brilliantly planned, inasmuch as the ladders' height had been specially calibrated to specification by counting the courses of bricks in the enemy counterfortifications. And the escapers had waited for a dark wintry night, even as the remaining garrison in Plataea provided diversions.

Each man went out with one foot bare to ensure good stability in the mud. Only a single Plataean was captured and a few others turned back; in all 212 Plataean men, over a third of the skeleton garrison, escaped. While their departure meant less mouths for the city's dwindling food supplies, it also left the desperate defenders with almost no ability to continue the watch on the ramparts, in theory a mere 267 men and women of dubious health to guard some fifteen hundred yards of parapet.

Each defender would now be responsible for over five yards of the circuit walls. The Spartans could take the skeleton garrison almost anytime they wanted, although they were still wary about storming the ancestral home of such an honored people. Thus, rather than go over the walls, they felt it wiser that the few Plataeans left sue for peace and surrender, inasmuch as they could later claim in any peace negotiation that the city had not been stormed and needed to be given back, rather in the manner of a convert that had voluntarily joined the Spartans and their allies.

At the very time the end was nearing for the trapped Plataeans, their Athenian benefactors a mere fifty miles away ignored the besieged and were instead concluding yet another successful assault of their own against the rebellious Mytileneans on Lesbos, across the Aegean. After the capitulation of the city, the Athenians executed over 1,000 of the ringleaders of the revolt and turned all their confiscated land over to Athenian settlers. Among the captives was a Spartan expeditionary officer, Salaethus, who asked to be spared on the condition that at the eleventh hour he could use his influence to call off his comrades' siege at Plataea. But the obdurate Athenians were more interested in killing an elite Spartan than in saving a few Plataeans who had foolishly taken them at their word of protection some four years earlier, during a time of peace when Pericles was alive and the plague unknown.

So Plataea fell shortly after the Athenians razed Mytilene, during the summer of 427, at the start of the fifth year of the war that had begun so much earlier with the Theban assault. The emaciated defenders left behind finally gave up, unable to meet one of the stronger Spartan probing attacks. Thucydides records the surrender negotiations, making special note of the poignant speech of the Plataean captives. They recited to the Spartans a litany of reasons why and how the entire calamity had begun years earlier when such a historically honorable people had been so unjustly attacked in a time of peace.

The Wages of Resistance

THE FURIOUS THEBANS demanded an opportunity to refute the captives as they insisted on collective death sentences. In the end the Spartans worried over the sheer embarrassment of it all, almost four years and thousands of man-hours wasted to capture a tiny garrison. Probably no more than a couple hundred men and women from the original defenders were still alive. Anger over their failure and the need to pacify the frustrated Thebans sealed the fate of the Plataeans.

The captives were asked once more a single question: had they done anything to help the Spartans in the present war? It was a silly inquiry: what chance had the Plataeans had to help either friend or foe while they were trapped inside their city for four years? When they each replied no, the adult males were executed on the spot. The women and children were sold into slavery.

Plataea itself, like Mytilene a few weeks earlier, was razed. The booty from its ruins was used to build a precinct to Hera, as if a symbolic act of piety could assuage the sins of invading a neutral city in a time of peace and executing the descendants of the heroes of the Persian Wars. The neighboring Boeotians, who had started it all by attacking sleeping civilians, rented out the surrounding farmland from the new Spartan owners, who desperately wanted some recompense for a costly fiasco that had gained them little strategic advantage. Thucydides ends the sad tale with the matter-of-fact statement "Such was the end of Plataea in the ninety-third year after she became an ally of Athens."[3]

The lengthy siege also fascinated the historian, who returned to the ongoing four-year saga of the garrison three times in his narrative. What can one learn from the poor Plataeans' debacle about the status of Greek siegecraft? First, it proved almost impossible to storm a walled city without artillery, movable towers, light-armed skirmishers on scaling ladders, and plentiful archers and missile troops. For all the impromptu ingenuity of the attackers, the Peloponnesians were the wrong type of besiegers, the majority of them clumsy hoplites, and they employed only primitive battering rams and covered sheds. The Plataean escapees, when lightly armed and equipped with ladders, proved more adept in going over the Spartans' elaborate double walls of circumvallation than the Spartans did in trying to break through the city's ramparts. Plataea's walls, like those of so many of the Greek city-states, seem to have been beefed up in the decades preceding the war on the assumption that the advantage in contemporary sieges was always with the defenders if they had strong stone ramparts.

Second, taking a city really meant starving the people inside. The only sure way to reduce a Greek garrison was through famine brought on by walling it off from both its own land and relief sorties from abroad. But a land power like the Peloponnesians was oddly ill-suited for such a task. Soldiers had their own harvest commitments back home. The moment an army arrived, the clock began ticking to determine whether the defenders or the attackers would first run out of food and water. The odds should have favored the besiegers. Yet their greater numbers, unfamiliarity with the local landscape, and worry about hostile relief forces could sometimes leave them as hungry, thirsty, and sick as those inside the city. In addition, in almost *no* case of any major siege, whether at Plataea, Mytilene, or Melos, did either Athens or Sparta commit sizable relief forces to save their respective beleaguered ideological allies. True, the Peloponnesians belatedly sent help to Syracuse, but only after a year of warring there, and more with the idea of hurting Athens than saving the Syracusans.

Sieges were ostensibly between conventional adversaries within and outside the walls. In fact, they were often precipitated by, and sometimes resolved through, the intrigue and treachery of zealots and foreign agents. The exorbitant expenses incurred at Plataea—most of the rural plunder had been carted off by the Boeotians and the vast majority of citizens had long ago left the city with their valuables—also had a catastrophic effect on the Spartans' willingness to engage further in such high-stakes intrigue. Plataea had cost much and, when taken, had given them back very little. Instead, as the war evolved sieges would increasingly become mostly a specialty of the Athenians, who were far better able to pay for them—and had far more subjects willing to revolt.

The Politics of Siegecraft

THE PELOPONNESIAN WAR, a supposed fight between the Athenian fleet and the Spartan hoplites, began with the siege of Plataea and ended almost three decades later with the blockade of Athens. In fact, even the precursors to this war involved sieges. The Corcyraeans surrounded the northwestern Greek city of Epidamnus, and the Athenians struck at Potidaea, as such naval powers sought to guarantee that subservient and tributary port cities stayed in line.

Attacking cities was not new in Greek warfare. It was as old as Troy and the mythical assault on Thebes by the seven Panhellenic heroes. Sieges were how the Athenian maritime empire was acquired and held at places as distant as Eion,

Sestos, and Samos. Yet the growing frequency of such long-term, elaborate blockades was also a result of the rising wealth of fifth-century Greece, which could afford such costly investments.[4]

Depending on how one defines a proper "siege"—whether a surrounded rural garrison is to be accorded the same status as an entire beleaguered municipality—there were probably at least twenty-one of them during the war, or almost one for every year of formal hostilities. Some were elaborate efforts against large cities like Potidaea, in northern Greece (431–429), or Syracuse (415–413), in Sicily, perhaps the largest state of the Greek-speaking world. Others involved smaller towns such as Plataea (431–427) and Melos (415). Sometimes sieges were little more than armies cutting off garrisons behind ad hoc fortifications, such as the Spartan attack on Oenoë (431) or the Theban assault on the sanctuary at Delium (424), both of which were full of soldiers rather than civilians.

The ubiquity of sieges cannot be appreciated by their mere numbers, but perhaps is far better indicated by the aggregate years invested by the combatants in besieging strongholds. For example, four years were spent at Plataea, three at Syracuse, two at Potidaea, and two at Scione. Most likely some city-state was under assault somewhere during almost every month of the Peloponnesian War, from Sicily in the west to Asia Minor far to the east, from northward regions of Byzantium to the southern Aegean. While her enemies were busy in the on-again, off-again operations against nearby Plataea, Athens was conducting far more extensive sieges at Potidaea and then Mytilene. With many more sieges than hoplite battles—twenty-one sieges versus two major hoplite battles—the practice of Greek warfare had changed almost overnight.

During some years of the war, numerous Greek cities and garrisons were under simultaneous assault. Between 424 and 423, the Athenians were blockading Megarian Nisaea, while up north they undertook a series of concurrent attacks on Torone, Mende, and Scione, even as the Boeotians were besieging the Athenian garrison at Delium and the Spartans stormed a fortress at Lecythus. In terms of overall battle casualties, while exact figures are few, during the war far more Greeks perished either at sea or attacking and defending cities than in infantry battle. Between 416 and 413, for example, the Athenians and their allies annihilated many of the male residents of Melos and Mycalessus, even as they lost nearly 45,000—many of them considered the best of the Athenian empire—in a vain effort to storm Syracuse. In fact, the greatest disasters in the history of the Athenian empire were due to the two colossal failures at Memphis, Egypt, before the war (454) and on Sicily, both failed sieges that may have together cost over 90,000 Athenian imperial soldiers. Add in the plague, and in a mere forty years the empire lost nearly 200,000 of its resident population as a direct result of warring apart from the traditional battlefield.

Some general trends during the war emerged from all of these bitterly contested assaults. First, most sieges were conducted by the Athenians. Although there were a few cases beside Oenoë and Plataea where the Spartans and their allies attacked smaller city-states and garrisons (more often at near the end of the war at Lecythus, Iasos, Naupaktos, and Cedreae), they very rarely tried to take major cities through formal assault. Something on the scale of the Athenian blockade of the port cities of Potidaea, Mytilene, Melos, or Syracuse was beyond the Spartans' expertise and resources, until they built a fleet with Persian money.[5] Yet at the very outbreak of the war, despite being completely incapable of conducting a siege against the walls of Athens or even a small rural Attic garrison at Oenoë, the Spartans showed some imagination at Plataea in fabricating a mound and some primitive rams and engines, before achieving capitulation by eventually starving the defenders out. So there is a better reason to explain why siegecraft during the Peloponnesian War was mostly an Athenian enterprise, and it involves the asymmetrical nature of the struggle itself.

For most of the war until its last decade, Sparta and its allies did not possess enough ships to patrol in force the Greek coast, much less the Aegean. Its ability to project power beyond the normal land routes was limited in comparison with that of Athens, which, in contrast, brought besiegers by sea to assault distant Potidaea, Mytilene, Minoa, Mende, Scione, Amphipolis, Melos, Syracuse, Chalcedon, and Byzantium, cities from Sicily to the Black Sea that were over a thousand miles apart.

Athens had displayed expertise in fortification with its vast circuit of walls surrounding its own city. Sparta, in contrast, had no ramparts; its port at Gythium was some thirty miles distant. A people that knows how to build battlements at home can better build or storm them abroad. Much of the Athenians' policy of walling besieged cities off from the sea was the reverse policy of their own construction of the Long Walls to the Piraeus, and so they were intimate with both the procedure and the psychological implications of having a fortified port.

The siege of Plataea was singular not merely because of its length and bizarre tactics but because there was nothing quite like it again, given that there were very few well-fortified inland city-states in southern or central Greece that were not already allies of the Spartans and Thebans. The great prizes in the Greek world—Syracuse, Athens, Corinth, Corcyra, Argos, Byzantium, Samos, and Mytilene—were either on the coast or connected to it by long walls. No state could attempt their capture without a large fleet that ensured naval superiority.

Unlike Sparta, in almost every case where siegecraft was called for, Athens assaulted its own rebellious tributary subject states, such as Potidaea and Mytilene. On rarer occasions, it sought to coerce neutrals, such as Melos or Syracuse, into the empire. Athens almost never conducted a large land invasion of Spartan, Corinthian, or Theban territory to carry on lengthy siege operations against an interior enemy city—impossible operations all, cases where its supply lines were untenable and its vast fleet of no use.

As the Athenians put it to the Melians in their famous dialogue in the fifth book of Thucydides' history, their chief worry was not really Sparta and its allies. Rather, the problem was Athens' own "subject peoples who might perhaps attack and defeat those who rule them." They further reminded the doomed Melians that it was precisely out of that fear of continuous revolts across the Aegean that they had sailed into Melos to set an example to any others entertaining such dangerous ideas of opposition to the "masters of the sea." In that context, by needs they had mastered the arts of siegecraft and boasted, "Never on a single occasion have the Athenians ever withdrawn from a siege due to the fear of any enemies," a brag that the ironic Thucydides was sure to emphasize on the eve of the disastrous failed siege in Sicily.[6]

Sieges—whether Sparta's successful attack on Plataea or Athens' ruination of Melos—were often not explicable in a traditional strategic calculus of cost versus benefits. After all, what did the possession of Plataea do for the Spartan cause? How was Athens made more secure, wealthier, or stronger by taking Melos? The rent from the farms of the Athenian colonists who settled in the surrounding countryside after the city fell could hardly have paid the cost of the long siege. Nor would the sale of captives into slavery recover the expenses of the besiegers. Instead, the efforts to storm recalcitrant cities seemed to confer enormous psychological implications on the reputation and competence of the two powers. Letting Plataea defiantly stand apart from Thebes or Mytilene boast of its independence was seen as a contagion that could weaken the entire system of alliances that had grown up after the Persian Wars.

As the war continued, a popular Athenian strategy was to preempt problem subjects. After the costly fiasco at Potidaea—by the outbreak of the conflict the siege there was well on the way to costing the Athenian besiegers nearly 2,000 talents (something like $1 billion in contemporary American purchasing power)—the Athenian fleet learned to use the iron hand quickly lest it get bogged down in expensive sieges. The most efficacious way, in other words, to conduct a siege may have been to tear down the walls of a neutral or friendly city in advance, on mere rumors that insurrection was brewing. In the case of the Potidaeans, the Athenians had asked them to pull down their fortifications rather than doing it themselves—and as a result became mired in the most expensive siege in classical Greek history.

In contrast, during the winter of 425 the Athenians made sure that they would have no more insurrections like that on Potidaea or Mytilene. Thus, the fleet sailed into nearby Chios and forced the islanders to dismantle their newly constructed walls on promises of no reprisals—a tough strategy that seemed to have precluded most trouble there for nearly two decades. The Thebans practiced the same preemption after the battle of Delium. Given the horrendous casualties taken by small Thespiae in the Boeotian victory over the Athenians, Thebans marched into the suspicious allied city and razed its fortifications merely on rumors of pro-Athenian sympathies. The last thing the Thebans needed was another expensive siege of a nearby neutral in the manner of recalcitrant Plataea, and so it was better to tear down the walls before the Thespians knew what hit them.[7]

The Holocausts

ASSAULTING CITIES IS the oldest, and often the most brutal, expression of warfare. The earliest Western literature begins with the biblical siege of Jericho and the Achaeans' attack on Troy. The most moving passages in Thucydides' entire history of the war—the Plataeans' pleas for mercy, the debate between Cleon and Diodotus over the fate of the Mytileneans, the Melian Dialogue, the butchery of the boys at Mycalessus, and the great siege at Syracuse—revolve around the assault on communities of men, women, and children when war came to the very doorstep of the Greek family. Indeed, Mycalessus proved horrific precisely because the Thracian mercenaries sought no real military objective other than the psychological terror of slaughtering children at school—the ancient version of the Chechnyan terrorist assault on the Russian school in Belsan during early September 2004, which shocked the modern world and confirmed Thucydides' prognosis that his history really was a possession for all time, inasmuch as human nature, as he saw, has remained constant across time and space.

There is something surrealistic about storming a city. Sieges are final, ultimate verdicts about not merely the fate of soldiers but of a very people. Noth-

ing is more chilling, for example, than the final hours of Constantinople—
10,000 people huddled under the dome of St. Sophia, praying in vain for the
angel of deliverance on the early afternoon of May, 29, 1453, as the sultan's
shock troops burst in to end for good the thousand-year culture of Byzantium.
In sieges, women and old men fight from the walls. Ad hoc genius is manifested
in countermeasures—history's array of missiles, flame, cranes, and flying roof
tiles—as the fate of thousands sometimes depends solely on their own collective intelligence and resolve. In the age of bombers, whose aerial weapons can
make walls superfluous, sieges might seem a thing of the past, until one recalls
that Leningrad and Stalingrad were two of the greatest and most costly sieges
of the ages.

Sieges also reflect a breakdown in the ability of soldiers to conduct war or,
rather, a failure of one side to offer resistance in the field and thereby to keep
the killing far distant from civilians and their homes. True, there are so-called
statutes of war; at least there were in the quieter times before the escalating
violence of the Peloponnesian War. The "laws of the Greeks," for example, assumed that upon the arrival of the enemy, besieged civilians in the ancient world
would usually be offered free passage out of their city, with the acknowledgment
that they must leave behind their property, their homes, and indeed their very
existences. Upon their refusal to submit, all bets were off, as if it suddenly became a moral act to kill adult males and enslave their womenfolk because they
either were not willing at the outset to give up or in the end could not protect
all that they had held dear.

What was the moral calculus in the mind of the defenders? They had only
four options once the enemy ringed their city: surrender, resistance from the
walls, counterattack with sorties, or escape. The Plataeans adopted all four
strategies at different times as their strength waxed and waned. During the initial Theban attack, the Plataeans rushed out and killed the intruders. Then they
refused terms for some four years. Half of the garrison broke out at night and
escaped. The rest finally capitulated and were either executed or enslaved.

What, then, was the degree of culpability of civilians inside the walls for
their own fates? If they did not actively fight on the ramparts, were they therefore considered noncombatants, and thus to be spared after capitulation or
simply executed by their peers as traitors as long as the walls held firm? Was
there a moral difference between supplying food for the defenders and actually
fighting from the parapets? Was it treason to offer no resistance, and did such
noninvolvement mean anything anyway once enemy soldiers poured into the
streets? Being besieged often had an ostensible effect of unifying the popula-

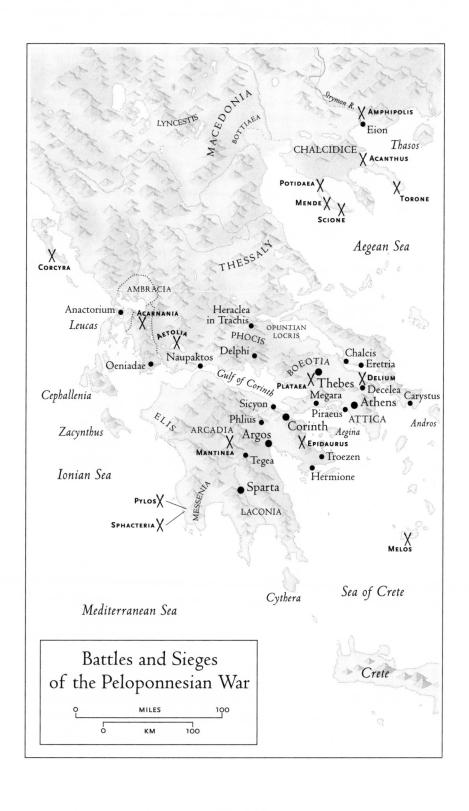

Battles and Sieges
of the Peloponnesian War

tion for better or for worse; since the victor might well apply collective punishment to the defeated, most inside the walls grasped that he must be resisted at all costs. For all the bickering at Athens, both Pericles and his successors were able to keep the population together as they watched ravagers from the walls, battled plague, and put up with overcrowding.

The ethical questions do not end there. Was a defending army morally culpable should it retreat back to its civilian base, as if deliberately to draw noncombatants into a war that it could not win on the field of battle? Or was it wise to shepherd soldiers inside ramparts rather than have them perish against overwhelming odds on the battlefield and so leave their cities defenseless, when instead they might otherwise have crafted a viable defense from the walls?

The Greeks were aware of all these contradictions and ambiguities, and assumed that there was rarely political unity even before they arrived at a city, and even less once the enemy's counterwalls rose and the pressure of hunger and disease raised tensions. Well before the Peloponnesian War armies had starved out towns and enslaved their citizens. Cities throughout the Greek world— Carystos (474), on the island of Euboea; Naxos (470), out in the Aegean; Mycenae (468), in the Argolid; the Aegean island of Thasos (465); the Boeotian town of Chaeronea (447); and Samos (440), off the coast of Ionia—that chose to resist the besiegers usually had their populations sold into slavery upon capitulation. On the very eve of the war the Corcyraeans had stormed Epidamnus, sold some of the population, and kept others as hostages—but had not executed the citizenry.[8]

A Harvest of Slaves

LINING UP AND murdering the surrendered adult Greek male population was still rare before the Peloponnesian War, and such slaughter became habitual only after the siege of Plataea. Then a discernible pattern emerged: free exit without one's property was offered to the besieged before the fighting started. After that window of choice closed, it was assumed that all guarantees were off, and death and enslavement loomed respectively for captured men and women. The fate of the vanquished, in short, belonged entirely to the victors—or as the dry, empirical Aristotle put it, "The law is a sort of pact under which the things conquered in war are said to belong to their conquerors." The playwright Euripides, who reflected contemporary events in the reworking of myths and produced his *Hecuba* in 425—two years after the brutal Athenian putdown of Mytilene—has Hecuba relate to the assembled Athenian audience the wretched fate of the defeated Trojan royal house: Hecuba enslaved, her daughter Polyxena sacrificed, Cassandra carried off as booty, Polydorus murdered, all following the death in battle of her sons Hector and Paris, and the execution of her husband, Priam.

"Look at me and examine carefully the evils I endure," Hecuba laments of her city's capture and her own enslavement. "I was once a ruler, but now am your slave. Once I had good sons, now I am old and childless. I am cityless, alone, the most wretched of mortals." Those in the audience who heard that were thinking of the poor Greeks of their own times, not mythical Trojans.[9]

Late in the war, as the tide of the conflict turned in their favor, Spartan generals sometimes announced that Peloponnesians did not believe in enslaving other Greeks. Yet such professed magnanimity was rarely intended to include Athenians. When Sparta sometimes released the vanquished allies of Athens, it was primarily for propaganda purposes and balanced against the singling out of Athenians for the special punishment of enslavement or death.[10]

Because ancient slavery was not based on the pseudoscience of genetic inferiority, all Greeks, like the royal Trojans Hecuba, Cassandra, and Andromache of myth, were in theory a city's fall away from servitude. The great supply of slave labor in the ancient Greek world was probably obtained through the storming of cities, a tactic that is eerily concomitant with the spread of chattel slavery itself in the seventh through fifth centuries.

It is hard to tell whether the Peloponnesian War resulted in a net increase or decrease in the number of Hellenic slaves, with so many cities stormed set against the number of freed slaves enrolled in armies and navies. For example, in contrast to those who were enslaved at places like Mytilene and Melos were the helots that were freed by Brasidas, far more who fled to safe zones like Pylos, Decelea, and Chios, and thousands emancipated to fight at battles like Arginusae. In any case, W. K. Pritchett once tallied all the instances of enslavement after battles and sieges during the Peloponnesian War as recorded in our literary sources. His incomplete list of some thirty-one instances still revealed a tally of several thousand Greeks who were sold into slavery. The Peloponnesian War proved the great example of human reversal in the history of classical Greece, as hundreds of thousands of former slaves were freed even as thousands more citizens were reduced to chattel status, a fact that in part explains the social chaos of the following century, when mercenaries replaced militias and postbellum disputes over property and citizenship dominated court proceedings. Fourth-century Greece also witnessed a surge of democratic frenzy, especially at Thebes and in the Peloponnese. And at Athens especially greater subsidies were given the poorer to participate in voting—a liberalization also reflective of the vast changes in political and social life during the war, in which slaves had became free and the free slaves.[11]

An Athenian Specialty

BESIDES PLATAEA, THERE were a variety of other sieges in the Peloponnesian War that ended not merely in defeat but in the complete annihilation of the inhabitants. In 423 the Athenians conducted a series of attacks against three towns in northern Greece—Mende, Torone, and Scione. All had revolted from their empire. Those insurrections were particularly galling to the Athenians since an armistice calling for a temporary cessation of military operations was claimed to be in effect. But all three towns, located on key peninsulas of the Chalcidice not far from the ill-fated Potidaea, were buoyed by the success of the Spartan insurrectionist Brasidas—the so-called liberator of Hellas—and sensed a weakening in the old Athenian resolve.

Brasidas was operating far from home in hopes of bringing key cities of the Athenians' northern empire over to the Spartans before the deadline of a general armistice took hold. In response, the Athenians eventually reduced all three and showed little mercy to the inhabitants. In the first instance, they were let into Mende by treachery, killed a number of the citizens, surrounded the rightist insurrectionists on the acropolis, and then allowed their allied democratic Mendeans to finish off the trapped revolutionaries.

Not long after, the Athenians returned in earnest to deal with the remaining two recalcitrant Chalcidian cities. They attacked Torone by land and sea, and entered the city following a retreating Spartan sortie that led them through the partially dismantled walls. All the women and children of Torone were enslaved; 700 of the males found still alive in the city were sent to Athens as hostages. At the formal acceptance of the later Peace of Nicias they were all returned.

Scione, however, was altogether a different story. The besieged city was to suffer a fate similar to Plataea's. In summer 421, the blockaded citizens finally gave up after a brutal two-year circumvallation. This time the Athenians accorded the victims the same treatment that the Spartans had dealt the Plataeans: executing all the adult males, selling the women and children into slavery, and turning over the abandoned land and city proper to those surviving Plataeans who had lost their capital when the Spartans began the siege of 429.

Scione, like Plataea, had ceased to exist as a city. The city had temporarily joined the Spartans, and so in the Athenians' logic it would now properly go as spoils to the Plataeans, whom the Spartans had likewise brutally expelled. Apparently, Scione was deliberately singled out to be a "paradigm" (*paradeigma*), inasmuch as the "Athenians wished to strike fear into those whom they suspected of planning revolts" and thus used the Scionaeans as an example to other Greeks of what could happen if a state left, or abetted those who attempted to leave, the Athenian empire.

The Athenians' vicious policy contained a certain predictable logic in this new no-holds-barred fighting of the Peloponnesian War. Many of those citizens not involved in planning the revolt who surrendered relatively soon, like those trapped in Torone or at Mytilene earlier, were allowed to live. Cities, however, like Scione that collectively chose to hold out to the bitter end would be accorded the same treatment that the Spartans had established at the war's beginning—a supposed sign of Athenian toughness that nevertheless made little impression on tiny Melos, which paid no heed to the fate of Scione and less than six years later met the same fate.

In the Athenian mind, the Spartans had initiated the cycle of executing surrendering citizens at the very outset of the war, and had continued that policy throughout the first decade of the fighting. In winter 424, for example, at the small outpost at Lecythus, Brasidas, who had none of the aristocratic restraint of Archidamus, had executed all the Athenian defenders who could not escape. The Spartans would go on to repeat such slaughter at Hysiae in 417 by killing all the free males of the doomed town.[12]

By the end of the first decade of the war the die was cast. With the reluctance of most belligerents to commit to hoplite battles, any Greek city might instead be besieged in a wider canvas of plundering, assassination, and general terror. The defenders had only one initial opportunity for surrender. Failing that, they could be executed when the city fell—a more likely certainty as the Peloponnesian War wore on. When the Athenians, desperate to end their expensive blockade of Potidaea, offered free passage out of the city to the captured populace, the assembly back home, reeling from the plague and the treacherous attack on friendly Plataea, was furious that harsher terms were not exacted. Even news that Potidaea was to be ethnically cleansed and handed over to Athenian settlers did not assuage the democracy, which probably indicted the generals for insubordination. Such "lenient" terms were never again offered to any defeated people by the Athenian assembly during the long course of the war to follow. So the engine of Athenian severity—whether on Mytilene or Melos—was driven not by rogue generals but, rather, by a majority vote of Athenian citizens themselves.[13]

Still, it was one thing to target insurrectionists such as those responsible for the revolts in Mytilene or Mende, quite another to kill every citizen who chose to resist and then obliterate all traces of an entire people's existence through razing their walls and resettlement with foreign interlopers. At Plataea and Lecythus the Spartans not only executed the garrison but demolished the city itself and consecrated the ground to the gods, a slightly less utilitarian policy than that of the Athenians, who preferred to erase captured cities but give the ground over to their own settlers.

About six months after the Spartans had marched into Argos to raze the democratic faction's incipient long walls and had stormed nearby Hysiae and butchered all the inhabitants, an Athenian fleet with 38 ships, equipped with a force of hoplites and archers numbering almost 3,500, sailed into the harbor of the tiny Aegean island of Melos. Even in summer 416, some fifteen years after the war began, the Melians remained an autonomous and quasi-neutral Dorian island city-state that for a decade and a half had astutely avoided taking sides in the fighting, although perhaps they were subjected to occasional Athenian exactions. The Athenians had earlier failed to take the island during the Archidamian War. Through a false reading of recent history, the Melians apparently thought they were more or less safe.

Yet to the Athenians there was a growing feeling that leniency toward neutrals was not appreciated but, rather, seen as evidence of their own weakness to be exploited. In their minds there was a certain logic that had led them to Melos: while the Spartans had butchered neutral Plataeans and assorted Greeks at Hysiae, the Athenians' own past generosity had led only to further rebellion. Allowing the captured Potidaeans to leave with their lives and money perhaps explained in part the revolt at Mytilene (427), a duplicitous subject state that opportunistically reckoned that Athens was weakened by the plague and would at least give moderate terms for the captured if its own rebellion failed.

The New Barbarism

THE ATHENIANS WERE now determined that the next siege would lead to the death of every captured male, not the sparing of either all or some, as had happened respectively in Potidaea and Mytilene. It may have been in the long term a counterproductive strategy, since many sieges depended on developing treachery from within, an impulse harder to encourage if the besieged thought they were all going to die indiscriminately. Scione had not convinced cities that opposition to the Athenians was synonymous with obliteration. Yet upon landing at Melos, the Athenian generals Cleomedes and Tisias immediately sent envoys to demand that the Melians either join the Athenian empire or perish, willing to do to them what their Spartan friends had done to the poor garrison at Hysiae. The Melians refused to let the Athenians address the popular assembly, lest the Melian poor find the offers of inclusion under the auspices of a democratic Athenian empire seductive to their own landless citizens. The dialogue as reported by Thucydides that followed between the Athenian envoys and the Melian elite, a magisterial exploration of moral right versus realpolitik, is one of the most famous passages in all of Greek literature. The once-underdog and idealist Athenians, who over sixty years earlier had saved the Greeks from the Persian horde, had forgotten their own past of fighting for ideals of independence and freedom against impossible odds.

Now as would-be conquerors like Xerxes before, the Athenians lectured the Melians about why they must accept the reality of power, give up hope ("danger's comforter"), relinquish their freedom, and thus submit, reminding them on the eve of their own greatest defeat of the war at Syracuse that "the Athenians never once yet have withdrawn from a siege." In Thucydides' hands, Melos comes after the Spartans had butchered the besieged at Hysiae, and yet right before the Athenian disaster to come at Syracuse, as the tragedy of the Peloponnesian War saw an endless cycle of violence and counterviolence, of bold conquerors unknowingly lecturing about their own fate shortly to come.

When the Athenian envoys were ready to depart after the fruitless conversation, they scoffed of the naïveté of the idealist Melians, who looked to hope rather than the formidable Athenian fleet in their harbor:

> Well, you alone, as it seems to us, judging from these resolutions, regard what is future as more certain than what is before your eyes, and what is out of sight, in your eagerness, as already coming to pass; and as you have staked most on, and trusted most in, the Spartans, your fortune, and your hopes, so will you most completely be deceived.

In their customary manner—by 416 the Athenians had starved out at least six other city-states since the war had started—the besiegers walled off Melos, left a garrison, and sailed home. Although the Melians were able to mount some successful sorties to bring in more food and pick off some of the occupying garrison, for the most part they were completely locked inside their city. About six months after the beginning of the siege, the Athenians sent back additional troops to tighten up the blockade and ensure the promised capitulation through starvation. Thucydides notes that some Melians may have allowed the Athenians inside through treachery, suggesting a democratic cabal that was never given an opportunity to argue for inclusion in the Athenian empire and sought to save their own lives by stealthy assistance. But in any case the city-state itself was doomed once it was walled off from its port and cut off from its agricultural land.

No mercy was offered. The Spartans no more came to help kindred Melos than had the Athenians earlier rushed out in force to protect Plataea. Instead, both powers concentrated their efforts on the weak and neutral defender rather than the strong and bellicose attacker. Upon surrender, most adult Melian males still alive were executed. The women and children were sold as slaves. Thucydides does not provide exact numbers of those killed or enslaved on Melos, but the total must have been in the several hundreds. The land itself was divided up among 500 Athenian colonists. Melos, like Scione, no longer existed. Ancient and modern critics deplored the slaughter and paid no attention to the fact that the Athenian generals were not allowed to present their offers directly to the Melian people, or that Melos was probably not as neutral as its oligarchic officials professed. Thus even the great defender of Athens, George Grote, once lamented, "Taking the proceedings of the Athenians towards Melos from the beginning to the end, they form one of the grossest and most inexcusable pieces of cruelty combined with injustice which Grecian history presents to us."[14]

One holocaust was one thing; a series of them finally made a profound impression on the Greeks. Again, after the killing of over 1,000 ringleaders of the Mytilene revolt, Euripides in his nearly contemporary *Hecuba* makes the heroine Hecuba curse the "murder vote" of the Achaean assembly that has brought an unwarranted death sentence to her daughter Polyxena. The tragedian offers a thinly veiled allusion to Cleon, "the honey-tongued," and the demagogues who swayed the mercurial contemporary Athenian assembly through a "clever trick" (*sophisma*) first to kill all, then, after reconsidering, to kill some of the Mytilene hostages: "A cursed race all you who seek honor through demagoguery. May not you be known to me, you who think nothing of harming your friends—if only you might say something pleasing to the mob."

But in Euripides' mind, what happened at Melos over a decade later was far worse. In his *Trojan Women*, performed during the spring after the Melian siege, he chronicled the horror that arises when the walls of a city fall and the attackers give no quarter. As he once more reworked the myth of Troy's fall into contemporary butchery, Euripides also predicted the Athenians' own disaster to come in Sicily even as they began to make preparations to sail: "Foolish is he who levels cities, temples, tombs, and the sanctuaries of the dead; as he sows destruction, so later he himself perishes."

Four years later, in his *Phoenician Women*, Euripides presented a lengthy description—"corpses heaped on top of corpses"—of the terror of being besieged by an unforgiving enemy. No doubt his long account of "a wretched city that has become utterly ruined" was in part a reaction to the Athenian string of slaughtering at Mytilene, Melos, and Mycalessus and its own disaster on Sicily. In his *Hecuba, Andromache,* and *Trojan Women,* Euripides chose to portray conquering Greeks as brutal and rapacious, and their Trojan victims as sensitive explicators of what servitude was like for the weak and vulnerable when their city fell.[15]

When the Spartans were on their way to sail into the Piraeus after their naval victory at Aegospotami (405), to end the Peloponnesian War, the Athenians themselves were gripped with the terror of nemesis. As the historian Xenophon put it, the Athenians had butchered so many innocent civilian Greeks at places like Scione, Torone, and Melos that they surely expected that the Spartans would do to them what they had done to other helpless and trapped garrisons. Had the Athenians won, the Spartans would have been equally afraid, remembering their own massacre of the free males of Lecythus and Hysiae, or Lysander's enslavement of the entire community of Cedreae in southern Asia Minor.[16]

From Siege to Slaughter

LESS THAN THREE years after the slaughter of the Melians, in summer 413 the Athenians unleashed some Thracian mercenaries under the leadership of the Athenian general Diitrephes. These light-armed skirmishers had arrived too late to join the relief armada that had set out for Sicily under Demosthenes. To recover some of their investment, the Athenians sought to use the Thracians along the nearby Boeotian coast to plunder and ravage. For a money-strapped Athens it was inconceivable to allow 1,300 mercenaries paid at a drachma a day—an aggregate outlay of 40,000 drachmas per month, or about the capital to maintain at least six triremes—to remain idle. Moreover, Delium had proved that it was impossible to defeat the Boeotians in pitched battle, and perhaps the only way to pay them back for their plundering of Attica and recent help to Syracuse was to conduct raids of terror.

Diitrephes went ashore near the small Boeotian town of Mycalessus, which, unfortunately, as an inland member of the Boeotian Confederacy never expected a sudden attack from seaborne outsiders. Its gates were open and much of its walls were in disrepair. Thucydides makes it a point to comment on the lack of good ramparts. In part he wants to explain the anomaly of an attacking force entering a city in the interior of well-guarded Boeotia so easily. Thus, the rapidly moving Thracians almost immediately broke through the dilapidated circuit. After looting the temples and shrines they began to cut down anything that moved:

> They butchered the inhabitants, sparing neither youth nor age but killing all they fell in with, one after the other, children and women, and even beasts of burden, and whatever other living creatures they saw; the Thracian people, like the bloodiest of the barbarians, being ever most murderous when it has nothing to fear. Everywhere confusion reigned and death in all its shapes; and in particular they attacked a boys' school, the largest that there was in the place, into which the children had just gone, and massacred them all.[17]

Athenian ships and an Athenian general, it should be remembered, had ferried the Thracians to Mycalessus. The Athenian assembly had paid the Thracians as hired terrorists to do as much damage as possible. The Athenians were nearly as guilty of the mini-holocaust as if they had accompanied the Thracians into the doomed schoolhouse. If the war had started off with the barbarous notion that besieged citizens received only one chance to surrender and walk out alive before the walls of circumvallation ringed their city, by its third decade Greeks sometimes went beyond even these tough protocols, assuming they could burst into a city without warning, loot, and kill at random horses, oxen, dogs, and anything else that breathed.

What was life like trapped inside the usually small circuits of blockaded city-states? In the case of Athens in 430, plague quickly broke out and the population was reduced to stealing funeral biers. At Potidaea the next year the poor city folk eventually ate the dead before surrendering their exhausted city-state. Cannibalism perhaps cannot be ruled out in any of the other sieges as well. Fighting among the garrison troops was common, both over food and the decision to endure or submit. Thucydides took a keen interest in the utter depravity of such mass killing. He records at length the debate over the fate of the captured at Plataea, and the preliminary discussion to the Melian siege. The flavor of these conversations resembles the show trials of the Stalinist era, as the powerful besiegers offer pretexts of inquiry and law as explanation for preset decisions to execute the innocent and weak.[18]

Again, how many died in these ghastly sieges of the Peloponnesian War?

There are no precise numbers, but it is likely that tens of thousands perished. The few figures that survive add up quickly: 1,050 Athenians lost taking Potidaea, with no exact figures of how many Potidaeans perished inside the walls; over 1,000 executed at Mytilene; about 45,000 Athenians and allies who did not return from the siege at Syracuse, along with an untold number of Sicilians, who were to be besieged not much later by the Carthaginians. Sources most often tally the Athenian losses but forget, perhaps, that as many Sicilians perished as well. Thousands more on both sides perished at Torone, Scione, Melos, and Mycalessus.

If one includes the execution of prisoners taken from captured ships, there were over twenty occasions in the Peloponnesian War when captured seamen or townspeople were summarily executed en masse. A recitation of such barbarity is salutary, if only to remind us just how frequent the killing became. Note especially the single year 427, when civilians were being simultaneously executed far to the west on Corcyra, on the mainland at Plataea, in the Aegean at Mytilene, and in Asia Minor by the Spartan admiral Alcidas.

Plataeans killed all Theban hostages (431). Peloponnesians did away with all Athenians found in ships off the Peloponnese (430). Alcidas slaughtered captured Athenians (427). Plataeans and Athenians were eliminated upon surrender of Plataea (427). The Athenians executed 1,000 Mytileneans (427). Corcyraean oligarchs were executed (427). Two thousand helots in Messenia were rounded up and killed (424). Aeginetans were captured at Thyrea (424). Megarian oligarchs executed democrats (424). Brasidas butchered all who could not escape at Lecythus (424). Spartans killed citizens of Hysiae. Mende was sacked (423) and Melos destroyed (416). Messanians were killed by pro-Athenian insurrectionists on Sicily (415). Even schoolboys were massacred at Mycalessus (413). The Athenians were surrounded and butchered at the Assinarus River and the survivors left to die in the quarries of Syracuse (413). Samian democrats murdered oligarchs (412); in turn, Chian oligarchs slaughtered democratic Chians (412). Lysander executed Athenians after Aegospotami (404). In addition, there were another 20,000 Greek soldiers who are recorded in our sources as taken prisoner and sold into slavery. Given these atrocities and the toll of the plague, in the sense of who died and how, the term "Peloponnesian War" appears a misnomer. A far better name might be "The Thirty Years Slaughter."[19]

How to Take a Polis

IN AN OBSCURE fourth-century military treatise about protecting poleis from besieging armies and intriguers within the walls, a shadowy Greek author,

Aeneas Tacticus, who may have been a contemporary Arcadian general, reviewed the intrinsic drama of the siege. Aeneas points out that should the besieged citizenry survive, they thereby send a powerful message to the enemies not to try such a foolish attack in the future. On the other hand, should a city fall, it presaged a fate far beyond that of a defeated army alone: "But if the defenders fail in their efforts to meet the danger, then there is not one hope of safety left."[20]

The word for siege or siegecraft in Greek was *poliorkia* (hence the term "poliorcetics," or "fencing in the polis"). Although there was an advanced science of taking cities by 431 involving rams, mounds, and fire weapons, walls themselves remained mostly unassailable, as they grew taller and thicker well beyond the old dimensions of ten to twelve feet in height and three to six feet wide, common before the mid-fifth century. The spread of ashlar blocks and regular courses of limestone, replacing mud bricks, rubble, and irregularly shaped stones, throughout the war widened the advantages of defense over offense even further. So there is yet another paradox about the besieging of cities in the Peloponnesian War, one that tells us a great deal about the overall nature of Greek society and culture: almost every assaulted city-state eventually capitulated, and yet almost *none* of them fell through storming the walls.

Instead, in a world where the art of defensive fortifications had far outstripped the science of offensive siegecraft, city-states like Plataea, Potidaea, Mytilene, Scione, and Melos were starved out only after months, or even years, of systematic circumvallation. The sieges were sometimes accelerated through treachery, mostly in the form of partisans opening the gates at night. Even the supposed experts, the Athenians, did not know all that much about attacking walls and towers directly, smashing through stone foundations, or battering down wooden gates.

Scaling a wall was not as simple as it sounds. Many city ramparts were twenty to thirty feet high. Ladders by necessity were tall, their height calibrated by counting the wall's stone or brick courses, and thus flimsy. All were easy for defenders to toss back, especially if assault troops were heavy hoplites perched on rungs in the air with sixty to seventy pounds of equipment. No army on either side yet knew how to craft wheeled siege towers with artillery and hinged boarding ramps that might provide a bridge over the fortifications—engines that would become ubiquitous only a century later, during the siege craze among the successors of Alexander the Great. The Athenians' clumsy attempts to build a primitive tower at Lecythus ended with its collapse.[21]

The last chance to breach the walls was to follow a beaten army inside the walls before the gates could be shut. Even battering rams—the Athenians purportedly first fashioned them, along with protective sheds, or "tortoises," at the prewar siege of rebellious Samos in 440—could not smash through reinforced wooden gates, at least not quickly enough to save the crews handling the ram from being picked off by stone- and missile-throwing defenders atop the walls. Primitive siege engines (*mêchanai*) were used not only by the Spartans at Plataea but also by the Athenians at Potidaea ("every kind of engine used in sieges"), and later in small skirmishes at Eresus and on Sicily. In all cases, such machines, probably no more than timber tipped with bronze on wheels, proved a failure, the crews sometimes wearing themselves out in vain efforts to batter down the fortifications. On other occasions they were vulnerable to capture or torching by counterassaults.[22]

Why was this so? Rarely were the approaches to ancient cities on flat ground. Instead, most often the targeted gates were on inclines. It was nearly impossible for crews to push ponderous rams over uphill rocky ground while under assault from the walls. A better solution was to knock the parapets down. But catapults and other sorts of artillery were not invented until *after* the Peloponnesian War.

There was no general in the fifth century comparable to the infamous Demetrius Poliorketes, nicknamed "the Besieger," who in his failed siege of Rhodes (304) employed catapults, moles, miners, and siege towers (including the infamous 130-foot iron-plated *helepolis*, or "city taker"). True, in three instances relatively early in the war troops employed fire—at Plataea, Delium, and Lecythus. But only at Delium did a strange hollowed-out beam, packed with incendiary pitch and its flame blown out by bellows, seem to work. That rare success was probably only because the target was a makeshift wooden rampart, not permanent walls of stone.

Mining was no doubt undertaken in most sieges of the war. Yet the dirty business seems to have been a tactic much feared—Aeneas Tacticus later gives us plentiful advice on how to stop it—but rarely successful. In theory, tunnels could provide secret access for besiegers under the walls. Barring that, wooden reinforcing braces could be burnt at preset times, forcing the subsequently unsupported subterranean passageway to collapse, and with it the foundation of the fortifications themselves above. On occasion, even bees and wasps were let loose into enemy shafts to sting and annoy diggers.

So tunneling was a tricky business. Greece is a rocky place where digging is rough under almost any circumstances. Sometimes cities had built substantial stone subterranean foundations that blocked underground entrance, or secondary interior moats to ensure that any diggers who got through emerged into trenches in full view of armed and waiting defenders. Nor was it easy to dig un-noticed from the walls. Tunnelers were forced to begin from great distances or to camouflage their excavations by building shelters over their initial holes.

In response, defenders could usually hear diggers. Often defenders placed inverted shields over the ground to intensify the sounds of pickwork; the be-sieged could then block off the tunnels, countertunnel to collapse them, fill them with smoke, or pour in dirt as fast as it was removed. Again, there was not a single instance in the Peloponnesian War where mining alone caused the fall of a fortified city.

Most cities, especially if they had provisions and strong fortifications, re-fused terms before the siege began. But if an army timed its arrival precisely dur-ing the grain harvest or grape vintage, depriving the defenders of their annual food supply or potential export income, then sometimes a few communities gave in at the very outset. Acanthus, for example, a wine-exporting community in northern Greece, in 422 surrendered at the outset to Brasidas rather than lose its precious grape crop.[23]

Betrayal

A POPULAR TACTIC was treachery, the reliance on agents inside the walls to open the city during a dark or rainy night and thus save the lives and property of the besieged. The Theban attackers who started the Peloponnesian War by their assault of Plataea entered the city only because sympathetic oligarchs inside unbolted the gates to their foreign co-conspirators. The fault lines between squabbling oligarchic factions, democrats versus oligarchs, Thebes against Athens, mistrust between friendly Athens and Plataea, and general hos-tility between Sparta and Athens all coalesced in this little town. These multi-faceted rivalries and tensions account for why the community was assaulted at night, prisoners murdered, oaths broken, and promised assistance not forth-coming.

Why did perfidy play such a prominent role in siegecraft? The explanation is both a general one and yet seems specific to the peculiar nature of the Greek city-state and the era of the Peloponnesian War. It was hard to maintain po-litical harmony among a cooped-up population of several hundreds or even thousands during a siege. Suspicion mounted that private deals might result in lenient consideration for opportunistic traitors after the city was taken. Con-servative farmers often trudged in from their fields and disliked their urban counterparts. The latter dominated the city and were more willing to sacrifice the fields of the wealthier than risk their own lives in providing defense outside the fortifications. In such cases, for men of property "patriotism" entailed the sacrifice of one's farm, while "treachery" reflected a desire to return to the countryside.

The fractious nature of Greek politics, especially by the outbreak of the Peloponnesian War, also ensured plenty of partisans on both sides in every city. Athens fought Sparta not merely as an Ionic culture pitted against the Doric people, or even a northern maritime state threatened by a southern infantry power. Rather, the divide was more sharply defined still by political fault lines, Athenian-style democracy against Spartan oligarchy.

Because democracy was the more revolutionary of the two creeds, and the Athenians more frequently the besieging party, it turned out that there were always either would-be democrats or Athenian agents ready to open the gates or, in contrast, a few oligarchic exiles who desperately wanted to find some way to restore their city to the men of property. Yet as ancient observers from Thucydides to Aeneas point out, ideological professions were often high-sounding cover for personal agendas—private feuds, concern over debts, petty envies and jealousies—that ignited whenever the social fabric was torn through sieges, which worked like plagues and revolution to strip away the patina of civilization.

Athens and Sparta were often hesitant to intervene, given the costs to the besiegers. At Potidaea, for example, a quarter of the attacking Athenians, 1,050 hoplites, perished from the plague alone. At Plataea, after four years of intermittent warfare and the eventual garrisoning of thousands of Peloponnesian and Boeotian troops, only 225 Plataeans and Athenians inside were officially reported as killed, less than the 300 Theban attackers who fell on the very first night of the assault in March 431! There are no figures of the additional hundreds of Spartans and Thebans who were injured or killed outside the walls in their nearly four-year effort to take the city.

Throughout history the attackers often paid the higher price. During the savage though unsuccessful siege of Malta in 1565, over 30,000 Ottomans perished, while killing only 7,000 of the defenders. At Vienna in 1683, the besieging Turks withdrew after suffering over 60,000 losses, twelve times the 5,000 deaths of the defending allied Christians. The Japanese took Port Arthur (1904–05) after a five-month siege, but only after suffering 90,000 dead and disabled from hunger, disease, and Russian fire—three times the casualties of the defeated Russian garrison. For all the misery of being inside a trapped city, it was sometimes worse to be exposed outside without permanent shelter, secure walls, and stockpiled food.

Statistical study of some sixty-nine recorded Greek sieges in the entire fifth century reveals that only sixteen citadels were taken through a forced blockade, while eleven involved some treachery inside the walls. But before one deprecates the art of siegecraft, in the other forty-two cases the city and its attackers came to some agreement that entailed a capitulation with terms, usually involving the besieged agreeing to hand over indemnities or give up on condition of guarantees for lives and property. So arose this paradox that exemplified the entire experience of attacking cities during the Peloponnesian War: few were successfully stormed, yet most came to some agreement to capitulate under threat of force and the specter of starvation.[24]

Postheroic Walls

WHY DID A people like the Greeks, steeped in the scientific method and adept at building majestic temples to precise designs, as late as the Peloponnesian War know so little about storming the impressive walls they so routinely built? From what little is known of the early history of the city-state from the eighth to fifth centuries, disputes were often settled by rural militias of heavily armed infantry who met each other in pitched battles. Under these rules of war, one side often threatened to ravage the cropland of the other to precipitate battle. Whereas early city-states may have had rudimentary walls of mud brick around their small citadels, most communities until the fifth century could not afford to encompass their entire living areas with stout stone fortifications. Why should agrarians spend labor and capital to extend the city's ramparts beyond its acropolis, especially to protect the poorer, who owned no land and lived in town? But after the trauma of the Persian invasion of 480, the subsequent cold war between Athens and Sparta for most of the mid-fifth century, and the spectacular construction of the Athenian Long Walls, an increasing number of Greek states slowly began to invest in fortifications, to protect against both a sudden march of Spartan hoplites and the unexpected arrival of the Athenian fleet.

Even today one of the most incomprehensible things about the antiquities of Greece are the plentiful remains of towers, walls, and temples in relatively flat terrain miles from quarries—proof, as it were, that the fragmented and warring classical Greeks lacked the unifying concept of nationhood (or even a word comparable to the Latin *natio*). Moreover, how the ancients cut stones with flimsy hand-held saws, then used teams to transport stones from quarries miles away seems miraculous, especially when it is kept in mind that even small stones not more than two feet in diameter might weigh nearly a ton.

Compared to the economy of hoplite battle, walls and the effort to capture them were an expensive investment. Thus, after the Persian Wars, futile calls went out to Greek states not to rebuild their circuits, or to tear down those walls that had survived. The Spartans claimed that they did not wish the Persians to have national redoubts should they return. In fact, they were more afraid that the Athenians might use fortifications to spread a creed of war without hoplite battle. Or was it that all sides conceded that the Greeks as a whole could better invest millions of man-hours in something more productive than cutting and carrying tens of thousands of stones to wall themselves off from one another?

For decades before the Peloponnesian War, the Greeks had sought to avoid something like what would transpire at the nightmarish siege of Potidaea, a two-year ordeal that cost the Athenians over 2,000 talents and over a quarter of their original besieging force, enough investment to have built two entire Parthenons, to have plated with gold Pheidias' monumental statue of Athena fifty times over, or to have staged *all* the plays that were presented in Athens during the fifth century. In that sense, much of the early cultural achievement of the Greek world was explicable in the relative economy of hoplite warfare, which required no investment in ships, dockyards, or walls, and limited fighting to a few grim hours.

Often the victors tried to reclaim some of the costs of a siege by expropriating the farmland and property of the vanquished, both before and after capitulation. For example, the Spartans claimed possession of Plataea and rented its land out to neighboring Boeotians. They probably ransacked houses, stampeded livestock, and made off with crops once the citizens had either fled inside the walls or to Athens. The Athenians gave captured Melos over to 500 of its own colonists. After the infamously expensive Potidaean blockade and the ongoing siege of Mytilene, the money-strapped Athenians not only gave the town and its environs to their own settlers but immediately sent out ships to collect much-needed revenue from their subjects as well as voting to tax themselves further.[25]

Booty sellers quickly descended on captured cities to market the spoils. Each woman and child, even when sold off en masse at depressed prices, might go for 100 drachmas, or about three months' salary for a besieger. For a state to pay for a year's siege, then, it would need to acquire about three or four healthy captives per each of its attackers—not counting the personal fortunes of the prisoners, which were often considerable. When the Athenian general Demosthenes surrendered his contingent to the Syracusan pursuers, the victors filled four inverted shields with coins, a sum estimated by present-day scholars to be about

55 talents, or the modern equivalent of about $27.5 million. If roughly 6,000 Athenians surrendered, then each man was carrying about two months of salary. So the capitulation of larger cities in some cases might mean an eventual profit for even the most costly of sieges. The trick was the initial outlay, or the confidence that a state had enough reserves to pay its besieging force on promises that the captured city would yield a profit to both the soldiers and the state.

Walls themselves were felt to be antithetical to courage and thus in the abstract always distrusted by agrarian conservatives. Morally, it was believed that fighting properly belonged to soldiers; practically, it was expensive to surround entire municipalities with fortifications. Hoplite phalanxes strengthened civic ties through solidarity in the ranks; in contrast, sieges brought out personal differences and accentuated political strife. All the major philosophers—Plato, Aristotle, and Xenophon—reflect a widely held moral skepticism of fortifications. Walls, the Athenian Plato wrote in the aftermath of the Peloponnesian War, were bad in every way: they weakened the collective health of the populace; they created a complacent city that lost confidence in its own muscular courage to repel the enemy; and they accentuated strife among the citizenry between those who wished to defend their farms outside and those who saw no need to protect what they did not have. Sieges, then, were as odious as naval warfare—expensive, cowardly, and a diversion from the heroic code of landowners fighting on land over land.[26]

The Heritage of Siegecraft

THE KEY COMPONENTS of successful siegecraft—movable towers, sophisticated rams, and catapults—appeared shortly *after* the end of the Peloponnesian War. The Greeks had learned that battle was now to be beyond the realm of hoplite warfare: the arrival of a crack army more often meant that an unsteady enemy retreated to its walls rather than trusted in open battle. Sieges usually eventually worked through starvation, but their start-up cost was prohibitive. Throughout the war, both sides had experimented with rams and fire guns, but only with mixed success.

Within just a few years of the war, bolder and more amoral men, like Dionysus of Syracuse and Philip of Macedon, unleashed a new siegecraft that was as ingenious as it was deadly, involving nontorsion and torsion catapults, siege towers to 120 feet in height, and mixed contingents of sappers, artillerymen, and rammers working simultaneously. Plataea lasted nearly four years after the first Theban attack. In contrast, the Macedonians could break through the walls of a city in a fraction of the time of the old laborious counterwalling, but they inherited a craft that was born on the heels of a twenty-seven-year war and the deaths of thousands. Had the Spartans had Philip's torsion catapults, they could have battered down Plataea's walls in a matter of days, 150-pound rocks crashing into the parapets in every direction, launched by artillery that were safely out of the range of arrows and missiles.

Epaminondas is remembered as the great victor over the Spartans at Leuctra, but his real legacy was the new science of fortification, which exploded in the aftermath of the Peloponnesian War. In some sense, the triad of newly demo-cratic and autonomous walled cities of Mantinea, Megalopolis, and Messene—perhaps all built along the similar blueprints of Theban engineers—reflected lessons learned in the later fifth century, when an infantry victory at Mantinea spelled the end of hopes of Peloponnesian autonomy. Had the helots, Man-tineans, or Arcadians possessed their later enormous circuits in the 420s, Sparta would have been rendered impotent a half century earlier.

Finally, Alcibiades, as one might expect, was involved in all the most notori-ous sieges of the war. Even before the fighting started, he was among the Athe-nians besieging Potidaea. Later authors attribute the brutal Athenian policy of reducing Melos by siege to Alcibiades' leadership. He was the architect of the failed Sicilian expedition. In his second incarnation, during the Ionian War, he successfully conducted the siege of both Chalcedon and Byzantium, and through treachery and negotiations achieved their surrenders.

So sieges framed Alcibiades' war. Nineteen-year-old Alcibiades began the struggle trying to break through the elaborate walls of Potidaea with a great army; some twenty-seven years later, as a tired, exiled, and discredited man of forty-five, he was shot down trying to keep a few assassins from entering his fortified house in an obscure town in Phrygia.

The greatest siege of the war, however, was not on the Greek mainland but on far distant Sicily. The effort to storm or starve out Syracuse required more money and men than any operation the Athenians conducted during the entire war. It followed immediately upon the successful effort on Melos and brought to bear all the experience and expertise drawn from a string of successful oper-ations at Potidaea, Mytilene, Scione, and Melos. Yet more Athenians were killed in the effort to take Syracuse than in all its previous sieges put together. After the disaster on Sicily, Athens rarely tried to take a fortified city again—laying to rest for good the old boast to the Melians that the Athenians had never once abandoned a siege.[27]

CHAPTER 7

HORSES

THE DISASTER AT SICILY (415–413)

The Big Idea

BY 415 THE war was still stalemated and now in its seventeenth year. During the shaky Peace of Nicias, Athens had lost a rare opportunity to galvanize a democratic revolt of Peloponnesian states against Sparta. The hoplite showdown at Mantinea was a catastrophic missed opportunity, in part as a result of Athens' meager contribution to the allied army. After Alcibiades' radical ideas were discredited with defeat of the coalition in 418, the temporizer Nicias—an expert at the half measure and the tactically successful but often strategically insignificant amphibious landing—was now once more ascendant.

Persia was not quite ready to antagonize Athens by committing money to subsidize the creation of a Peloponnesian fleet. Meanwhile, in the Greek Third World the successes of Pylos and other Athenian outposts around the Peloponnese were offset by the defections from the empire caused by Brasidas' insurrectionary activity in the north around Amphipolis. Athens was still stuck with a two-front war against Thebes and Sparta after its failure at Delium, while the Spartan fleet had performed miserably and seen its efforts to subvert Corcyra fail after a bloody rampage of civil strife.

Many of the war's leaders and their successors—Archidamus, Brasidas, Pericles, and Cleon—were now dead. Thousands had perished from the plague at Athens, while Sparta hemorrhaged from constant helot flight to Pylos, and yet neither side felt the war was really over. While Spartans contemplated ways of creating a fleet to destroy the Athenian empire, some Athenians were crafting an even wilder plan to gain advantage during these years of respite. What they came up with changed the entire course of the war, although in ways the Athenian assembly never imagined.

Great invasions of faraway places evoke our worst fears. Communications are difficult; by the time most Frenchmen heard Napoleon had taken Moscow, his retreating army was already near ruin in the snows of Russia. Given the great distance, the fragility of logistics, and the danger of extended transport, losses in transit can be as severe as battle casualties. Safety, especially in long-distance amphibious operations, lies in having a way to get back home. And a secure return most often resided, in the age before petroleum, in either ships or horses. After his fleet was sunk at Salamis, Xerxes understandably worried whether his pontoon bridges across the Hellespont were still intact. In contrast, a defiant Cortés burned his ships in the harbor of Veracruz to remind his men that military defeat meant not failure but their own destruction. In such great gambles, victory usually does not hinge merely on success in battle but demands the complete subjugation of the invaded, who in turn are fighting for their survival, not just against conquest.

It is only within this grand and risky context of seeking to conquer a city eight hundred miles away, one as great or greater than Athens itself in population, size, and wealth, that a full appreciation is possible of the disaster of the Sicilian expedition. The trauma to Athens arose not merely from its material and human losses that followed from the defeat; it suffered worse fatalities from the plague and would lose far more in the great sea battles of the Ionian theater to come. Rather, the debacle was spiritual as well, the sheer horror of within just two years tapping the empire to send over 40,000 men so far away either to conquer or to die trying.

Why, in the autumn of 416, well into the sixth year of an armistice with Sparta, did the Athenian assembly vote to attack Syracuse, the capital of Sicily? Classical scholars have collated the ostensible reasons given by Thucydides and other ancient sources. They are legion and remain baffling. First, the Athenians claimed that they were treaty-bound to honor the requests for help from the small Sicilian states of Segesta and Leontini, which were ostensibly threatened with absorption by a growing Syracusan (and Dorian) empire on the island. Both looked desperately for outside succor from an ethnically and politically akin benefactor to preserve their autonomy.

Yet in the realities of war not all promises are always kept, as the poor Melians had learned the year before, when they had put their hope in Spartan aid. The otherwise busy Athenians had reasons other than mere justice and promises to sail so far away.[1] Instead, the common people at Athens smelled money in the proposition: profit through promises from the aggrieved states to cover their expenses and greater hopes of plunder once Syracuse itself was conquered. Some Athenian imperialists, Alcibiades most prominently, envisioned Sicily as a stepping-stone to even greater acquisitions in North Africa and Italy. They had already shrugged off the plague, and now saw the beginning of some sort of trans-Mediterranean empire stretching from Asia Minor to Gibraltar, which would have predated the Roman imperium by four centuries. In fact, after the Athenian defeat in Sicily, neutral states breathed a sigh of relief. Most had apparently been convinced that an Athenian victory might have meant that they were next on the long list of targets.[2]

Meanwhile, the debate over Sicily became the arena for the renewed rivalry between the pro-Spartan Nicias and the imperialist Alcibiades. After the earlier defeat of the pro-Athenian alliance at Mantinea, the elder Nicias' policy of caution seemed to have eclipsed Alcibiades' wilder schemes. In response, the Athenians, the imperialists argued, should see victory in Sicily as integral to the current *bellum interruptum* with Sparta, a way of preempting any Sicilian aid to Sparta at a time of general tension as both sides sought to gain advantage during a phony peace.

Controlling the grain supplies of Sicily—to the modern visitor, the farmland of the island is striking in its clear superiority and size to anything found in southern Greece—might end the Peloponnesian importation of foodstuffs. Contrast the parched Peloponnese or Attica with verdant Sicily, and the additional idea that Athenians were also interested in imported grain for themselves makes good sense. The population and military assets of the island also could come in handy when the war with the Peloponnesians resumed, as it inevitably would in even greater fashion. In any case, the earlier expedition against the island (427–424) had been aimed at denying grain imports to the Peloponnese.[3]

The renegade Alcibiades, who would betray the Athenian cause a few weeks after arriving in Sicily, was smart enough to understand that when he switched sides in 415 and made his way to Sparta, he had to make some dramatic connection between the survival of Syracuse and the self-interest of his new host city. The best way to enlist Peloponnesians to help defeat his former countrymen at Syracuse was to assure them that the Athenian invasion was really aimed at Sparta. "If this city shall be taken," Alcibiades told the Spartan assembly, "then all of Sicily is theirs, and immediately Italy as well. And that danger that I just now spoke about from there would in no time fall upon you. Thus, let nobody think that you are deliberating only about Sicily, but also about the Peloponnese."[4]

Athens had not been in an active battle with Sparta in six years. The city was starting to recover from the losses of the plague. It was now full of young fire-brands who had only a dim childhood memory of either the funeral pyres in the city or Spartan hoplites trampling amid the vineyards of Attica. Athens also had just pulled off a successful siege of a Dorian protectorate of Sparta, the island of Melos, without reigniting the war with Sparta. Steady tribute, the absence of offensive operations for nearly five years, and a restoration of trade had all meant that Athens was almost as well off as during the years before the war. For all these reasons the citizens were once more ready to reassert them-selves militarily.[5]

The campaign was both practicable and mad at the same time: doable in the sense that Athens' military potential was so great that it had restored sufficient power despite plague and war, while unhinged in the sense that its own subjects, especially in the Thraceward region, were on the verge of revolt, even as Sparta was both unpredictable and unconquered. The pro-Athenian but weak Segesta and Leontini were dubious, if not duplicitous Sicilian allies. The sheer distance and impossibility of easy communications and supply made the operational as-pects of the expedition daunting.

Nicias, in overly dramatic fashion, set out all these reasons why Athens should not go to Sicily and achieved the opposite result of inflaming the Athe-nian citizenry, not unlike the sexagenarian King Archidamus on the eve of the war almost two decades earlier, who had predicted a tough fight only to be dis-regarded by the Spartan assembly. In the last analysis, one does not defeat the proximate oligarchic enemy by sailing eight hundred miles distant to attack a democratic neutral.

What is striking about the casus belli for the Sicilian expedition was that Syracuse, while Doric and Sicilian, was *not* oligarchic. Well before the war even broke out, an anonymous conservative observer remarked that anytime Athens did not support democracy abroad, it fared poorly, given its natural affinities for popular governments. The Syracusans may not have been as radically dem-ocratic as Athens, but their constitution was liberal in the ancient sense. A sov-ereign Syracusan popular assembly ensured free give-and-take between the poor and the well-off, meaning that the Sicilian expedition was at the outset a be-trayal of professed Athenian values of promoting Panhellenic democratic cul-ture. To the conservative Thucydides the anomaly was not merely that Athens had forsaken its ideological agenda of protecting democracies from reaction-aries, but that for the first time in the Greek experience two large maritime democracies were at war. They would bring into the fray all the military assets that such imaginative and resourceful societies characteristically possessed. And these advantages—ships, money, manpower, and popular leadership—were many and not to be lightly dismissed.

Democratic states involved the entire citizenry in their decision making. They did not stake their collective defense on farmland for the sake of a hoplite class. Because such governments empowered the poor, encouraged social mobility and immigration, experienced higher rates of population growth, instilled greater civic discipline ("as is the way of a democracy"), and created capital for both fleets and fortifications, they made war far more formidably than their oligarchic counterparts (dubbed by Thucydides as "slow" and "timid").

As Thucydides further put it: "Of all the cities that Athens had gone to war against, the Syracusans alone were the most similar to Athens, being democratic like themselves, and strong in ships, horses, and size." He later concluded, "Because the Syracusans were most similar to the Athenians, they made war against them the most successfully." Despite the horrors of the plague and over a decade of war, there were thousands of young Athenian men who willingly took up the challenge of sailing dangerous seas to fight mostly unknown fellow Greeks, in a struggle to storm the largest city in the Greek-speaking world. While one may recoil at their madness, their sheer audacity is even more arresting.[6]

Because Thucydides devoted two entire books of his history to the campaign—25 percent of his entire narrative dealing with just three of the twenty years chronicled—there is a good record of the main events of the disaster. After two acrimonious assemblies, the Athenians voted to send a massive armada to Syracuse in June 415. A troika of generals would command: the reliable veteran Lamachus, the old conservative but timid Nicias, and the ever intriguing Alcibiades. Whereas the initial idea was to send out a moderately sized force of some 60 triremes, about the same number that had sailed years earlier in a fruitless attempt to intimidate Syracuse between 427 and 425, in a subsequent assembly inflated rhetoric and acrimony prompted a complete, and what would prove disastrous, reappraisal.

Unlike the earlier invasions of Sicily, now the Athenians in a moment of zeal mandated an even larger force: 134 ships (100 of them Athenian), including over 90 triremes, and 5,100 Athenian and imperial hoplites. Arrangements were made for an assortment of 480 archers, 700 slingers, 30 horsemen and mounts, and 30 cargo ships.[7]

In material terms, what had been envisioned as another punitive raid was now redefined as an attempt at conquest and annexation. However overwhelming the ostentatious armada might have appeared on parade in the harbor of the Piraeus as it set sail, the fleet was perhaps rather small to subdue an entire island the size of Sicily, especially if it did not take immediate and decisive action on arrival and thus establish a deterrent presence. Scholars sometimes talk about the oppressive nature of the Athenian empire, but its aggregate force in 415 was somewhat pathetic—the allies of some 200 states contributing only 2,850 of the 5,100 hoplites. The Athenians experienced the false security of all departing armies that judge the extent of their own power by the impression they make upon themselves rather than solely on the enemy.

What was stunning about the Athenian expeditionary force was its initial luck. The fleet enjoyed good weather in transit. It made the tricky voyage across hundreds of miles of sea without losses or delays, and thus there is scant detail in Thucydides' narrative about what could have been an especially perilous trip. Despite its extravagant and public send-off, the triremes arrived at Sicily to the almost complete surprise of the Syracusans. In contrast, during the next two years, the Peloponnesian reinforcements had far less luck in reaching Syracuse, and were often blown off course, shipwrecked, or delayed by stormy weather. In other words, in this first wave the Athenians had probably transported over 25,000 combatants across the open seas without any real losses and arrived in good shape to the utter astonishment and terror of their enemies. Yet almost immediately tragedy inexplicably began to unfold.

Paralysis

AT THE VERY heart of the disaster was the flawed nature of the tripartite command. It was not just that battle responsibility was divided among three generals, rather than the more normal two. The suspicious Athenians, after all, were notorious for sometimes having too many squabbling commanders in the field at once. The problem was that the three were temperamentally so different, and in addition brought considerable political baggage along on the voyage. The senior officer in charge, the naturally cautious Nicias, was in poor health and had been against the expedition from the beginning. Thus for the next two years he fought only haphazardly and always in fear of being charged back home with dereliction. Such was the peculiar nature of Athenian command that sometimes generals who did not approve of expeditions were put in charge of them, on the dubious logic that they would provide a critical accountability both in the field and, later, at home.

Alcibiades was shortly recalled on allegations of sacrilege. On the eve of sailing, dozens of young right-wing firebrands, in a fit of drunkenness and politically inspired audacity, had been accused of public sacrilege that cast ill omens over the expedition's impending departure. Perhaps their real intention was to spook the superstitious voting poor into rescinding the expedition altogether. Only that way might Athens ensure that an oligarchic Sparta remained neutral and its army thus kept away from the Attic heartland. While Alcibiades may have been involved with the pranks that defamed the secret fertility rites at Eleusis, he probably had nothing to do with the bolder escapade to mutilate the herms, stone totems sacred to Hermes that dotted the Attic landscape to ensure divine protection for travelers and private households. In any case, the fleet left under a cloud, but the irony remained that by charging Alcibiades in absentia with a capital crime and then seeking his recall from Sicily, the outraged Athenians perhaps played right into the hands of the conspirators: the man most responsible for leading the democracy on a vast imperial adventure would be sabotaged by his erstwhile supporters from carrying out their own radical ideas.

Shortly after arriving in Sicily, Alcibiades received the summons to return home. Grasping that extradition was the equivalent of a death sentence, he evaded his jailers and sailed instead to the Peloponnese. There he soon ended up at Sparta, urging it to renew the war both through aid to Sicily and the garrisoning of Attica. Meanwhile, back on Sicily, the no-nonsense Lamachus apparently lacked the political stature or wealth to convince the other two to enact his prescient plans for immediate attack on Syracuse. Within the year he was killed in battle while besieging the city. His impotence and later death were tragic, since under his leadership Athens not only might have shocked an ill-prepared Syracuse into surrender or panic but would have captured a great deal of plunder out in the countryside before it could have been evacuated.

The Athenians almost immediately ignored the cardinal rule of any great invasion: the need for direct action. Upon arrival in enemy territory there is only a finite time for victory, as stalemate weighs in favor of the defenders. Yet the Athenians did not, as Lamachus advised, head straight for Syracuse upon discovery that most of the Sicilians were not so eager to be liberated, that Athens' few allied states were neither wealthy nor resolute, and that the Syracusans themselves were not shocked and awed as they began to see an impressive fleet more hesitant and dilatory than resolute and aggressive.

Nevertheless, the Athenians fought courageously for the next two years in almost every imaginable fashion, as befitting an ingenious democratic people. But never again after their arrival in late summer 415 would they regain what the American general George S. Patton once called the "unforgiving minute"— that brief window of opportunity when lightning action can stun the enemy, win an entire theater, and bring dramatic results without great carnage. The moment the surprised Syracusans discovered that they were not the immediate object of the Athenian armada, the emboldened citizenry recovered and demanded offensive operations against the Athenians.[8]

The Athenians did little upon arrival. Instead of attacking Syracuse, after heated debate they sailed to Rhegium. Once there, they got no help. Worse, they soon learned that their purportedly opulent Segestan allies were broke. With neither much allied money nor many troops forthcoming, they now headed for the town of Catana, some fifty miles to the north, to make a base for further operations against Syracuse.

Their first success after months of dawdling was the capture of the small community of Hyccara. After their experiences of nearly two decades of storming small cities from Potidaea to Melos, the Athenians had little trouble in taking the insignificant town. Under the new protocols of war, they sold every inhabitant into slavery. But by now it was nearly autumn and the first four months of the campaign had accomplished almost nothing: Alcibiades had been recalled, escaped, and was advising the enemies of Athens; the slothful Nicias was in virtual command; and the Athenians had yet to attack an ever more confident Syracuse.

The Struggle for Mounted Supremacy

MEN WHO KNEW war well at Athens mostly misjudged the type of forces necessary for victory on Sicily, a distant island whose wide plains and greenery were more like the landscape of Thessaly than that of Attica or the Peloponnese. Intelligence about the nature of Sicilian warfare, the reliability of allies, and the resources of the enemies was either flawed or nonexistent. In perfunctory fashion Nicias had warned the Athenians that they would require mounted troops, but as a traditional soldier he predictably still gave far more attention to the need for hoplites. Even Alcibiades, the experienced cavalryman, had assured the Athenians that they could easily defeat Syracuse precisely because Sicilian states were notoriously weak in infantry! Yet almost immediately upon arrival, the Athenians discovered instead that their thousands of hoplites were mostly irrelevant for victory, and that they lacked the one resource—plentiful horsemen—that might have given them the protection needed for a successful siege. There was little excuse other than hoplite chauvinism to account for such strategic naïveté. After all, the Athenians already knew that more horsemen would have played a critical role at Spartolos (429), and through cavalry they had kept the Spartans under constant attack in Attica—operations that both Nicias and Alcibiades has been integrally involved with.[9]

Once ensconced at Catana, the Athenians grasped that Sicily was huge and required nearly constant communications with its network of cities. For an invader to have any chance of success against Syracuse, a city-state as large as Athens with hundreds of skilled horsemen, mounted supremacy was critical. Instead, Syracusans routinely rode up to the Athenian base at Catana and insulted the encamped Athenians, deliberately trying to provoke an invader who himself within a few weeks of arrival seemed more like the besieged than the real aggressors. To win this war, Athenian cavalrymen were needed in massive numbers to protect the stonemasons and skirmishers who alone could cut off Syracuse from its hinterlands by fortifications.

If the Syracusans were to emerge for a conventional hoplite battle, Athenian horsemen would be necessary to protect the flanks and conduct pursuit in the plains of Sicily. And when Athenians began to ravage the countryside and deny farmers access to their fields, cavalrymen were again essential. Lamachus, as an old veteran of fighting the Spartans in Attica who knew something about raiding and plundering, believed that upon arrival the Athenians should have immediately scoured the Syracusan countryside to find supplies from the unguarded farms and to shut off the city's access to its vital hinterlands.

Something drastic had to be done to provide deterrence against what would prove the largest corps of enemy horsemen the Athenians had faced since the Persian invasions over a half century earlier. Yet cavalry was the one asset that the Athenians were woefully short of on Sicily. Either out of fear of the great seas between western Greece and southern Italy, or perhaps realizing the need to keep a cavalry patrol to guard the Attic countryside should the Spartans return in their absence, the Athenians had initially brought along only a single horse transport and 30 riders. Perhaps that was understandable for anyone who has made the voyage from western Greece to Sicily in moderately heavy seas: imagine an armada of 10 or so horse transports—300 ponies on converted triremes with decks a mere few feet above the water—riding the waves that often sicken contemporary tourists on mammoth modern ships. Athens was not likely to risk its entire fleet of horse-transport ships and almost a third of its vital mounted defense force of Attica on the open seas.

After discovering from their base at Catana that their hoplites and skirmishers could not destroy Syracusan agriculture any better than the Spartans had ruined Attica, the Athenians sought to find some way of getting back down to Syracuse without being constantly attacked by horsemen. Finally, through false information they tricked the Syracusans into committing their land forces. Meanwhile, they stealthily sailed down the coast unopposed to Syracuse. There they disembarked in safety before the fooled cavalry could return. Although successful, this stratagem was ominous: a few hundred horsemen had kept tens of thousands of Athenian troops confined to their base. Only by deception could the Athenians even approach the very target of their entire expedition—and they had to sail, not march overland.

Even when the Athenian phalanx assembled in front of the surprised city, it was careful to deploy only on terrain where "the Syracusan cavalry could least of all harm them both in the actual battle and before." One ancient source believed that the desperate Athenians actually set spiked horse traps on the sides of the army to keep back the dreaded mounted enemy—a humiliating admission that heavy infantrymen no longer fought on the "best and most level ground." And why not, when the furious deceived Syracusans would ride back in full force, some 1,200 horsemen eager to pick off anyone out of formation? Although in the ensuing actual battle Athens' hoplites broke the more inexperienced Syracusan infantrymen—who were apparently terrified by the sound of thunder and unused to war on foot—they could not destroy them, given the cover once more of this enormous mob of horsemen. At no time in the Peloponnesian War had the Athenians ever fielded a force of more than 600 cavalry at once. The very idea that 1,200 enemy horsemen would roam the Greek battlefield at will was something beyond their comprehension.

Even this tiny hoplite battle was predicated on the idea that only a trick could allow the Athenians to muster in peace, that only wise use of geography could protect them in battle, and that victory could never be fully exploited as long as a mounted enemy ranged the battlefield. Overnight on Sicily, Hellenic war as the Greeks knew it had changed. The presence of 1,200 Syracusan horsemen salvaged a standoff from an utter rout. Overwhelming numbers of horsemen turned the rearguard action into a victory when the Athenians sailed back to Catana and gave up operations for the winter. Once back at their base, the stunned Athenians made preparations to find as many cavalrymen as quickly as they could.[10]

The Athenians' only hope under these surreal conditions of Sicilian warfare was to cobble together an adequate mounted counterforce of their own from their allies or somehow find reinforcements from home. Once the Athenians obtained mounted superiority, they could move, forage, and fortify at will; but should they fail, the besiegers might well be confined to camp and thus become besieged.[11]

Despite living in makeshift quarters, thousands of Athenians now had to prepare to spend the winter outside Catana, while Nicias made ad hoc arrangements to acquire horses as quickly as possible, and to send out embassies to potential allies. He naively expected that both Sicilians and Carthaginians might aid an invader who had won only a small hoplite battle. In contrast, the Syracusans were hardly depressed by a minor setback, but rather buoyed by the near mastery of the countryside provided by an ever more haughty cavalry. While the Athenians dallied, the Syracusans revamped their command and set to work to reinforce the city's fortifications for the inevitable siege to come. They sent encouraging news to the distant Spartans, soon to fall under the spell of their newfound advocate Alcibiades, that it was time to restart the war and finish off a now hemorrhaging Athens.

After escaping Athenian custody, Alcibiades had immediately reinvented himself in the Peloponnese into a doughty Laconian and spun fantastic tales that the Athenians had all along sought to renew the war and obtain hegemony over the entire Mediterranean: Sicily first, then Italy, followed by Carthage itself. From Alcibiades' mind poured out even more yarns: such conquests would win new allies from Iberia, triremes built from the forests of Italy, and money from conquered peoples. Did a Carthaginian expedition exist only in his mind, or was it the logical successor to a Sicilian victory? Answers vary, but surely such visions of Athenian imperial democratic aggrandizement could rile paranoid Spartans to renew the war—and for the moment that was in the exiled Alcibiades' own interest.

With the zeal of the convert, eager to pay back his countrymen, to save his own skin, and to ingratiate himself with his new hosts, Alcibiades further ter-rified his stunned Spartan audience with tales of fantastic Athenian plots to surround the Peloponnese by land and sea. He finished his treachery by outlin-ing the only way to destroy his native city, in a manner as sober and judicious as his stories of Athenian imperial aims were probably wild: the Peloponnesians should promptly invade Attica and fortify a base at Decelea, send help to Sicily, and foment insurrection in the Aegean.[12]

Back in Sicily, when spring arrived the Athenians attempted a few raids. But mostly they were waiting for the requested horsemen from Athens. Eight months at Catana were essentially lost. From Athens at last came 250 expe-rienced riders, 30 mounted archers, and 300 talents to purchase horses from Segesta and Catana. The fact remained that the Athenians had essentially ac-complished nothing since the prior summer. Through inaction they had em-boldened the Syracusans and very soon also their old Peloponnesian enemies on the Greek mainland. Nevertheless, with the arrival of a few Sicilian horse-men, Nicias had cobbled together a makeshift force of 650 cavalrymen, enough cover to allow his siege engineers to start the assault on Syracuse itself.[13]

Despite the near-fatal laxity on the part of Nicias, the Athenians still pos-sessed a number of advantages that might well have snatched victory from the jaws of defeat. With the departure and treachery of Alcibiades, Lamachus, the always reliable third general, slowly came into his own and was able to galvanize the Athenians to sail back to Syracuse and at last begin the real war that should have been started on the first day of arrival.

There they could use their newfound cavalry to protect besiegers while they started the campaign of building fortifications in earnest to hem in the city. After the Syracusans refused another pro forma offer to meet in hoplite battle, the Athenians suddenly showed signs of their old skills, which had reduced a score of cities from Potidaea to Melos. They almost immediately seized much of the heights of Epipolae, the upper portions of the citadel, and began a sophisticated plan to wall off from above the entire city from its hinterlands. To this end, they quickly built a round fort ("the Circle"), and began to use this nexus as a base from which to send out walls of circumvallation both to the sea at Trogilus and also southward to the Great Harbor of Syracuse, and thus partition off the city proper from infantry or naval reinforcement.

After successfully dealing with five invasions of their own territory, and storming Potidaea, Mytilene, Scione, and Melos, the Athenians had gained a great deal of both offensive and defensive experience in combined land and sea operations. Unlike the city of Athens, Syracuse had neither a well-fortified harbor like the Piraeus, a superior fleet, or anything like the Long Walls. Should the Athenians finish their ramparts around the upper city, patrol the southern walls to the sea, keep their newfound cavalry and hoplites busy in the countryside, and guard the exits from the Great Harbor, Syracuse really could be cut off from both home-grown and imported supplies, and thus the war won.

With at least an adequate supply of horses, the tide of battle slowly began to turn the Athenians' way as they began freely to roam around the targeted city. Perhaps hunger and plague would soon follow, given that Syracuse would be more easily cut off than was Athens of 430, which had descended into epidemic and chaos. Rumor had it that as the wall inched toward the city, the Syracusans were on the verge of capitulation, ready to concede that the belated Athenian attempt to cut them off from their hinterlands spelled doom for the city.[14]

Growing Despair

WHAT WAS TRAGIC about the next year of failed Athenian operations was not the combination of stupid mistakes and lost opportunities but, rather, how often Athenian courage and audacity almost nullified the blunders of command and nearly won the day. Nicias had made no effort to stop the Syracusan counterfortifications during the winter of relative inaction. He had allowed the newly arrived Spartan general Gylippus to bring an allied army of relief overland into the city. The Athenians let a Corinthian naval squadron under the Corinthian admiral Gongylus sail into the harbor at Syracuse. They failed to assault the enemy counterwall in its first phases of construction, and then labored on a meticulous double wall of circumvallation rather than immediately cutting off the city first with an ad hoc single fortification. Yet despite all that, the Athenians almost took Syracuse a few weeks after they began serious investment, in spring 414.

Because of some attacks on the Peloponnesian coast, Sparta now had the pretext that the Peace of Nicias was broken. It began freely to organize a steady stream of reinforcements to Sicily as it also prepared to invade Attica for the first time in over a decade. Sparta had agreed to the peace in winter 421 as a demoralized state, full of gloom over Pylos and failures in Attica and the northwest. But after the victory at Mantinea and the growing enemy quagmire in Sicily, it now saw no reason to wait to finish Athens off, especially when a major Athenian defeat might convince Persia to subsidize a Spartan fleet in earnest.[15]

After finishing their circular fort, Athenian horse and infantry immediately beat off a Syracusan counterassault. With superior infantry discipline and the newfound support of horsemen, the Athenians systematically attacked the Syracusans on the heights of their upper city known as Epipolae, in a tragicomic war of rival fortifications: one side sought desperately to finish its walls over the rocky terrain to the sea, while its enemies threw up perpendicular lines of obstruction. In this odd mix of simultaneous attempts at construction and destruction, Lamachus was killed in a brief skirmish, robbing the Athenians of their sole gifted general.

Worse still, Nicias dawdled at the most critical moments and seemed to underestimate the psychological significance of the arrival of the Peloponnesians. He had no appreciation of the critically brief window of opportunity he had to finish the walls before the despairing Syracusans rallied at the sight of fresh Peloponnesian hoplites and ships. Given that Nicias had perhaps 10,000 laborers available for the task and about five miles of fortification to build on either side of the circular fort, there was no reason why a determined general could not have finished the project before reinforcements from the Peloponnese eroded both his psychological and numerical advantages.

Earlier in the war, the Athenians had built walls far more rapidly at Nisaea, Delium, and Pylos. Even the supposedly slow Spartans had surrounded Plataea with a double wall in less than three months. Almost five centuries later Titus walled off Jerusalem with a fortification of about the same length as the Athenians' on Epipolae, using not many more men and in just three days. So despite the rough terrain and stubborn resistance, the Athenian line failed to reach the sea mostly because of lackluster leadership.

Nicias continued to dally. The two sides fought over ramparts on the heights. And almost imperceptibly an often idle Athenian navy, the only means of getting back home safely, deteriorated: its waterlogged ships and deserting allied and servile crews meant that the Athenians were no longer capable of either an ironclad blockade or an automatic victory in the Great Harbor should the Syracusans' fleet and their newfound Corinthian allies finally come out to fight.

The appearance of the Corinthian fleet followed Gylippus' overland relief march. This sudden arrival of Peloponnese manpower and leadership not only added military resources to the Syracusan cause but also began to win over neutral Sicilian cities. In a matter of days, Syracuse was thus saved from sure defeat. In response, Nicias, ailing from some sort of kidney disease, compounded his already long train of errors at summer's end by sending home a request to be relieved. Facing the possible choice of dying on Sicily or being executed at home when he returned from a military catastrophe, Nicias sought to shift the responsibility for the campaign's fate once more back to the Athenian assembly. Thus he advised the Athenians either to recall the entire expedition or to send him massive reinforcements.

In one of the most memorable scenes in his history, Thucydides begins his famous seventh book with the appearance of Peloponnesian succor at the eleventh hour of the siege, just as the Syracusans were on the verge of surrender:

> Gylippus happened to have come at the critical moment when the double wall of seven or eight stades [almost a mile] had already been completed by the Athenians down to the Great Harbor—except for a short distance near the sea where they were still building. In regard to the remainder of the encircling wall, for most of the course that ran to Trogilus and the outer sea, stones had already been deposited and some parts were half completed while others were already finished. Thus, so near had the Syracusans come to catastrophe.[16]

The interruption of the critical final Athenian fortification above Syracuse by the Peloponnesians proved the most important moment of the entire conflict. Both sides now sought to pour additional forces into the confused and often nonstop battle on the heights above the city: the Athenians desperate to finish

The Athenians
Attack Syracuse,
414

MILES

KM

SICILY

Syracuse

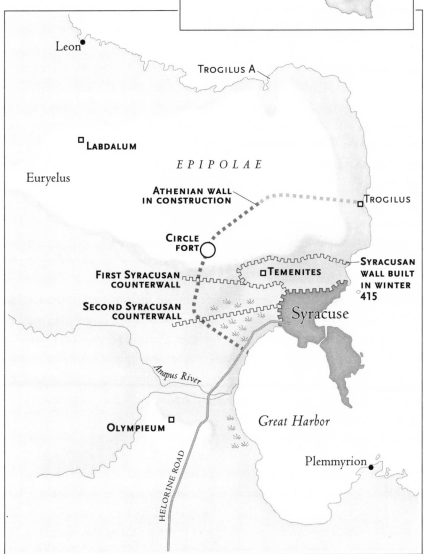

Leon

TROGILUS A

□ **LABDALUM**

EPIPOLAE

Euryelus

**ATHENIAN WALL
IN CONSTRUCTION**

□ **TROGILUS**

**CIRCLE
FORT** ○

**FIRST SYRACUSAN
COUNTERWALL**

□ **TEMENITES**

**SYRACUSAN
WALL BUILT
IN WINTER
415**

**SECOND SYRACUSAN
COUNTERWALL**

Syracuse

Anapus River

OLYMPIEUM □

Great Harbor

HELORINE ROAD

Plemmyrion

their double wall to the harbor and their longer rampart on Epipolae, the now energized Syracusans equally anxious to block their progress while they simultaneously harassed the enemy construction crews.

Despite occasional tactical victories, the war of the walls was a struggle that Nicias ultimately lost as Gylippus adroitly barred his path with a series of forts and counterwalls. The Syracusan cavalry on one occasion was instrumental in routing the Athenians. They charged hoplites on rough ground, sending the entire army back behind their unfinished fortifications. Such interruptions essentially ended any chance that the Athenians could ever break through the counterwall and extend the key final segments of their own circuit to the sea on either side.

Nicias alleged a number of reasons for the army's failure in his interim written account to the Athenian assembly back home, from the lack of sufficient cavalry to the constant wear and tear on ships and crews. But ultimately the problem lay with the thin margin of error allowed by a total force of only 45,000 in both the first and second armadas. The expedition had really always been a great gamble that an Athenian fleet of little more than 200 ships could take out one of the largest cities in the Greek-speaking world some eight hundred miles distant across the seas—one always predicated on audacious and resolute leadership.

True, the careers of both Alexander the Great and Julius Caesar proved that forces of fewer than 50,000 could conquer and occupy successfully huge tracts of enemy land, but such a bold military calculus demanded even bolder commanders who grasped that morale, will, and an offensive spirit alone could nullify an enemy's numerical superiority. In that regard, Nicias—old, sick, by nature timid, and on record against the entire invasion—was sorely wanting and thus naturally sought ever greater resources to supply an edge that his own leadership could not. Poor generalship is often synonymous with frequent requests for more troops.

The Horns of a Dilemma

WORSE FOLLY ENSUED. The uncharacteristically dense Athenians back home once more misconstrued their general's cautionary assessment as sober advice about obtaining victory rather than a thinly veiled cry for retreat. They readied a second armada to arrive sometime the next spring. To be fair, the Athenians were on the horns of a dilemma: pulling out would only embolden their enemies, while sending more reinforcements raised the specter of turning a manageable tactical defeat into a military catastrophe.

By early 414 most of the Greek world was slowly learning of the growing quagmire in Sicily and preparing to get in on the kill in a variety of ways. States as diverse as Corinth, Sicyon, and Boeotia were adding their own hoplite contingents to another Spartan expeditionary force slated to sail to Syracuse. A growing Peloponnesian fleet dispatched more ships to Syracuse. Gylippus now found additional surrounding Sicilian states as eager to help Syracuse as they had once been interested in joining the Athenians when the city was on the verge of capitulation. While the Greek world rallied to defeat the Athenian expeditionary fleet, the Peloponnesians prepared to invade Attica and fortify Decelea.[17]

Athens never flinched. In majestic defiance or folly the Athenian assembly sent Demosthenes—the hero of Pylos, the scapegoat of the Delium campaign, and more or less unheard from for over a decade—with an auxiliary imperial fleet of yet another 65 triremes and 1,200 hoplites, supported by additional allied contingents. And by the time Demosthenes arrived in Sicily, in ostentatious fashion as pipers and coxswains blared out his arrival, his combined forces had grown by over 70 fresh triremes and another 5,000 hoplites, augmented by more light-armed auxiliaries.

Once again the Athenians could hardly afford to bring either horsemen or mounts to replace the exhausted Athenian cavalry, which was increasingly unable to ward off its superior Syracusan counterparts. Altogether, in less than two years Athens had thrown into the fray almost 45,000 men and 216 ships, well over half of all the available military assets of the empire. This madness was at a time when Spartans were camped thirteen miles from the walls of Athens, thousands of slaves were deserting from Attica, and tribute-paying allies from the Hellespont to the southern Aegean were on the verge of revolt.

It was precisely this resiliency that so amazed Thucydides. He repeatedly emphasized the incredible resources of Athens and its ability to carry on the fight despite overwhelming losses and a growing list of adversaries. Moreover, at the very time thousands were besieging Syracuse, Persian satraps were also plotting to finance a new Peloponnesian fleet to tear apart the maritime empire. Thucydides might have been appalled at the foolish logic behind such a grand mistake, but he was also in awe of the democratic spirit that nevertheless went ahead with the gamble, and amazed that Athens could have pulled it all off.[18]

Demosthenes was as audacious as Nicias was timid. But once the Athenians had mobilized a second relief force and made their way to Sicily, they discovered that things on the island had become even worse than when Nicias' had sent the bleak letter home the prior autumn. Frustrated up on Epipolae and unable to break through the counterwalls of the enemy, Nicias had abruptly turned his attention to the sea and plotted a new strategy: the navy would now take the offensive in the Great Harbor of Syracuse while ground troops were stalemated on the heights.

Yet in a series of brutal sea battles in and around the Great Harbor, the Athenian triremes were manhandled by the less skillful Corinthian and Syracusan fleets. The enemy—learning from the battle of Sybota (432), where the Corinthians had found success against the more expert Corcyraeans by turning a fight at sea into a land battle of boarding and head-on attacks—had reinforced their rams and found the confined conditions inside the harbor to their advantage.

Even worse, Nicias had lost a key fort at Labdalum, up on the northern crest of Epipolae, that was critical to supplying forces to protect the ongoing construction of the wall. In response, he had moved his base of operations to Plemmyrium, on the south entrance to the harbor—a nearly indefensible spot that had little water and less fuel. But then Nicias had already given up on sealing off the city. He was more worried about securing a base in which to outfit his triremes for a quick departure home should things get any worse. That poorly selected fort was quickly lost as well, along with most of the rigging and supplies for the fleet.

The Athenians' earlier efforts to use battering rams to knock down the Syracusan counterwall failed. It was this increasingly bleak scenario that the newcomer Demosthenes immediately surveyed, and it influenced him to make that drastic decision to attack the Syracusan counterfortifications by night. Only for a moment, Demosthenes reasoned, had Athens regained the momentum and perhaps local superiority in manpower, and they could ill afford to throw away this second but fleeting chance at victory.

The attack was a disaster, as one might expect of thousands of heavily armed soldiers marching up unfamiliar rocky heights to fight an unknown enemy in the middle of the night. Demosthenes' fresh reinforcements soon found themselves in full retreat down the slopes, lost in the darkness, often falling and fighting one another, and eventually butchered by the ever vigilant Syracusan cavalry. Two thousand men may have been killed in just a few hours, nasty deaths for Athenians who a few weeks earlier were strolling in their agora at a time of relative peace.

In one of the most famous pronouncements about the confusing nature of Greek infantry battle, Thucydides concluded of the nocturnal Athenian calamity on Epipolae that "it was not easy to ascertain from either side what precisely had transpired; of course, things are clearer in the daytime, but even then those who are present hardly know everything that goes on—except what each person senses with difficulty in his own vicinity." Utterly demoralized, Demosthenes now pondered a variety of options before concluding that it was probably wisest to gather both forces up and sail home. The Athenians, he figured, still had ships and a tenuous naval superiority. And the Spartans gathering in Attica, not democratic Syracuse some eight hundred miles distant, posed the greater danger to Athens. The new dilemma was not one of winning or losing but, rather, a choice between defeat and ruin.[19]

Utter Destruction

AFTER LENGTHY DEBATE and needless delay, both sides made ready for a final grand sea battle in the Great Harbor, one even greater than the initial fights a few weeks earlier, which had on occasion involved some 160 ships. The Athenians put to sea everything they had left, some 110 triremes. Thucydides implied that it was the most crowded and desperate battle in the history of Greek naval warfare. He may have been right, since there were well over 20,000 Athenian and imperial sailors on the water, along with missile troops and marines on the decks. Perhaps as many infantrymen and slaves were watching from the shore. But the invaders were already a beaten force well before the battle even started, inasmuch as most enterprises that they had begun on Sicily—the effort to rally the island's neutral states, the attempt to wall off Syracuse, the sea battles with the enemy fleet, and the political intriguing to win Syracuse by treachery—had already failed. Even occasional victories, whether besieging minor cities or beating Syracusan hoplites in the field, had not led to strategic success.

By day's end, the Athenians were thoroughly defeated. The last battle in the harbor of Syracuse was an authentic Greek tragedy as the assembled Athenian soldiers watched the two enormous fleets go at it—now swaying and screaming from shore, "We are winning"; now in dejection shouting, "We are losing." At last, realizing that their own superior seamen could take full advantage neither of their numbers nor of their skills in such confined waters of the harbor, sailors and hoplites alike grasped that their fleet's defeat was not a setback but a death sentence. Those triremes, after all, were the only way to get back home.[20]

Nicias and Demosthenes then chose to march their still enormous combined army of 40,000 survivors on a meandering course west and then south across the island in hopes of finding refuge among friendly allies. For all the calamity, Demosthenes and Nicias still commanded more troops than the Peloponnesians and Sicilians combined. True, in two years of attrition, the Athenians had lost many in battle and to disease. Yet the startling fact remained that perhaps four out of five combatants who had arrived at Sicily were still alive and determined to find sanctuary somewhere on Sicily. It was no idle hope: a little over a decade later a far smaller force of 10,000 Greek mercenary hoplites fought their way to safety, against far greater odds, from the middle of Mesopotamia to the Black Sea, despite being outnumbered and constantly attacked by an array of Asiatic horsemen and tribal peoples.

This was still the largest army that Athens had fielded in the entire war. Indeed, it was perhaps the greatest Greek force that had been marched en masse since Archidamus had invaded Attica, almost twenty years earlier. But if alive and mostly well, most soldiers were nevertheless defeated men, demoralized that their once magnificent fleet was gone and, with it, the only way home. The Athenians were in hostile, unfamiliar territory, constantly pursued, and forced to march without easy access to water under the late August sun.

The Syracusan horse rode them down mercilessly. Infantry and light-armed troops harried them without end. The retreat soon became a rout and then a slaughter. Some eight days of marching and twenty-some miles later, they ended up in the riverbed muck of the Assinarus River, thirsty, demoralized, and incapable of going on. How many imperial troops ultimately returned home is unknown. The captured allies and slaves were sold off, while 7,000 Athenians were taken alive and interred in the quarries of Syracuse. Diodorus believed that 18,000 men were killed in just a few hours, a horrific figure that, if true, would represent the greatest single-day fatality rate in the history of classical Greek warfare and, indeed, rank with the Roman nightmares like Trasimene, Cannae, and Carrhae, or even modern bloodbaths like the first days of Antietam or the Somme. Both Demosthenes and Nicias surrendered and were executed, and their once grand expeditionary force quite literally ceased to exist, meeting not so much defeat as annihilation. Syracusan demagogues argued that after the Athenian barbarism at Scione and Melos, the captives deserved no clemency for trying to repeat their savagery on Sicily.

An entire mythology at Athens arose in later years surrounding this lost generation. Only a few notices of the dead emerge from extant Athenian casualty lists on stone—less than 200 of the tens of thousands who perished, with names like Nicon, Euages, Blepyrus, or Athemion. One can read of a Phrynus killed and a Carpides dead, but will never know how or where they died.

Yet some diehards purportedly fought on as guerrillas avenging their comrades' deaths. Others ransomed themselves by reciting verses from Euripides, who was much in vogue among the Syracusans, perhaps because he was seen as an antiwar voice who aroused sympathy for the victims of Athenian aggression. In the most gripping passage in his entire history Thucydides records the last moments of the desperate Athenians struggling to stay alive in the muddy waters of the Assinarus River, as they were picked off by their enemies from the banks above. The force that had left in such celebration at Athens and arrived in equal pomp at Syracuse now met its destruction from drowning, enemy missiles, and one another:

> Inasmuch as they were forced to move in a dense mass, they fell on and trampled one another. Some of them immediately were killed by being run through by their own spears and becoming bogged down amid their equipment. Others were swept away by the current. The Syracusans were standing on the opposite steep bank, and hit the Athenians from above with missiles. But they were busy drinking greedily and tangled up in the hollow bed of the river in great confusion. Then the Peloponnesians descended to the water and cut them down, especially those in the river itself. And the water immediately became fouled, but nonetheless was drunk—mixed as it was with mud and dyed red with blood. Indeed, it was fought over by most of them.

In the gore were thousands of men from the far reaches of the Athenian empire and friendly states—Chalcidians, Euboeans, Argives, Aegean Islanders, mercenaries from Crete, Arcadia, and Italy—all of whom, a few months earlier, had had no idea what fate would meet them in far-off Sicily against an enemy they knew very little about. The final destruction of the Greek forces was an eerie spectacle that affected Thucydides as no other battle disaster did. Reading it today reminds us of Plutarch's gruesome account of the Roman triumvir Crassus' end at Carrhae in 53 B.C., when nearly the same number of legionaries were surrounded and slaughtered by mounted Parthian archers. History is unfortunately replete with these awful scenarios of veteran infantrymen far from home who are destroyed by mounted enemies whom they cannot draw into pitched battle—a thirsty Crusader army cut apart by Saladin's 12,000 horsemen at Hattin in July 1187 or Napoleon's retreat before Russian Cossacks. The Athenians had arrived on the island in late summer 415 only to discover that they needed cavalry, and they had perished in August two years later, still regretting that they lacked enough good horsemen to make good their retreat. The incongruity that so many thousands were reduced to a mob by enemies whom they could not engage not only appalled but saddened Thucydides:

> This was the most remarkable occurrence of all those that transpired during the war—indeed as it seems to me of all the Greek events that we know of—

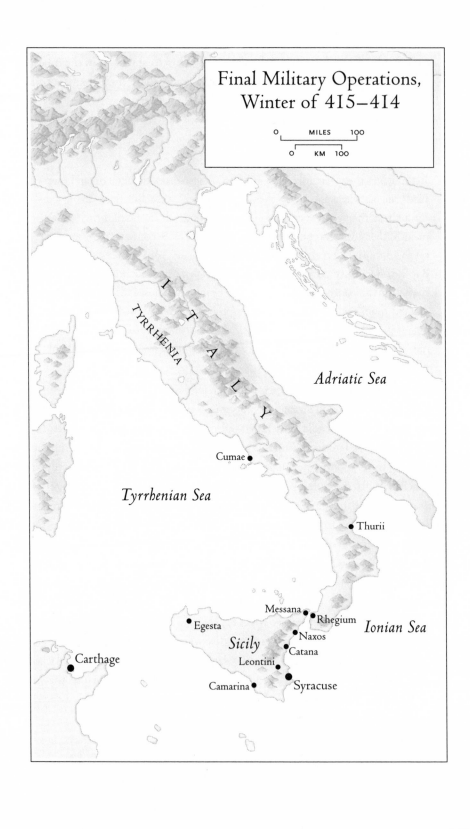

Final Military Operations,
Winter of 415–414

0   MILES   100

0   KM   100

ITALY

TYRRHENIA

Adriatic Sea

Cumae

Tyrrhenian Sea

Thurii

Messana
Rhegium
Egesta
Naxos
Sicily
Catana
Carthage
Leontini
Camarina
Syracuse

Ionian Sea

one most illustrious for the conquerors and for the defeated most ruinous. As for those defeated utterly and in every respect and meeting with no small setback in any manner—but rather as it is said with an utter destruction—their land forces, fleet, and everything else perished, and few from many came back home. Such were the events that happened in Sicily.[21]

Pony Battle

WHAT DID HORSEMEN of the Peloponnesian War look like, these deadly riders who killed hundreds of Athenians and ruined their imperial hopes in Sicily? The typical knight of the later fifth century was hardly a medieval conquistador in full mail or even a raider of the steppes with a string of mounts. Instead, imagine a young aristocrat, with a breastplate, helmet, and high leather boots—young, proud, and privileged, like the stone horsemen captured for eternity on the frieze course of Pericles' Parthenon. Few carried shields in battle. Such protection might mean an additional weight of fifteen to twenty pounds and could thus unbalance the rider and interfere with the reins.

Riders were not much over five and a half feet tall, 120 pounds. They were perched on ponies about four and a half feet above the ground (13½ hands at the withers). These tiny mounts, mostly stallions, were only partially protected with light cloth padding over the face, thighs, and chest, and harder to ride than geldings. Without the aid of stirrups, riders required strenuous training in how to grip the sides of the animal with their thighs. Most riders carried a short thrusting spear and either one or two auxiliary javelins. For close-order fighting, a small saber proved effective for downward strokes to the heads, necks, and backs of foot soldiers. Mounted bowmen were prized but rare, inasmuch as they drew on the combined skills of both horsemanship and archery.

On vase paintings, horsemen seem to be riding down infantrymen as often as bombarding them from afar with missiles. The disastrous loss of Lamachus on Epipolae reflects what could happen to fleeing or pursuing veteran hoplites should they find themselves out of formation and confronted with even a single horseman. If death by trampling seems unlikely given the small weight and height of the ponies, it is important to remember that infantrymen themselves were about the same size as modern twelve-year-olds rather than contemporary adults, and fought as clumsy hoplites without javelins or bows.[22]

While in theory cavalry of most Greek city-states were loosely organized into large regiments of 500 or so—and later in Hellenistic times would mass in tactical rhomboid formations of 120 to break light infantry—for most of the

Peloponnesian War, smaller subgroups rode out in bands of 30 to 50, often in loose rectangles. True, they were probably deployed in dense formations in pitched battles at Solygia, Delium, and Mantinea; but just as often classical horsemen scattered to attack small pockets of ravagers or skirmishers. Heavy cavalry and lancers charging in concert with infantry were the later achievements of Philip and Alexander, almost a century after the outbreak of the Peloponnesian War.

Despite the superior speed of cavalrymen and the ability of mounted armies to travel hundreds of miles at sustained daily clips of over thirty miles, for a variety of reasons prior to the Peloponnesian War horses had, strangely, not mattered much to Greek militaries. Of course, they were always valuable for surveillance and reconnaissance. As ancillaries in hoplite battle, a few horsemen could also protect the unshielded wings and could stab at the backs of fleeing infantrymen during pursuit—places and times when cavalrymen were not confronted with serried ranks of spears. But there was a variety of reasons why the Greek city-state never put much emphasis on mounted forces in the eastern Mediterranean, where wars had traditionally been decided by great chariot collisions in the Middle East or the dreaded charges of Persian horsemen on the vast plains of Asia.[23]

On the Greek mainland, it made little sense to raise horses in small valleys. Pasturage was rare and rocky hills common. Eating horseflesh was considered wrong, reflected by the general deference for the horse in Greek religion and mythology. Oddly, the auxiliary and subordinate role of horses in Greek society cast an aura of reverential exceptionalism upon them, making their position there different from that on the steppes, where they were seen in more pragmatic and utilitarian ways. Moreover, in an age before sophisticated harnesses, oxen under yokes proved the more reliable and economical draft animals, whether pulling wagons or plows. An acre devoted to wheat, barley, vines, or olives would support a family much better than turning the land over to pasturage for sheep, goats, or cows—much less horses.[24]

Cavalry Calculus

COST IS ALWAYS mentioned in any discussion of horse rearing, a profession confined to the rich, who, in turn, publicly complained about its ruinous expense. By the end of the war, even an average pony might cost the equivalent of almost a year and a half's salary for the average unskilled worker. The price of a typical horse might instead support a family of six for almost two years. A mount was clearly a luxury that only a small fraction of the population could afford. The average Athenian who walked into town or plowed with an ox saw a horse not as a critical asset but as a luxury, one that in a radically democratic society perhaps gobbled communal Athenian resources away from the more needy. The simple truth was that there were not thousands of acres of communal grazing land around most city-states on which herds of horses could graze cheaply.

The acquisition cost for some of the better mounts might exceed 1,000 drachmas, illustrating another dilemma for democratic Athens: as the war wore on and horses were proving more critical for collective survival, only the very rich could afford to patrol the homeland. And if the additional costs of feeding the horse are added in—and often a groom, who accompanied the cavalryman on a cheaper mount to carry supplies and equipment—a knight might need almost a drachma a day to buy barley rations. True, the state often provided partial subsidies for horse acquisition and upkeep, but as imperial revenues declined, Athens found itself broke and ever more dependent on private largess to ensure that cavalrymen continued to scour the countryside.

In theory, only a wealthy state like Thessaly or Syracuse, with a surrounding lush countryside, could afford to put into the field a gigantic force of 1,200 horsemen, which represented an initial investment of at least 100 talents, in addition to over 5 talents a month in collective upkeep. For that kind of money, a state might instead field a hoplite army of 20,000 infantrymen for a month, or even outfit a fleet of 100 triremes.[25] Cavalry was thus a luxury most states—other than Syracuse, Boeotia, and Thessaly, which all enjoyed wide expanses of pastureland—could not afford. Most generals would reckon that a trireme or 60 suits of heavy bronze armor were far wiser outlays than the equivalent investment in a mere 12 horses.[26]

Yet what is nearly inexplicable is that under the practices of the typical polis before the Peloponnesian War, hoplite and agrarian snobbery *extended to the very wealthy as well*, the elite who owned farms of perhaps 100 acres or more and so could manage to own a horse or two. There are few, if any, other ancient societies in which a wealthy citizen could brag to the assembly that he dismounted and chose instead to serve the state as a soldier in the ranks, despite the valuable and privileged role horsemen played in the defense of infantry. At the outbreak of the war Greeks thought that cavalry service was easy and riders were less than resolute compared to hoplites. At Sparta there was essentially no formal cavalry force until the seventh year of the Peloponnesian War. And at Athens, even by the outbreak of fighting in 431, there had only recently been raised about 1,200 horsemen, drawn from less than 3 percent of the voting citizen population.[27]

For one of the rare moments in history, landholding for the period of the polis was comparably egalitarian. Thus the very wealthy did not enjoy automatic prestige, and certainly were not accorded deference in political and military matters. Their land might have been ten, but surely not one hundred, times the size of the average farm owner's. This relatively equitable landscape was a vast difference in land tenure from that of the horse lords of Thessaly or the Macedonian princes who raised entire herds on vast estates.

In contrast with the north, even at oligarchic Sparta the state was run by an elite number of Similars. These infantrymen owned equal shares of land and took up identical slots in the phalanx, the real basis of their prestige. At Athens the landless thetes gradually assumed the predominant role in the politics of the city, a fact that explains everything from Pericles' massive building program to state subsidies for government service to an enormous fleet and the primacy of the Long Walls. At agrarian Thebes, despite the flat plains and a rich heritage of *hippotrophia* (horse raising), the real power likewise resided with hoplite farmers, who by the fourth century would become fully democratic and the most dreaded military in Greece.

The two oligarchic revolutions that overthrew Athenian democracy, those of 411 and 403, occurred during and at the close of the war, following the military catastrophes at Sicily and Aegospotami, which were blamed on the radical democrats. In contrast, the so-called knights were the privileged horsemen who had taken on an increasingly vital role in, and paid a high price for, the city's defense during the struggle, cleaning up, as it were, the mess created by their inferiors. Indeed, in almost every land engagement that Athens fought—Spartolos (429), Solygia (425), Delium (424), Amphipolis (422), Mantinea (418), Syracuse (415–13), Ephesus (409), Abydos (409), and Kerata (409)—the Athenian cavalry had had a critical role and had won a strange sort of admiration from the usually hostile majority of poorer citizens. During most expeditions a tenth of the Athenian aggregate force was made up of cavalrymen.

Besides such political and economic considerations peculiar to Greece, there were other more pragmatic and general military explanations for the inferior role of cavalry. Ubiquitous rocky terrain meant that unshod horses often went lame or were restricted to bottomland. Because Greek horses stood less than five feet off the ground, in an age without saddles, stirrups, or horseshoes, they were not equipped to carry even a small mailed knight at a gallop into shock battle. Whether one turns to jokes in ancient comedy or warnings in equestrian literature, there are frequent references to the dangers of falling off horses, even without the worry of attacking and defending during battle.

Bareback riders can be lethal warriors (witness the Native Americans). But it is still a difficult skill to ride and stab or shoot without a modern saddle and the expertise acquired by years of training of the sort Xenophon outlined in plentiful detail in his treatise on ancient horsemanship. The city-state, unlike a nineteenth-century nation, could not put thousands of raw recruits on ponies and, with standard-issue saddles, stirrups, or horseshoes, then expect them to become serious lancers that could break apart the ranks of hoplite spearmen. Instead, more often the wealthy few alone grew up on horses and learned to throw the javelin, shoot the bow, or stab with a short spear while mounted on a simple blanket—but not, in the later manner of Alexander the Great, to co-ordinate attacks with fellow infantrymen.[28]

The New Horsemen

THE PELOPONNESIAN WAR changed most of this existing equestrian protocol, as military efficacy, not social stereotypes, economic rationalism, or political considerations determined how men now fought. Horses did not suddenly grow larger. Stirrups were not magically invented, and aristocrats did not gain control of the reins of government. As the war progressed, and traditional strategies from agricultural devastation to hoplite battle were proved wanting, city-states began to learn that horsemen were vital to all sorts of operations that would play major roles in determining the outcome of the war, from rid-ing down fleeing hoplites and light-armed troops to patrolling the countryside and keeping the enemy away from camps, fortifications, and farmland.

Unlike most of the battle experience of the previous decades—the Greeks had won at Salamis and Plataea with ships and hoplites, and fought one another for the next fifty years in classic pitched battles at Sepea, Tanagra, Oinophyta, and Coronea—horsemen appeared everywhere in the Peloponnesian War and killed far more thousands of Greeks than did those in the hoplite phalanx. Typ-ically, cavalry would gallop upon small groups of infantrymen, who were either marching loosely or scattered in twos and threes. They rode up, often at short bursts of speeds of thirty miles per hour, cast a javelin or shot an arrow, and then easily outran pursuit, hoping to tire any infantryman foolish enough to offer chase.

Because the rider was throwing with his arm alone and thus could hardly ap-proximate the two- to three-hundred-foot range of a skilled javelin thrower on foot, he might at most have cast his weapon thirty to forty feet, and then found safety only in retreat given his mobility and speed. When horsemen outnumbered infantry groups—on Sicily this was not uncommon, given the enormous size of the Syracusan mounted contingents—they could ride in formation and spear their inferiors from the back or sides, not unlike German fighter pilots of World War II, who swarmed American B-17s that fell out of protective formation.

Athenian cavalrymen attacked Spartan ravagers in Attica on five separate occasions in the Archidamian War (431–421). They accompanied every Athenian army during the annual invasion of the Megarid, participated in many of the seaborne raids of the Peloponnesian coast, wore out their mounts harassing the Spartan permanent garrison at Decelea, and were active in the last decade of the war in Ionia. During the Megara campaign of 424, 600 horsemen protected thousands of infantry, providing the sort of cover that they would desperately need in Sicily a decade later. In the Megarid they held off the more feared Boeotian cavalry, which likewise appeared 600 strong, as over a thousand mounted troops on both sides battled it out to a draw.[29]

Thucydides, at least, believed that in a number of instances the presence of Athenian horsemen ensured victory, such as at Solygia in the Corinthian plain during the battle there of 425.[30] At Cleon's final battle at Amphipolis, where both he and Brasidas perished in the summer of 422, at least 300 cavalrymen were present. The value of horsemen in the first decade and a half of the war suggests that the Athenians grasped that they would be critical on Sicily. Still, for some reason, they miscalculated the ease of securing mounts from their allies, and had no real idea of the effectiveness or size of the Syracusan cavalry.

The outcome of entire theaters occasionally hinged on horsemen. For example, at the battle of Delium, Thucydides makes the Athenian general Hippocrates claim that a defeat of the Boeotians would put an end altogether to the Spartan invasion of Attica, inasmuch as the Boeotian cavalry would never again venture into Attica to protect Spartan ravagers. In the battle itself, horsemen were largely responsible for the Boeotian victory. As reserves they surprised the victorious Athenian right wing and collapsed the morale of the entire army. Only the presence of a few hundred Athenian cavalry kept the Athenian flight from becoming a complete disaster as they desperately tried to shield fleeing hoplites from being speared from the rear by mounted pursuers. In the only other major hoplite encounter of the war, that of Mantinea in 418, Thucydides observed that had the Athenian cavalry not been present, the Athenians might have lost more than their 200 dead and 2 generals.[31]

The enormous force of Sitacles's that invaded Macedonia with 150,000 troops comprised 50,000 horsemen. In response, the Macedonians fought back with heavy cavalrymen, men with breastplates equipped with stabbing spears and riding horses with body protection. Sitacles' invasion must have been the greatest cavalry fight of the ancient world in the era before Alexander the Great.

Postmortem

THE ATHENIANS HAD set sail for Sicily in spring 415. Then they were still at peace with Sparta and in the midst of an ongoing recovery from the ravages of the plague and war, as well as buoyed by the recent conquest of tiny Melos. Two years later, between 40,000 and 50,000 Athenians, allies, and slaves were dead, missing, or captured. Some 216 imperial triremes were lost. The Athenian treasury was broke. For the first time in the war, Athens could no longer afford to patrol the coast of the Peloponnese. Its old strategy of proactively hitting the enemy to the rear was now over with. Allies and tributary subjects were talking of revolt at precisely the time Athens needed their money, materials, and imperial crewmen to build an entirely new fleet. After expending well over 3,000 talents in a failed enterprise, Athens earned only a renewed war with an ever-growing Peloponnesian alliance. There was to be a permanent Spartan fort in sight of the walls of Athens, a newly envisioned alliance of Persia, Sparta, and Syracuse, and the specter of a Peloponnesian fleet far larger than its own now augmented with a few Syracusan triremes.

Oddly, Syracuse fared little better. The two-year siege had cost the state almost as much money as it had Athens. Despite enemies on and south of the island, Syracuse was now itself obligated to the Spartans to send troops and ships from its exhausted citizenry eight hundred miles back to the other war in the Aegean. Within five years the Syracusans were faced with a massive Carthaginian invasion, inasmuch as the North Africans had watched the internecine Greek bloodletting with glee.

There was further irony still. The poor in the fleet and among the light-armed felt that they had played an underappreciated role in the victory, one every bit as important as that of the more recognized aristocratic horsemen. In response, in 409 they stripped the moderates of power and altered the conservative Syracusan democracy into something more resembling the radical government of their Athenian oppressors. Hermocrates himself, the astute statesman who had crafted the successful Syracuse defense, was exiled and later killed in domestic unrest.

Yet this more radical Syracusan democracy did not last even four years. In 406, in Syracuse's moment of crisis against Carthage, only the tyrannical vision of the strongman Dionysius would unite Sicily, saving all but the western part of the island from Carthaginian subjugation. Again, the paradox was had the Athenians pulled off their hegemonic enterprise, Sicily would probably have been united earlier under the very democratic auspices it later welcomed. It would have remained mostly autonomous from Carthage—just as the Peloponnesians probably would have sued to continue the armistice of 421 in fear of this most recent display of Athenian power. The Punic invasion of Sicily following the defeat of Athens was one of the most savage encounters in Greek history, a sort of mini–Peloponnesian War in which at various times the Carthaginians ceremoniously in a few hours executed 3,000 Sicilians, razed Himera and Selinus, butchered tens of thousands of civilians, and then lost half their entire force to the plague.[32]

There was one final legacy from the Athenian invasion. Once the tyrant Dionysius consolidated his tyranny over the Syracusans, he mustered them en masse in 401 to guarantee that no foreign power would ever be able to wall the city off from Epipolae above—ex post facto perhaps proving that the Athenians had earlier had enough men but had lacked the audacity to do in two years what Dionysius did in less than a month. Some 60,000 Sicilians, along with 6,000 pairs of oxen, built almost four miles of stone fortifications in just twenty days, so traumatic were the lingering effects upon the Syracusans of the Athenian effort to destroy their city from its own heights.[33]

In theory, the Spartans were the main beneficiaries inasmuch as their small expeditionary contingent under Gylippus had energized a massive response against the Athenians that had caused more enemy losses than any single battle of the war. Yet for all the vaunted size and reputed wealth of the island, the exhausted Syracusans later contributed only 20 ships to the growing but distant Peloponnesian fleet in the Aegean—a commitment that nevertheless strained the fragile political equilibrium and led to the destruction of the oligarchic party, the very stalwarts Sparta had hoped to promote by its intervention. While it might be logical to assume that such a paltry Syracusan role in the renewed Peloponnesian War in hindsight makes the Athenian case for intervention weak, one must remember that Athens' attack on Sicily took an enormous toll on the enemy, and better explains why Syracuse could contribute so little to finish the Athenians off.

Lessons of Sicily

WHAT, THEN, IS one to make of Sicily? The problem was not just the cost. The imperial Athenians had lost as many men and ships before the war, in Egypt—

and later would suffer even more casualties in the Ionian War. If the plan to conquer Syracuse was mad, it was nevertheless not intrinsically unfeasible. The island was not easily defensible and was conquered often in history—the Romans in 211 B.C., the Muslims in A.D. 878, followed by a succession of Franks, Spanish, Normans, Italians, and the allies under George Patton and Bernard Montgomery in 1943. Even the nearly suicidal tripartite command structure, the ongoing witch hunt back home, the treachery of Alcibiades, the illness of Nicias, and the renewal of the war with Sparta did not inevitably doom the Athenian plan. The effort, after all, had been a close-run thing, perhaps just days away from success before the unexpected arrival of the Spartans and Corinthians.

As for an ultimate benefit-to-risk analysis, in hindsight the invasion of Sicily seems absurd. True, had the Athenians won they would have acquired enormous prestige, terrified the Spartans, and cut them off from Sicilian trade, and perhaps found some material rewards, additional grain, and more allies. But Sicily was far distant and pushed to the limits any idea of the "indirect approach" of defeating enemies without meeting them head-on in conventional battle. So while there was something to gain in Sicily for the Athenians if everything went right, there was also far more there to lose if anything went wrong in the larger war itself. That ambiguous assessment seems to be Thucydides' own, when paradoxically he acknowledges that the Athenians might have prevailed, but the way the campaign unfolded nevertheless constituted its greatest mistake of the war.[34]

What went wrong?

At almost every key juncture the absence of sufficient cavalry ruined the Athenians. While the theater was a multifaceted campaign involving sieges, hoplite battle, agricultural ravaging, terror, and dramatic trireme battles, in the end it was the unheralded cavalry skirmishes that made much of the difference. In the first months of the campaign, the Athenians were stymied by Syracusan horsemen from doing any damage from their base at Catana. Only deception that for a few days fooled the enemy cavalry forces permitted them the safety of even approaching Syracuse; once they were there, an important hoplite victory brought little strategic success, given the presence of 1,200 riders who stopped the minor defeat from becoming a serious rout. These horsemen—we know neither names nor any other details about them—stunned the victors. Coupled with their earlier patrols, they demoralized the Athenians, in large part explaining the virtual cessation of hostilities during the winter of 415, when the Athenians sheepishly kept close to their quarters at Catana.

In contrast, once the Athenians gathered even a small force of 650 horsemen, the pulse of the campaign changed radically. Cavalry allowed the Athenians to ascend Epipolae and begin work on fencing in the city from above. The ensuing yearlong war on the heights was often determined by mounted troops, most notably when the Syracusans beat back Lamachus' offensive and killed him in the confusion. Gylippus' overland march from Himera—the real turning point in the war—was safeguarded by cavalry. Had the Athenians had a mounted force the size of the Syracusan cavalry, they might have turned it back and won the war outright with the completion of their fortifications. In any case, Gylippus' only subsequent setback was due to his foolish decision to attack the Athenians without mounted escorts, a rash mistake that he regretted and did not repeat.

In the final year the Athenian loss of its fortified base at Plemmyrium, on the harbor south of the city, stemmed in large part from the constant raiding of hundreds of Syracusan horsemen, who rode down any Athenian who ventured out of the ramparts for water or firewood. This forfeiture of that naval base and its supplies did much to begin the ruin of the Athenian fleet. And Nicias had turned his attention to blockading the city by sea only because of the prominent role of enemy cavalry around the approaches to Epipolae, which ensured that he could never storm the counterwall that stymied the advance of his own fortifications. Demosthenes' bold plan to take Epipolae at night was a failure. The deadly nocturnal pursuit of the Syracusan horse turned it into a bloodbath, destroying the morale of the army itself and putting an end to offensive operations by land.

A mere 1,200 Syracusans tipped the balance of the war, and ensured that 45,000 enemy invaders would lose. The experience of horse warfare on Sicily in and of itself did not immediately lead to the integration of cavalry and infantry mastered by Philip and Alexander. Yet despite the peculiar circumstances of Sicilian terrain and culture, the stunning defeat taught the Greeks that the days of hoplite exclusivity were ended. Gone too was the parochial idea that aristocratic knights were to remain prancers on the flanks of the phalanx rather than packs of mounted killers who, if not met by like kind, could limit the operations of even the largest forces—and alter the very course of sieges and naval engagements.[35]

Alcibiades was thirty-five when the Athenians landed on Sicily. If any single person was responsible for the birth and death of the Sicilian idea, it was surely he. His oratory and demagoguery were instrumental in convincing the volatile mob to sail in the first place. Yet his hope that an entire island could be subdued through intrigue rather than blood and iron proved as catastrophic as the timidity and inaction of Nicias. Ploys and deception were certainly vintage Alcibiades, who earlier at Mantinea had lined up an alliance of democratic states to dethrone Sparta from the hegemony of the Peloponnese—only to fail to galvanize the Athenians themselves to send the necessary force to guarantee victory.

Personal excess, arrogance, licentiousness—call it all what you wish—gave ammunition to his enemies, who recalled him from Syracuse for both good and bad reasons, involving legitimate and trumped-up charges of impiety and indecency. Whether Alcibiades was always lying or disclosed accurate strategic information to the Spartans is not clear, but without his presence in the Peloponnese the Spartans might well have tarried in their aid. Remember, had either Gylippus or Gongylus arrived a few days later, Syracuse would have already been lost.

Despite Alcibiades' courage at the siege of Potidaea, his service in Attica during the invasions and plague, his heroism at Delium, and his machinations that led to Mantinea and perhaps Melos, the war was turning away from the great personalities and now hinging more on manpower and matériel. Horses would have won Sicily for Athens—and now ships would decide the last phase of the war, a struggle that Alcibiades was to reenter but in a most unexpected and ultimately tragic way.

There is a final, sad epitaph to the Sicilian nightmare. In a fitting tribute to the cavalrymen who had won the war, the Syracusans branded the foreheads of the thousands of Athenian captives they took—by burning into the flesh of each the mark of a horse.

CHAPTER 8

SHIPS

THE WAR AT SEA (431-404)

The Gathering Storm

SICILY DID NOT end but, rather, reignited the old struggle with Sparta. Suddenly the entire war was on again, and its focus abruptly shifted from the west to far eastward, in the coastal waters off Asia Minor. The Athenian disaster would be followed by a final naval Armageddon in the eastern Aegean as a triumphant Sparta won over enough allies and Persian money to make good on its boast some twenty years earlier of winning by creating a massive fleet. Still, in the immediate aftermath of Sicily, there was a general consensus that Athens was immediately doomed—without enough ships, citizen warriors, or capital to keep enemies out of the Piraeus.

If the Peloponnesians could not storm a weakened Athens or destroy its hoplites, then it would squeeze the city and hope to wreck its seapower through a showdown on the Aegean. King Agis at Decelea ordered his allies to raise funds immediately to construct a fresh armada of 100 triremes to coordinate a joint land and sea strategy for finishing off the wounded adversary. What had happened to the previous Peloponnesian fleet during the first two decades of the war is not clear; but even the new plan to launch 100 triremes was not all that ambitious—and yet was dependent on Persian subsidies that would involve years of concessions and negotiations.

During this uncertain period immediately after the disaster in Sicily, subject states of Athens, initially the powerful Euboeans, Lesbians, and Chians, began to conspire with Sparta about defecting from the empire, even as the Persian satrap Tissaphernes sent his envoys to Sparta to offer his support for Peloponnesian maritime supremacy. Athens' allies sensed that the end was near, and were furious anyway that the imperial city had led so many of their sons to mass slaughter in Sicily. Meanwhile, across the border in Thebes, the Boeotians stepped up their plundering of Attic farms and made ready to take back the disputed borderlands of the Oropus, a move that would enhance the success of insurrection on the nearby island of Euboea. "Everyone," Diodorus concluded, "assumed that the war had come to an end—since no one expected that the Athenians even for a moment could endure such severe setbacks."[1]

At Athens itself, a special board of auditors (the *probouloi*) was appointed to craft ways to save the city and circumvent the assembly from proposing any further reckless adventures. The contingency fund of 1,000 talents, untouched since the outbreak of the war, was now tapped to begin reconstructing the fleet. This new idea that appointed senior Athenian statesmen—the aged playwright Sophocles was among them—would offer sober checks to the popular will foreshadowed widening splits among the citizenry and, indeed, the oligarchic revolution of 411 to come. Meanwhile, with the growing force of Peloponnesians at Decelea still kept out by the walls of Athens, with no hope of a final phalanx battle on the plains of Attica, and with the attention of all of Greece now turned to the flow of food and capital into the Piraeus, the outcome of this last chapter in the Peloponnesian conflict would hinge mostly on thousands of Greek seamen embarking on strange oared ships to kill one another far across the Aegean.

A Most Peculiar Ship

THERE HAS PROBABLY never been as bizarre yet successful a galley as the Greek trireme. Certainly no such oared vessel like it had been constructed and rowed on the Mediterranean before that time, nor has one since. If hoplite battle before the Peloponnesian War may have had a prior history of some two and a half centuries, trireme warfare was relatively new. Triremes themselves probably first appeared only in the middle and later part of the sixth century. Although the Phoenicians or Egyptians perhaps first mastered the art of building triremes, it was the growth of the Athenian empire in the mid-fifth century that saw the emergence of sophisticated naval tactics.

Lightness and balance, not seaworthiness and protection, seem to have been the chief aims in building good triremes. If middle-class landowners were almost invulnerable inside their traditional hoplite armor, the landless fought absolutely defenseless as they rowed nearly naked across the seas in these relatively novel ships. Although the trireme was not a particularly large platform, about 120 feet from bow to stern and 20 feet wide amidships, it could nevertheless carry 200 sailors, officers, and marines. The crew could row at nearly fifty strokes a minute to achieve short bursts of fighting speeds of almost ten knots as it delivered devastating force with its ram. A sail was used to rest the seamen while in transit when combat was unlikely.

So unique was the vessel's tripartite system of oarage that until the last few decades scholars still could not even agree on how the trireme (from the Greek *trieres,* "three-fitted") was powered. Because triremes were unusually buoyant and rarely equipped with ballast, they never really completely sank to the bottom—thus ensuring that there are presently few remains for underwater archaeologists to examine. What exactly is the significance of the "tri-" in the ship's nomenclature? Did three men sit side by side on one bench, pulling jointly on a single oar? Or did three rowers pull three oars? Or, as is most likely, were there three banks of oarsmen, sitting at three levels, hitting the water from three different elevations and angles with their like-sized fourteen-foot oars?

Much of the puzzle that had evoked heated debate since the Renaissance was supposed to have been solved in 1987, when a joint British-Greek research team launched *Olympias,* a modern full-sized replica of a classical Athenian trireme. Despite problems in the performance of *Olympias,* even its limited sea trials confirmed that the often-conflicting ancient testimonia about triremes probably meant that there could be three levels of oarsmen, each rower with his standard-sized oar. But the simulations on *Olympias* also reminded us of just how miserable naval service was for thousands of seamen—despite not being shackled and chained like Roman galley slave rowers—and how tricky it was for rowers to synchronize their strokes with their light firwood oars. Indeed, so far the modern craft has never quite achieved levels of performance commensurate with those of ancient ships as suggested by classical texts.

The most cramped and unpleasant positions in the 120-foot-long ship probably belonged to the 54 thalamites. These poor crewmen rowed from deep in the hold (*thalamos*), crammed in a scant eighteen inches above the water. Leather pads in their oar holes in theory kept the waves out. But seawater always splashed in anyway—the ship was honeycombed with over one hundred such holes—and bilge water also seeped through the planking near their feet. Sailors were probably soaked on and off throughout the entire voyage. As a rower pulled and leaned back and then pushed forward, his rear scooted to and fro along the bench, explaining why seamen considered seat cushions as important as good oars—and why rump blisters were a common complaint.

Because of the crossbeams and the other seamen rowing directly above their heads, the thalamites could see almost nothing. The sweat from the two superior banks of rowers—the posteriors of the seamen above were more or less in the thalamites' faces—drenched them as well. The comic poet Aristophanes joked that the thalamites were often farted upon and even showered with excrement from the straining oarsmen above, a scatological reference that he may have derived from the common and collective real-life miseries of the veterans in the theater audience. Sweat, thirst, blisters, exhaustion, urine, and feces—all this was in addition to the billows of the sea and the iron of the enemy.[2]

Yelling, confrontation, perhaps even outright fights were common as rowers elbowed one another. Anyone who has tried to put on football gear in a jam-packed, steamy August locker room can get some idea of the petty squabbles and temper tantrums below the deck. Sometimes crewmen fouled each other's oars, or encroached on another's cramped rowing space. By the end of the war, after thousands of citizen rowers were long dead, the poor, foreigners, residents, and slaves were drafted and all sat together, finding a messy equality on benches that was unknown even in the democratic assembly.

Crewmen always preferred striking calm seas to achieve the greatest efficiency. Yet because of the disharmony of three tiers of oarsmen, only 30 of some 170 rowers ever really hit completely undisturbed seas. Most rowers, then, were pulling their oars in the wake of others and found it difficult to hit choppy and swirling waters squarely with any force.

Right above the lowly thalamites sat the middle bank of 54 zygiante oarsmen, who were perched on the ship's main crossbeams (*zyga*). They, too, could not see the water and rowed through portholes. But at least these "crossbeamers" in the middle bank had more room and did not have to contend with the legs and the rumps of the oarsmen above.

The top row of two banks, the most prestigious slots and so often the best paid, was occupied by 62 thranites in total, port and starboard. These elite rowers were above the splashing of the seas and enjoyed constant breezes. They sat on an outrigger, and besides the fresh air, sunlight, and greater room could alone of the crew see their oars hit the sea and communicate with the rowers below. If they were the most vulnerable to enemy missiles, thranites were also the most likely to get out of the ship alive if it was rammed and sank.

Presumably those rowers with either the greatest experience or demonstrably superior skills, whether judged by consistently hitting the water with a full stroke or stamina in maintaining a steady pull for hours on end, were selected for these favored benches on the ship. Thranites seemed to have set the pulse of the oarage for the entire crew. They were those most attuned to the vagaries of wind and current, nearby ships, and their combined effect on the trireme's speed and steadiness. Indeed, because of the elite rowers' expertise and experience, nominal thranites may have sometimes been scattered throughout the ship on all three banks to ensure that such steady role models were never far away.

The competence of rowers varied widely within a fleet. Sometimes oarsmen could be culled out and assembled together to create a small elite flotilla that could achieve speeds consistently greater than normal. Experience seems to be the requisite for rowing excellence. So it is probable that many of the best rowers were in their thirties and forties and—at Athens, at least—veterans of dozens of campaigns when the war broke out.[3]

Battle Afloat

WHEN A PHALANX—thousands of men in polished armor arrayed in neat columns—lowered its spears in unison, it was lauded as a fierce hedgehog raising its bristles. For the Greeks the banked oars of a fast-moving trireme swishing in perfect rhythm in and out of the sea lent an equally profound impression of a living, breathing entity. As dozens of such eerie vessels bore down on an enemy in matched order and cadence, crews and onlookers alike were caught up in the spectacle. On the ships' prows, painted or inlaid-marble apotropaic eyes glowered like sea monsters at the doomed target ahead.

Part of the trick in turning mundane wooden triremes into frightening visual spectacles centered on their multifarious decorations: eyes, nameplates, painted figureheads, and various ornaments. Perhaps the only way to tell one state's trireme from another's was the wooden statue of the particular tutelary deity affixed above the ram—in the case of Athens, representations of Pallas Athena. Because many of these ships were paid for and outfitted by private citizens, there was a natural rivalry among the wealthy to launch the most impressive trireme in the fleet, one that might not only startle potential enemies but also encourage the better oarsmen to sign up as rowers.

Fleets could become symbols of national power and were often specially adorned to galvanize public support and acclaim. Returning admirals often garlanded their triremes, decked them out with captured arms, and towed dozens of captured ships into port—such as Alcibiades' magnificent return to the Piraeus from triumph in the Hellespont, when the Athenian fleet arrived hauling in 200 captured Peloponnesian triremes.[4]

"A terror to enemies" and "a joy to her friends," Xenophon wrote of an oared ship in ramming mode, the chief method of attack. The swish of the oar, the *rhothion,* of a rapidly advancing trireme was famous. Both the sound and the look added to the drama, and presaged something terrible to come. Thucydides emphasized "the fear of the swishing" (*phobos rhothiou*), which only compounded the scary sight of a trireme bearing down. Triremes, like later full-masted men-of-war, were beautiful and occasionally noisy vessels, and they captured contemporaries' imaginations in ways most other more workmanlike warships, from Roman galleys to ironclads, did not. With a length six or seven times its width and a massive ram, the sleek trireme in one sense was simply a floating spear.[5]

The protocols of sea battle by intent resembled a hoplite encounter on water. The generals harangued their troops before embarking. Both sides usually sought to ram and smash each other. Combatants chanted a war cry. Upon conclusion, the dead were given up under truce, and a trophy was erected nearby on shore. If Greek infantrymen ran into battle yelling, *Eleleu!* or *Alala!,* sailors kept mostly silent, at least until the final seconds. Sometimes as they went into their ramming strokes for the last few thousand yards before collision they chanted in unison, *Ryppapai! Ryppapai! Ryppapai!* and *O opop! O opop!*—or so Aristophanes wrote.

Just as often, as if they were hoplites in the phalanx, they broke out in a longer, more formulaic war cry or chant, the paean, to keep cadence, promote élan, terrify the enemy, and ward off evil. As triremes approached the enemy, trumpets would sound, the war cry would reverberate throughout the fleet, and general shouting would erupt, veteran rowers especially eager to be the first to strike the enemy fleet.[6]

Order and unity were critical on board oared ships, amid the distractions of the loud swishing and the piper's tune to guarantee good rowing time. Idle chatter and its resulting inattention might mean that a Greek trireme's 170 oars—broad, short shafts for the calm waters of the Mediterranean—would soon fall out of synchronization. In a matter of seconds, the relatively light ship could stall or become buffeted by winds. So, for example, in 429 the Athenian admiral Phormio reminded his sailors as they set out for a second engagement against the Peloponnesian fleet in the Corinthian Gulf, "Be careful to keep order and silence"—the keys to battle success—"especially in sea warfare." The challenge for trireme warfare was not just enemy ships but also the very intricate mechanics of oared propulsion itself.[7]

Most trireme sailors rowed blindly, not just by rote and practice but also through the sheer inability to see the sea below. Indeed, 108 of the 170 rowers, those in the two lower vertical banks, sat enclosed inside the hull. They could not even steal a momentary glance to see their own oars hit the water. To learn where and how far away the enemy was, these sightless oarsmen counted on the warnings of the coxswain, and perhaps even the top bank of rowers, perched on the outriggers. The latter might for a few seconds lift their heads up to scan the oarage and warn of problems, periodically apprising the rest of the crew of the efficacy of their own blind strokes.

Yet given the low ride of a trireme in the sea, even the officers and seamen in the top bank of oars could take in very little of the battle. Greece's ubiquitous headlands and promontories often cut off sight lines in battles, which were typically fought close to shore. In the case of the Ionian theater, especially in the battles in the Hellespont at Aegospotami, Cynossema, Cyzicus, and Sestos, triremes were often rarely more than two or three miles from the coast. Unlike land warfare, there were no hills from which trierarchs might look down upon the nature of their deployment either before or during the battle—or the tall masts of later men-of-war, by which the pilot could send up lookouts to shout coordinates to officers below.

The blind world of a Greek warship suddenly ended when the trireme either hit the enemy or was rammed itself. "Quite simply, over the entire harbor arose the crash of the colliding ships and the cry of desperate struggling men, killing and in turn dying," Diodorus wrote of the Athenian fleet as it smashed into its Syracusan counterpart in the Great Harbor. "No one could hear any of the commands once the boats hit each other and their oars smashed together, and at the same time was added the racket of the men fighting on the ships and their supporters on shore." Diodorus reminds us, "When a ship was caught by several triremes, and struck in every direction by their massive rams, once the water poured in, the ship and its entire crew were swallowed by the sea."

When triremes collided, men were immediately jarred from their seats, and bedlam followed. If they were on the attack, the orders—how the boatswain's commands could be heard in the midst of battle is unknown—went out to back immediately to disengage the ram from the struck ship, lest the doomed enemy seamen and marines swarm onto their own decks.

In turn, if struck broadside at ten knots with a wooden ram weighing four to five hundred pounds and sheathed and tipped with bronze, seamen either jumped into the water or boarded the attacker in the few seconds before their own trireme, penetrated at the waterline, was partially submerged. When the Athenian assembly voted to put down the rebellion at Mytilene or to launch an armada against Sicily, most of the 6,000 to 7,000 voters crammed onto the rocky Pynx—the meeting place below the Acropolis—were themselves veterans of this macabre warfare at sea: rowers and rammers first, participants in democracy second.

At top speed a trireme could power into a targeted hull with fifty tons' worth of destructive force and send in thousands of gallons of seawater in seconds. Indeed, sometimes the first hit put such an enormous hole in the enemy hull that the ship was immediately swamped. But a Greek warship could attack only in one direction. Even its own few missile troops offered little offense amidships. In some cases skilled crewmen could orchestrate ramming attacks against a number of ships that found themselves unable to turn about, knocking apart targeted triremes even as they sought to flee past, to shore.

Free-for-All

PREPOSITIONING IN TRIREME fighting was everything. Amid wind, waves, and other ships, once battle commenced it could take critical minutes to turn around such a large oared ship to face an attacking enemy. On a normally outfitted ship, only about 4 or 5 archers and some 10 or so marines on deck hit passing ships with missiles, or were ready to board and fight on enemy decks once a trireme came into range. If the fight was in the calm waters of harbors, crews could stockpile stones. Then when two ships were stuck in a death grip, dozens who were not trained archers or marines might pelt their adversaries, in hopes of killing the enemy's available oarsmen. This auxiliary crew of soldiers was vital: if a ship lost its own infantry defenders, enemy hoplites could easily slaughter the packed crew trapped below as it scrambled to climb out, the men for the most part half-naked and without arms. And when a trireme went down, enemy sailors might hover around to spear defenseless oarsmen who frantically reemerged, gasping for air. At the battle in the Great Harbor at Syracuse (413), "those who were swimming away from their sunken ships were wounded by arrows or killed outright when struck by spears."[8]

Admirals usually commanded the fleet from the lead ships. There was no flagship full of officers at the rear. Some of the most well-known commanders —in the manner of Lord Nelson—died at sea, like the Athenian Eurymedon at Syracuse and the Spartan Mindarus at the battle of Cyzicus. On rare days defeated commanders killed themselves, and their bodies were washed ignominiously to shore—such was the case with the Spartan Timocrates at the second defeat in the Corinthian Gulf in 429.[9]

The rowers had to sense the pulse of the battle, since most verbal orders were impossible to hear when wood hit wood. Most sailors were probably trained to row blindly and adjust their rhythm to what they felt and sensed rather than saw or heard. Being rammed in the vulnerable broadsides was not the only worry. Sometimes ships hit each other head-on and got locked together, victory in that case going to the vessel that could pull out more quickly and had suffered less from the leakage caused by a damaged ram. In theory, a dozen or so crewmen scurried around with extra oars, planking, and rigging to plug holes and ensure that a disabled ship could stay afloat. In fact, even a small leaking hole would partially submerge a trireme in minutes. In engagements of 200 to 300 ships—and there were several such showdowns in the latter Peloponnesian War—40,000 to 60,000 men, the equivalent of a large Greek city, were at once hurling missiles, rowing, boarding, clinging to wreckage, and swimming to shore. So in minutes the seas were flooded with the flotsam and jetsam of broken triremes, bodies, and men splashing and clinging to debris.

Because there were no uniforms or clear naval insignia—oarsmen probably wore little more than a loincloth during summer sailing—crews sometimes even attacked their own ships, killing friendly sailors in the heat and panic of battle. Often ships were grappled and snagged. Then the sea fight "of the old style" might better resemble a land battle, as both marines and rowers joined in the confused melee. The immediate goal was to kill more enemy sailors than you lost friendly seamen, and then to choose the more seaworthy of the two craft and try to disentangle and row away from the wreckage. Thucydides concludes of the battle of Sybota, fought two years before the war, that the killing was so tumultuous, no one could hear anything at all in the clamor; he adds that victory hinged more on force than on skill:

> The sea battle was brutal, not so much due to skill, but rather because it more resembled an infantry battle on land. For whenever they crashed against each other, the ships could not easily be separated, partly because of the sheer number and crowding of the vessels, but still more because they trusted in the hoplites deployed on the decks, who stood and fought while the ships remained motionless.[10]

The Peloponnesians and, later, the Syracusans learned that to defeat the Athenians it was necessary to neutralize their superior seamanship—inasmuch as almost all Greek maritime states throughout the eastern Mediterranean had "gone trireme" and built ships that were remarkably uniform in size and construction. Overcoming Athenian expertise was sometimes accomplished by fighting in the narrows, employing head-on crashes with reinforced rams, or using small boats with missile troops to row alongside and shower the enemy with javelins. Just as the Athenians had learned never to meet Spartan hoplites in a so-called fair fight on a level plain, her enemies acknowledged that it was equally perilous in the early years of the war to take on the experienced Athenian fleet in open waters. The key to understanding the Peloponnesian War is not just that Athens was a naval power and Sparta fought by land; rather, of the 1,500-some city-states Athens was by far the strongest seapower, while Spartan hoplites were the preeminent infantry in Greece.

Only superbly trained crews could maintain their triremes in any formation, given the vagaries of wind and current and the fear of enemy attack. The Athenian admiral Phormio, for example, at the first battle of Naupaktos completely encircled the Corinthian fleet and left it in confusion, buffeted by panicking sailors struggling to row in seas that were choppy and full of confused triremes. One of the problems of waging the Ionian War in or near the Hellespont was that the strong current of the strait often made operations nearly impossible.

Even when fighting started, the running, hurling, and jumping of even a half dozen combatants on the deck, in addition to their sheer weight, must have made the careful work of the rowers beneath almost impossible, explaining why the triremes were often "motionless" as the deck fighting proceeded. Rarely in the history of sea warfare has the range of options been so severely curtailed by the fragile nature of the craft involved. Often defeat at sea is attributed not to enemy action but to the simple confusion and misdirection of desperate rowers trying to keep their ships in proper attack formation against the variables of wind and current. For example, the Spartan general Gylippus assured his crews at Syracuse (413) that the Athenian plan to load their triremes with extra marines—to turn the battle in the Great Harbor into a sort of infantry tumult—would be counterproductive precisely because so many men scrambling on deck and their lack of training at throwing javelins while sitting would confuse the rowers and put the ships off keel.[11]

Modern simulations have suggested that even the presence of a single man moving about on the canopy deck of a trireme could adversely affect the rowing. And the accuracy of such missile troops was not very good anyway except at very close ranges, given that both platform and target were rolling on the waves. Part of the crew's training, then, was not merely rowing but the ability to work without extraneous movement that could interrupt offensive operations of the ship, and even jeopardize the ship's safety while in transit.

All sides tried to apply innovations to the standard trireme design to gain an advantage in what was mostly a collision between like ships. As triremes raced into battle, crews often put up side screens (*pararumata*) to deflect missiles with flat trajectories from hitting the top bank of rowers (the thranite seamen) or to keep arced shots from raining down among the entire crew. The idea of such airborne assault was not to kill all the crew but perhaps to stun, wound, or disable enough oarsmen to disrupt the very movement of the ship, since a trireme's smooth strokes could be ruined by losing key rowers to wounds or panic.[12]

In other instances, ship-to-ship engagements were not even the focus of sea battle. Instead, sometimes in harbor battles divers drove stakes into shallow waters to tear out the hulls of unsuspecting triremes. In response to these close-to-shore tactics, specially outfitted triremes were equipped with cranes to pull such obstacles from the bottom of harbors, while forces on land fought over forts and docks, on the assumption that at some point the fleet would have to come in, be resupplied, and undergo repairs.[13]

The same ingenuity of response and counterresponse that had characterized the siege of Plataea was extended to sea, or at least to fighting on calmer waters near land. Merchant ships might cluster around harbors or places of refuge to offer safe haven for their own retreating triremes. On rare occasions crews hung enormous lead weights ("dolphins"), or even heavy stones, from their much longer spars, which could then be dropped opportunely onto enemy triremes as they raced in, plunging through the benches and decks, and tearing holes in the hull.[14]

Even straightforward sea fights rarely resulted in simple contact between two opposing triremes. More often it was instead a matter of three ships hitting two, or four against one—and being rammed while ramming the enemy. Besides ramming and boarding ships, there was a third way to ruin a trireme: cutting off its path to the open seas and gradually forcing it landward, where it could be driven onto shore, beached, and its crew rendered temporarily helpless as land-based infantry rushed into the surf to cut down sailors struggling to leave the ship.

Thucydides emphasizes just such chaos at the infamous battle of Sybota, on the eve of the war, when the Corinthians had no idea whether they were winning or being conquered by the Corcyraean fleet. Out of this bedlam within an hour or two a general consensus arose that one side—in the first few years of the war usually the more skilled and numerous Athenians and their allies—was destroying more ships than it was losing. Then the call went out among the defeated for each ship to save itself and row in frenzy back to base. Because triremes were costly and, like bronze panoplies, universally used by all sides in the Peloponnesian War, disabled ships and even floating wrecks were precious. They were also easily salvageable, since without ballast ruined vessels rarely were lost, but bobbed about only partially submerged. Because triremes relied on speed rather than stability to guarantee survival there was very little sand or stone in the hold as ballast, and water jugs were probably all that was carried to provide stabilizing weight.

Trireme buoyancy explains why ancient descriptions of sea battles are replete with broken ships and planks fouling the surface. The victors immediately tried to rope and tow away any ship worth possible salvaging on the theory that these showy trophies were far less expensive to repair than the construction of entirely new triremes and might offset the enormous costs involved in naval warfare. As in the case of hoplite panoplies, the equipment of trireme warfare was recyclable, the winners sometimes ending even hard-fought battles with more ships than when they'd begun. The aftermath of a trireme engagement must have been a strange sight, as dozens of wrecks were tied to the victors' ships, which rowed off with tow cables. Indeed, so similar in appearance were the respective fleets that both sides were often unsure whether sudden reinforcements were friendly or hostile.

In general, sea fights lasted far longer than hoplite battles, inasmuch as marching forward to spear and slash in heavy armor was a more exhausting task than to row at sea.

Lots of Ways to Die

GREEK SAILORS WERE familiar with the seas, and in almost every maritime battle the fighting took place within a few thousand yards of shore. Mass drownings should have been relatively avoidable, unlike the debacle at Salamis, where perhaps 40,000 Persians and their allies, many fully clothed and unused to the water, were lost amid the wreckage. The scandal at the battle of Arginusae, after which six of the victorious Athenian generals were executed for allowing hundreds of their kindred sailors to drown while clinging to debris in storm-driven seas, was an aberration, thus explaining the unusual wrath of the Athenian assembly, which could not be assuaged even by the fact of the enemy's far greater losses.

Frequent drowning was relatively common inasmuch as few Greeks swam on a regular basis to guarantee their survival in rough seas. When a ship was hit, it was not easy to get out from the cramped rowing bench, climb through dozens of panicky seamen, avoid jagged wooden debris, missiles, and boarders, and then swim the thousands of yards to shore. On a crippled ship, the key to survival was to manage to disengage, row away, and allow the crew to jump overboard well distant from the enemy—such as the Athenians who escaped after their defeat at Notium in 408, losing 22 ships but saving most of the sailors.

What percentage of a ship's crew was lost when a trireme was submerged is not recorded. Yet there are plenty of descriptions in Greek literature to suggest that on occasion a ship's entire complement of seamen could be killed, lost, or taken prisoner. Inclement weather—as, for example, off Cape Athos in 411 (12 of 10,000 saved) or at the battle of Arginusae in 406—seemed to ensure that sinking warships would doom their entire crews.[15]

It was not an easy thing for the wounded and bleeding to be picked up by friendly ships or to swim to land. And very few of the uninjured could climb out of the cramped hull safely and quickly—not when the task of merely embarking took several minutes, as the crew tried to find their proper places. Even if oarsmen made it out of a damaged ship without major injuries, they were not home free. Rough seas, foul weather, the cold, and more could easily ensure that thousands went down even when clinging to floating debris.

Drowning was considered the most nightmarish of deaths in Greek popular religion. It was angst over that dreaded end of hundreds of their comrades that led the Athenians to put their own generals on trial after the victory at Arginusae in 406. Thousands back home lamented their kinsmen's souls roaming the netherworld without rest while their unclaimed bodies rotted without proper burial observance. The scapegoating after Arginusae, along with the vote and revote concerning the fate of the prisoners on Mytilene and the postbellum trial of Socrates, is usually recalled as one of the worst moments in the history of Athenian democracy. One of the most eerie scenes in Aristotle's *Constitution of the Athenians* is his account of the show trials: the inebriate demagogue sauntering into the assembly hall, decked out in his breastplate, ready to denigrate, browbeat, or accuse any who stood between him and butchering the very men who had given Athens its greatest victory. In any case, the people soon repented their stupid and immoral action. Callixeinos, the proposer of the illegal motion to try all the Arginusae generals on death charges en masse, "was hated by everyone and died of starvation."[16]

Often the victors were more brutal than the chilly and choppy seas. Rowers, after all, like aircraft-carrier crews, were also premium military assets who took months to train and who, once lost, were not easily replaced. Although the rules of war in theory protected prisoners at sea, as the conflict wore on clemency was ignored and the more savage protocols of the siege and ambush took hold. Often it made better sense to row away and leave the wounded of the enemy to the seas. Only that way could the manpower pool of skilled oarsmen be permanently reduced, without incurring the odium of violating understood conventions that might prompt retaliation—the sea, not men, killing the defenseless in the water.

Yet sometimes captured crews were brought ashore and either cut down or maimed—often grotesquely, by cutting off the right hand or thumb to guarantee that they could never row again. It is unclear which side began to initiate such brutal practices. But in the later part of the Ionian War, the Athenian general Philocles persuaded the Athenian assembly to go on record as allowing trireme captains to chop off the right hand of all prisoners taken at sea. Presumably his idea was that only such tough measures would stop the desertions of imperial seamen tempted to join the Spartans by promises of higher pay.

Philocles himself was known to have ordered captured oarsmen thrown overboard on the high seas, which explains why the Spartans executed almost every Athenian they got their hands on after their final victory at Aegospotami—a staggering number that might have reached 3,500. On an early-fifth-century black-figure vase, prisoners at sea are shown bound with rope, thrown overboard, and then pushed underwater with sticks and spears—suggesting that such a cruel fate was not uncommon.[17]

The execution of the Athenian prisoners after Aegospotami—Philocles himself was executed on Lysander's orders—may have ranked as the worst single-day execution of Greeks in the entire war. More were probably butchered than those cut down at Mytilene, Scione, and Melos and exceeded the number of those murdered by the infamous Thirty Tyrants, who overthrew the democracy at war's end. The toll from Aegospotami was not matched until Alexander the Great killed almost every Theban male when he razed Thebes in 335 or cut down most of the Greek mercenaries in the aftermath of Granicus, a year later. Lysander would have done better to spare the crew, sell them into slavery, and share the profits with his own oarsmen, a practice that was common by war's end as well.[18]

Perhaps the most common method of dispatching defeated seamen was to sail amid the wreckage and spear them like fish. The accepted idea was that the battle was not quite over, and thus men clinging to enemy wreckage were still fair game and could be killed without moral censure or fear of reprisals. After the battle off the Sybota Islands, the Corinthian ships rowed among the wreckage killing all the Corcyraean survivors they could find. So intent were they on finishing off the helpless enemy that they ignored towing back the damaged ships and finally even inadvertently began murdering their own men in the water. At the second battle off Naupaktos a contingent of Athenian ships got cut off and was driven to shore. Once beached, all the crewmen who could not lumber out of their triremes were executed on their benches by boarders.[19]

Two millennia before the victorious Christians at Lepanto (1571) had scoured the wreckage to execute any Ottomans found alive in the water—after that battle at least 30,000 Turks were presumed killed—the Greeks of the Peloponnesian War accepted the brutal calculus that the murder of helpless sailors meant less chance of meeting such trained rowers in the next round of battle. Hoplites on all sides were farmers or property owners; in contrast, rowers were the poor and foreigners—even, at times, slaves—who shared no gentlemanly pretensions about some mythical common agrarian status. Often it was the marines, mostly hoplite soldiers themselves, who did much of the spearing of trapped rowers—and who would have been the first to have perished in their breastplates once the ship was swamped. Most of those killed on deck may well have been lost to missiles rather than drowning. Yet because Thucydides and other historians almost always record naval losses by triremes destroyed or captured, it makes it nearly impossible to translate such generalization into any accurate number of killed or wounded. The particular condition of the seas, the nature of nearby land, the attitude held toward the enemy, and the status of the ship could all determine how many sailors escaped a doomed trireme.[20]

Reputation and Fear

THE SPARTANS WERE essentially wiped out at the sea battle of Arginusae. The Athenian fleet ceased to exist after Aegospotami. In the former case, the Athenians enjoyed immediate naval supremacy and the Spartans sought peace. In the latter, the Athenians lost the war in a single day as Lysander's fleet made ready to sail into Athens.

Entire fleets that acknowledged their seamen to be inexperienced were often scared that a superior navy would make short work of them. It was precisely that fear that prompted Athens to keep a reserve fund of 1,000 talents and 100 of "the best" triremes to protect the Piraeus, as a last resort should the Peloponnesians ever achieve naval supremacy and thus cruise freely in the Aegean and then right into their home port. Even the Athenians accepted the fact that at sea anything could happen, that whole fleets with thousands could go down in a few hours.[21]

Because there was no way to stop Pericles' navy in the early years of the war, Corinthian ships were often terrified at the very approach of the Athenian triremes. Against Phormio in the Corinthian Gulf they became so confused by superior Athenian seamanship that they gave up defending themselves and tried to row away to safety. In response to the acknowledged asymmetry, the Syracusan Hermocrates conceded to his followers the superior proficiency of his Athenian enemies—"the skill of the enemy that you so especially dread"—but insisted that their own greater number of ships and courage could still trump such Athenian advantages if they confined the battle to favored locales. *Phobos*, or fear of "the dreadful Athenian presence," is often alluded to as a prime factor in all sea battles with the Athenians before their catastrophe in Sicily, as if most other Greeks admitted that they had little chance of survival in a fair fight against such seamen.[22]

When the war broke out the Athenians themselves proved arrogant, convinced after the fifty-year administration of a maritime empire that they were de facto invincible at sea, "lords of the sea," as they were generally acknowledged. Like the nineteenth-century British navy, the Athenian fleet felt that its qualitative superiority meant that it could attack any enemy at any time—whatever the theater imbalance in numbers. At the famous battle in the Corinthian Gulf in 429 Phormio told his men to disregard the size of the enemy armada: "Inasmuch as they were Athenians, they would never retreat before Peloponnesian ships, however great their number." In the Athenian mind, victory now paid dividends later, since the rest of the Hellenic world would be constantly reminded of the futility of challenging Athenian ships. As Phormio further put it, "When men have once experienced defeat, they are not willing to maintain the same ideas about facing the same dangers."

Ironically, that truism was never more valid than after the Athenian calamity in Sicily; the Athenians became as paralyzed with fear as the Spartans had been over a decade earlier after their own debacle on Pylos. Immediately the Athenians lost their confidence at sea. For the first time in two decades they systematically began to lose ships to the newly constructed Peloponnesian fleet. For two years, imperial seamen were fearful of battle altogether, until the victory at Cynossema in summer 411 restored some of their old swagger.[23]

Because naval battles took place among frail ships in often unfriendly waters and involved tens of thousands of combatants, the real lethal theaters of the Peloponnesian War turned out not to be hoplite battlefields or even sieges. The historian Barry Strauss once systematically counted only the precise fatality figures for Athenian infantrymen and their landless counterparts as recorded by contemporary sources—a fraction of the actual number, since most ancient Greek historians far more often use vague words like "many were lost" or omit casualties figures at specific battles altogether. He nevertheless observed that over twice as many Athenian thetes (who were mostly sailors) died than hoplites during the twenty-seven-year war, most of them in the brutal final decade of naval fighting. If the hoplites and cavalrymen had suffered inordinately in siege and amphibious operations during the first decade of the war, the greater losses after 413 were almost all among the rowers. When one speaks of the Peloponnesian War, the specters of Sicily, the plague, and the executions at Melos and Scione haunt our imaginations. Yet the real carnage came late in the war and at sea battles whose names are now mostly forgotten.[24]

The Crews

THE MOST BIZARRE facet of ancient naval power was the general method of manning the triremes, a mixture of private and public finance and control that was common practice in most of the city-states. Each year at Athens, for example, four hundred of the wealthiest citizens were put on notice as being liable for obligation as trierarchs (trireme commanders), which entailed, among other responsibilities, active command of a warship at sea. Because the fleet during the war numbered about 300 ships—at one point in the war 250 triremes were at sea at the same time—three out of four annual designees were then further selected and proceeded to the dockyards at the Piraeus to take control of their allotted ships for one year.

The state usually supplied the hull, the fittings, and the crew, although in a few instances some rich men bought and outfitted their own warships altogether. But the trierarch was mostly responsible for much of the ship's daily expenses—repairs, food, and water for the crew—and usually served as the de facto captain while on patrol. Although a few grandees sought to skimp on expenses, more often trierarchs spent far more than was required, in keen rivalry with one another to find the best rowers and helmsmen. Such, apparently, were the wages of military philanthropy.

Private largess lavished on public ships—better rigging, hiring the best pilots, and adding bonuses to the daily wage of the rowers—might not only bring trierarchs renown but also increase the odds that in battle they themselves would survive. Thucydides says that when the Athenians left for Sicily, they departed with the best crews, ships, rigging, and figureheads. In both fighting ability and appearance, the flotilla of 415 was far more impressive than any prior armada, even those past great expeditions to Epidaurus and Potidaea at the beginning of the war, which had nevertheless set out with "poor equipment."

At first glance such private initiative seems out of character for an all-inclusive state government like that of imperial Athens. In fact, the trierarchy was a forced contribution on the part of the wealthy to the state, what the Greeks called a liturgy. Besides finding a way to tap the capital of the rich, the polis also wished for its most wealthy citizens to serve side by side with the poorest while at sea. Some hoplites and cavalrymen, owners of farms and conservative in their political thinking, might resent the rise of a naval state. Yet the richest of all in times of war found themselves being honored for serving at the cutting edge of Athenian power. The trireme, in other words, was an extension of the democratic Athenian state and served the larger civic interest of acculturating thousands as they worked together in cramped conditions and under dire circumstances.[25]

Throughout classical literature the need for skilled rowers is a constant refrain. Three men from different elevations plying about the same length oars would have to maintain a synchronized sweep, always hitting the water, never striking a nearby oar, thus insuring what the Greeks called the "simultaneous hits of the oar" (*kôpês xynebolê*). Practice in rowing in unison was a constant requirement, and apparently a skill easily lost through inaction. It was not just that rowers had to have strength and learn to row in synchronization; they also had to get used to hitting rough seas with their oars, become accustomed to the crash and roar of battle, and expect to cruise for long hours in both heat and cold.[26]

States in the Peloponnese were always looking to reach nautical parity with Athens or Corcyra by promises that they could outbid competitors on the open market and that way hire away experienced mercenary rowers from what was an apparently limited pool. But even Peloponnesian leaders acknowledged that matching long-held Athenian rowing expertise "would take time." So they agreed with Pericles' confident prewar prediction that sea power was "a full-time occupation," something not so easily acquired by farmers and amateurs. That for twenty years Spartan triremes had little chance against the Athenians bears out his cocky assessment, just as the early-nineteenth-century Napoleonic fleet found its wonderfully constructed ships still no match for centuries of British naval mastery. Pericles apparently was prescient when he warned that there would be little opportunity for the Spartans to gain belated expertise in a real war—as if enemies could suddenly learn to row when the Athenian fleet was systematically scouring their shores. At war's end, when Spartan parity with the Athenians was reached, it is difficult to ascertain whether the Peloponnesians had become qualitatively better as oarsmen or, after the losses to the plague and at Sicily, the Athenians had gotten far worse.[27]

Swamping Triremes

WHAT WAS THE goal of the classical Greeks, then, in adopting such an awkward method of naval construction and operation, a nautical science that seems to have reached its apex at Athens shortly before the war broke out? Clearly, the desire for speed and power relative to displacement was a central driving force: sea battles were to be decided not always by marines but by quick ships that could ram, withdraw, and nimbly maneuver to strike again. To achieve ramming power required speed, and speed in turn necessitated 170 actual rowers on a relatively light vessel—and that near-impossible calculus of weight, speed, and manpower explains the complex method of banking three oarsmen to allow so many men to fit in such a small space. Impressed philosophers often commented on this peculiar method of rowing, calling oared ships "mills," a crowded factory that turned out as its product sheer muscular propulsion.

The Athenians, who screamed freely among their betters in the assembly, christened their triremes with names (apparently always in the feminine gender) not merely like "Empire" (*Hegemonia*) or "Most Powerful" (*Kratistê*) but also "Freedom" (*Eleutheria*), "Democracy" (*Dêmokratia*), "Free Speech" (*Parrhêsia*), and "Justice" (*Dikaiosynê*). Perhaps the frequent references to Athenian maritime excellence do not arise out of the state's commitment to building numerous triremes or even the long service accrued from overseeing a maritime empire. At least at the start of the war, at Athens the rowers were for the most part all free voting citizens in a manner not true of the Peloponnesian fleet, suggesting that their unique élan at sea was a reflection that oarsmen felt that they had a stake in the very society they rowed to defend. In any case, wide-scale mutinies were rare in the Athenian fleet, but perhaps more common among the Peloponnesians, even in the last decade of the war, when things were beginning to go Sparta's way.[28]

The Athenians—who put a far greater premium on nautical skills than on the presence of hoplites and boarders on their triremes—mastered two general methods of ramming. Both required well-trained crews and quick, light ships. When employing the *diekplous* ("sailing through and out"), a row of ships tried to blast an enemy line of triremes. Once through, the attackers could then ram their targets from the inside of the enemy formation. In contrast, under the more subtle *periplous* ("sailing around"), the fleet tried to outflank or even encircle the enemy. Most fleets lacked such seamanship, and if it was a question of ramming Athenian triremes in a fair fight, the Peloponnesians would usually lose, suggesting the more desperate alternative of boarding and missile attack.

The Athenian object was, again, to maneuver into the line of exposed ship sides that could be rammed by columns of fast-moving triremes—a sort of "crossing the T" in the pre-dreadnought age. The Athenians believed that in the relatively open seas the greater maneuverability and speed of their own ships would eventually ensure that the usually more inept enemy would become confused and exposed to easy attack. In other words, under optimum conditions the contest would be a true naval battle rather than a land fight between hoplites and missile troops on pitching decks close to shore.[29]

In Hollywood films sometimes one galley smashes the oarage of another. Many classical scholars doubt that this was possible. How, after all, could a trireme perfectly navigate to within a few feet alongside another, the attacker's rowers giving a final strong pull before yanking their oars from the water, while their vessel glided on by its adversary, knocking off the enemy's unsuspecting oars in succession? Yet while it was no doubt a rare tactic contingent upon a skilled crew meeting up with a more poorly manned trireme, sometimes oar slicing seems to have worked. Off Mytilene in 406, for example, the Athenian admiral Conon was forced to retreat—but not before "shearing off the oars of some ships."[30]

Often crews resorted to grappling hooks. They were probably on board every trireme. Attackers sought to catch an enemy and pull him over for boarding, in the expectation that their own rowers could provide superior power and pull rather than be yanked instead. And if a targeted ship was damaged or some of its crew killed, it might be hooked and towed away, either toward the fleet or to friendly shores, where the crew would be captured or killed. Boarders preferred to come alongside and spear the enemy; but just as often they might jump over to the enemy and finish the business with swords.[31]

Trireme fighting became a real show. The skill of the pilots in maneuvering their triremes for hits, the cohesion of the crews in pouring on the speed in the last moments before the collision, and the explosive impact of 170 rowers smashing into their enemy counterparts—no wonder Diodorus called all that "an amazing spectacle" (*kataplêktikon*). Sometimes thousands of spectators lined the beaches to gaze at dozens of ships ramming, boarding, and showering each other with missiles. Soldiers were eager to watch the deadly business, rooting their respective sides on, slogging into the surf to help out, and finishing off or aiding any crews that beached their vessels. Nowhere was the grisly fighting at sea more notorious than in the Great Harbor at Syracuse. There, in a succession of sea battles, thousands of Athenians fought the Sicilians in almost every imaginable manner—ramming, boarding, missile warfare, grappling, driving ships to shore, dropping stones from cranes, and employing underwater stakes. Although the seas washed away the flotsam and jetsam of battle, at least in the immediate aftermath of a major sea fight, there could be thousands of bodies and hundreds of wrecks in the waters, while the shores were quickly made a grisly scene of bloated bodies and debris.[32]

In a sea battle two years before the Peloponnesian War that broke out between the Corinthians and Corcyraeans, both sides fought in the "ancient fashion." That is, javelin throwers and archers boarded ships and in a conflict "more like a land battle" showered the crews. The subtext of Thucydides' description is how inferior both fleets were to the Athenian navy, which would never have allowed its ships to be grappled and boarded since their superior oarsmen could easily win a battle of maneuver and ramming.

The Spartan general Brasidas once summed up the respective naval strategies of the two fleets: Athenians relied on speed and maneuverability on the open seas to ram at will clumsier ships; in contrast, a Peloponnesian armada might win only when it fought near land in calm and confined waters, had the greater number of ships in a local theater, and if its better-trained marines on deck and hoplites on shore could turn a sea battle into a contest of infantry. A character in a contemporary comedy of Aristophanes' says of this naval dominance, "Athens is where the good triremes come from." Most Greeks agreed. For the Athenians, rowing was "second nature," a skill learned "from boyhood."[33]

In the first major sea battle of the war off Naupaktos (430), Phormio with a mere 20 Athenian ships attacked and routed a larger Corinthian contingent of 47. Such superiority was to last nearly twenty years, until the disaster of Sicily weakened Athens, necessitating a crash program to rebuild ships and hire green crews. That unforeseen catastrophe prompted Sparta to renew her efforts to acquire a top-notch fleet, and thus set the stage for the last decade's climactic deadly battles in the Aegean, which would end the war.

At some point navies began to reinforce their rams with lateral side beams designed to ensure that the heavier trireme might survive a head-on collision. Such was the case late in the war off Naupaktos, when some specialized Corinthian triremes managed to disable seven Athenian ships by ramming them head-on. Throughout the war the less skilled navies of the Peloponnesians sought such ways to nullify the advantages in Athenian seamanship: if the Corinthians were less adept at maneuvering for a more difficult broadside ram, then perhaps at the battle's outset they could charge directly into the oncoming Athenian fleet in expectation that their heavier rams might give them the best of the collision. So while the Athenians practiced long and hard in mastering the more difficult but survivable lateral hits, their enemies counted on superior naval construction to blast ships head-on. Thucydides seems to assume as much when he reminds us that "the Corinthians considered themselves as winners if they were not decisively beaten, and in contrast the Athenians accepted that they lost if they were not clearly victorious."[34]

Yet throughout the war it was the Peloponnesians, not the Athenian masters of the sea, who showed themselves most adept at adopting new tactics and modifying their ships to nullify traditional Athenian superior seamanship. The Athenian tragedy in the Great Harbor at Syracuse was the story of complacence and even arrogance. The scrappy Syracusans and their Peloponnesian allies fitted out new rams to hit their more nimble enemies head-on in confined waters, as well as driving stakes into the harbor bed, chaining off the harbor entrance, and deploying stone throwers from the decks. Only at the end of the war did the Athenian admiral Conon take special measures to prepare his ships in a manner unprecedented by past fleets, apparently to ensure that his triremes were as seaworthy and reinforced as the enemy's.

Unskilled rowers did not back their ships well. When ramming, such poorly manned triremes often stayed enmeshed in the target vessel, in the hopes that hoplites and light-armed troops could kill the enemy crews and eventually free the ship, along with its captured trophy. Sometimes the concussion of the hit knocked officers and marines overboard, given that there were no rails on the suddenly unstable deck. Such was the fate of the Spartan admiral Callicratidas, who fell off his ship at Arginusae when it was rammed in battle.[35]

A Zero-Sum Game

TRIREMES WERE OFTEN deemed "fast" or "slow" depending on the quality of the crews, the nature of their construction, and the conditions of the hulls. In theory, newer ships, fully manned by 170 seasoned rowers, were far more nimble and faster than older triremes with leaky or waterlogged bottoms manned by rookies—a deterioration that could set in within months if boats were not allowed to dry on shore between voyages, and their hulls periodically scraped and caulked. In fact, the skill of the boatwright, the quality of the timber, and modifications in design all influenced the speed of a trireme in addition to its age and upkeep.

Still, all the criteria that made for a "fast" trireme are not clear, but it was an acknowledged fact that "the excellence of crews lasts only a short time." After only a brief period at sea, given the likelihood of illness and physical exhaustion, there remained only a few skilled seamen who could keep a ship in steady motion and "keep the oar strokes in time." Even within fleets on the high seas there was often a culling that went on to put the best rowers on a few select triremes that could serve as a sort of advanced flotilla to speed on ahead of the main armada. The assumption was that there were always a few rowers who were stronger or more experienced—or both—than most.

A ship's officers were critical to its performance. Besides the trierarch (who was the official commander of the vessel) and the *kybernitês*, or helmsman, who oversaw the rowers and gave orders, success hinged on the quality of the *proratês* (pilot) at the helm and the *keluestês* (rowing master), who either yelled out the rowing beat or hit stones together to keep time for the oarsmen. They were to the crew as the maestro is to the orchestra, and for much of the war Athens possessed thousands of such veterans who had crisscrossed for decades the seas of the empire.

There were several other drawbacks for such an elegant vessel, one that weighed probably little more than twenty-five tons empty, and not many more than fifty when fully manned. First, a trireme when fitted out as a pure warship could carry beside the rowers only about thirty crewmen and combatants, including marines, archers, captain, helmsman, boatswain, piper, and assorted crewmen in charge of gear, sails, and repairs. That meant that to convey any larger land forces, the 170 rowers would have to double as infantry of some sort, resulting in either oarsmen or infantrymen who were less than expert.

Alternatively, the number of rowers could be reduced, perhaps by two-thirds, and the ship essentially turned into a slow-moving troop transport or "hoplite carrier." Usually the thranites on the top benches alone rowed, as hoplites with their heavy equipment sat in the lower two banks. To what degree a "hoplite carrier" meant that none, some, or sometimes all infantrymen helped out in the rowing is not known.

In the Athenian fleet, some 10 or so specialized triremes, with as few as 60 rowers, were used as horse transports. They could carry as many as 30 mounts for short distances if all the benches of the lower two banks were removed. A fleet of 10 such transports would have given Athens the ability to move about 300 horses in an emergency. As the conflict continued, troops of all sorts were increasingly often moved around theaters by sea. Indeed, one of the great fears of the Athenians on Sicily was the rumor that the Peloponnesians were sending sizable numbers of their best hoplites and freed helot troops on merchant ships.[36]

So it was impossible to cheat the arithmetic of such a zero-sum game: to transport any large number of infantry, the ship would have to be so reduced of oarsmen as to make it slow and vulnerable. In contrast, retaining a full rowing crew ensured speed, but only a handful of quality infantry. To have hoplites or light-armed troops row meant that they could not be used at sea, and since they were mediocre rowers, they only hampered the optimum use of the ship. If skilled sailors were to become hoplites on landing, then the quality of the ensuing army was questionable from the start.

Because waves of three feet or so might swamp the vessels, fleets were often kept on shore in even light storms. A number of ancient commentators reflected the ancient maxim that "a sea battle could only be fought in calm waters." Thucydides, for example, recalling the fight in the relatively quiet Corinthian Gulf between the Athenians and the Peloponnesians, remarks how the latter were sent into fatal confusion once a small wind came up and the seas grew choppy:

> They at once fell into confusion: ship fell foul of ship, while the crews were pushing them off with poles, and by their shouting, swearing, and struggling with one another, made captains' orders and boatswains' cries alike inaudible, and through being unable for want of practice to clear their oars in the rough water, prevented the vessels from obeying their helmsmen properly.

The vast majority of naval engagements in the Peloponnesian War took place in three or four areas of relatively protected seas: the Corinthian Gulf, the harbor at Syracuse, the strait of the Hellespont, and the protected waters between the coast of Asia Minor and the large Aegean islands right offshore. While all these regions could experience sudden choppy seas and high winds, they were at least safer than miles out in the Aegean.

There was not a single major trireme battle on the high seas in either the Mediterranean or the Aegean, in the same manner that all of history's great sea engagements—such as Salamis, Lepanto, Trafalgar, Midway, and Leyte Gulf—were fought relatively close to either islands or the mainland. Admirals, ancient and modern, like calm seas, nearby refuge, and close ports of call. And if a sudden storm came up without warning, trireme battle ceased as crews almost immediately headed for shore; they found it impossible to ram or even navigate in choppy seas—as Alcibiades learned when he approached the Hellespont in 411 and was met with such rough water that he quit all pursuit of the Spartan fleet.[37]

It is hard to speak in the normal sense of a true "blockade," or even "voyage" or "patrol," in the Peloponnesian War, since triremes could venture out for only a few hours each day. They were entirely dependent on friendly shores to provide food and water each evening. There was very little room to stow food and water in the ships, given the number of rowers and the need for spare rigging and parts. Yet almost two gallons of water was needed per man per day to prevent dehydration. How the rowers were given periodic rations and water while stationed at their benches is not known, but every captain had to berth his trireme each night someplace where fresh water was abundant. In most cases, oarsmen brought some of their own rations and stowed them near their berth. If rowers were kept too long at sea without a meal, fatigue quickly set in. The precise calculation of the effects of heat, sunlight, and lack of ventilation on the efficacy of oarage is unknown, but modern simulations suggest that a trireme's speed could be markedly reduced if its crew was exposed to constant summer sunlight, denied refreshing breezes, and shorted on drinking water.[38]

Common was the sudden ambush of and attack on sailors who were foraging for food, water, and firewood—especially by horsemen and light-armed troops. Indeed, provisioning was a prime reason for the Athenians' defeat on Syracuse. Their sailors had to bivouac and search for supplies. The Syracusans, in contrast, had plenty of horses to hunt them down. The verdict of the entire war finally hinged on questions of logistics: learning very little from the disaster at Sicily, the Athenian fleet made no preparations for easy provisioning at Aegospotami and thus was ruined when Lysander surprised the crews, most of whom were off finding food.[39]

To travel even short distances, triremes needed safe ports at intervals of fifty miles or so, where ships could find food (barley bread, onions, dried fish, meats, fruit, and olive oil), water, wine, and shelter for their crews to sleep in. Not all ports were equal. Most often ships were forced to beach on the sand or venture into streams or rivers, with sometimes disastrous results. Lamachus, for example, nine years before he was killed on Sicily, in 423 sought refuge for his small fleet of 10 Athenian triremes near Troy, in the river Cales, which flows by Heraclea. But a sudden storm came up and created such a strong current that the triremes were torn loose and completely destroyed on the rocks in a purportedly protected inland river.

Even a small fleet of some 20 to 30 triremes might entail an aggregate force of well over 5,000 crewmen—larger than most city-states in Greece—all descending on a port at once in search of food and water. If there was not careful planning, the resources of seaside communities could be overwhelmed when a fleet approached over the horizon. Most small communities did not mind the lucrative business of selling provisions to desperate sailors—as long as such suspect seamen kept clear of town and confined themselves to ad hoc markets on the beach.[40] Much of Athenian foreign policy, including its efforts to maintain an overseas empire in the Aegean, cultivate allies such as Argos and Corcyra, and establish dependencies at distant Amphipolis and Potidaea, was predicated on just the need to create permanent bases to facilitate long-distance cruises. Trireme harbors were not unlike the British Empire's network of coaling stations throughout Africa and the Pacific to service its late-nineteenth-century global fleet.

The Limitations of Triremes

MODERN *OLYMPIAS* FOUND that the trireme had to be cleaned every five days or so, so bad was the smell from just the collective sweat of 170 rowers, who at least left their benches to use toilet facilities rather than relieve themselves, ancient style, in the hold of the ship. In Venetian times, returning galleys were periodically sunk in friendly harbors to rinse the hold of excrement, trash, and vermin. Few things for soldiers in the Peloponnesian War could have been as unpleasant as rowing for any length of time, given the vagaries of wind, cold, the sun, and the human miasma of 200 men crammed into such small quarters for hours on end.

Hulls became quickly soaked, waterlogged, and leaky if not periodically brought up on shore to dry.[41] Frequent reference to the constant refitting of triremes in the middle of campaigns suggests that the ropes, oars, rudders, masts, and sails needed continual attention as well. The need to dry out the hull on the beach often left an entire fleet vulnerable in the late evening and early morning, should an enemy come upon the ships without warning. In one of the longest continual deployments in Greek history, the Athenian imperial fleet of over 200 triremes was, except for brief beaching on the shores surrounding Syracuse, in the water almost constantly from the time it left the Piraeus in 415 until its final destruction in September 413 in the Great Harbor.[42]

Even excellently maintained ships lasted only about twenty-five years. At that rate of attrition, during peacetime Athens had to build 20 craft almost every year just to maintain a fleet of 300 triremes. That optimal number had been reached during the intended Thirty Years Peace of 446–431, when Athens had not only kept up regular maintenance and replacement of its 200-ship navy, which had won the Persian War, but added another 100 triremes to its armada. The shores around the port of Athens were perennially littered with the wrecks and hulls of old triremes that were left to rot once they were beyond repair, in a continuing cycle of Athenian abandonment and building of triremes. The challenge for the Athenian maritime bureaucracy was not just that in theory 60,000 seamen—Athenian poor, some farmers, resident aliens, allied and subject rowers, freedmen, and slaves—were on call to man 300 ships, but that perhaps as many as another 10,000 to 20,000 workers were busy in the dockyards of the Piraeus building and repairing the hulls and rigging of such an enormous fleet.

The most moving story of seasonal erosion in the seaworthiness of a fleet is found in the Athenian general Nicias' pathetic account of how quickly the once magnificent armada wore itself out on constant sea patrol outside the harbor of Syracuse, with a myriad of problems that markedly diminished its combat efficacy. "The ships," Nicias lamented, "are waterlogged since they have been at sea for such a long time, and the crews have wasted away. The reason is that it has not been possible to drag the ships onto the shore and dry them out." In contrast, the Syracusans inside the blockade at least could periodically maintain their hulls.[43]

Trans-Mediterranean voyages, as were possible in the age of Venetian galleys, were almost unheard of—and when attempted, often disastrous. The Athenian fleet that headed for Sicily plotted a leapfrogging course along the Greek and Italian coastlines, inasmuch as it had to follow the shortest route across the Adriatic of some eighty-four miles from Corcyra (modern-day Corfu) over to the heel of Italy. It never contemplated plying the straight voyage from Greece to Croton (some two hundred miles), which would not have allowed any overnight stops.

Depending on winds and currents, triremes might move easily under muscular power for six to eight hours at four to five knots an hour—or a steady thirty or so strokes per minute. In rare cases, if they encountered no headwinds, ships could row even longer and cover distances of fifty to sixty nautical miles. But should a stiff wind of, say, twenty knots arise, it could almost nullify the effort of the rowers and force the vessel to shore to avoid being buffeted endlessly at sea. Superb crews and new ships on rare occasions could row for sixteen hours, and thus cover 120 miles in a day. Thucydides records the singular achievement of a messenger ship dispatched to Mytilene that made it from the Piraeus to Lesbos (184 miles) in twenty-four hours, at a clip of almost eight nautical miles per hour. Yet this feat of rowing across the Aegean by an elite crew in one bold stroke was clearly exceptional. In fleets of 70 to 100 ships, the armada usually had to move at the speed of the slowest ships in order to maintain formation. And pilots had to be careful not to wear out their crews prematurely; sometimes overzealous pursuit could result in exhausted seamen, who in turn could not maintain formation and thus fell victim to an opportunistic enemy counterattack. Pacing a trireme's oarsmen was critical, since any warship with worn-out rowers was left for several minutes essentially dead and helpless in the water, entirely dependent on wind to sail away to safety—and not even that recourse was possible if the rigging had been left on shore in expectation of battle.[44]

There is also no recorded instance of "power cruising," in which sails and oars were used simultaneously—perhaps because of the near impossibility of coordinating the rowers' strokes with the unpredictable breezes. Any winds approaching fifteen knots would require ships to pull down their sails and head for shore to keep an even keel and avoid seas splashing into the lower oar holes or over the sides. In most cases, ships sailed whenever possible under wind power at a slow clip of about three to four knots, from port to port. Triremes then usually relied on oarage only when heading out to battle, when masts and sails were either stowed or more likely left behind on land.

Naval warfare in the Peloponnesian War, however, was not merely subject to the limitations of these fragile oared ships at sea. The construction of triremes was also costly, usually requiring the equivalent of some 6,000 man-days of labor. For a state like Athens to launch a fleet of 300 triremes consumed about the same outlay as outfitting an enormous hoplite army of 18,000 with full armor. But even that is a facile comparison: hoplites usually bought their own panoplies, and marched to battle and back within a few days, thus requiring little further logistical expense from the state.

Each trireme, in contrast, cost one talent for construction and another talent of both private and public expenditure per month to keep afloat. If Athens had on average two-thirds of her ships at sea for the 240 days during the eight sailing months, from March through October, these 200 ships might in theory cost the city 1,600 talents, or more than twice the entire annual tribute from the empire. That cost was unsustainable for more than a year or two. To wage a multifaceted naval war, in which such a sizable fleet went out on annual patrol for some twenty-seven years from Sicily to Corcyra to the Aegean and Ionia, could have cost over 43,000 talents, seven times the entire financial reserves of Athens at the beginning of the war and more than its aggregate imperial income over some three decades. Did the empire exist to provide a navy or did the navy create the empire—or both?

Wealthy Versus Poor

THE TRIERARCHS ON board also took on some of the expenditures for maintenance. Thus a large part of the state's military budget was covered by private contributions that did not figure in the state's fiscal accounting, explaining why the fleet could cost more than the income of the city. Perhaps more than half of all Athens' expenses came from the forced donations of wealthy citizens. In that context of skyrocketing naval costs, exacerbated by catastrophic defeats at sea at Sicily and Aegospotami, it was natural that reactionaries in both the revolutions of 411 and 404 sought to curtail the power of the naval lobby and seek some type of peace with Sparta. When, after 413, the landed elite were often barred from their own estates in Attica, insult was added to injury by asking them to pay to replace a fleet lost eight hundred miles away, one that would do nothing to protect the soil of the city-state from Spartan ravagers a few miles off.

So the war quite literally was bankrupting the rich conservatives of Athens, who paid to employ the poor for what seemed like a perpetual war that devoured hundreds of Athenian triremes. These revolutionary movements at home in some sense could mark the most important events of the war: should Athens, the beacon of democracy and the font of imperial aid to radical egalitarians throughout the Aegean, "flip" and become oligarchic, there would be no ideological basis for an empire at all, at least one that professed its reason to be the protection of the "people" from coercive elites. Such radical change later on was always the hope of rightists like Plato, for example, who felt that the moral decline of the city had begun with Themistocles' creation of a navy and the diminution of hoplite warfare—a process accelerated by the Peloponnesian War and only to be curtailed through revolution.[45]

Yet the financial challenge was not just building ships and paying crews. There was also an enormous investment required in dockyards and ship sheds as well. Since the materials for construction had to be imported (mostly from northwestern Greece), stored, and protected from the elements, a veritable arsenal at the Piraeus—almost two millennia before the extravagant galley factory at Venice—was constructed to launch and repair ships. There was nothing like it in the ancient world; and the inventory of ship parts and the sophistication of its arsenals explain why Athens alone of the city-states could build and maintain a fleet of 300 seaworthy triremes. Long-term maintenance involved thorough cleaning of the planks beneath the waterline of ships, which quickly became encrusted with marine life, waterlogged, and worm-eaten. To keep an expensive trireme afloat for some twenty years meant that it had to be drawn up on land and protected in a covered shed, where maintenance work on the delicate craft was nearly constant.

A Precious Investment

THE FASTEST VESSELS were probably built of silver fir, or in some cases of either pine or cedar, lighter materials that lacked the strength and resiliency of the occasionally employed hardwoods like oak. Modern reconstruction has also revealed how quickly the multitude of a trireme's intricate parts can break.

Olympias was no quicker put to sea than immediate maintenance and repair were needed. Just assembling some 300 to 400 triremes in one place, as happened in the last gigantic battles of the Peloponnesian War, was an amazing feat of logistics, as thousands rowed on fragile and temperamental craft across the Aegean without sure provisions, navigation, or any real sense of meteorology.[46]

The chief problem in trireme warfare, however, was always manpower. In theory, Athens itself had over 20,000 thetes who would customarily row. But that number could man only a hundred or so ships, even if every citizen left municipal employment or his own private job to serve for months in the Athenian fleet. So to man an imperial fleet of 200 to 300 triremes, tens of thousands of rowers were needed from subject states in the Aegean, along with resident aliens and on many occasions thousands of slaves, if not off-season farmworkers. Toward the end of the war, after tens of thousands were lost to the plague and at Sicily, non-Athenians may have made up as much as 20 to 30 percent of some of the crews. To pay for such a horde was one thing; to lose it at sea was catastrophic, weakening the very stability of the empire.

Unlike hoplite battle, which was rarely ruinous—the average fatalities in such land engagements were usually around 10 to 15 percent of the combined forces—naval warfare held the potential to take out a city's entire fleet and its enormous human investment in a single clash. Besides the disaster at Sicily, the numbers involved in battles on the eve of and during the Peloponnesian War were staggering: Sybota (433): 300 ships, 60,000 seamen; Cynossema (411): 162 ships, 33,000 seamen; Arginusae (411): 263 ships, 55,000 seamen; and Aegospotami (404): more than 300 ships and 60,000 seamen. So such losses at sea could in theory nearly bring down an entire state in a few hours. The 216 ships, 45,000 men, and perhaps over 3,000 talents in wages, capital investment, and provisions that were lost in the two armadas sent to Sicily changed the course of the war, representing as it did a sum almost the equivalent of the city's entire financial reserves present on the eve of the hostilities, capital acquired through some fifty years of empire. The Athenian disaster at Aegospotami almost a decade later immediately brought the war to a head in late 405, once a depleted Athens had gambled on putting to sea its last reserves of 180 ships with 36,000 men. In not more than an hour or so they lost 170 ships and the vast majority of the crewmen, who were either killed, captured, or scattered throughout the Hellespont. Aegospotami was a one-day financial disaster of some 400 talents alone in lost capital and wages—and the added expense of lost thousands of man-hours of labor, both military and civilian, for years to come.

The Advantage of Sea Power

GIVEN THE DANGERS and the horrendous costs of trireme warfare, why fight at sea at all? Thucydides apparently felt it necessary to explain in rather explicit terms why ships were so valuable. He starts his history off with a lesson about the early Greek thalassacracies ("sea powers"). And his long account of the war abruptly ends nearly in mid-sentence hundreds of pages later, with the Athenian victory at Cynossema in 411. Thematic throughout is his belief that money, walls, and ships represented a new horizon in warfare, one not envisioned until the rise of powerful maritime states. Their commerce and strong central government emerged in the half century of prosperity after the Persian War, and alone could fuel sufficient manpower and capital to create real navies. Yet did the Peloponnesian War prove Thucydides right about the advantages of sea power? Prewar Sparta, after all, at far less cost had created a system of land alliances in the Peloponnese that rivaled the power of Athens.

True, late-fourth-century Sparta managed to maintain a large fleet; but it was still eventually emasculated only by Theban spearmen, not rowers. In general, throughout history, one can count on one hand the world's formidable commanders—Themistocles, Don John of Austria, Nelson, Jones, Nimitz—in contrast to dozens of great captains like Alexander, Hannibal, Caesar, Genghis Khan, Saladin, Cortés, Napoleon, Wellington, Grant, Rommel, and Patton. Entire wars—the Second Punic War, the Crusades, the American Revolutionary and Civil Wars, the western fronts in both World War I and World War II—have been fought mostly without decisive sea battles. People, after all, live on land, not water; most food is grown in the soil, not the sea; and men need not build vessels to fight on the ground. Victorian England could blockade imperial Germany; but victory was possible only with the destruction of the formidable German army. In turn, Germany probably could have won both world wars on the Continent without defeating the British fleet. The Soviet Union was kept alive by the American and British merchant marines, but the battles that broke the Third Reich on the eastern front were all fought on land.

Why then do states, ancient and modern, if they are to be great and imperial, look to the sea? The dilemma of ships versus infantry is best resolved not in an either-or proposition but, rather, in terms of a cost-benefit analysis. In a strictly military sense, did building and maintaining a large fleet bring advantages to justify the enormous human and material investment, as well as the risk of losing such aggregate capital in a single bad day? Alexander, Caesar, Napoleon, and Hitler might argue otherwise; their power, after all, was created and maintained by infantry forces largely acting alone against like armies. But then the latter two eventually came to ruin, and the former often won only through maritime support and transport.

At the most basic level, ships gave to a state a vast array of alternatives, both military and economic. With the addition of a potential fleet of more than 200 active and 100 reserve ships, Athens found that within a three-hundred-mile radius it could unite, or rather coerce, nearly two hundred Greek states—perhaps comprising almost a million people, and all reachable by a fleet of triremes in a little over three or four days. Island states that had surrendered their navies, unlike land powers, were easily kept separate and isolated, and had no mechanisms for uniting. In turn, their imperial ruler could coerce all piecemeal with its magnificent fleet, making a maritime empire easier to control than its landed counterpart. It was a difficult task to cut off and surround a landlocked city, but not so much an island, which could be blockaded and separated from trade, commerce, and help.[47]

Athens alone of Greek states had the ability to reach even farther abroad, to additional millions of Mediterranean peoples in Cyprus, Egypt, southern Russia, Italy, and Sicily, in much the same manner that tiny sixteenth-century Venice was enriched by scores of trading outposts in the eastern Mediterranean. But what is meant by "reach"? Perhaps that maritime commerce was possible only through the presence of warships that could protect merchant ships from pirates and hostile powers and provide a degree of coercion to establish favorite trading relationships. Out of such free, safe trade arose an Aegean economy that was integrated through constant export and import of goods— and humans as well.

The Piraeus, and the Long Walls that linked it to the city, became almost a secular religious entity in Athenian thinking. Throughout the war there was a paranoid fixation on the harbor's safety, this vital emporium of the empire in the Aegean. Thucydides once remarked that an aborted Peloponnesian attack against the Piraeus created among Athenians "a panic as great as any throughout the war."[48] Aristophanes used almost reverential tones to describe the chaos at the port when the Athenian fleet made ready to sail: captains shouting, money being paid, ships' figureheads being gilded, food and water being carried on board, farewell parties, fistfights, and last-minute repairs. An anonymous conservative Athenian critic, sometimes called the "Old Oligarch," hated his city's naval power and the democratic culture it fostered, but then waxed eloquent about how it ensured a lucrative trade and vibrancy unmatched in the Greek world.[49]

Thus, the Athenians realized that such fortifications were the linchpin of an entire way of democratic and prosperous life. Despite having their fleet wiped out, facing famine, and with the Spartans camped outside the walls and demanding surrender, the Athenian assembly nevertheless initially made it a crime for any Athenian citizen to agree to Spartan armistice demands to tear down large sections of the Long Walls—and, with them, the real and symbolic guarantor of the entire idea of radical Athenian democracy.[50]

Militarily, maritime Athens could do more than landlocked Sparta: send troops to Pylos, raid the coast of the Peloponnese, supply a sustained war in northwestern Greece, put down revolts on the island of Lesbos, and blockade rebellious cities on the shores of the Chalcidice. As Pericles put it, sea power could not be compared to "the use of houses or agricultural land." Rather, it represented a strength altogether different, something unrivaled that gave Athenians the freedom to go wherever they pleased, one matched by neither the king of Persia nor by "any other nations of those now on earth." What he meant by such majestic rhetoric was that the Athenian fleet allowed the city to achieve numerical superiority in almost any local theater without the muster of a huge, ponderous land army of the type that had lumbered into Attica in the first decade of the war.

Athenian maritime flexibility, coupled with the protection of the city proper offered by the Long Walls, was the theme of almost all of Pericles' speeches outlining Athenian wartime strategy. At the very beginning of the war, the Athenians thought that by winning over neighboring states and gaining key islands off the coast of the Peloponnese—Cythera, Corcyra, Cephallenia, and Zacynthus—"they might encircle the Peloponnese and conquer it."

In addition, food, supplies, weapons, and troops themselves—all these could be transported by sea at a fraction of the cost of land support. Other than helot attendants, the Spartan army essentially had no "lift" capability whatsoever, and could operate abroad only to the degree that it could bring along a few days' supply of food and scrounge the rest from the surrounding countryside. The Greeks deprecated the Spartan ability to conduct sieges, but inherent in that perceived weakness was their inferiority in ships, inasmuch as assaults were most often conducted against port cities. Nor was Greece a Mesopotamia or Nile Valley, where overland travel entailed level marches on well-watered ground; rather, it was a mountainous and often inhospitable country, and even today some of its mountainous coastal communities are accessible only by sea. King Agis moved against Athens from the Spartan base at Decelea only when Lysander's triremes were in its harbor. Land powers could fight each other without warring at sea. Thebes and Sparta, for example, would later do just that for nearly thirty years during the first half of the fourth century. But they could make little headway on land against a sea power with urban fortifications.

The Burdens of the Athenian Navy

ONLY WHEN WARFARE turned into a true transcontinental enterprise did the value of plentiful triremes diminish somewhat. For example, in the fourth century, after the loss of empire and tribute, the Athenian fleet reached its greatest size ever, 400 triremes by 300 B.C. But in a world where the new composite army of Alexander—heavy cavalry, missile troops, phalangites, and sophisticated logistics—was designed to march thousands of miles into the interior of the Persian Empire, the old parochial harbors and choke points of the citystates became irrelevant and, with them, the value of triremes themselves.

Even in the heyday of the fifth-century trireme, naval superiority came at a cost. The expense could nearly bankrupt a maritime state in a few seasons, as the British almost learned at the beginning of the twentieth century and the Russians discovered at its end. During some years Athens sent out between 200 and 250 triremes at once, and the expense nearly exhausted the state.[51] The single naval catastrophe at Egypt in 457, a nightmare where at least 100 triremes were lost and, with them, in theory as many as 20,000 imperial sailors and support troops, sent aftershocks throughout the Athenian empire. The destruction of so many ships and men so quickly probably explains why in the disaster's aftermath the Delian treasury was moved for safekeeping to Athens, the land war on the mainland was curtailed, the empire in the Aegean was tightened up, and peace feelers were extended to Persia.[52]

The philosophers weighed in negatively against the social effects of sea power. A disgusted Plato scoffed that the sea was a "bad neighbor" and that the glorious victory at Salamis, which had started it all, made the Athenians "worse." It would have been better, he huffed, to send Athenian youths to the mythical Cretan Minotaur than for the city to find its autonomy and safety through a hated armada! Aristotle also could not deny the value of navies, but he urged that the seamen be kept away from the city, quarantined in an apartheid existence in a secluded port, to preclude the mongrelization of society that maritime life ensured. How insidious was a city built on sea power: paying its slaves to row, offering them freedom after victory, empowering the poor. The chaotic result, according to such abstract critics, was that a proper gentleman walking along an Athenian street could not distinguish a free man from his servant, much less expect a slave to step out of his way![53]

Yet in the end it seems incredible that Athens could build and lose at least two entire fleets, pass up at least three Spartan entreaties for peace, and press on with the war for twenty-seven years. But it was not just the defeat of Athens that was at stake. Rather, for 20,000 poor Athenians, half the city's citizenry at war's outbreak, victory meant freedom and prosperity, while defeat was thought by many to presage a return to powerless existence under a hated landed oligarchy. Poor people, not reactionary elite horsemen or conservative yeomen farmers, wanted the Peloponnesian War, and the assurance that their bulwark of radical democracy, an imperial fleet, and an empire of tribute-paying democratic subject states would be the future of Greece. Accordingly, the last decade of sea fighting was so violent and savage precisely because hundreds of thousands of poor Greeks, in places like Byzantium, Chios, and Samos, now understood that they would either continue to vote under the aegis of an often stern Athenian imperialism or, with Athens' defeat, be forced to accept oligarchic rule.

The wealthy in Athens felt that they had only so much capital that could be taxed. Despite the riches generated by state-owned silver mines, additional income from abroad was needed if the triremes were to stay afloat. By the second or third year of the war, the city was already nearing financial insolvency as a result of constant patrolling around the Peloponnese. In response, measures were taken to increase tribute and imperial revenue as early as 428. But with continual naval action off Sicily, Melos, and Mytilene, by 426 the costs of triremes grew voracious. The old prewar annual assessment on some 200 imperial subjects had been around 500 to 600 talents, as Athens was a protection racket that billed its clients for the cost of providing their own security. Yet by just the fourth year of the war, the assessment had skyrocketed to 800 talents.

After all, if 200 ships were, in theory, in service for eight months a year and thus could consume almost 2,000 talents to outfit and man, even more tribute was required. By 425 the imperial levy soared to somewhere between 1,200 and 1,300 talents. And still the hungry triremes of Athens were short of money. A city that had once engaged in a twenty-year conundrum over the excessive cost of 1,000 talents for temples on the Acropolis was consuming more than that expense every year and showing very little progress in the war for all the sacrifice.

All that futile expense was to change in the last decade of the war, when Sparta at last came out to meet the Athenians at sea. More Greeks would fight and die in the Aegean after 411 than had during all the battles of the first two decades of the conflict, as the combatants finally agreed to meet each other in decisive battles and settle the war for good.[54]

CHAPTER 9

CLIMAX

Trireme Fighting in the Aegean (411–405)

Sparta Builds a Fleet

AFTER THE DEFEAT of much of the Corinthian fleet by Phormio in 429, the Peloponnesians had essentially given up the idea of defeating the Athenians at sea, much in the same way as the latter avoided pitched battle with Spartan hoplites. In response, the Athenians were often given a free hand to patrol the empire. They would do so with near impunity for almost the next sixteen years; the Peloponnesians, in contrast, resembled more the smaller German navy of the two world wars, venturing out to terrorize merchants and neutrals only when the British fleet was elsewhere or asleep.

Then, suddenly, the unexpected Athenian catastrophe of 413 in Sicily—216 imperial triremes (perhaps at least 160 of them Athenian) and almost 45,000 men of the empire were lost or captured—gave new impetus to Sparta's efforts to catch up and build a new Pan-Peloponnesian fleet fueled by Persian money. The vast armada of Athens had always been a fluke beyond what should have been the limited resources of any single city-state. Indeed, its creation in 482 was a result only of a rich strike in the silver mines of Laurium, and it was later sustained by the imperial tribute of hundreds of subject states. In contrast, without mines or tribute-paying subjects, Sparta's old pipe dream at the beginning of the war of creating a vast armada of 500 ships could be realized only by an unholy alliance with the empire of Persia.

It was not just that Athens had lost two-thirds of its once magnificent imperial fleet or that the roughly 100 reserve triremes that remained in the Piraeus were in various states of unreadiness. Instead, the greater dilemma was that the human losses at Sicily, coupled with the thousands of dead from the plague, had wiped out an entire generation of experienced Athenian rowers, teachers, and students of the sea, all almost impossible to replace at once. In a similar example, after the defeat of Lepanto (1571), the Ottoman catastrophe was not just the loss of almost 30,000 seamen and 200 galleys—or the thousands more sailors who were unaccounted for. Rather, the destruction of thousands of trained bowmen, archers who made Turkish ships deadly but took years to train properly, ensured that even after the hasty reconstruction of their fleet by the next year, the Ottomans would rarely again venture into Italian-controlled waters.

A third to half of the thousands of imperial rowers who were lost at Sicily were probably Athenian citizens and resident aliens. The death or capture of the remaining 20,000 foreigners and allied seamen not only drained the empire of manpower but also created waves of resentment against Athens among bereaved subjects. Long gone was the memory of the festive spectacle of cheering and merriment, and expectations of easy loot and glory on the cheap, when the grand flotilla had sailed from the Piraeus in 415. Sailing with the Athenians could quite literally get you and your sons killed.

Something had also come over the Greeks after Sicily. Perhaps it was the length of the war; it was now almost twenty years since Sparta had invaded Athens, and both desperate sides were beginning to sense that the end could not be too far away. Or maybe the increasing savagery was attributable to the mounting losses and the barbarism unleashed at Scione, Torone, and Melos. In any case, in the Archidamian War one does not sense that Spartans and Athenians hated each other. But in the last phase of the conflict, there is a real feeling of growing fury on both sides, that trireme war in the eastern Aegean was perhaps more like the Japanese, rather than the European, theater of World War II, when most soldiers gave no quarter and harbored a deep visceral and racial dislike of their enemies.

If an islander were to row in the future, it might be wiser to enlist for higher pay in the new and larger Peloponnesian fleet, which was likely to patrol in greater numbers in the eastern Aegean, which was now increasingly empty of the old Athenian triremes. As the war heightened in the eastern Aegean and the limits of Greek manpower became clear after some two decades of steady combat losses, the final sea fights became as much a bidding war for mercenary oarsmen as a test of seamanship. In other words, the war would descend into a one-sided financial contest between the limitless gold of Persia and an impoverished Athens.[1]

Athens started the war with 5,000 talents in reserve. But after Sicily it now had less than 500 in its treasury, scarcely enough to build 100 triremes and keep them at sea for even four months. The special emergency reserve of 1,000 talents to guarantee the safety of the Piraeus was suddenly not so sacrosanct. Thucydides concluded that besides the absence of men to make up the losses and the few triremes left in the ship sheds, there was also "no money in the treasury." In addition, the two traditional sources of Athenian naval financing—silver from Laurium and tribute from the Aegean—were now imperiled by Spartan ravagers and ships. Most Greeks thought that after Sicily "the war was over." Thus, should Sparta somehow find the capital to build a fleet and pay for its new crews, there was a good chance that by 413 its rowers would be no more inexperienced than most Athenian replacement oarsmen.[2]

After a few years of valuable help to the Peloponnesian navy, the Persians decided to take a far more active role when the maverick Spartan admiral Lysander and the renegade teenaged Achaemenid prince Cyrus struck a partnership of convenience in 407, one that meant the Peloponnesians would have a nearly unlimited supply of capital to build ships and hire crews. With overwhelming numerical superiority, the Spartans could afford to keep challenging the Athenians at sea, backed up by the assurance that their losses would be made good as they wore down the Athenian fleet in a theater vital to the continuance of imported food and precious tribute.[3] Even earlier, after the defeat at Cyzicus in spring 410, the Persian satrap Pharnabazus had encouraged the demoralized Spartans to remember that there was plenty of timber for ships in Persia, and lots of replacement arms, money, and clothing to reequip any sailors who survived the defeat.[4]

In the immediate aftermath of the Athenian catastrophe at Sicily, when it came time to pony up for Peloponnesian triremes, the Boeotians, Corinthians, Locrians, Phocians, Arcadians, Megarians, and the states of the Argolid sent out no more than 75 ships. Along with the Spartans' own paltry 25 triremes, that still made up a combined fleet of only about 100 ships. The Sicilian allies proved an equal disappointment. Despite having been saved by the timely arrival of a Peloponnesian fleet in the harbor at Syracuse, in recompense they added little more than 22 vessels to the Spartan cause—given their worries over a nearby aggressive Carthage. So there loomed the chance that in 412 the Peloponnesians might soon achieve numerical parity at sea, a situation in the short-term that meant Sparta could at least engage the green reconstituted Athenian fleet with an equal number of ships and crews no more inexperienced.

The inclusion of seasoned naval officers from Syracuse and Corinth who long had organized fleets might account for some sharing of nautical experience among the high command of the grand Peloponnesian fleet. At times, for example, there is special mention of skilled navigators like Ariston the Corinthian, who was "the best pilot of the Syracusan fleet." He had devised a stratagem for feeding his seamen rapidly on shore and getting their triremes back in action as quickly as possible. The same innovator was most probably responsible for attaching shorter and lower rams to the Syracusan ships, to ensure that they struck below the waterline and with greater force.[5]

Nevertheless, what has never been adequately explained is how a landlocked reactionary state like Sparta, one that not only had little experience with the sea but openly loathed the entire social cargo that accompanied naval power, in the space of less than a decade turned green crews and brand-new triremes into a formidable and seasoned opponent of the great fleet of Athens. The creation of an eastern Aegean Spartan flotilla, alongside the Roman armada during the Punic Wars and the Japanese imperial fleet at the beginning of the twentieth century, ranks as one of the great naval achievements in history.

Ancient observers remarked on the sheer audacity of Spartan naval power, usually through acknowledgment by Spartans themselves that they had no real idea of what they were doing. "Sending out men who had no experience with the sea" to replace "men who were just beginning to understand naval matters" summed up Spartan policy in the eastern Aegean—as if one Spartan hoplite on deck was as good as another.[6] Contemplating Spartans out in the middle of the Aegean on rocking triremes, one might paraphrase Samuel Johnson and wonder not that it was done well, but that it was done at all.

Bloodbath

YET IF THE Aegean had been relatively quiet since 429, suddenly from 411 to 404 the Athenians met the Spartans and their allies in at least seven major engagements. Across time and space, rarely are rival fleets willing to engage each other repeatedly until one side is not merely defeated but annihilated. Such is the conservatism of admirals who so jealously protect their precious assets while on the high seas. Like the British systematic destruction of the Napoleonic armada or the American Seventh Fleet's brutal death struggle with the Japanese, which finally ended with the utter annihilation of the most lethal carrier and battleship force of the pre–World War II world, both Athens and Sparta now no longer sought mere tactical advantage but were willing to risk their all to finish off the enemy.

To win, Sparta had to kill off, capture, or scatter a final cohort of at least another 50,000 or so Athenian and allied sailors and sink another 200 ships, which otherwise, over a decade, might replace the losses of Sicily. These last battles across the Aegean—they are often lumped together and called the Ionian War—were decided in the waters off western Asia Minor (Ionia) and in or near the Hellespont (the modern Dardanelles). If Boeotia, home of nine major hoplite battlefields by the fourth century, was once dubbed by the Theban general Epaminondas "the dancing floor of war," one could call the Hellespont and the adjoining Propontis (the Sea of Marmara) "the seas of death." In those environs alone 50,000 men were probably killed, missing, or captured in just three battles at Cynossema, Cyzicus, and Aegospotami, all within a sixty-mile radius. In addition, between 412 and 404 thousands more Athenians, Persians, and Peloponnesians died in ambushes, seaborne attacks, and random killing up and down the Ionian seaboard.[7]

With the establishment of a permanent garrison at Decelea, the new Peloponnesian fleet was confident that it now had muscle enough to block grain ships from arriving at Attica. Thus, this time under a year-round combined land and sea assault, the city, it was thought, would shortly go bankrupt if not starve: keep Attic farmers away from their land, destroy ships that imported food, deny access to grain-growing areas abroad, assure subjects that they can revolt in safety and withhold tribute, and all the while sink Athenian triremes. Decelea was the antithesis of Archidamus' earlier failed strategy, which had offered no permanent presence and no ancillary naval strategy.

Not long after the defeat in the Great Harbor of Syracuse, an emboldened and reconstituted Spartan armada engaged what was left of the Athenian fleet in a series of inconclusive sea battles in the Aegean, at Spiraeum (412), Syme (411), Chios (411), and Eretria (411). Whereas losses at these rather obscure sea battles on both sides were minimal, the succession of collisions began to wear on a shaky Athens and had the practical effect of destroying another 30 or so Athenian triremes.

More importantly, perhaps 5,000 seamen were killed, scattered, or captured. Despite spending its final 1,000-talent critical reserve on rebuilding the fleet, strategically Athens could no longer control even the seas off its own coast. It was also on the verge of losing much of Ionia and, with it, a tribute-rich empire. After the defeat at Eretria in nearby Euboea—the Athenians lost 22 ships and most of the crews were killed in battle or captured—a panic descended upon the city that was greater than the near riot that had broken out after the news of the Sicilian disaster reached the Piraeus, two years earlier.[8]

The final phases of the war next turned to the northern coast of the Hellespont. There, near the peninsula called the Thracian Chersonese, the Spartans now tightened the noose, hoping to cut off the sea-lanes between Propontis and Athens. In summer 411 at Cynossema, 76 Athenian ships, under the brilliant general Thrasybulus, beat back the larger Peloponnesian fleet of 86 triremes. Perhaps 32,000 seamen were involved. At least 36 ships were lost in fighting that spanned some eleven miles of the strait. The total casualties are unknown—though as many as 7,000 may have been killed, scattered, or wounded. The Athenians claimed victory on the basis that they had at least kept their last fleet intact. They had regained morale in their first major fight after the disaster in Sicily, defeated a fleet that included several hated Syracusan triremes last encountered in the disaster of the Great Harbor, and ensured that commerce with Athens remained open. As Thucydides rightly put it, "They stopped considering that their enemies were worth much in naval matters."[9]

Yet in such battles of attrition, the greater resources now were starting to tip toward the Peloponnesians. Their newfound pluck at sea would encourage more contributions from their allies and closely observant Persia. In contrast, to win the war on the seas the Athenians would have to inflict crushing losses on the Spartans while losing almost none of their now precious triremes. Thucydides, for example, said of the Athenian victory at Cynossema (fought not far from Gallipoli) that it came "at just the right time," inasmuch as small losses to the Peloponnesians in the prior two years and the great catastrophe on Sicily had made them "afraid of the Peloponnesian fleet."[10]

To compound the Peloponnesian misery, not far away, at Abydos, a few weeks later the Spartans once again forced battle. There they were to lose another 30 ships, along with thousands of crewmen. Still, Alcibiades—in 411 he had returned to Athens in yet another incarnation, as chief Athenian admiral—summed up the Athenian dilemma best before the battle of Cyzicus. After explaining why his crews had "to fight at sea, fight on land, and fight against walled fortresses," he finished with the admission of a bitter reality: "The reason is that there is no money among us, while the enemy has all they wish from the king of Persia."[11]

Sparta was not to be deterred by the loss at Abydos in its ambitious efforts to destroy what was left of the once grand Athenian fleet. In between battle and revolution, the Spartans offered Persian bonuses for oarsmen on the open market, rightly figuring that higher pay in the Peloponnesian navy would cause desertion from the Athenian fleet, which now depended on mercenary rowers.[12]

About six months later, in March 410 and thirty-five miles distant from

Cynossema, the Spartan fleet unabashedly forced battle again, near Cyzicus. In this third consecutive battle of the Ionian War, after Cynossema and Abydos, the Peloponnesians suffered yet another setback, despite their now accustomed numerical superiority. Inspired leadership by the veteran generals Thrasybulus and Alcibiades and remarkable seamanship by a new generation of Athenian oarsmen, who went to sea in a storm and performed flawlessly the difficult *periplous*, explain the remarkable victory. In fact, Cyzicus proved one of the greatest naval disasters for any Greek fleet during the entire war. Yet it was the beginning, not the end, of the bloodbath in the Aegean.

Another 60 ships, including 20 Syracusan triremes, were now lost, some of which their dejected crews burned after seeing the defeat of their allies. The casualties are not known, but they must have been high. Perhaps well over 10,000 seamen were captured, scattered, or killed, including the Spartan general Mindarus. The historian Xenophon, in one of the most famous passages in his Hellenic history, quotes a laconic letter sent back home to Sparta from the surviving vice admiral Hippocrates—intercepted by the victorious Athenians—that read: "The ships are gone. Mindarus is dead. The men are starving. We are at a loss what we should do."[13]

What to do? In less than a year, Sparta had suffered staggering losses. Somewhere between 130 and 160 triremes were gone—almost the entire contribution two years earlier of its Peloponnesian and Syracusan allies. How many were dead, wounded, or lost is not recorded. In theory, between 20,000 and 30,000 seamen were on those ships that went down; in reality, no doubt at least a few thousand probably escaped or were captured.

Suddenly the entire course of the war began to change. After Sicily, the Greeks had assumed that Athens was finished. Now they were not so sure. Athens' food supply was still safe. Rebellion among the allies was less likely. Athenian naval prestige was once again unquestioned. And most importantly, generals like Thrasybulus, Theramenes, and Alcibiades had proved that they were far better tacticians than almost all the admirals that had accompanied the Spartans to the Aegean.

After Cyzicus, a dejected Sparta apparently remembered why it had not sought naval engagements against Athens some twenty years earlier. In frustration, Sparta quickly sent out peace feelers to Athens: "We want to have peace with you, men of Athens," their ambassadors pleaded in offering a return to the prewar status quo. But the Athenian assembly, perhaps led by rabble-rousing demagogues like Cleophon, was now aroused, drunk on success and paranoid after the failed oligarchic coup of 411. For the first time in some three years, the

Athenians had thoughts of reclaiming the entire Aegean. Maybe they really could destroy the Spartan fleet for good, and drive the Persians out of Greek affairs. Unsure how to follow up their spectacular successes, the Athenians unwisely played defense for nearly four years, between 410 and 407, while the Spartans rebuilt their forces and found themselves a true military genius in Lysander, albeit one who did not emerge in a major role until 407, near the end of the war.

Unfortunately for the Athenians, few of the city's politicians saw the true complexion of this new Ionian War, and ignored the advice of the three brilliant generals, Alcibiades, Thrasybulus, and Theramenes, who had brought them such stunning victories. The truth was that the war had now changed dramatically and could no longer be seen in terms of the old simple Spartan land/Athenian sea dichotomy of decades past. The newfound Spartan ability to tap into the imperial treasuries of Persia, through the direct succor of its western satrapies, ensured the enemies of Athens an inexhaustible supply of mercenaries, new triremes, and money to hire crews who were experienced rowers, not rustic farmers from the Peloponnese.

To nullify the Spartan advantage in numbers and its determination to prompt battle repeatedly, Athens had to rely on superior seamanship and command *in every major battle*, without any margin of error. It could not fight on the defensive, since it was trying to maintain an empire, which involved more than just keeping out the Spartan fleet. And an unforeseen result of the Athenian victory at Cyzicus was a reexamination of the Spartan command, leading to the appointment of a new admiral, Lysander, who, even more so than Brasidas, would prove to be the unqualified military genius of the entire war on either side, the most ruthless, brilliant, and multidimensional battle leader Greece had produced since Themistocles. Most Spartan generals were fighters (with tough names like Thorax, "Breastplate," and Leon, "Lion"), but rarely was one both heroic and full of strategic insight about how to defeat something as insidious as the Athenian empire. The presence of Lysander—a man cut from the same cloth as Brasidas and Gylippus (none of them were Spartan royalty and thus all were considered somewhat expendable)—along with a greater infusion of Persian capital was felt almost immediately as the Spartan maverick systematically hunted down grain ships, stormed Athenian strongholds, and enslaved captured peoples. In the next major battle, at Notium (spring 406)—the Spartans had used the three-year hiatus in naval confrontation to rebuild their fleet—Alcibiades temporarily left command to Antiochus, a minor captain, with strict orders to avoid an engagement in his absence.

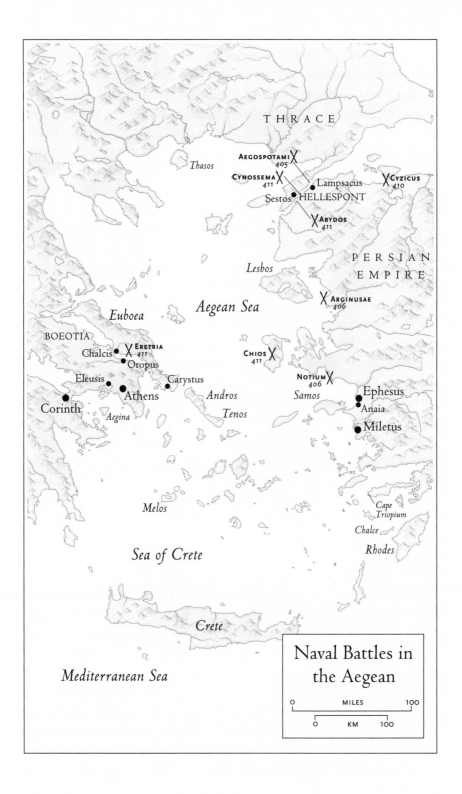

THRACE

Thasos

AEGOSPOTAMI X
405

CYNOSSEMA X
411

Lampsacus

X CYZICUS
410

Sestos • HELLESPONT

X ABYDOS
411

PERSIAN

EMPIRE

Lesbos

Aegean Sea

X ARGINUSAE
406

Euboe

BOEOTIA

Chalcis • X ERETRIA
411

Oropus

CHIOS X
411

Eleusis •

Carystus

NOTIUM X
406

Corinth •

Athens •

Aegina

Andros

Samos

Ephesus •
Anaia

Tenos

Miletus •

Melos

Cape
Triopium

Chalce

Rhodes

Sea of Crete

Crete

Mediterranean Sea

Naval Battles in
the Aegean

0   MILES   100

0   KM   100

Instead, the Athenians rashly fought Lysander off Ephesus, and right away lost 22 irreplaceable ships. By any measure this was small potatoes after the stunning string of victories at Cynossema, Abydos, and Cyzicus. On the other hand, every Athenian trireme was now precious. Despite the fact that when Alcibiades returned to Notium after the defeat of his subordinate the Athenians still had as many ships as Lysander, the loss caused outrage at a desperate Athens, raising the specter of Alcibiades' past machinations and triangulations.

Once more Alcibiades was banished, and with that Athens lost its most capable and popular admiral. True, Athens had lost few ships, and its fleet of 108 remaining triremes was roughly the same size as the Peloponnesian armada. But Athens' dilemma was not merely that it had to stop the Persian fleet but that it had an empire to protect in Ionia as well, a fact that in strategic terms meant that superiority, not parity, in ships was required.[14]

A few months later at Mytilene, the Athenians under Conon lost another 30 ships to a Spartan fleet that once more had grown to somewhere between 140 and 170 ships. In response, the Athenians began a desperate search for even more manpower, putting old and young, slave and free, poor and wealthy on triremes in hopes of manning enough ships to thwart the Spartan juggernaut. By late spring of the same year, the death struggle continued as the fleets once more sailed to engage each other off the Ionian coast. In the previous five years, at the smaller battles of Spiraeum, Syme, Chios, Eretria, and Abydos and the three great fights at Cynossema, Cyzicus, and Notium, at least 84 Athenian triremes had been lost, along with perhaps as many as 16,000 seamen. Sparta, in turn, had suffered nearly double those casualties—160 ships sunk or captured and, with them, perhaps as many as 30,000 sailors.[15]

The Last Battles

ALTOGETHER, THE FIRST unheralded years of the Ionian War had proved more catastrophic than the better-known Athenian disaster in Sicily. Almost 50,000 aggregate Greeks drowned or were captured, killed in action, executed, or scattered, along with nearly 250 triremes—the equivalent in actual, rather than relative, human losses for the huge American navy of losing 10 modern aircraft carriers along with their crews of 5,000 sailors. And the worst was yet to come.

By late summer it made no difference to the Athenians that over the last seven years they had given better than they had taken. What mattered now was that after the last two losses of Mytilene and Notium the fleet had been reduced to fewer than 80 triremes and might not be able to ensure grain imports from the Crimea or to hold on to the tribute-paying Greek city-states in Asia Minor. Rather than giving up their empire, in desperation the Athenians somehow manned and launched 60 new triremes—slaves and freedmen alike embarked as rowers—and rushed them to Ionia to join what was left at sea. Shipwrights had built dozens of green triremes in just over a month, as the city scavenged the precious metal veneers from the statues on the Acropolis and melted them down to issue coinage to build and man the slapped-together warships. The hope was to reconstitute a fleet of over 140 triremes that might have some chance against the ever-growing Peloponnesian fleet. That was not an impossible feat given that some seventy years earlier (between 483 and 480) Themistocles, with far less experience, had built the first great Athenian fleet of some 200 triremes in just over two years. In fact, with aid from the Samians, the new armada now reached 155 triremes, an astounding number in light of the recent disasters.

Sparta's launching of a series of new fleets is understandable given their Persian capital and their relatively light losses during the first two decades of the war. But how Athens after the plague, Sicily, and continued attrition in the Ionian War could project such naval forces near the end of the third decade of the war staggers the imagination. Few contemporaries had envisioned that by 406, after twenty-five years of war and thousands of dead, Athens would launch a fleet almost as large as any in Greek history.

Off the Arginusae Islands, despite the preponderance of inexperienced replacement crews (thousands of Attic slaves now enlisted on promises of freedom even as the wealthiest horsemen in the city volunteered to row) and hastily constructed ships that were qualitatively inferior to those of the Peloponnesian fleet, the Athenians enjoyed the old numerical superiority for the first time since the Sicilian disaster. Some 120 Peloponnesian triremes were assembled to meet them under Callicratidas, who most recently, at Mytilene, had defeated the skilled Athenian admiral Conon. Other than citing a numerical advantage of a few dozen triremes, to this day scholars are perplexed about how the Athenians, with green triremes, crews augmented with slaves, and coming off defeat, could have so decisively annihilated the veteran Peloponnesian fleet.

Arginusae proved to be the most violent sea battle of the Peloponnesian War. The engagement marked perhaps the largest collection of warships in one encounter since Salamis, as over 270 triremes and 50,000 rowers collided. Diodorus thought it was the greatest naval battle of Greek against Greek in history, as Athenian triremes rowed in large part by slaves gave the democracy its greatest victory since Salamis.

After a brutal collision of ships, the Athenians destroyed some 77 Spartan and allied triremes at a loss of only 26 of their own, an astounding 3-to-1 kill ratio. Sixty-four percent of the Peloponnesian fleet was destroyed in a few hours, well over twice the grievous loss rate earlier at Abydos, Cynossema, and Cyzicus, which had reached an unsustainable average of 28 percent. With this loss of over two-thirds of their forces at Arginusae, Sparta and her allies in the space of a mere five years had now suffered 250 ships sunk that were manned by 50,000 rowers and marines, in a rarely recognized disaster that dwarfed that of the Athenians in Sicily in 413.

The difference, however, was twofold. Spartan commanders reported back to an oligarchy, where the average citizen could hardly shout down a speaker and whip up the crowd. Second, most of the money lost and the crews killed were not Laconian but mercenary seamen and Persian-financed triremes. This disparity may explain why the Athenians in hard-fought triumphs went into despair, while in catastrophe the Spartans continued on their policy of steady attrition.[16]

The paradox of Arginusae was not that the Athenians had nearly annihilated the Spartan fleet but that they had lost some 26 triremes with most of their crews in the process. Lurid stories soon filtered back to Athens of the abandonment of survivors in the "thousands" bobbing in stormy water and clinging to wreckage, along with the "abandoned" corpses of the dead, which were likewise not retrieved. In the uproar that followed, 6 of the 10 generals were executed for dereliction of duty (among them Pericles' last surviving son). The rest, who were the most talented officers in Athens, fled into exile in fear of a similar death sentence.

Still, even the small loss of 26 Athenian ships at Arginusae, or 16 percent of the fleet, less than a decade after the loss of 200 imperial ships in Sicily and another 100 in the Ionian War, was a setback. Sparta, in yet another moment of despair, may now have once more sent envoys asking for peace, offering to evacuate Decelea and leave the truncated Athenian empire alone. And the democracy in the aftermath of the engagement may have won a key victory in the greatest trireme battle in half a century; but the throng in the assembly still felt more anguish after than before the triumph. Thus, they rejected peace feelers and yet failed to follow up the victory with another direct attack on the Spartan fleet, in essence squandering hard-won momentum as relish to destroying its own top command.[17]

A city that often blamed itself more in victory than defeat was showing manifestations of a terminal illness, conducting postbellum hearings to assess blame in the midst of a war for its survival. In the real monster battles of the Ionian War, like Cynossema, Cyzicus, and Arginusae, Athens had won every time. But it now somehow felt more demoralized than Sparta, which had suffered twice its losses, as each sailor was seen to be irreplaceable and thus every elected general was held responsible for any loss. The war, as Archidamus had once warned, would ultimately hinge on money; but even he had had no idea that a quarter century later his own Spartans, not imperial Athens, would have the greater reserves of money and manpower and, in Lysander, a commander far more audacious and versatile than any of the most experienced Athenian admirals.

Two years later Athens' luck finally ran out at Aegospotami ("Goat Rivers"), a few miles to the north of Arginusae. With generals like Alcibiades and Thrasybulus exiled or driven out, there was a dearth of command talent, but somehow still plenty of green crews, slapped-together triremes, and an array of amateurs eager to command and fight for the idea of imperial Athens. Not far from Sestos, on the Hellespont, Lysander came upon a complacent Athenian fleet on or near the beach; most crews were convinced, after four days of Spartan feigned inaction, that a showdown was unlikely. But on the fifth, Lysander suddenly struck and caught thousands of Athenians scattered on shore, searching for food and supplies. Unwisely the admirals had encamped over two miles (some fifteen stades) from their supplies at Sestos, and thus found logistical support constantly at odds with battle readiness. Only a few ships made it out to sea to meet the surprise Spartan attack. Most of them had only one or two banks fully manned.[18]

The result was an abject slaughter. The Spartan fleet destroyed, disabled, or captured 170 of 180 triremes, dispersed thousands of the oarsmen, and then executed 3,000 to 4,000 of the captured Athenian crews, sparing only the allies and slaves. The butchering of the victors in a few minutes exceeded the toll of all those who had perished during the two great hoplite battles of the war, at Delium and Mantinea. This most decisive naval defeat in the history of any Greek city-state was not even really fought at sea, and in some sense was not a battle between triremes at all. Rather, Lysander's triremes surprised thousands as they ate, slept, and lounged on the beach. And nearly all the Athenian ships that managed to leave shore were sunk in the shallow surf.[19]

In the aftermath of the battle, Lysander's victorious armada swelled to 200 ships, perhaps the largest single concentration of a city-state's triremes to sail in unison since the Athenian fleet joined the allies at Salamis nearly eighty years prior. The new monster fleet of the Peloponnesians systematically sailed throughout the Aegean, stationing triremes at key ports and declaring the Athenian empire to be over. Aegospotami ranks with the destruction of Xerxes' triremes at Salamis (480), the obliteration of the Ottoman fleet off Lepanto (1571), the ruin of the Spanish Armada during the battle and retreat of 1588, and the French disaster off Trafalgar (1805) as one of the most decisive naval engagements in European history. Unlike earlier naval catastrophes, Aegospotami is one of the few battles in history in which such a grievous setback led not only to withdrawal and retrenchment but to the veritable collapse of an entire imperial state.[20]

What of our Alcibiades, who as a nineteen-year-old had started off the war so heroically at the siege of Potidaea? While another Alcibiades, his namesake cousin and fellow exile, was caught in the aftermath of the battle at Notium by the Athenian general Thrasyllus and stoned to death as a traitor, Alcibiades himself proved once more a survivor.[21]

The bloody Ionian War made him hero, scapegoat, and, finally, irrelevant. The genius and heroism that had first catapulted him to fame as a teenager at Potidaea were never more evident than at Cyzicus, when the newly arrived Alcibiades played a key role in defeating the Spartan fleet and ending the career of the admiral Mindarus. Between 410 and 408 Alcibiades integrated skilled oarsmen into the Athenian fleet, began raising money from Pharnabazus, the Persian satrap in the Hellespont, and was responsible for capturing the key cities of Chalcedon and Byzantium.

At age forty Alcibiades was now at the height of his powers, versed in some twenty years of political intrigue and a host of campaigns. He was decorated at the siege at Potidaea, patrolled the Attic countryside, manned the rearguard at the defeat at Delium, crafted a political alliance at Argos, engineered the Sicilian expedition, created a fleet ex nihilo for Sparta, and sought to win over Persia by promising the ruin of both Athens and Sparta.

Quite literally, there were very few key battles of the entire war that Alcibiades missed. In 411 he returned triumphantly to the side of Athens, as the crowd forgave Sicily, returned his property, and praised him for the resurrection of the Athenian fleet off Ionia. But given his own flamboyance and the fickleness of the assembly, such a simple reconciliation could not last. After leaving his triremes at Notium with the lowly subordinate Antiochus, who unwisely engaged Lysander and lost, in 406 Alcibiades was once more cursed and relieved of command. Two decades of the old charges resurfaced—public immorality, triangulation with Persians and Spartans, dereliction of duty—and both out of envy and for good cause he now left Athens for the second and last time.[22]

Alcibiades' end was a fitting metaphor for the entire Athenian experience of this awful three-decade war. For the last two years of the conflict (406–404) he was in exile at one of his private strongholds around Thrace, no doubt plotting some fantastic third return. Aegospotami, ironically fought in sight of his temporary residence on the Ionian coast, precluded all that. Once more, in the hours before Lysander's attack he offered sound tactical advice to the generals, only to be refused on grounds that had everything to do with envy and distrust of this proven resource and little to do with the acuteness of his military thought.

At this late date, the one single Athenian who perhaps could have saved or ruined Athens was told to leave. The competent generals ignored his wise counsel to instill discipline among their foraging crews and move immediately to a more defensible position, and thus they lost Aegospotami, their fleet, and the war itself. Alcibiades was murdered in Phrygia shortly after the surrender. Whether the responsible parties were rightist agents of the Thirty Tyrants, who feared his popular appeal with the Athenian masses; assassins of the Persian satrap Pharnabazus, who worried that Alcibiades would disclose his own intrigue against the king; envoys from Lysander who remembered the old treachery against Sparta; or the enraged male brethren of yet another young virgin he had seduced is not known. No Athenian had displayed such an ability both to save and to ruin his mother city, and no one had so many powerful friends and dangerous enemies. Like Athens' own experience in the Peloponnesian War, so too Alcibiades' life mirrored the conflict and, in the same tragic manner, proved a colossal waste. At the end, both the city and its most flamboyant and gifted citizen shared an identical fate of enormous potential ruined rather than fully realized.

Yet in the bitter aftermath of the war the dream still would not die. In the nadir of summer 403, when Spartan hoplites patrolled the Acropolis and the Thirty Tyrants ran the city, it was said that Athenians still did not despair as long as they knew that somewhere the exiled Alcibiades still lived:

> Nevertheless, despite their present plight, some vague hope yet prevailed that the affairs of the Athenians were not completely lost so long as Alcibiades was alive. In the past he had never been willing as an exile to live an idle and quiet life, nor now would he—if there was just a mechanism available to him—overlook the arrogance of the Lacedaemonians and the madness of the Thirty Tyrants.[23]

But this time both the once majestic fleet and the legendary Alcibiades were long gone, the mere phantoms of a shocked population that could not really accept that somewhere there was not another armada of triremes on the horizon.

The Dream Ends

AFTER AEGOSPOTAMI, THERE were no more Athenian ships between the Spartan fleet and the Piraeus. The war and Athens itself were now for all practical purposes through. One of the most moving passages in Greek literature is the historian Xenophon's eyewitness report on the calamity at Athens when the news of the disaster at Aegospotami first reached the Piraeus:

> It was at night that the *Paralos* arrived at Athens with an account of the disaster and wailing ran from the Piraeus through the Long Walls into the city proper as one man passed news to another. And during the night no one slept, not only in grief about those who were lost, but far more still for themselves, wondering whether they would suffer the exact things they had done to the Melians, the colonists of the Lacedaemonians, after reducing them through a siege, and also to the Histiaeans, and the Scioneans, and the Toroneans and the Aeginetans, and many other Greek peoples.[24]

By any fair reckoning, the carnage of Aegospotami was a fitting end to the Ionian War, a decadelong disaster in which more than 270 Athenian ships and over 50,000 imperial seamen were captured, lost, routed, or killed. In total, 500 Hellenic triremes were probably sunk or damaged in the theater. Perhaps 100,000 casualties were inflicted on both sides.

In terms of luminaries, the Ionian War was no less a bloodbath. The Spartans lost generals, tough men like Callicratidas, Mindarus, Labotas, and Hippocrates, while the Athenians, between 412 and 403, either sacrificed in battle, banished, or executed almost every talented admiral left in the city. After Aegospotami there was not a single experienced naval commander around. *All* of the old veterans were either dead or exiled—Alcibiades, Aristogenes, Aristocrates, Conon, Diomedon, Erasinides, Lysias, Pericles the Younger, Protomachus, Thrasybulus, and Thrasyllus. For one who wishes to understand why Athens lost the Peloponnesian War and Sparta emerged in no real position to enforce her will, the bloodbath of the Ionian War, both sailors and commanders, will probably explain quite a lot.

After the October 405 defeat at Aegospotami, Athens did not surrender for about six months, until March 404—blockaded by Lysander's fleet of some 150 triremes, while its wall was approached by two Spartan kings, Agis from Decelea and Pausanias, with a huge force marching up from the Peloponnese. Yet the city's fortifications were still impregnable, given the rudimentary nature of Greek siegecraft. So instead the Spartans waited for famine and political dissension to take effect.

Six months after Aegospotami, hunger and revolution at last prompted Athens to seek terms of concession. Some oligarchs won Spartan guarantees that the city itself would not be razed, despite the fury of the Thebans, the Corinthians, and a host of others eager for an end to Athens. Erianthos, the Theban admiral at Aegospotami, had proposed that Athens—in the manner of the infamous plan of the American secretary of the treasury Henry Morgenthau for turning postwar Germany into a perpetually pastoral state—not only be leveled but that all the Athenians be enslaved and the site devoted to pastureland. In the end it was enough that imperial Athens and all that it stood for was to be no more—as the city agreed to tear down its Long Walls, dismantle the fortifications at the Piraeus, free its tribute-paying subject states, maintain a navy no greater than 12 ships, allow the return of the right-wing exiles, establish an oligarchy, and enter into a military alliance with Sparta.[25]

CHAPTER 10

RUIN?

Winners and Losers (404–403)

Death or Renewal?

Was Athens—or Greece itself—destroyed by the war? An entire industry of classical scholarship once argued for postwar Hellenic "decline," and the subsequent tide of fourth-century poverty, social unrest, and class struggle as arising after the Peloponnesian War. Victorians, in turn, felt the loss was more a "what might have been," a conflict that had ended not just the idea of Athens but "the glory that was Greece" itself and the Hellenic civilizing influence in the wider Mediterranean.

Bernard Henderson, for example, ended his military history of the Peloponnesian War with the melancholy reflection that the romance of Greek history "for a half-century illumined the Imperial Democracy of Athens and the people's leaders. Athens falls, and the gleam lights on her no more. The City, for all Demosthenes' fiery if mistaken eloquence, lies henceforward in perpetual shadow." Alfred Zimmern, a utopian who was deeply involved in the work of the League of Nations, summed up best the Victorian view that the war had been the tragic divide of ancient, and indeed world, history.

For a wonderful half-century, the richest and happiest period in the recorded history of any single community, Politics and Morality, the deepest and strongest forces of national and of individual life, had moved forward hand in hand towards a complete ideal, the perfect citizen in the perfect state. All the high things in human life seemed to lie along that road: "Freedom, Law, and Progress"; Truth and Beauty; Knowledge and Virtue; Humanity and Religion. Now the gods had put them asunder.[1]

In the short term, perhaps such bleak assessments rang true. Soon after the fighting stopped in autumn 405, democracy, saddled as it was with the humiliation of military defeat and the loss of thousands of unfortunate supporters who had gone down in the Aegean during the nearly decadelong Ionian War, began to unwind. After the formal capitulation of spring 404, it was replaced by a narrow and mean-spirited oligarchy (the Thirty Tyrants), as Athens' old tributary subjects abroad were "liberated" and left to their own devices. Aegospotami marks the official end of direct Athenian-Spartan hostilities, yet the war was not formally concluded until a besieged Athens gave up the democracy in spring 404.

In place of an enlightened democratic hegemony, an incompetent Spartan protectorate clumsily tried to impose on Athens' former subjects oligarchies that left the most vulnerable states in Asia Minor open to either direct or insidious Persian suzerainty. In peace, the conquering Lysander quickly proved to be a different sort of statesman from Pericles, an oligarchic rather than a democratic imperialist whose brutality was not mitigated by any sense of majesty.

After a brief civil war and the overthrow of the Thirty Tyrants, by late 403 democratic government was firmly once more in control at Athens, in glorious fashion. It would provide another six decades of relative tranquillity and stability, if not a dangerous laxity, before the onslaught of Philip of Macedon in the 340s. A second Athenian maritime league, without the odious tribute or forced confiscations of land, was in place in 378, within thirty years of the war's end. The Aegean was to be patrolled by yet another fleet of some 300 active triremes, and reminiscent more of the balanced Delian League than the old exploitative empire. Athenian citizens were even now paid to attend the assembly, perhaps because so many of the urban poor who had once routinely done so had been killed off in the sea battles of the Ionian War.

Some scholars even believe that the fourth-century Athenian fleet at times grew larger than that of the fifth. The walls that Lysander had once pulled down to the music of flute players were rebuilt within eleven years, along with a growing line of refitted Attic border forts, which allowed the city more strategic flexibility and in theory the chance to stop enemies before they reached the richer cropland around the city. Since the real wartime damage to Attic agriculture had been confined to annual losses of grain and an inability to reach fields, almost immediately after the war agrarians were back at work in their vineyards and orchards. Once Athens had capitulated and the six-month siege was lifted in late spring 404, there was surprisingly little postwar famine, nor a massive pool of ruined Attic farmers eager to list abroad as mercenary hoplites.[2]

In the troubled world after the war, the old imperial Athens did not look so bad after all. In comparison, the real threat of Persia reappeared, Sparta proved cruel, and there was less imperial largess for plays and majestic temples. Despite Mytilene, Melos, and Sicily, it remains one of the great controversies of history whether, in fact, the old Athenian empire that Sparta destroyed really was a coercive hegemony that extorted money and trampled on local autonomy. Or was Pericles' Athens a cultural engine for Greece that channeled capital into the arts even as it served as an aegis for the poor and dispossessed throughout the Aegean?[3]

For their own part, Sparta and Athens soon enjoyed a reconciliation based on their mutual suspicion of the growing power of Thebes and its resurgent and reunited Boeotian Confederacy. Twenty years after the Peloponnesian War's conclusion had the ruin and genocide of the past merely become a bad dream? In such a revisionist view, did Thucydides (the supposed determinist, who may well have lived into the early 390s) cease his history in medias res in 411 for reasons other than illness or an untimely death? Perhaps as he toiled in the 390s to finish up his grand tale of Athenian folly and its inevitable punishment and decline, the resurrected democracy instead right before his eyes arose from the ashes of war and oligarchy, calling into question many of the historian's sweeping pessimistic judgments forged during his wartime exile.

Xenophon, whose narrative takes up at 411, seems to have been one of the few contemporary historians who accepted Thucydides' notion of a twenty-seven-year-long war beginning in 431 and ending in 405 with the defeat at Aegospotami, followed by the capitulation of the city in 404. Other observers, like the historians Theopompus and Cratippus, felt that the Peloponnesian War did not really end until 394, a thirty-eight-year war in all. In this view, hostilities actually ceased when the Spartan fleet was defeated by Athens at the sea battle at Cnidus (394). Then its expeditionary army was forced home to Sparta from Ionia to meet a new rising threat from Thebes, while the Long Walls of Athens were rebuilt, thereby ending once and for all the saga of the old fifth-century bipolar world of Athenian and Spartan hegemony.

The histories of Theopompus and Cratippus are lost except for a few fragments. Yet they might have reflected a generally held view that Athens did not lose the "Peloponnesian War" in 405–404 as much as suffer a two-year setback—not unlike the Sicilian disaster—before pressing ahead to find rough parity and permanent peace with Sparta somewhere around 394.

The End of the Great Century?

VERY EARLY IN his history, Thucydides justified his lengthy narrative in part by the magnitude of suffering that took place in the conflict:

> But the length of the Peloponnesian War was drawn out over a long time; and in the course of the war, disasters unfolded in Greece such as never had occurred in any comparable space of time. Never had so many cities been taken and left in ruins—some by Barbarians, others by Greeks themselves as they warred against each other. Indeed several of those cities captured suffered a change of inhabitants. Never had so many human beings been forced into exile or had there been so much bloodshed—either as a result of the war itself or the resulting civil insurrections.[4]

Clearly something had been lost in the twenty-seven years of fighting of what was, in fact, the first great civil war in Western history. But precisely what was this damage that might explain why Athens, which had once spearheaded a Panhellenic coalition to trounce a Persian invasion of some 250,000 combatants, could not by the mid-fourth century protect itself from another northern invasion of a mere 40,000 Macedonian combatants? Between the brilliant victories over the Persians at Marathon and Salamis (490 and 480) and the traumatic rout by Philip and Alexander at Chaeronea (338) looms the Peloponnesian War, whose steep costs were as much psychological as material trauma.

Much of the present-day notion of a lost brilliant classical fifth-century Hellenic culture was the creation of fourth-century Athenian orators themselves. Rhetoricians like Demosthenes and Isocrates habitually reminded their audiences how eminent their grandfathers had once been before the outbreak of the great Athenian war. That was the catastrophe, according to an understood consensus, that had reduced the Greeks to small men like themselves who now kowtowed to, rather than routed, the king of Persia and a half-Greek thug from the badlands of Macedon. A half century after the end of the war, Isocrates could still remind an Athenian audience of the carnage that awful war wrought on the city in bombastic, if often inaccurate detail.

> In the Decelean War they lost 10,000 hoplites of their own and the allies, while in Sicily 40,000 and 260 ships. Finally, in the Hellespont 200 ships were lost. But who could count up those ships that were destroyed in groups of five, ten, or more—or the men who perished in armies of one or two thousand?[5]

In Isocrates' worldview, empire and arrogance had wrecked Athens and later Sparta as well, once the Greek city-states abandoned their Panhellenic alliances against the common enemy of Persia. A resurrected fourth-century Athens, despite the still towering presence of its intact Parthenon, the genius of Aristophanes and Plato, and the florescence of red-figure ceramic art and idealistic marble sculpture, was altogether a different place. Ostensibly the decline was from the loss of tribute, the destruction of and cost to rebuild a fleet, the consumption of thousands of talents of reserves, political turmoil, and the humiliation of an occupied homeland. The combination of suffering from the plague and the nightmare of Sicily and the awful losses of the Ionian War, coupled with the violence wrought against Mytilene, Scione, and Melos, which haunted the citizenry, had also made Athens a different city.

Such an idea of a declining Hellenic postwar culture is the general consensus, then and now: fifth century great, fourth in decline, and the Peloponnesian War the great dividing line between the two. Of course, some of this thinking is also arbitrary, an artifact of the modern calendar. Our current system of dating, which replaced the older reckoning of Greece and Rome—classical systems based, respectively, on the founding of the Olympics and the date of the establishment of Rome—was worked out only sometime in the sixth century A.D. Then an odd historical artifact emerged: the past was seen through a series of distinct "centuries" delineated by the birth and death of Christ. Thus, ancient Athens had lost to Sparta sometime near the "end of the fifth century B.C." Was there a proper connection between defeat and a fin de siècle transformation?[6]

For at least fourteen centuries, students of Greece thought so. Hence Westerners have loosely equated the close of the great Athenian hundred years that started roughly after the victories over Persia with the finale of the Peloponnesian War. Because moderns put stock in value-laden ideas about the uniqueness of centuries—eighteenth-century America, nineteenth-century values, twentieth-century modernism—they have become accustomed to seeing fourth-century B.C. Athens as somehow decadent and a pale imitation of its grand fifth-century predecessor, which was decimated by a hideous war that ended in 404.

Add that Socrates, embodiment of the fifth-century Athenian enlightenment, was executed in 399, and the picture of a sharp departure (or, rather, downturn) from the previous majestic hundred years is nearly complete. In this way of thinking, a great man like Pericles and his sober counterpart Archidamus had started the war. But it wound down with the likes of a different sort in Alcibiades and Lysander, who were both more versatile and more reprehensible than the older generation of Athenians and Spartans.

In addition, the master playwrights Sophocles and Euripides probably both died in 406. This coincidence reinforced the common belief that the lofty triad of Aeschylus, Sophocles, and Euripides were fifth-century, not fourth-century, minds. Did the excellence of tragedy pass away once the singular atmosphere of imperial Athens was brought down by Sparta? And did fifth-century Old Comedy end with Aristophanes' final plays in the decade after the war?

Surely modern perceptions would be different had the war begun in 470 and ended in 440. But then there is an equally disturbing afterthought: Did the chaos and suffering of the Peloponnesian War itself have something to do with the explosion of Greek accomplishment in the last third of the century? Can Thucydides' genius be explained only by the conflict, Euripides' greatest plays—*Medea, Hippolytus, The Trojan Women,* and *Bacchae*—as a response to the ongoing brutality at Athens, the thinking of Plato in the 380s and 370s likewise as a product of both the teacher Socrates' wartime prowling through the city and the student's own alienation during the prior strife, and Aristophanes' best comedies—*Acharnians, Peace, Lysistrata*—as reactions to the ongoing setbacks of the war? Such ideas of war alone producing works of genius are perhaps too disturbing to be taken seriously, especially given the fact that intellectuals like Antiphon, Gorgias, and Thucydides were not merely affected by the conflicts but key players in the drama itself. Still, what precisely in human and material terms was lost during the awful twenty-seven years?

Flotsam and Jetsam

By MATERIAL STANDARDS, the immediate damage to the Greek world from this three-decade-long civil war was staggering. For that reason radical material recovery within a decade was all the more astonishing. The roll call of ruin and death makes depressing reading. Almost an entire generation of Athenian leaders was consumed by the war, its members, who ventured abroad more widely than their Spartan counterparts and lost far more battles, either killed in action, exiled, or somehow destroyed by the political fallout from the conflict. In this regard, Isocrates was not really exaggerating when he claimed that the "great houses" of Athens, which had survived the earlier nightmares of revolution and occupation by the Persians, were wiped out. Few of the most prominent Athenians died a natural death, or at least met an end that was separate from the events of the war that they helped wage.

At Athens almost *every* statesman who assumed a role of major political or military leadership during the conflict perished. A brief review of dead generals and political leaders is appalling, as the death toll was steady year by year throughout the entire war: Alcibiades (d. 404; twice exiled, assassinated in the war's immediate aftermath); Androcles (d. 411; assassinated at Athens); Antiphon (d. 411; executed at Athens); Asopius (d. 428; killed on Leucas); Charoeades (d. 426 in Sicily); Cleon (d. 423; death at Amphipolis); Cleophon (d. 404; killed at Athens); Demosthenes (d. 413; executed on Sicily); Euripides of Melitus (d. 429; killed while in command at Spartolos); Eurymedon (d. 413; killed in naval battle at Syracuse), Hippocrates (d. 424; killed at Delium); Hyperbolus (d. 411; murdered at Samos); Laches (d. 418; killed at Mantinea); Lamachus (d. 413; killed on Sicily); Melesander (d. 429; killed in Lycia); Nicias (d. 413; executed on Sicily); Pericles (d. 429; plague); all three of his sons (lost to the plague or executed at Athens); Philocles (d. 405; executed after Aegospotami), Phormio (d. 428; after being charged with corruption), Phrynichus (d. 411; assassinated at Athens); Procles (d. 426; killed in Aetolia), Thrasyllus (d. 406; executed with the generals after Arginusae); and Xenophon (d. 429; killed at Spartolos).

While at least 22 Athenian elected generals were killed in combat or the immediate aftermath of battle during the war, the carnage among the leadership at Sparta was marginally lighter, due only to the fact that for the first two decades of the war the Spartans did not send their commanders all over the Greek world—and then Sparta eventually won the conflict. Nevertheless, the sharpest Spartan military minds (not always an oxymoron) were mostly gobbled up by the war, often in its last decade in the eastern Aegean: Alcamenes (d. 412; killed at Spiraeum), Brasidas (d. 423; killed at Amphipolis); Callicratidas (d. 406; drowned near Mytilene); Chalcidaeus (d. 412; killed near Miletus); Epitadas (d. 425; killed at Pylos); Eurylochus (d. 426; lost at Olpae); Euthydemus (d. 413; killed on Sicily); Hippocrates (d. 408; killed at Chalcedon); Labotas (d. 408; killed at Heraclea); Macarius (d. 426; at Olpae); Mindarus (d. 410; killed at sea in the Hellespont); Salaethus (d. 427; executed at Athens); Thorax (d. 404; executed for financial impropriety); Timocrates (d. 429; killed off Naupaktos); and Xenares (d. 420; killed in northern Greece). In the text of Thucydides alone, 22 Spartan or Athenian infantry generals are explicitly noted as being killed in some sort of land battle.

How many ordinary Greeks died in the war? In ancient sources, the adjectives "a great number" (*polus arithmos*) or "many" (*polloi*) are more frequently used than exact figures. Such generalizations refer to tens of thousands of Greeks whose lives remain forever anonymous and forgotten. Nevertheless, if one were to count up all the explicit figures of the dead as reported by Thucydides, Diodorus, and Xenophon during the twenty-seven-year war, from well over 150 engagements, ambushes, sieges, executions, and various assorted types of combat, there are some 43,000 Greeks listed as killed in battle proper—again, a fraction of the true total, since in the vast majority of battle reports that wind up in ancient historians' accounts, no figures at all are given.

For Athenian combat losses at least, Barry Strauss once made a similar effort to collate all our literary evidence, combined with commonsense conjectures, and arrived at a minimum and very conservative figure of some 5,470 hoplites killed in battle, along with at least 12,600 from the poorer thetic class. In some sense, the fact that the last decade of the war proved to be a bloodbath for the poor who rowed in the triremes that were lost across the Aegean might explain why Athenian democracy was somewhat more tranquil in the fourth century after the war. It was then another legacy of the Peloponnesian War that the critical balance between landless poor and middling hoplite citizens was altered by inordinate losses at sea, reducing the thetes by perhaps 20 percent in relationship to the better-off middle and upper citizens.[7]

But even the conservative figure of about 20,000 Athenian fatalities in recorded combat is just the tip of the iceberg. The adult-male-citizen population of the city, either from the effects of extended service, plague, or hunger, itself shrank from some 40,000 at war's outbreak to around 15,000 by the surrender, or a 60 percent loss over some three decades. If, in addition to the hoplites, at least some 80,000 residents of Attica of all ages who perished from the plague are tallied (there are no figures on those lost to hunger or disease in other years), well over 100,000 Athenians of all classes (well apart from imperial subjects and allies) died as a direct result of the war. To imagine in contemporary terms the effect on Attica of losing an aggregate third of the population, assume that the United States suffered not a little over 400,000 combat dead in World War II out a total population of roughly 133 million (.3 percent), but rather over one hundred times that figure—or some 44 million killed in combat in the European and Japanese theaters.

Thebes, in contrast, which was never occupied and never risked its hoplite strength in any battle encounter after Delium, came off pretty well. Its light losses in comparison to those of its traditional rivals, along with Boeotia's eventual democratization, in part explain its growing prominence in the fourth century. The Thebans also plundered at will across the border in rural Attica, a region that had become legendary in antiquity for its bounty. Only 500 Boeotian hoplites perished at Delium and an additional 1,000 light-armed troops. Perhaps another 1,000 or so Boeotians were lost either attacking or defending small towns such as Plataea, Mycalessus, and Thespiae. In any case, the war was good to Thebes and bad to Athens and Sparta, and the political events of the following thirty years would reflect that reality.

Just as Sparta and Athens had fallen out after spearheading the Panhellenic victory over Persia, so too Thebes and Sparta almost immediately were at each other's throat as soon as Athens was vanquished. Ostensibly they fought over the ample shared spoils taken from Attica that had accrued at Decelea. But the problem that would divide Greece for the next half century was intractable: Thebes was as powerful as Sparta; its infantry was both larger and, soon, superior; and its political institutions were becoming more liberal as exclusive Sparta's regressed into even greater insularity.[8]

There is little information on the number of those killed in the other city-states. For example, how many allies died when an aggregate of almost 500 Athenian and Peloponnesian triremes went down in the eight years of the Ionian War is simply unknown. Much less is there recorded any exact number of those Greeks butchered at Mytilene, Corcyra, Scione, or Melos, or the total who perished from over twenty-one sieges, hundreds of skirmishes and raids, or the Sicilian expedition that took almost 45,000 Athenian and allied seamen and hoplites, with an untold number of Sicilians as well.

Material losses were equally severe, but they are even harder to calibrate. The Athenian fleet at war's end was no more than 12 triremes. Perhaps well over 400 or 500 Athenian ships, even apart from those of the imperial allies, were lost during the war. For Greece as a whole, the losses may have been double that number. The entire financial reserves of Athens were depleted. In the fourth century, liturgies for the building of ships were shared among several wealthy citizens, the implication being that there were no longer hundreds of Athenians of sufficient wealth who could outfit a trireme for a season.

While the agrarian infrastructure of Attica was not permanently destroyed by the annual Peloponnesian invasions—trees and vines, for example, were too numerous and too difficult to eradicate to ensure systematic agrarian damage— many of the wealthiest farms in the Athenian plain had been plundered for nearly a decade. Ancient sources speak of 20,000 slaves who fled to Decelea, and they comment on the growing wealth of neighboring Boeotia, once its robbers and raiders had a free hand for the last years of the war.[9]

Other Greek cities, like Melos, Scione, Torone, and Plataea, ceased to exist. Their physical infrastructures were either leveled or their abandoned houses resettled by foreign populations. Some major states, such as Argos, Chios, Corcyra, Lesbos, and Samos, were torn apart by civil war. Others, including

Amphipolis, Corinth, Mantinea, and Megara, had been crisscrossed by armies and were the scene of constant fighting. Megara had been invaded twice a year for most of the Archidamian War. It probably suffered more rural damage than did Attica or, indeed, any other region of Greece—provisioning thousands of Peloponnesians as they passed through on their way to and from Attica and then in their absence being ravaged by furious, revengeful Athenians.

Dreams Lost?

YET THE RESULT of the killing, looting, and disease was not that Greece was reduced to abject poverty, much less that its farms were ruined for a half century, or that the countryside was depopulated because of the war deaths. Rather, the cost was more in terms of the material surfeit and the intellectual energy of Greece that were depleted. Thus, the prosperity and affluence accrued from the prior centuries were gone. In the years following the war there was hardly any margin of security to fund and subsidize the artistic and literary endeavors of the past. The psychological wound of the Peloponnesian War—the myriad ethnic hatreds, political factions, and private vendettas—would plague Greeks for decades, even though its consequences came to light only through bits and pieces of incidental anecdote and gossip in later extant literature.

The postbellum comedies of Aristophanes, Xenophon's minor treatises, and Plato's utopian literature all reflect some sort of crisis of confidence in the Athenian state. Implicit political or economic advice is offered about how to resurrect lost glory through elevation of the public over the private good. Athenian oratory of the fourth century, for example, perhaps reflects this sense of eternal wrangling over a shrinking pie—with stories of once prosperous families who were undone by the war, their petulant orphans and descendents still lamenting the lost fathers and uncles or property confiscated or destroyed. Again, the perception of lost splendor and wealth, rather than abject poverty, seems to characterize postbellum angst.[10]

Sparta, for a time at least, felt it had done well despite its terrible losses in the Ionian War. As the Athenians had warned the doomed Melians, Spartan rhetoric was never quite matched by action and sacrifice, at least when there were real risks in deploying Spartiates far from home. Other than raids on the Peloponnesian coast, the motherland of Laconia escaped the war virtually unscathed. When Epaminondas torched it a half century later, a variety of sources recorded the shock in the Greek world of a landscape that had previously been *"aporthêtos"* ("unplundered") for nearly seven hundred years.

War, however, can alter winners as much as losers with a variety of unintended consequences. Republics, whether Rome of the third century B.C. or America of the 1940s, that are drawn into global wars can find their ensuing success, both the wealth that accrues and the resources needed to meet new-found military responsibilities, as challenging as defeat. So Sparta learned that in the 390s it was psychologically, economically, and culturally incapable of administering an empire, even one far smaller and less demanding than the one Athens had ruled for a half century. Its parochial elites were easily corrupted abroad, in direct proportion to the length of time they stayed away from the mess hall and the amount of gold they were offered by a variety of Persian grandees. As Spartan hoplites took on new responsibilities in Asia Minor, the helots back home grew stronger and the Spartan state weaker. By 398, a disenfranchised Spartiate, Cinadon, was found guilty of organizing a massive rebellion of all non-Spartiates in Laconia and Messenia against the Spartiates, whom, he claimed, his supporters wished to "eat raw."

Within thirty years of the conclusion of the war, overseas service abroad and constant campaigning to preserve their newly won empire had created a permanent class of Spartan proconsuls and generals, the net effect of which was a rapid decline in the number of Spartiates. Forty percent of all the land in Messenia and Laconia was soon to be owned by women, not surprising given the deaths and long absences of the shrinking Spartan elite. The number of Spartiates sank to a mere 1,500 by the time of the battle of Leuctra (371), while Athens, the loser of the great war, in its aftermath recovered to a population of over 25,000 citizens.[11]

Military Lessons of the War

OVER THREE DECADES of fighting unleashed the creative talents of thousands of Greeks in the singular effort to kill one another without ethical restraint or much ostensible deference to past protocols. Just as the horror of World War II even today still prefigures all current military strategy and practice—from strategic bombing and atomic weapons to massed tank assaults and carrier war—so too innovations over thirty years of fighting ended old concepts and for the next three centuries, until the coming of Rome, unleashed the Greek creative talent for killing.

RULES OF WAR ARE TO BE BROKEN
Before the Peloponnesian War the Greeks at least paid lip service to the notion of protocols, or the "laws of the Greeks" (*nomima*). These were murky and supposedly widely shared Hellenic ideals that had arose to mitigate the destruc-

tiveness of war. While there were always violations and atrocities in the past centuries, there was nonetheless the dream that war could and should still be decided by two opposing land armies in an open battle. It mattered little whether such reactionary idealism actually was true in all wars between the city-states. Rather, the nostalgia tended to retard military innovation and curb the brutality and length of many wars.[12]

The Peloponnesian War—in the manner that the carnage of World War I, with its massive conscript armies, machine guns, gas, and artillery, ended the romance of a good nineteenth-century fight—put such parochial notions to rest. More than sixty years after the war ended, the orator Demosthenes lamented how the old understandings of a past age had not survived into his own time:

> Whereas all the arts have made great advances, and nothing is the same as it was in the past, I believe that nothing has been more altered and improved than matters of war. . . . The Lacedaemonians, like all the others, used to spend four or five months—the summer season—in invading and ravaging the territory of their enemy with hoplites and civic armies and then retire home again. . . . They were so bound by tradition or rather such good citizens of the polis that they did not use money to seek advantage, but rather their war was by rules and out in the open.[13]

War "by rules and out in the open" was rightly seen as an impediment to the sheer efficacy of killing as many as possible given the constraints of time and space. Winter campaigning was common on both sides. After Delium, Athenian dead from Sicily to Asia Minor were left to rot. Captives, whether in Plataea, Melos, or Scione, were often butchered, perhaps cumulatively in the several thousands over the course of the war. Civilians were the only targets at Mycalessus.

The tenets of the Peace of Nicias were almost immediately violated. Slaves were critical to the fleets of both sides, as their desertion and emancipation were key strategies in the war. Sanctuaries, whether at Delium or on Sicily, were not considered sacrosanct. Those who surrendered were either butchered or mutilated after Aegospotami, and held hostage with threatened execution after Pylos. Generals like Demosthenes and Nicias were executed after defeat—something that did not occur in the earlier wars of the fifth century in Boeotia. Even the reactionary Spartans early on in the war recognized that the old hoplite protocols had become "moronic" (*môria*) and irrelevant, echoing the Persians' earlier slurs that the pedestrian Greeks had once fought "foolishly," "without wisdom," and "absurdly."[14]

Spartan hoplites not only lost their battle on the island of Sphacteria to once despised light-armed troops but also surrendered and were willing to become hostages, an act that would have shamed Leonidas and his 300 a half century earlier at Thermopylae. The hoplite myth was over. To win the Peloponnesian War, Sparta not only built a fleet but also enrolled thousands of helots and created a large corps of horsemen. In the war's fourth-century aftermath fighting became far more deadly, amorphous, and concerned with the ends rather than the ethical means.[15]

Good-bye to All That

Status, wealth, and reputation—"all that" was integral to how war was waged in Greece prior to 431. Yet by the war's end an Athenian's wealth or parentage no longer necessarily determined the nature of his military service. This too was a revolutionary breakthrough and throughout the next centuries would soon improve the overall ability of Greek militaries. Of course, aristocracies never quite die, and their twin offspring of influence and nepotism always favor those blessed by money or birth. But for the great majority of Greeks, the old prewar social calculus—the wealthy on horses, agrarians as hoplites, the poor as rowers and skirmishers, slaves as baggage carriers, infantry attendants, and cooks—was rendered obsolete.

The losses from the plague, Sicily, and the slaughter of the Ionian War all meant that bodies were needed, with scant attention paid to wealth or status. Furthermore, it was not clear that a horseman was always more valuable than an infantryman, or the latter in turn more deadly than a rower. The result was that in times of crisis the wealthy sometimes fought as infantrymen, farmers rowed, and the poor were equipped by the state as hoplites.

Because such newfound forces were actually superior to the old class-demarcated services, the ultimate wage was an increase in military efficacy and a democratization of warfare. A half century later, the new national army of Philip of Macedon was the beneficiary. Although he was a thug, he was also a military visionary who could not care less whether his hired killers were rich, poor, citizens, or former slaves; but he did worry a great deal about whether they could be trained to fight his way and follow his orders.[16]

The Peloponnesian War taught Westerners that the logic of military efficacy should trump tribalism, tradition, and arbitrary constructs of wealth and power. Plato, who wrote in the aftermath of the three-decade disaster, saw this more clearly than any other Greek thinker—and resented it bitterly.[17]

THE OTHER

Before the Peloponnesian War, a fundamental expression of full citizenship was infantry or cavalry service. Aristotle thought the very rise of the polis was a direct result of a growing class of small landowners who could afford arms. That way the farmers established a more inclusive citizenship by a property qualification in lieu of birth, the new cutoff line being those who could obtain their own heavy armor and thereby fight as hoplites in the phalanx.[18]

After the devastating losses from the initial years of the Peloponnesian War, the limitations of such a parochial idea were soon transparent. At Athens, there may have been over 20,000 resident alien males of military age, many of them prosperous and intensely patriotic. Their numbers were dwarfed by more than 100,000 slaves—adult males and quite capable of fighting. Sparta for its part sat atop a volcano of 250,000 helots. Even Corinth, Argos, and Thebes all had sizable numbers of rural servants, who often carried the armor and supplies of hoplites on brief campaigns.

The trick was to tap such huge manpower reservoirs without undermining the rather exclusive civic premises of the parochial city-state. The Greeks soon found themselves in some of the same dilemmas as the tottering old Confederacy during the American Civil War: in times of crisis slaves could be valuable combatants; but should they fight well, then their very courage might undermine the entire logic of their purported inferiority. Outside of Messenia, chattel slavery in Greece was not predicated on race or ethnic identity. Thus, it escaped the paradoxes brought on by an unsupportable pseudoscience of racial inferiority. People became slaves through accidents—a captured city, a lost battle, or a servile parent. Nevertheless, once the unfree were allowed to fight in exchange for their freedom, a natural question arose: what exactly was the capricious logic that made them remain forever inferior?

Brasidas, for example, drafted thousands of helots and extended freedom to them. The ultimate dividend from such emancipation may not have been just increased Spartan manpower but a subsequent rising unrest among the helot population in the decades after the war, when such stalwart Brasideans returned home and constructed their rather vicious fallen commander as a great crusading "liberator."

At Athens, from the very start of the conflict resident aliens, or metics, served as reserve and garrison troops, while slaves probably rowed far more often in the imperial Athenian fleet than was noted by the aristocratic Thucydides. At Arginusae the assembly promised freedom to any slave who would embark on a trireme. Thousands went on to prove that they were indispensable for the Athenian victory. Prebattle observers may have thought the Peloponnesians had the far better crews; but the Athenian victory proved that there was something about the democratic élan of the empire that could turn slaves and the poor into rowers as good as Sparta's more experienced and skilled mercenary seamen.[19]

Later Greek and Roman history reflects this additional revolutionary legacy of the Peloponnesian War, as the fourth-century Greek, Hellenistic, and Roman armies were multicultural, multiracial, and professional. The militaries of both Sparta and Athens in the war's aftermath were full of mercenary slaves and ex-slaves, without which they could never have replaced the manpower losses of the prior thirty years. In the chaos following the war, the Ten Thousand mercenaries who accompanied Cyrus the Younger on his quest to claim the Persian throne were a motley assortment of Peloponnesian War veterans, ex-slaves, and resident aliens, united only by their skill at arms, their shared need for money, and the notion of being Greek.

Before the war, far more adult male Greeks were noncitizens than citizens of the city-states. But it took the war to strip that veneer of pretense away, and show that a man's status did not predetermine his value on the battlefield. War, then and now, is a destroyer of protocol, privilege, and tradition, and that is not altogether always a bad thing.[20]

MONEY

In Book 1 of Thucydides' history Pericles outlines the limitations of the Peloponnesian adversaries. They had no capital. Unlike the Spartiates, most of the allies in the Peloponnesian coalition were agrarians who needed to farm at precisely the time it was best to fight. In contrast, Athens was a sophisticated polis with vast sums of coinage in both circulation and as specie on reserve. Pericles' adversary, King Archidamus of Sparta, agreed, and so warned his rural Peloponnesians that they were not equipped to fight a long, multifaceted war with even a seasonal militia. This new conflict, he warned, was quite different: "War is not so much a matter of men as of monetary expense." He proved absolutely right.[21]

The great irony of the war was that the very requisites for victory—an enormous fleet, money for rowers' pay, and officers deployed overseas for long periods of imperial service—were inimical to the historic assumptions of rural and isolated Sparta, which heretofore had had no monetary economy. Persia finally filled the void, gave Spartan generals untold amounts of gold, and made up losses in men and matériel almost immediately. As long as Greeks were killing Greeks, the satraps of the Persian Empire were happy to subsidize the carnage.

Yet in the war's aftermath, with the Persian subsidies gone, the implosion of the Spartan empire was directly attributable to its new financial responsibilities of administering a fleet and distant subject states that were so at odds with its old insular moral code. Money and manpower, not always just courage and class, quite literally won wars. The Peloponnesian War offered another bitter lesson, one that would also arise during the transition of Rome from republic to empire. Consensual government started in Greece as a limited enterprise. These constitutional states were predicated on a civic militia cloaked in amateurism and localism, and determined to protect the property of a minority of its citizens. But as the invective of Athenian conservatives from Plato to Aristotle illustrated, war over decades and across thousands of miles required mobilization, weaponry, and capital—and only the new resources of a more centralized and powerful state could meet those vast burdens.[22]

TECHNOLOGY

In the Greek psyche wars were traditionally purported referenda on courage and discipline, not to be decided by tricks, the quality of weapons, or accidents. Add to that code the intrinsic aristocratic distrust of rote labor so common in Greek thinking. Factor in also the ubiquity of slavery, whose cheap labor tended to discourage technological innovation. Thus, a good case could be made that for all the genius of the Greek city-state, until the later fifth century it was remarkably slow in applying its clear achievements in science, philosophy, and architecture to a practical crafting of weapons of destruction. A society that could sculpt the Parthenon friezes and easily lift them high up on the architraves of the temple apparently had no means of tearing down a simple enemy wall during a siege.

That stagnation too began to end in the Peloponnesian War, as both sides scrambled to invent new siege techniques at Plataea, weird devices like fire cannons at Delium, and constant naval modifications at Syracuse. Innovations from horse transports to the idea of forward fortified bases (*epiteichisma*) and swarms of missile troops were commonplace throughout the war, and often deeply resented. Thucydides reports the lamentation of one Spartan prisoner on Sphacteria, who, when chided about the surrender of Greece's best infantrymen to poor javelin throwers and archers, snapped that the old hoplite courage was not worth much when an enemy showered his phalanx with arrows and missiles, killing the brave and cowards alike.[23]

The major sieges left an indelible impression on both attacker and besieged, especially when the belligerents had experimented with siege towers, flame-throwers, and elaborate circumvallation. As a result, within four years of the end of the war, Dionysius of Syracuse, during the siege of Motya (399), crafted the first true artillery in history, crude nontorsion catapults that were known as "belly bows" (*gastraphetes*), and resembled something like oversized medieval crossbows.

Such ad hoc artillery soon led to true torsion catapults, perhaps first crafted by the engineers of Philip II of Macedon in the 340s. Considerable propulsive power could be stored by twisted hair, rope, or sinew through the use of stocks, winches, or springs. On release such machines might hurl stones or specially crafted bolts over three hundred yards, as efficiently and accurately as seventeenth-century gunpowder artillery. All this innovation marked not just a technological continuance of the ingenuity shown at the sieges of Plataea, Delium, and Syracuse but was made possible by the liberation from traditional moral restraint upon war making that had occurred during the Peloponnesian War. The success of the war's major campaigns, from Potidaea and Plataea to Mytilene and Syracuse, depended on craftsmen who could either build or tear down walls in the most efficient and rapid manner.

Defensive engineers were also quick to grasp the lessons of the value of fortifications and the need to counteract them with even more powerful artillery, as a veritable arms race ensued, characterized by constant response and counterresponse. Most of the present-day ruins that dot the Greek countryside date not from the fifth century but from the fourth and later, as the arts of military construction and destruction accelerated, hand in glove.

The vast circuits of the Peloponnesian cities of Mantinea, Megalopolis, and Messene and rural forts on the frontiers of Attica, Megarid, and in the Argolid were constructed in just this period of the early and mid-fourth century. The chief improvements learned from trial and error during the Peloponnesian War consisted of a systematic use of ashlar blocks, binding courses, embrasures, internal trussing, more extensive foundations, and drafted corners to assure wall stability at vastly increased heights and breadths. Forts were framed with towers over thirty feet in height that housed small antipersonnel nontorsion catapults to prevent besiegers from approaching too near the circuits. Some of the embrasure windows were equipped with elaborate shuttering systems designed to open and close as wheeled catapults laid down continuous fire.

Historians could argue over whether the rush for both urban and rural fortification in the postwar period was an unwise diversion of Greece's finite resources, or itself spurred on economic activity while providing needed defense. But the archaic dream that Greece should remain unwalled was dead forever. Citizens, not just soldiers, began to plan for their collective defense in wars that were as likely to break out at their doorsteps as in distant fields.[24]

THE NEW COMMAND

Before the Peloponnesian War it was rare for Greeks to entrust too much power to the hands of any one commander. It was neither a Spartan nor an Athenian trait but a Panhellenic custom that most generals led the army or fleet from the first rank and so frequently died in battle, a fact that precluded both long military careers and evolving tactical innovation. The old ideal was perhaps best reflected in the seventh-century poet Archilochus' encomium to the hoplite brawling leader: "short and bandy-legged, firmly set on his feet, full of heart and courage."[25]

But throughout the three-decades-long war, commanders discovered that a general could do more to kill large numbers of their enemies than by merely wielding a spear on the right wing of the phalanx, displaying the cardinal virtues of sobriety and self-control (*sophrosynê*). Armies were no longer the glue that held together the consensual government of the old polis but became simply military assets that carried no particular civic or political weight. Personalities such as Alcibiades, Cleon, Demosthenes, Thrasybulus, Brasidas, Lysander, and Gylippus were not anonymous warriors but leaders who were expected to exercise intellectual options that might achieve victory by superior logistics, tactics, finance, or public relations. A man like Brasidas or Lysander (each of questionable background) was seen as a valuable asset in his own right, whose worth was almost impossible to calculate but now appreciated as never before.[26]

Pagondas, for example, was more responsible for the victory at Delium than was the strength of his Theban agrarian infantry, in the same manner that Sphacteria and Pylos were Athenian victories due largely to the vision of Cleon and Demosthenes. Without Alcibiades and Lysander, Sparta would never have successfully built a large fleet. Only Gylippus' arrival at Syracuse saved Sicily. To marshal the new diverse forces of mercenaries, slaves, and combined arms, thinkers, not just warriors, were needed.

A veritable revolution in the idea of generalship unfolded in the Peloponnesian War and its aftermath, especially in the hysterical reactions to it, as philosophers and rhetoricians debated the proper credentials for military leadership.[27]

Before the war generals were considered regular folk; afterward they often appeared publicly as mounted horsemen and were feared and worshipped. The careers of Epaminondas and Alexander the Great are testament to the idea that single men could galvanize an entire state—democratic or otherwise—and through sheer brilliance and audacity raise sophisticated armies of invasion.

Whatever the controversy, immediately following the defeat of Athens there appeared an entire genre of military literature for the specialist. Some itinerant sophists, like the Dionysodoros of Xenophon's *Memorabilia*, promised that they could teach one "how to be a general." In the war's aftermath, veterans often enlisted as mercenary commanders—men, for example, like Phalinos of Boeotia, who claimed that he was an "expert on tactics and arms-drill." Fourth-century utopian literature stressed the new need for professionalization, specialization, and careful training.[28]

At Athens an entire array of mercenary captains, such as Iphicrates, Timotheos, Chabrias, and Chares, took over the military in a way undreamed of in the prior fifth century, when Nicias and Alcibiades had debated as politicians first and generals second. One of the great mysteries of the Peloponnesian War is why inward and blinkered states like Sparta and Thebes produced brilliant strategists and tacticians like Brasidas, Gylippus, Lysander, and Pagondas, while liberal, freethinking Athens entrusted so many of its critical commands to timid dullards like Nicias; inspired but often reckless entrepreneurs such as Alcibiades, Cleon, and Demosthenes; or anonymous functionaries whose names are known only by reason of their death in defeat, such as the otherwise obscure Hippocrates or Laches. Perhaps it was the intrusion of the assembly into military decision making, a factor inherent in the radical democracy at Athens, or a naval tradition that great commanders of the past—like Themistocles, Pericles, and Phormio—were admirals, not infantry generals. In any case, the Peloponnesians, not Athens, produced the better military minds. At key junctures—Sicily and Aegospotami stand out—the outcome of the war itself hinged on just such superior leadership.[29]

WAR AS EVIL

Not all the legacies of the Peloponnesian War were material, social, or political. There was ideological and philosophical fallout as well. Much of Greek literature both before and after the Peloponnesian War, whether the pre-Socratic philosopher Heraclitus' dictum that "War is the father of us all" or Plato's postbellum appraisal in his *Laws* that war is a more natural phenomenon than peace, envisioned war as tragedy, but not therein necessarily evil. Rather, the moral landscape of the times—who fought whom, why, how, and with what result?—determined the ethical appraisal of wars that had been mostly short and economical.

Again, the growth of such a Greek tragic acceptance of war, so common from Homer to Sophocles, was also predicated on two more practical realities. Most wars of the eighth to fifth centuries between Greeks had probably been both short and seasonal. The rare cosmic struggles for national survival, such as the Persian conflicts between 490 and 479, were conducted exclusively against foreigners and still ended with a single climactic pitched battle.

The Peloponnesian War was different. When the Greek world tore itself apart in national suicide for almost three decades, some Greek thinkers—in the manner of the postwar 1920s generation, who recoiled at the trenches of World War I—began to associate their own dissatisfaction over the conduct of this particular war with the nature of war itself. Thus, wartime plays such as Aristophanes' *Acharnians, Peace,* and *Lysistrata,* as well as Euripides' *Andromache, Helen, Hecuba,* and *Trojan Women,* while they betray no love for the Spartans, seem to offer a new wrinkle in Greek attitudes toward war: such conflicts themselves are awful human experiences that transcend the reasons for hostilities. The farmers and women of Aristophanes' *Acharnians, Peace,* and *Lysistrata,* like the captured and suffering civilians of Euripides' *Hecuba, Trojan Women,* and *Andromache,* reveal that everyday Greeks found shared experiences across the battle line. Thus the playwrights offer the idea that there is something wrong with war per se—not just with the Spartans.

While the totality of postbellum thought never became therapeutic, much less pacifist or utopian, the Peloponnesian War at least introduced into Western philosophy the comprehensive idea that war was not always noble or patriotic but often nonsensical, suicidal, and perhaps intrinsically wrong, especially when it lasted twenty-seven years, not a few hours on a summer day. Homer, of course, had questioned the morality and logic of motives and sacrifices of unthinking warriors in the *Iliad,* but Achilles did not doubt the nobility and heroism inherent in armed conflict.

Fourth-century Greeks, however, realized that the Peloponnesian War had been something uniquely awful in the Hellenic experience. It destroyed the idealism and spirit of Panhellenic unity that was so critical in the defense of Greece against the Persian invader. The war left in its wake the more self-interested idea that Greeks, if they were going to kill so savagely, should at least kill Persians, the mantra that Philip and Alexander would soon so brilliantly manipulate. In any case, to win the war the Spartans had used Persia to destroy

Athens—a strategy brilliant in the short term but calamitous in the conflict's aftermath, when Spartan hoplites were stationed in Asia Minor to check the Persian resurgence in Ionia that they had ensured by earlier bringing the satraps into the war effort.

Why Did Athens Lose?

GIVEN THE ABSENCE of resolute action or inspired Spartan leadership in the twenty years before the Ionian War, one asks that question rather than "How did Sparta pull it off?" Thucydides himself emphasizes how rare capable men like Brasidas, Gylippus, and Lysander were at Sparta, and how Athens, despite the advantages that democratic government brings to war, made mistake after mistake.

In his narrative there emerge four reasons why Sparta triumphed; none of them can be attributable to the oligarchy's strategic insight or imaginative tactics. The plague was nature's bane. Sicily was Athens' own strategic mistake and was compounded by tactical blunders. The creation of a fort at Decelea and the use of Persian capital to build a fleet are attributed by Thucydides and Xenophon to the advice and machinations of Alcibiades, an Athenian. So naturally observers look to what Athens did wrong rather than to what Sparta did right to explain how such a dynamic imperial city was not merely beaten but nearly ruined.[30]

Yet Athens no more lost its war with Sparta than Nazi Germany did its offensive wars with France or Poland. By 425, in the seventh year of the conflict, almost all of Athens' limited objectives had been achieved in line with Pericles' original goal of a temporary stalemate—or perhaps more charitably seen as not losing in a war of exhaustion. Athens' empire was still intact. It exercised continual naval supremacy over all potential enemies and, indeed, would finish the first decade of the war with its fleet still at its prewar level of 300 ships. True, the problems with Sparta were not solved, only postponed; but the city at least had shown that its own destruction might be beyond the capabilities of Sparta's original alliance.

Athens, after all, had proved to Sparta that hoplite invasions of Attica, despite the horrific plague, would not bring the city to its knees. With the capture and detainment of the Spartiate prisoners from Sphacteria, who were to be executed the moment a Peloponnesian army again crossed the borders of Attica, the general outline of the Peace of Nicias, which would transpire four years later, was already established. Pericles' vision, though tattered and torn, seemed fulfilled. Contemporaries in 421 thought Sparta was checked and demoralized after Pylos and the failure to make headway in Attica. Whether a shaky peace and a return to the status before the war was worth the cost of a decade of fighting and the plague is another matter altogether.

In contrast, the reasons for Athens' later and utter defeat after the failed peace were probably twofold. First, even before the Sicilian expedition Athens had not simply fought Sparta but for a decade of the Archidamian War was holding off Sparta, its entire Peloponnesian alliance, and Corinth and Thebes. These two latter states proved their vehemence by not even becoming signatories of the shaky peace achieved in 421. In the trireme fighting in the Corinthian Gulf, at Solygia, and at Delium both allies had frequently fought Athens mostly on their own, without help from Sparta.

The powers formally allied with Sparta for most of the conflict were not weak. Peloponnesian states like Elis, Tegea, and at times even a reconstituted Mantinea and Argos provided hoplites for a Spartan-led enterprise or later occupation at Decelea. The Boeotian army was as formidable as the Spartan. Its bitter hostility ensured a two-front war, a permanent condition after the failed Athenian effort at Delium. Corinth controlled much of the lateral sea traffic in and out of the Gulf, and all routes to and from the Peloponnese by land. The continual Athenian failure to take over the Megarid only ensured the Peloponnesians perpetual access to Attica anytime they thought they could devise some better strategy than the earlier failed annual invasions, such as the final occupation of Decelea.

In the first few years of the war Athens conducted massive operations abroad, but quickly learned that the permanent deployment of some 100 to 200 ships was exhausting its treasury without bringing decisive results. But with the capture of Pylos and Sphacteria in 425 it achieved a stunning psychological victory, made all the more so once the Spartans were shamed by the surrender of their crack hoplites and were willing to withdraw from Attica for good.

Once more, by 421 the Athenians had not won; but they had proved that even after suffering horrendous losses to the plague they could find innovative new methods of not losing the war. Yet the city-state's most creative thinkers, from Alcibiades to Demosthenes, gauged stalemate a disappointment rather than a windfall. Thus they began to devise further probing operations in the Peloponnese that might weaken Sparta without taking on her formidable hoplites. The result was a doubly disastrous policy, a renewed war with the Peloponnesians and misplaced faith in expanding the theater of conflict in lieu of confronting and defeating the Spartan army outright as a way of freeing the helots and dismantling Spartan apartheid.

Second, despite taking on all at once the three largest of the city-states, Sparta, Corinth, and Thebes; losing well over a quarter of its population to the plague; and not destroying the hoplite or naval resources of any of its three adversaries, in 415 Athens invaded Syracuse. Immediately it found itself at war with a larger city than its own and almost as democratic. Not only had Athens diverted its precious resources to a far distant campaign at a time when Spartans were soon to be thirteen miles from its walls, but in attacking democratic Syracuse it also weakened its propaganda that its war was in large part ideological, taken up on behalf of democratic peoples and their resistance to foreign-imposed oligarchies.

Sicily drew blood, and the hemorrhaging attracted a whole host of new enemies. Perhaps worst of all, after Sicily Athens was in a war against itself, as the revolution of 411 and the failed oligarchic putsch proved. By 412 Persia was soon to be a de facto belligerent. Without Persia's vast capital for crews and triremes, Sparta could never have prosecuted the Ionian War, which eventually forced Athens to capitulate. In that narrow strategic regard, Athens really was like the Germany of World War II, which fought the old European allies of France and England, took on the vast industrial might of the United States, and tried to invade Soviet Russia. Hitler might have defeated or obtained a draw with any of the three powers individually or in succession, but never two, much less three, in combination.

It was the belief of Thucydides that if democracies brought multifaceted advantages to war, their raucous assemblies, constant second-guessing, grandstanding, and hypercriticism severely hampered military operations. Only a towering figure such as Pericles could rein in the raw emotions unleashed in open forums and, as first citizen, by sheer power of his moral authority run the country by near fiat and still take full advantage of democratic dynamism. Whether that pessimism of the historian was warranted or fair to democracy, it was certainly clear that Sparta had more patience with an occasionally lax Brasidas, Agis, or Lysander than Athens ever did with its own generals.

True, Sparta could execute generals like Thorax and shun the returning prisoners from Pylos, but in comparison to Athens it gave latitude to commanders in a way unknown at Athens. If Thucydides was exiled for failing to save Amphipolis from Brasidas, later in the same theater Brasidas most surely was not recalled to Sparta after failing to reach Torone in time and thus losing the entire city to Cleon. That the Athenian assembly exiled, executed, or fined almost every notable general it ordered on campaign did not make commanders more accountable as much as timid and prone to second-guessing. Thus, after any setback, whether in the Delium campaign or at Arginusae, they would most likely not come back to Athens, in fear of a trial. So the city did not often learn from its mistakes but almost always scared generals into being too cautious or reckless, their decisions based on anticipating what the voters back home might approve on any particular day.

A Possession for All Time?

WHETHER THUCYDIDES ENTERTAINED preexisting views about the nature of war and sought to use the events of the Peloponnesian War to confirm his pessimism, whether his philosophy emerged inductively from the mayhem that he witnessed over three decades, or both is not really known. But his history is more than a narrative of now obscure battles and massacres. Instead, as he predicted, it serves as a timeless guide to the tragic nature of war itself, inasmuch as human character is unchanging and thus its conduct in calamitous times is always predictable.

If the Peloponnesian War still teaches us something about men at war, it is the lesson that interim armistices may quiet down the fighting but cannot with any degree of consistency end the conflict unless they address why one party chose to go to war in the first place. More often resolute action, for good or evil, can bring lasting peace, usually when one side accepts defeat and ceases its grievances through a change of heart or government—in either freedom or tyranny. In that sense of how to make a war end for good, the no-nonsense Lysander understood the nature of this awful conflict far better than the stately Pericles or naive Nicias.

Both states initially went to war unsure of how to defeat the other. Yet after nearly twenty years of futile killing, the war was resolved in about seven years when Sparta realized how Athens could be vanquished (keep its people inside the walls, its tribute and food outside, and sink its fleet). The disturbing message here is that discussions follow the sway of the battlefield, and diplomatic solutions work best when they accurately reflect military weakness or strength.

It is common to label this appreciation for power and its role in state affairs "realism" or "neorealism." But Thucydides—and this is why he is truly a great historian—is too discerning a critic to reduce strife down simply to perceptions about power and its manifestations. War itself is not a mere science but a more fickle sort of thing, often subject to fate or chance, being an entirely human enterprise. *The Peloponnesian War*, then, is not a mere primer for international relations studies, and the historian does not believe that "might makes right." Tragedy, not melodrama, is his message.

Yet Thucydides does recognize that humans are also subject to other inexplicable emotions that make them do things that do not quite make sense, whether that means Spartans who "fear" Athenian success, the poor Plataeans who choose to resist the siege, the supposedly stern Spartans who panic after the fall of Sphacteria and cease all their invasions into Attica on news that a mere 120 of their elite might be executed, the Melians who in vain hold out for Spartan support, or the once haughty Athenians who sail to Syracuse and persist in folly with the same reliance on "hope" that they had earlier damned the naive Melians for entertaining. If moderns wonder why entire countries of several million people can be held hostage when masked criminals threaten to behead a single one of their citizens on global television, we could do worse than to remember why panicked and shocked Spartans simply abandoned their entire strategy of invading Attica.[31]

For a writer who is supposedly interested in power rather than tragedy, Thucydides misses no occasion to note how heartbreaking the losses of particular armies were. What seems to capture the historian's attention is not, as is so often claimed, the role of force in interstate relations but the misery of war that is unleashed upon the thousands—the subject of this book—who must fight it.

Thucydides sometimes opines that a particular campaign was wise or foolish, but he nearly always adds enough detail and editorializing to convey to us that the soldiers who believed in the cause for which they were dying deserved commemoration in terms that matched their sacrifice. So one discovers that the Thespians who perish at Delium are not around the next year to save their city when their erstwhile allies, the Thebans, tear down the walls. The town of Mycalessus loses not merely its schoolboys but even its animals—and we, his readers, should know that and mull it over. The Athenians are not merely slaughtered at the Assinarus River but perish as they fight one another to drink the blood and mud of the river. Whereas historians search for messages about the "lessons" of Thucydides embedded within his text, the general reader has no problem in sensing immediately what his history is about precisely from those memorable passages that will never go away, reminding us of the passions and furor that are unleashed on otherwise normal men when they go to war.

The young men of Athens, on the eve of the initial Spartan invasion or during the debate about Sicily, are always eager for war, inasmuch as they have had no experience with it. In contrast, "the older men of the city," the more experienced, who know something of plagues, assassinations, terror, and sinking triremes, always are reluctant to invade, and thus often strive to give the enemy some way out during tough negotiations that otherwise might leave war as the only alternative. Thucydidean war can have utility and solve problems, and it often follows a grim logic of sorts; but once it starts, it may well last twenty-seven years over the entire Greek world rather than an anticipated thirty days in Attica and kill thousands at its end who were not born in its beginning.

Such recognition is not necessarily cause for pacifism; rather, to Thucydides it calls for acceptance that thousands will end up rotten in little-known places like the Assinarus River and Aetolia, the logic that follows from decisions made far away in the hallowed assemblies of Sparta or Athens. A wild-eyed Sthenelaidas or sophistic Alcibiades might rouse his volatile assembly to war without good cause, while an Archidamus or Pericles might think that his own sobriety and reason will either preclude or mitigate the killing. But between emotion and logic resides the fate of thousands of the mostly unknown—Astymachus and Lacon executed at Plataea (427), the Tanagran Saugenês cut down at Delium (424), Scirphondas butchered at Mycalessus (413), and the Spartan Xenares falling at Heraclea (419)—who will surely then and now be asked to settle through violence what words alone cannot. Remember them, for the Peloponnesian War was theirs alone.[32]

APPENDIX I: GLOSSARY OF TERMS AND PLACES

ACROPOLIS · the fortified hill and center of a city-state; most often used in reference to Athens and the great temples built by Pericles.

ARGOS · the renowned large city-state in the northeastern Peloponnese that for most of the war was democratic, independent of Sparta, and often allied with Athens. The surrounding peninsula that extends from the northeastern coast of the Peloponnese into the Aegean is known as the Argolid.

ATTICA · the geographical area surrounding and controlled by Athens, a hinterland encompassing one thousand square miles.

BOEOTIA · a large agricultural region north of Attica in central Greece. Most of the cities of its nearly one-thousand-square-mile countryside were united politically into an oligarchic confederation headed by its largest city, Thebes. Throughout the fifth century Athens sought to weaken its neighboring rival by periodic occupation, fomenting democratic revolution, and encouraging Boeotian states like Plataea and Thespiae to remain autonomous.

CORINTH · a traditional maritime rival of Athens and stalwart ally of Sparta that drew its wealth and prestige from its control of the Isthmus, which governed Greek maritime traffic east and west and land travel north and south.

DECELEA · a small hillock in the Athenian plain about thirteen miles from the walls of Athens, fortified by the Spartans in 414–413 to serve as a permanent garrison of occupation in Attica and a clearinghouse for continuous plundering.

DEMOCRACY · "people power," or government characterized by inclusion of the landless poor into the voting citizenry and rule by majority vote of the assembly. From 507 to 338, ancient democracy was nearly synonymous with Athens, the most powerful and influential of the democratic city-states.

DRACHMA · the most common unit of Greek money, often equivalent to the top daily wage of a well-paid worker. Six **obols** equaled one drachma. One hundred drachmas made a **mina.** A **talent** was equal to 6,000 drachmas or 60 minas. If current semiskilled adult labor is often compensated at about $10 (U.S.) per hour, we can envision a drachma having the approximate contemporary worth of about $80. Direct comparisons are impossible, but a talent in present-day American money might consequently be equivalent to something like $480,000—or about the cost of a large urban house in both Athens and America.

HELLESPONT · the modern Dardanelles, or the very narrow strait of water that connects the Aegean via the Sea of Marmara to the Black Sea, and thus divides Europe from Asia. It was the scene of horrific Athenian-Spartan sea battles in the last four years of the war.

HELOTS · hereditary indentured and publicly owned rural serfs of Laconia and Messenia, who worked in forced servitude to supply food and provisions for their Spartan overseers.

HOPLITE · a heavily armed Greek infantryman deployed in the phalanx. Originally a voting, property-owning citizen of the polis who supplied his own armor, the hoplite was eventually defined as a soldier of any class who fought in close rank with body armor, shield, and spear. The name derives either from his large circular shield (*hoplon*) or his panoply in general (*hopla*).

IONIA · the Greek-speaking western seaboard of Asia Minor (modern western Turkey), whose northern inhabitants claimed common ancestry with Athens. Not to be confused with the Ionian Sea, which is an ancient name for the southern Adriatic, between Italy and western Greece.

ISTHMUS · the thin strip of land connecting the northern Greek mainland to the Peloponnese, and settled and governed by the Corinthians, who profited enormously by their control of north-south land traffic and east-west maritime trade between the Aegean and the Gulf of Corinth.

METICS · privileged resident aliens who might serve in the military even without full rights of citizenship. The term is used most frequently in reference to foreigners at Athens, where by the mid-fifth century some 20,000 metics resided.

OLIGARCHY · consensual government restricted to those who owned property or had ample capital, hence "rule of the few." Oligarchs were championed by Sparta in its ideological war against democrats, the poorer and often landless supported by imperial Athens.

PELOPONNESE · the southern part of Greece, consisting of the large peninsula south of the Gulf of Corinth. The majority of states in this area of some eighty-five hundred square miles were ethnically Doric and either allied to or subjugated by Sparta. The area gave its name to the war because of the Athenocentric nature of our sources: to Athenians their war was against Sparta and its allies—loosely defined as the Peloponnesians.

PELTASTS · light-armed troops, later often mercenary and foreign, equipped with a javelin and light crescent-shaped shield (*peltê*) and trained to fight as skirmishers on rough terrain.

PHALANX · a columnar formation of Greek heavily armed spearmen (hoplites). The mass was used to batter away at its like counterpart in open land battles.

PIRAEUS · the port and harbor of Athens, some five miles from the Acropolis and connected most prominently by the two parallel Long Walls, which established a safe corridor for the importation of maritime goods into the city.

POLIS (PL. POLEIS) · any self-governing city-state of ancient Greece; the term serves to describe both a political entity and the geographical area surrounding the municipal center.

SATRAPY · a Persian provincial state. The term refers most often to those districts in northern (Hellespontine) and central (Sardis) Asia Minor that for the latter part of the war were run by Pharnabazus and Tissaphernes, respectively.

SPARTA · an oligarchic city-state that led the Peloponnesian alliance. A variety of terms are used to loosely describe Sparta and its empire. **Lacedaemon** is both a political and a regional connotation denoting those surrounding city-states and towns in the southeastern Peloponnese that were directly governed by the Spartans. **Spartans** refer to residents of the city and its environs of various statuses. Some men were further distinguished as **Spartiates;** these full citizens constituted a small elite. **Laconian** is more an ethnic and geographic rubric employed to describe the land around and the people residing in and surrounding Sparta, while the far broader adjective **Peloponnesian** roughly includes all those city-states situated on the mainland south of Corinth, most of which were allied with Sparta. **Doric** is a broad ethnic and linguistic category of southern Greeks, mostly referring to the Peloponnese, Sicily, the southern Aegean, and Asia Minor.

THETES · the lowest census class at Athens, composed of the poorer citizens, who owned little or no land and usually either rowed in the fleet or fought as skirmishers outside the phalanx. By the outbreak of the war thetic adult males at Athens may have numbered over 20,000.

TRIREME · a swift war galley powered by three banks of oarsmen and armed with a bronze ram. Triremes usually carried about 170 rowers and another 30 assorted officers and could employ an auxiliary sail during transit and patrol.

ALCIBIADES · (450–404) the most controversial general at Athens; his tragic fate mirrored the decline of Athens itself. The architect of the ill-fated Sicilian expedition, he fled a sure Athenian death sentence only to urge the Spartans to build a fleet and fortify Decelea outside the walls of Athens. Later he sought to ingratiate himself with the Persians by harming the interests of both Athens and Sparta, and was variously championed and exiled by the Athenians for an assortment of purported crimes before being murdered in Phrygia shortly after the end of the war.

ARCHIDAMUS · (ruled 467–427) one of the two hereditary kings at Sparta at the outbreak of the war. He led the first invasion into Attica; thus the ten-year fighting from 431 to 421 later came to be known as the Archidamian War. Thucydides records a number of insightful speeches by Archidamus; yet his record in the field reveals Spartan conservatism rather than the élan of a later Brasidas or Lysander.

ARISTOPHANES · (ca. 460–386?) Athenian comic poet whose eleven surviving plays caricatured many of the prominent Athenians of the later fifth century and often provide valuable information about wartime life in imperial Athens during the Peloponnesian War.

BRASIDAS · (d. 422) perhaps the most gifted foot soldier that Sparta produced; his expeditionary forces of Spartiates, allies, freed serfs, and helots caused havoc for the Athenians in northeastern Greece. His sudden death at

Amphipolis curtailed Spartan offensive efforts abroad for nearly a decade and helped lead to the stalemate of 421–415.

CLEON · (d. 422) the infamous Athenian demagogue who, Aristophanes and Thucydides felt, was emblematic of the dangerous rabble-rousers coming to the fore following the death of Pericles. He was a vigorous supporter of imperialism, won a stunning victory at Sphacteria over the Spartans, and opposed Nicias' efforts at the armistice in 422 before dying in battle at Amphipolis.

CYRUS THE YOUNGER · (d. 401) second son of King Darius II and a claimant to the Persian throne. At the close of the Peloponnesian War, Cyrus exercised authority over much of Asia Minor, and his close association with and subsidies to Lysander explain the miraculous creation of the Spartan fleet that eventually won the war.

DEMOSTHENES · (d. 413) innovative Athenian general (not to be confused with the fourth-century orator of the same name) whose daring and unconventional tactics brought stunning success at Amphilochia, Pylos, and Sphacteria but contributed to disaster during the Aetolian, Delium, and Sicilian campaigns. He was unceremoniously executed by the Sicilians after the Athenian surrender in 413.

DIODORUS · a Sicilian historian of the Roman Age who wrote circa 60–30 B.C. His universal history in forty books is mostly a compilation from lost Greek historians (most notably Ephorus) but often offers detail about the fighting of the Peloponnesian War otherwise unknown from Thucydides.

GYLIPPUS · the gifted Spartan general whose sudden arrival at Syracuse in 414 with a Peloponnesian relief force turned the tide against the Athenian efforts to take the city.

LAMACHUS · (d. 414) the epitome of tough, soldierly competence at Athens, he often led Athenian troops successfully in the field before dying heroically in the battle for Syracuse.

LYSANDER · (d. 395) the brutal Spartan admiral most responsible for the competence of the Spartan fleet during the Ionian War and the ultimate victory over the Athenians in a series of bloody sea battles in the Hellespont and off the coast of Asia Minor. He survived the war but was slain in a minor clash against the Boeotians nine years later at Haliartus.

MINDARUS · (d. 411) successful Spartan admiral who transferred his base of operations from Ionia to the Hellespont to garner more Persian subsidies and disrupt Athenian grain importation. His death in battle at Cyzicus was a setback for Spartan hopes of maritime supremacy.

NICIAS · (470–413) a sober, conservative Athenian statesman who opposed the radical democrats in the power struggle following Pericles' death; the peace of 421–415 bears his name. His legendary caution led him to oppose the Sicilian expedition. Yet once he was chosen general, his initial demands for massive forces, coupled with his timidity in using them, turned a probable tactical defeat into an unnecessary strategic catastrophe.

PERICLES · (ca. 495–429) as an annually elected general and political leader, he led the Athenians for almost thirty years, and was most responsible for the decision to build the monuments on the Acropolis, expand the Athenian empire, and go to war with Sparta. He died from the plague in the second year of the war, with disastrous consequences for the empire he had helped create.

PHARNABAZUS · (d. 370) Persian satrap of the Dascylium area around the Hellespont who took a more actively pro-Spartan stance than his rival provincial governor Tissaphernes, to the south.

PLUTARCH · (ca. A.D. 50–120) Greek biographer of the Roman period whose *Parallel Lives* compares illustrious Greek statesmen and generals with their likely Roman counterparts. His *Alcibiades, Lysander, Nicias,* and *Pericles* are valuable ancillaries to Thucydides' history.

THUCYDIDES · (460–395?) the great Athenian historian whose narrative covers the origins of the war, its outbreak, and each year's events, from 431 until 411, where it abruptly breaks off. Thucydides himself was an elected Athenian general but was exiled in 424 for twenty years, ostensibly for allowing Brasidas to capture Amphipolis.

TISSAPHERNES · (d. 395) Persian satrap, or governor, at Sardis of the central coastal provinces of Asia Minor who championed the policy of playing

Sparta and Athens off against each other, while professing support for the creation of a Spartan grand fleet.

XENOPHON · (428–354) Greek historian, philosopher, and military writer whose Hellenic history continues the narrative of Thucydides from 411 to the end of the war in 404, and then continues Greek history until the second battle of Mantinea (362).

NOTES

References to Thucydides' The Peloponnesian War are cited by book and section number only. Other ancient historians, such as Diodorus, Herodotus, and Polybius, are referred to by name alone if they are authors of only one titled work.

1. For the dramatic description of the end of war, see Xenophon's account in *Hellenica*, 2.2.19–25. Thucydides (2.8.4; cf. 1.139.3) reminds us that the Spartans originally proclaimed that they were going to war to "liberate Greece," a slogan that, despite consistent Spartan brutality, most Greeks apparently rallied to at the conflict's end. Yet elsewhere Thucydides seems to suggest that many city-states were not very ideological at all. Most simply wished to be left alone ("either democracy or oligarchy was fine, provided that they were free"), and thus predicated their allegiance to the Spartans on the idea that they might win, and in victory prove less able to reinstitute a coercive empire; e.g., 3.82.2–3, 8.48.5.

2. 1.23.4; cf. 3.23.5. Before we fault Thucydides for associating natural phenomena in some loose way with the war, we should consider that even in our own time earthquakes and famine are often seen in close connection with ongoing conflict. In late December 2003, a massive earthquake at Bam in northern Iran was immediately discussed in the Western press in association with the ongoing war against terror—and the degree to which the disaster and the presence of Western aid teams would strengthen or weaken the theocracy and its alleged support for terrorist enclaves.

Chapter 1

1. On criticism of the neoconservatives and their purported use of Thucydides to bolster efforts to take America to war in the manner of Periclean imperialism, see Gary North, "It Usually Begins with Thucydides" (http:www. lewrockwell.com/north/197.html) and the critiques from different perspectives by D. Mendelsohn, "Theatres of War: Why the Battles over Ancient Athens Still Rage" (*New Yorker*, January 12, 2004). Cf. L. Miller, "My Favorite War" (*New York Times Book Review*, March 21, 2004). For allusions to Clemenceau and Venizélos, see Lebow and Strauss, *Hegemonic Rivalry*, 2–19.

2. Isocrates, *On the Peace*, 4, 88, mourned the loss of prominent Athenians over the three-decade course of the war, aristocrats who would have done far better to use their talents against the common Hellenic enemy, imperial Persia. Isocrates' argument is similar to that of those who now regret the First World War, which is seen as a tragic European suicide that wrecked the imperial mission of a civilizing Britain. See, in general, N. Ferguson, *The Pity of War* (New York, 2000), 457–62.

3. 1.22.4. This bold assertion is perhaps the most famous phrase in Thucydides' entire history—one of striking confidence that the historian's views will live beyond the importance of his own subject matter. Meanwhile, some twenty-five hundred years after he wrote *The Peloponnesian War*, English translations of Thucydides' history sell about fifty thousand copies in America each year.

4. See his comments on Pericles: 2.65; Brasidas: 4.81.2; the oligarch revolution of 411: 8.97.2; and Antiphon: 8.68.1–2. Those whom Thucydides appears most impressed with—Pericles, Nicias, and Antiphon—were aristocratic in nature and harbored a distrust of the collective wisdom of the common people as it was manifested on any given day in the assembly.

5. 4.65.3–4. For references to Athens as America, see Sabin, "Athens," 237–38.

6. Xenophon, *Hellenica*, 2.2.23. The discussion of Athenian popularity abroad is complex, involving the contrasting views of the poor and the more prosperous inside every city-state and the physical proximity of a particular state to either Athens or Sparta. It would not be too cynical to assume that had Athens won the war, the same Greeks who were gleeful when the Long Walls were torn down would have been equally pleased with a Spartan defeat—as, in fact, they were when Epaminondas' massive Panhellenic army swept into the Peloponnese three decades later to destroy the Spartan empire. G. E. M. de Ste. Croix, *Origins*, 42–44, most famously discusses the popular perceptions of Athens.

7. 2.8.4–5. The goodwill of the Greeks toward the Spartans arose only after the

latter gradually withdrew from the alliance with Athens following the Greek victory in the Persian War. The less the Greeks saw of the Spartans, the more they liked them. Indeed, at one time the Ionians and other Greeks "begged" the Athenians to become hegemons to curtail a Spartan presence abroad; cf. 1.95.1–2.

8. See the complaints from the Athenian envoys at Sparta (1.76.4) who remind their opponents that "even our sense of equality has very unfairly subjected us to criticism rather than approval." The Athenian demagogue Cleon reiterated the same theme in the debate over the hostages at Mytilene (3.37) when he made the eerily modern argument that the liberal Athenians were ill-equipped for the harsh exigencies of empire. In their own domestic comfort and security they apparently wrongly assumed that the world worked according to the same principles out in the Aegean.

9. The famous phrase—a war "like no other" (*hoia ouch hetera en isô chronô*), from which the title of this book is taken—is found at 1.23.1; cf. 1.1.1. The Greek refers literally to the "sufferings" (pathêmata) from the war, which were unique in Greek history.

10. Whereas the Greeks had always been aware of these differences between strife and war, it was precisely the nightmare of the Peloponnesian War that led philosophers like Plato and Isocrates to draw a distinction between the two phenomena: foreign wars against people like the Persians being sometimes good, internal strife among Greek city-states always being bad. See Plato, *Republic*, 470B; and the long discussion by Price, *Thucydides and the Internal War*, 68–73. By the fourth century, the long-distant Persian conflict was the "good war," the recent Peloponnesian "the bad"—not unlike our present construction of World War II and Vietnam into respective noble and controversial efforts.

11. 1.1.2. The notion of a "shaking up" is an interesting one, implying social unrest, terror, revolution, plague, and a host of other catastrophes that transcend the normal military casualties associated with battles of a conventional war. Thucydides was not a religious man, but his inclusion of earthquake, pestilence, and tidal wave as part of the upheaval lent dramatic effect to his tale of a self-induced Armageddon. At least he was aware that in times of terrible war people would loosely associate a host of natural misfortunes in some way with the human struggle at hand.

12. Attica, her land allies, and the subject states across the Aegean perhaps numbered a million people. For figures on some modern wars, see Keegan, *Warfare*, 359–61.

13. 1.23.6, 1.86.5, 1.88, and 1.118.2. Note the emphasis on perceptions of power

rather than carefully delineated real grievances, and the role honor and status play in the Spartans' sense of inevitable decline. This feeling of perceived grievance is perhaps greatest in an insular, parochial, and traditional society, in which the views of its elder ruling elite are rarely questioned or exposed to fresh ideas from abroad.

14. Fear of both sides: 1.44, 1.118; Athens' size: 1.80.3. For the benefits of empire, see [Xenophon], *Constitution of the Athenians*, 2.12. There is a perceptive discussion of the Spartan angst in Cawkwell, *Thucydides*, 26–39. Popularity was not the only issue that determined the stability of the Athenian empire: in most Greek states for much of the fifth century the poor counted on seeing Athenian triremes in their harbor far more often than the rich could expect a phalanx of Peloponnesian hoplites marching up to the city gate. For the idea that the Spartans were both capriciously cruel and harsh abroad, see, for example, 4.80.4–5 and 4.81.3 (Brasidas as a different sort of Spartan). Dorians fighting for Ionian Athens: 7.57.

15. 3.61.2. Just as globalization is characterized by the spread of the English language, American popular culture, and the U.S. dollar, so too "Atticization" was marked by intrusion into the Aegean of Athenian coinage and the Attic dialect, as well as imperial triremes and knowledge abroad of Athenian tragedy and comedy.

16. [Xenophon], *Constitution of the Athenians*, 3.10–13. The anonymous author of this contemporary treatise on Athenian society displayed a certain ironic approval of the logic of Athenian democracy quite apart from his own oligarchic prejudices, perhaps in the same fashion that an aristocrat might be appalled at Wal-Mart and rap music but at least would concede that such popular institutions and tastes appeal to the material and entertainment needs of the masses far better than do small family shops, museums, and opera.

17. For the innate political differences between Sparta and Athens that led to the war, see 3.39.6, 3.47, and 3.82.1. The Corinthians reprimanded the Spartans for their inability to counter the restless culture of Athens, ending in the famous appraisal of the Athenians as a people who "were born for the purpose of themselves neither having any peace nor allowing other men to enjoy." Cf. 1.70.9, 1.76–77, and 4.55.2. For a review of the ancient evidence attesting to Sparta's fear and Athens' desire to preempt, see de Ste. Croix, *Origins*, 64–67.

18. 2.64.3. There is a modern echo of post–Persian Wars Athenian control in the current use of what the former French foreign minister Hubert Védrine called *l'hyperpuissance américaine*—the overweening influence of the United

States that has arisen in the post–Cold War world after the fall of the Berlin Wall. By 431 the Persian Wars were too far distant in Greek memory for much vestigial amity predicated on a former alliance against the common threat—Athens was too powerful and the old enemy was seemingly long gone.

19. The Spartan demands are listed at 1.139.1–4. For the radical transformation of Athens from an agrarian polis to a rich, urban, and imperial powerhouse, see Hanson, *Other Greeks*, 351–96. The reactionaries longed for a return of the Solonian state, when a century earlier Athens had had no empire and had been run on the basis of a constitution favoring property owners.

20. 7.18.2; cf. 1.33.3, 1.76.2, 1.102.2–3, and 5.20. Regardless of the grievances of each side, in the end it was the Spartans, not the Athenians, who first crossed a rival's borders.

21. See Kagan, *Origins of War*, 8–9 and 567–73; he best discusses these primordial emotions and their role in Thucydides' interpretation of the war's outbreak.

22. 1.86–87. Note that for all the previous grievances against Athens listed by her enemies, the official Spartan vote hinged on Spartan "honor" and fear of Athens' "power."

23. Herman, *Idea of Decline*, 14–19. For Roman imperial authors such as Petronius, Suetonius, Tacitus, and Juvenal, social "decline" or the natural "aging" of a state is seen as arising from luxury, leisure, and general affluence rather than a result of shaggy barbarians, plague, famine, or invasion.

24. 1.123. There is irony in the Corinthians' assertion inasmuch as the most luxurious of the Greeks at the outbreak of the war were the Corinthians themselves, the most rugged still the Spartans.

25. For Socrates' military record at these battles, see Plato, *Symposium*, 220E, 221A–B; *Laches*, 181B; *Apology*, 28E. His opposition to the Sicilian campaign is found at Plutarch, *Nicias*, 13.7. Socrates may have fought at three battles and sieges while in his mid-forties. But after 421 we hear of no further service, and should imagine that he spent the last two decades of the war, while in his fifties and sixties, on guard duty with the older hoplites and resident aliens.

26. Plato, *Protagoras*, 359E. There is little of pacifism in any of Plato's dialogues, which instead assume that war is a tragic but nonetheless natural event. His criticism of wars per se is pragmatic rather than what we would recognize as moral, and instead arises over particular modes of fighting that involved Greeks being killed by Greeks, or good hoplites brought down by their social inferiors in less than heroic skirmishes and at sea.

27. Cf. 1.44.2 and 1.144.3. Pericles is often and accurately compared to Churchill in that by the end of their long careers, both old aristocratic imperialists had

seen too much to have any illusions that the appeasement of a garrison state and its antidemocratic coalition would bring peace.

28. 1.122.1. After the Corinthians berate the Spartans for their backward-looking foreign policy, they advocate an immediate invasion of Attica—advice incumbent on the most reactionary of all strategies, that of agricultural devastation in hopes of prompting hoplite battle. The Spartans had turned back in 446 on their own accord from invading Attica. They were sure that in 431 there was nothing stopping them from entering Athenian soil, as if that fact in and of itself would either precipitate battle or harm Athens to any great degree. Here they wrongly equated the successful tactic of overrunning Attica with the nearly impossible strategy of turning such force dominance in Attica into long-term advantage.

29. An entire subfield of Greek history exists to ascertain why the Peloponnesian War erupted when it did, and which side was at fault for finally breaking the peace. The arguments damning Athens are found in E. Badian, *Plataea*, 125–62. For the Athenian position, see the famous apology of G.E.M. de Ste. Croix, summarized briefly in *Origins*, 290–92. Kagan, *Outbreak*, 345–74, is fair and comprehensive in reviewing a century of scholarly controversy. Nevertheless, he has doubts about Thucydides' rather deterministic views that the war was inevitable, given Spartan fear of an ever more powerful Athens.

30. 1.68.4. It is hard to discover any Peloponnesian recognition that the rapid growth of the Athenian fleet in the decades before the war demanded a countereffort to match trireme for trireme. The Athenian decision to build 300 warships certainly prompted no arms race like the notorious Anglo-German dreadnought rivalry of the early 1900s, which nearly bankrupted the two empires. In our sources, it is almost as if the Peloponnesians discovered belatedly at the outbreak of the conflict that in this new war ships will be critical—and that they have very few of them.

31. 2.8.1. Thucydides' assessment of inexperience was true enough for Sparta. But Athens, in fact, had fought almost continuously by land and sea throughout the early and mid-fifth century. For example, in the two decades before the outbreak of the war, Athens had campaigned in Boeotia (447), put down revolts in Euboea and Megara (446), and besieged Samos and Byzantium (440). The idea that the young rashly rush into war without past experience of its horrors is thematic in Thucydides' history, and explains in part why in 416 an inexperienced generation of youths paired off against its elders in demanding to go to Sicily.

32. 2.65.7; cf. 2.13.2 and 1.144.1. For a critique of Pericles' strategy, see Kagan, *Archidamian War*, 352–55. Nowhere in our sources is there any Athenian war plan remotely akin to the daring of the later Epaminondas, who assumed

that the only way to beat Sparta was to march into its homeland, dismantle its system of apartheid, and ring its territory with a circle of friendly democratic citadels.

33. 1.10.2. Again, it is notable that in the prewar deliberations, Sparta contemplated organizing a fleet to defeat Athens by ruining its armada and sailing into the Piraeus, while Athens never planned to create a massive army to storm into Laconia.

34. 1.71 and 1.141.3; cf. 1.142.3. At least Pericles' prewar prognosis of Spartan impotence was mostly correct, and in sharp contrast to the last decade of the war, when Persian money changed the entire complexion of the conflict. On these and other passages, see Hanson, "Hoplite Battle," 215–16. At the war's outbreak Sparta had no missile troops, few horsemen, no light-armed contingents, and almost no ships—the very type of contingents that would be necessary for victory.

35. 1.102. The Athenians had come to Sparta's help thirty years before the outbreak of the war, to put down the helot uprising of 462 on the slopes of Mount Ithome, in Messenia. Both their skill and their revolutionary character frightened the Spartans, who abruptly sent the Athenians home lest they become more of a problem than part of the solution.

36. 1.36.3. It was odd in this war how often the actual fighting belied prewar assumptions, especially how much attention both Sparta and Athens gave to ensuring the goodwill of Corinth and Corcyra, respectively, and how little each side later actually contributed to the eventual outcome of the conflict. Both states were not unlike Mussolini's prewar Italy, which was thought to be a valuable potential ally by both Churchill and Hitler, but one that proved to offer little military advantage once the war actually started.

37. See 8.2–7 for the efforts of Sparta to create a fleet, and cf. Kagan, *Fall,* 14–16.

38. Later remarks about mercurial helots: Aristotle, *Politics,* 1269A; Xenophon, *Hellenica,* 3.3.6; cf. Thucydides, 1.101–02 and 4.80.3 Most Greeks owned slaves of varying statuses and nationalities. But at Sparta the helots were exclusively a rural people, without exception Greeks, and in the case of the Messenians endowed with a proud national heritage. Thus, while Athenian slaves rowed and carried the baggage of their infantrymen masters, there was far less chance that they would enjoy common affinities with one another that might transcend their servile status and thus lead to rebellion en masse.

39. King Archidamus warns about the demographical advantages that Athens enjoyed: 1.80.3. For the myriad ramifications of helots and demography on Sparta's ability to wage war against Athens, see Cartledge, *Agesilaos,* 37–43.

40. Cf. 1.80.3, 1.81.1, 1.114.1, and 1.101.1. Most classical armies took along only three days' worth of rations, so speed and timing were essential: an army that was

waylaid or arrived after the harvests had been evacuated had very little tactical latitude. In some sense, Greek armies before the age of Alexander shared the same vulnerabilities as early escort fighters in World War II, whose dog-fighting over the target was curtailed by limited fuel reserves and thus often lasted for only a fraction of the total time of the mission.

41. Cf. 4.85.2, 5.14.3, and 7.28.3. Aristophanes' plays (e.g., *Acharnians*, 182–83, 512) emphasize the shame of Attic farmers impotently watching the enemy ravage their property, and especially their inability to alter the official Periclean policy of restraint.

42. Xenophon, *Hellenica*, 1.1.35. By 411, Sparta had a fleet, capital, and new allies and thus could be assured that it could stay in Attica permanently without much worry that the Athenians, as in the past, could seriously frighten the Peloponnese. A real debate rages over the degree of Athenian self-sufficiency in food. Garnsey (*Famine and Food Supply*, 105–06) may well be right in his contention that classical Attica could supply almost half the grain needed by the late-fifth-century Athenian state.

43. 1.144.4. The evacuation of the Attic countryside before Xerxes' onslaught was often evoked as proof of Athenian courage and sacrifice—even as the Athenians made arrangements never to suffer such an indignity again.

44. 1.80.3 and 1.82.2. We owe to the genius of Thucydides this paradoxical portrait of Archidamus, the one astute Spartan who warned against the very strategy he subsequently followed, and who was forever associated with the first decade of the war that he sought to avoid.

45. Long Walls at Argos and Patras: 5.52 and 5.82; cf. 1.93.1. Irony abounds: Nicias (7.77.6) argued that walls did not matter, but rather the men behind them. Yet they did at Syracuse: just a few more thousand feet of fortifications on Epipolae and his now disheartened mob would have cut off the city and been in control. Corinth seems to have used long walls to connect its ports to the city without falling to the democratic virus, but it had a long prior tradition of aristocrats engaging in trans-Isthmus trade and, given its strategic geography, never associated fortification with the deliberate abandonment of farmland.

46. 1.69.1; cf. 1.90–93. Athenian conservatives had always opposed the Long Walls and had hoped that the Spartans would intervene to stop their construction; cf. 1.107.4.

47. For Athenian finances, see 2.13.3–5. It is a testament to the costly nature of the new war—mostly sieges and wages for rowers—that by the fifth or sixth year of the war, Athens was essentially out of money and was seeking new sources of income (as well as reduced expenditures) to avoid capitulation.

48. 1.19.1. For the size of the empire, see Aristotle, *Constitution of the Athenians*, 24.3, and Cawkwell, *Thucydides*, 101–02. We can only speculate on the future of Athens had it avoided war in 431 but instead continued to augment its reserves and ensure its tribute—what-ifs similarly entertained by a few British Tories who felt that their empire was lost by a needless internecine struggle with Germany between 1914 and 1918. Alcibiades in extremis outlines all sorts of imperial conspiracies to the Spartans, suggesting a soon-to-be-greater Athenian empire that would shortly absorb Sicily, Italy, and Carthage (e.g., 6.90.2–3)—even after tens of thousands had been lost to the plague and fifteen years of prior war.

49. [Xenophon], *Constitution of the Athenians*, 1.10–12. For Athenian population growth, see Sallares, *Ecology*, 95–99.

50. 1.81.2; cf. 2.13.6, and [Xenophon], *Constitution of the Athenians*, 2.1–3. Rather than destroy the subject states of the empire, the Spartans eventually realized that ruining Athenian assets might give psychological impetus to local oligarchs, who, in fact, throughout the war caused the Athenians enormous grief at Samos, Lesbos, and Chios. The exact number of Athenian subject states is under dispute, but contemporary Athenians considered the empire huge—so the comic poet Aristophanes (*Wasps*, 707) offers up the impossible number of one thousand tribute-paying states.

51. Thucydides thought Athenian latitude for unilateralism was a real advantage in the war (e.g., 1.141.6); but it cut both ways. A single setback like the plague or Sicily could induce immediate revolt, inasmuch as subjects felt that they had little responsibility for such poor planning and much to gain by distancing themselves from an apparent loser. On the shortcomings of Athenian strategy, see Henderson, *Great War*, 47–68.

52. To survive (*periesesthai*): 1.144.1 and 2.65.7; cf. Lazenby, *Peloponnesian War*, 32–33. For the Spartan pipe dream at the war's beginning of creating a huge navy and the allied contributions, see 2.7.2; cf. 1.121 and 1.27.2. The thought apparently did not much scare the Athenians (e.g., 1.142.6).

53. The role of the Athenian empire and its popularity as a protector of local democrats against oligarchic exploitation were the focus of the life's work of the great, though eccentric historian G.E.M. de Ste. Croix. See especially his brilliant, often hyperbolic arguments in *Origins*, 34–49. For Sparta's efforts at imposing oligarchy, see 5.81.2. Athens likewise sought to spread democracy by force: 5.82.1–4.

54. See budget figures in Kagan, *Peloponnesian War*, 62–63; these suggest Athens could not sustain full deployment of its fleet for more than four years.

55. See 5.26.2–5 for Thucydides' famous defense of the idea that the twenty-seven

years were to be seen as a cohesive period of war rather than a series of theater conflicts. The "Ten Years War" was often later known as the Archidamian War (431–421). The Pachean War (431–425), the Peace of Nicias (421–415), and the similarly distinct Mantinean War (419–418) followed that first decade. The intervening Sicilian War (415–413) led to a third phase of the conflict, often in two simultaneous theaters known on land as the Decelean War (413–404) and at sea as the Ionian War (411–404).

Chapter 2

1. 3.26.3; cf. Xenophon, *Hellenica*, 4.5.10 and 5.3.3; Polybius 18.6.4. "Suckering" is an annual job of any tree or vine farmer, who must send crews into the orchards or vineyards each spring to cut off unwanted shoots that spring from the trunk.

2. [Xenophon], *Constitution of the Athenians*, 2.14. Thucydides could have added that the poor also looked to profit in war from state pay for service and opportunistic plunder, perhaps on the expectation that the city itself could survive despite annual attacks on its landowning classes' exposed cropland.

3. For examples of landlocked states that faced real problems after having their harvests ravaged, see Xenophon, *Hellenica*, 5.4.50 and 7.2.10. Both sides in the present-day Israeli-Palestinian conflict seem to embrace the importance of olive trees as symbolic capital that has value far beyond producing olives. Throughout the years 2000–2002 the Palestinians cited the Israelis as bulldozing some fifteen thousand of their olive trees—about one hundred acres at normal planting densities—to clear paths along strategic areas to prevent sniper attacks. Yet the *Christian Science Monitor* (December 8, 2000) reported that both the destroyers and the owners, as traditional Mediterranean peoples, were depressed by the tactic: "We were educated not to uproot a sapling, and for us as Israelis, this has left a bad taste," remarked Yoni Figel, an Israeli government official. In turn, the Palestinian mayor of Hares lamented, "Olives are like water to us. You cannot imagine a home without olive oil. The olive tree is a symbol of our people, surviving for centuries on these hillsides" (*Daily Telegraph*, London, November 3, 2000).

4. See, in general, Aristophanes, *Peace*, 511–80. The hero of both his *Acharnians* and *Peace* is the archetypal "little guy" farmer, whose good sense, practicality, and salt-of-the-earth morality are at odds with a new commercial and radically democratic culture.

5. Xenophon, *Oeconomicus*, 6.9–10. In another paradox of the highest order, for the romantic Xenophon the paragons of Hellenic virtue were the Spartans,

who themselves did no farmwork at all, while his archenemies were the Thebans, the agrarians par excellence of the Greek world.

6. Sophocles, *Oedipus at Colonus*, 694 ff.; Euripides, *Medea*, 824. The sense of the sanctity of Attica's soil was reflected in art as well. On the west pediment of the Parthenon, Poseidon vies with Athena for dominion over Attica, while a sacred olive tree is prominent nearby on the Acropolis.

7. *Supplementum Epigraphicum Graecum* 21 (1966): 644.12–13; Xenophon, *Memorabilia*, 2.1.13; Plato, *Republic*, 470A–471B; cf. 5.23.1–2 and 5.47.3–4; Aristotle, *Rhetoric*, 2.21.8, 3.11.6; Isocrates 14.31. For these and other passages, see discussion of these citations in Hanson, *Warfare and Agriculture*, 9–13.

8. 1.121.2–3. The Corinthians apparently had some affinity with Athenian innovation by reason of their own long walls, sizable fleet, and maritime economy. Yet, despite all their natural endowments and prized location, oligarchic government lacked the dynamism of radical democracy, and thus by the fifth century Corinth itself was abjectly weak compared to the Athenian empire. For democracies and oligarchies in war, cf. 1.118.2, 2.39, 4.55.3–4, 6.18.6–7, 6.93.1, 7.55.2, 8.1.4, 8.89.3, and 8.96.5; cf. Herodotus 5.78. On the advantages of ancient democracies in wartime, see the review of ancient citations in Hanson, "Democratic Warfare," especially 17–24.

9. Short war: 5.14.3 and 7.28.2. It is not clear whether these initial wildly optimistic estimates were based on anticipated starvation accruing from devastation, the exhaustion of Athenian financial reserves, a hoped-for destruction of the Athenian phalanx, or panic and capitulation on the part of the Athenians. For Brasidas, see 4.85.2; cf. 3.79, 5.14.3, and Hornblower, *Commentary*, 2.38–61.

10. 1.114.1 and 2.21.1. Rumor had it that King Pleistonax had earlier been bribed by wealthy Athenians to go home, which might explain the later stories that Pericles' own estates were to be saved in a similar private deal or through collusion with Archidamus. In fact, Pleistonax had quit at Eleusis because of advance word that the Athenians would grant sizable concessions to Sparta, which explains why King Archidamus tarried in hopes of a similar brokered deal in 431.

11. 1.124.1; cf. 1.121.4. The Corinthians' confidence was perhaps grounded in their own experience with long walls across the Isthmus, which had a poor record of keeping enemies out of Corinthian territory—an expanse, however, that was far more difficult to fortify and defend than the Athenian-Piraeus corridor.

12. 1.81.6. Whether Archidamus really said that in 431 or whether, years later, after the verdict of the Archidamian War was in, Thucydides put such "pre-

scient" words into the mouth of one of his favorite Spartans we are not sure. But the sentiment was probably widely shared by at least a handful of pessimistic conservative Spartan elites who had gotten word of the growth of both Athenian fortifications and a 300-trireme fleet. See also 2.11.6–8, 2.12.1, and 2.18.5.

13. The reserve fund: 2.24.1; the Spartan sneak attack: 2.93.3. It would have been far cheaper for the Athenians to meet the Spartans in the plain of Attica to wage hoplite battle than to send hundreds of its ships on patrol in the Aegean and around the Peloponnesian coast to monitor the allies and attack enemy villages. Far from being merely passive, Periclean strategy was ambitious and thus enormously expensive.

14. For the promise that a defeat of the Thebans would keep Sparta out of Attica, see 4.95.2. This irony is noted in Krentz, "Strategic Culture": a Spartan force designed to harass and thus to prompt battle was so formidable that it had precisely the opposite effect of ensuring that no one in his right mind would march out to confront it.

15. See Thorne, "Warfare and Agriculture," 249–51, which offers interesting though theoretical scenarios on the difficulty facing Athenian farmers evacuating their harvests into Athens. Much of his revisionist work argues that we underestimate the damage that could be caused by torching grain; i.e., that it was not that difficult to time an invasion right at the combustible period of wheat and barley maturity, while much harder for the defenders to harvest it and bring it inside the city in time. These are interesting hypotheticals, but many of his arguments—e.g., that ravagers in a parched Attic countryside could have poured sufficient amounts of water into grain granaries to spoil stored crops—seem unlikely.

16. Plutarch, *Pericles*, 33.4; cf. Thucydides 1.143.5. Athens' youth or, rather, a new generation of inexperienced Athenian hotheads, posed a challenge for Pericles as well: the older hoplites had known conflict in Boeotia and Megara, before the war; but the younger were the most likely to rush out foolishly to fight the Spartans; cf. Diodorus 12.42.6, and de Ste. Croix, *Origins*, 208–09. For Agis, see Diodorus 13.72–73, who locates the incident in 408.

17. Cf. Diodorus 12.42.7–8. Cf. Thucydides 2.25.1–2, 2.26.1–2, 2.30.1–2, 2.56.1–6, and in general Westlake, "Seaborne Raids." In terms of destroying large amounts of Spartan war matériel, the raids accomplished little. Yet Peloponnesian farmers were subject to the same fears as their Attic counterparts. Thus, the notion that Athenian seaborne raiders were attacking the rural communities of Peloponnesian ravagers back home was unsettling.

18. 6.105. Thucydides said the ravaging of Laconian soil gave the Spartans a

"rather more plausible excuse" (*euprophasiston mallon tên aitian*), inasmuch as the crop devastation violated the peace treaty in "the most manifest way."

19. Aristotle, *Politics*, 1269B. The best account of the Spartan paranoia over the helots, and how that fear played into the hands of its enemies, is still found in Cartledge, *Agesilaos*, 170–77.

20. 3.18.5; cf. 1.101.2. The Mytileneans could say that in 427, but only in light of four failed Spartan invasions of Attica. Before the war maritime states such as the Corinthians had, in fact, urged an invasion of the Attic hinterlands as a mechanism to relax the Athenian grip on its overseas empire. Cf. 1.122.1.

21. Plutarch, *Pericles*, 33.4–5. Cf. 1.43.5. We have no information that Pericles ever, in fact, contemplated a scorched-earth policy. Had the Athenians been able to destroy all their crops, the arriving Spartan ravagers were nevertheless just a few miles from the border of the friendly and especially rich heartland of Boeotia.

22. Euripides, *Medea*, 824; Plutarch, *Pericles*, 31.1–2. Cf. 3.851; 4.84, 88, 130; 5.84. It was another irony of the war that much of civic-inspired tragedy and comedy inside the walls would have a larger audience in the early years of the war only because of the forced evacuation of thousands from the countryside— and thus for perhaps the first time began to portray rural themes in earnest.

23. For the trauma of the evacuation of Attica, see 2.17 and 2.52.1; Diodorus 12.45.2; and Aristophanes, *Knights*, 792–93. Thucydides focuses on the emotion and pain of the first withdrawal into the city in 431. But there were four other such evacuations that he does not mention in any such graphic way, and these treks may have been just as difficult. In general, the historian describes fully a "typical" siege, battle, or civil strife, and then assumes that the reader is familiar with the details of subsequent events that are more cursorily noted.

24. 2.54.1. We do not quite know what Pericles meant by such a bleak assessment. Presumably Athenian countermeasures after 430 might have been even more muscular and effective around the shores of the Peloponnese had the state not been so devastated by disease. Plutarch believed that had the plague not hit, Sparta might shortly have given up the idea of defeating Athens altogether (Plutarch, *Pericles*, 34.2).

25. On Alcibiades' warning: 8.18.7. There has been a long controversy among scholars about the actual legal basis of Pericles' enormous power, a debate nicely summarized by Hamel, *Athenian Generals*, 9–12. One of the indirect means of running Athenian politics was the decision about whether or not to convene the assembly. Obviously, in times of crisis and acrimony a sober general like Pericles would prefer to postpone debate, cool down tempers,

and not subject state policy to the collective wisdom of 7,000 or so enraged citizens crammed onto the Pynx.

26. 2.65.9; cf. 2.65.4, 4.83.3, 6.17.2, 6.63, 8.2. Elsewhere Thucydides uses the terms *ochlos* and *homilos* in a manner that is not always pejorative but perhaps reflects the potentiality, rather than the inevitability, of the "people" to be fickle and mercurial. Cf. Cawkwell, *Thucydides*, 7–8.

27. 2.12. Cf. 2.10.1–2. Although Thucydides began the second book of his history with the March 431 Theban attack on Plataea, he apparently felt that the war proper started only with the direct confrontation of Spartan and Athenian troops more than two months later. See Gabriel and Metz, *Sumer*, 104, for the length of marching armies of about 65,000.

28. 2.8.4. It is also unclear to what degree such anti-Athenian sentiments were based on a cynical assessment of being on the winning side—that Sparta might well either beat or at least humiliate Athens in a brief, cheap, and lucrative campaign. On the farms of Attica, see the *Hellenica Oxyrhynchia*, 12.3–5. The anonymous historian suggests that the Athenians themselves may have stocked their farms in part from the plunder and booty from military operations abroad. Cf. Hanson, "Thucydides," 212–26. What exactly was rural "plunder" in the ancient world? Most likely anything valuable left behind, from household fixtures (furniture, wooden doors, window frames) to roof tiles, wagons, farm implements, and stock animals. On evacuation and the difficulty in burning grain, see Foxhall, "Farming and Fighting," 140–43.

29. For eleventh-hour discussions at both Athens and Sparta, see Kagan, *Outbreak*, 310–42.

30. Plutarch, *Pericles*, 33.3. For the nature of the deme of Acharnae and its relationship to Athens, see Jones, *Rural Athens*, 92–96. See Foxhall, "Farming and Fighting," 142–43, for the idea that Archidamus sought to provoke domestic friction and strife by targeting the farms of conservative Athenian hoplites.

31. Plutarch, *Pericles*, 33.5. There is surely irony here: the angriest of all Athenians, the farmers of Attica, rarely served in the cavalry or the navy, and thus sat tight while others risked their lives to take revenge upon their enemies.

32. An entire corpus of literature has emerged assessing Pericles' strategy: Was it really all that passive? Was it effective? Did the cavalry and sea patrols constitute an offensive mind-set? See a review of the arguments in Ober, "Thucydides," 186–89, and Spence, "Perikles," 106–09, which credit Pericles with a strategy that was more sophisticated than is usually acknowledged. Krentz ("Strategic Culture," 68–72) believes that the Spartans ironically appeared with such a large force that they precluded any chance of their hoped-for Athenian hoplite response. For Pericles as strategist, see the classic treatment of Delbrück, *Warfare in Antiquity*, 135–43.

33. Later the Athenian general Hippocrates urged his troops on the eve of the battle of Delium to remember that a victory over the Boeotians might rob Peloponnesians of cavalry support and thus ensure that the enemy would never invade Attica again—an odd statement since by autumn 424 they had not been in Attica for almost a year and a half, and would not return for over a decade. Cf. 4.95.2.

34. Isocrates 7.52; cf. Aristotle, *Constitution of the Athenians*, 16.5, and Alciphron, *Letters*, 3.31. We assume that the ubiquitous phrase "the Athenians" included residents of Athens; but, in fact, perhaps two out of every three "Athenians" actually lived in rural Attica, either in small villages or isolated farmhouses outside the walls of the city. These rural folk may have rarely come into Athens at all.

35. 1.82.4. Archidamus' advice reveals that even after the outbreak of the war, there was something still phony about the conflict. The Spartans believed that there was room for discussions should they not attack the Athenian countryside without restraint.

36. 2.13.1. Thucydides (2.55) and Diodorus (12.45) often talk of "all" the land being ravaged even as they assume that it was not seriously damaged (e.g., 3.26 and 7.27.4). In almost every contemporary comedy of Aristophanes' there is some reference to the devastation of Attica, an experience that must have traumatized the Athenians for many years. See Hanson, *Warfare and Agriculture*, 138–43.

37. 2.14.1–2 and 2.16.2. The problem with the Long Walls was that while they followed the successful Athenian strategy of withdrawal before a superior land army, the sacrifice now fell largely on the country folk, rather than, as before the battle of Salamis, on the urban and rural population alike. On the radical cultural and social changes that came about from the evacuation, see the arguments of Jones, *Rural Athens*, 195–207. For premonitions of a Spartan invasion, see Lazenby, *Peloponnesian War*, 23–24.

38. Ravaging tools: Plutarch, *Cleomenes*, 26.3. For ancient passages about the devastation of Attica: Aristophanes, *Acharnians*, 232, 509–12; *Peace*, 319–20. Cf. Hanson, *Warfare and Agriculture*, 164. The Persian occupation of Attica left tangible records of destruction, most prominently on the Acropolis and the shrines of Attica that were burned. In comparison, there is almost no archaeological evidence of the five Spartan invasions of the Archidamian War—or, for that matter, from the effect of the near-decade-long occupation of Decelea.

39. Cf. 3.26.3, 7.27.4, and *Hellenica Oxyrhynchia*, 12.4. Of course, it is possible that the anonymous fourth-century B.C. historian was, in fact, drawing on Thucydides himself as a source for marginal damage during the Archidamian War.

40. For Aristophanes, see *Acharnians*, 1089–93; *Peace*, 557–63, 573, 1320–25. The nature of the Aristophanic evidence for agricultural damage is discussed at length in Hanson, *Warfare and Agriculture*, 138–43. On the indestructibility of the olive tree, see Sophocles, *Oedipus at Colonus*, 694 ff. "A terror to its enemies" perhaps makes sense to anyone who has started the unenviable task of chopping down or uprooting an olive tree.

41. 2.57.2; cf. 2.65.2 Thucydides seems not terribly interested in these latter four invasions. His description of the plague, the revolution at Corcyra, and the Pylos campaign all merit more attention. Before 425 the Spartan army was used briefly at the siege of Plataea and for combating a few raids in the Peloponnese. But the idea of constant war making during the first seven years is absurd inasmuch as real infantry battle did not start until 425, with the subsequent clashes on Sphacteria, at Delium, and near Amphipolis.

42. See Pericles' outline of strategy on the eve of the war at 1.141.3–7. Once Sparta failed in Attica, the poverty of its strategic thinking was apparent: besieging the marginal town of Plataea, giving only nominal support to the critical insurrection on Lesbos, and parrying Athenian attacks in the Peloponnese. Not until Brasidas' long march to the Chalcidice was there anything inspired about Spartan military planning that might change the course of the war.

43. 3.26.1–4. For the Spartan anger over the fact that Athenians were down in the Peloponnese while they were up in Attica, see Diodorus 12.61.3.

44. 3.15.2–16. One of the common themes of Aristophanes' contemporary comedies is the Panhellenic revulsion for the destruction of property and crops. In both his *Acharnians* and *Lysistrata*, Greeks flock together from the countryside to protest the stupidity of destroying property.

45. Other than Acanthus, it is hard to cite any city that simply capitulated in fear of losing its crops. On Sicily, the Athenians, we are told, "burned the grain" of some of the nearby allied towns of the Syracusans, but such ravaging seems to have had no effect in either drawing hoplites outside their walls or in inducing starvation. In general, see 4.84.1–2 and 4.88.1–2; for the luxuriousness of the Sicilian countryside and the systematic efforts to evacuate it during times of invasion, see Diodorus 13.81. And cf. Herodotus 5.34.1, 6.101.2.

46. 4.66.1–3, 2.31.2; for the proverbial sufferings of the Megarians, cf. Aristophanes, *Acharnians*, 535; *Peace*, 246–50. The passes over Megara were always a source of contention, as the Athenians realized that their occupation meant that a Peloponnesian army might be preempted or even stopped before arriving in Attica. See de Ste. Croix, *Origins*, 190–95.

47. Decelea clearly fascinated Thucydides, who makes much of the strategy of *epiteichismos* inside Attica (1.122, 6.91.6–7, 7.18.1). For the effects of Decelea, see Hanson, *Warfare and Agriculture*, 153–73. Most famously, 20,000 slaves were said to have left Attica for Decelea, the majority of them probably from the countryside of Attica. See Hanson, "Thucydides," 225–28. Agis arrived in Attica "earlier than ever before" (7.19.1), inasmuch as he was building a permanent fort, not engaging in seasonal devastation.

48. For this repeated theme of "fear," see 1.236; cf. 1.881, 1.118.2, and 1.75.3. Cf. Van Wees, *Greek Warfare*, 258n4. Donald Kagan has often emphasized the accuracy of Thucydides' assessment; see *Origins*, 8–9, 71–74. And for a spirited defense of Pericles' strategic thought, see Delbrück, *Warfare in Antiquity*, 135–39, and, in general, his *Die Strategie des Pericles Erläurtert durch die Strategie Friedrichs des Grossen* (Berlin, 1890). Emotions, not reason, are often cited for the motivations of states; cf. 1.75.3 for the Athenians' own excuse for empire: "Fear was our motive, afterward honor and finally self-interest." See also 1.76.2 for the importance of honor (*timê*), fear (*deos*), and advantage (*ôphelia*).

49. 1.121. For the table of Athenian expenditures, see Zimmern, *Greek Commonwealth*, 437. Money seems to have been thematic in all early discussions of the war, and the asymmetrical nature of the two adversaries' reserves became a primary reason for Pericles' antebellum optimism. For this new idea that money, not courage, numbers, or traditional warfare, was the arbiter of military success, see Kallet, *Money and Corrosion*, 285–94.

50. Alcibiades and the ephebic oath: Plutarch, *Alcibiades*, 15.1; Hanson, *Warfare and Agriculture*, 5. For information about the property, family, and early life of Alcibiades, see Davies, *Athenian Propertied Families*, 20–21. In Thucydides' account (7.91.6), Alcibiades is one of the strategic architects of the Decelea operation. Perhaps as an earlier cavalryman he understood how difficult it might have been to stop Spartan ravagers had they stayed on in permanent fortifications.

Chapter 3

1. 1.23.3. Thucydides' statement on the plague is quite astonishing; what he implies is that the disease was the greatest disaster to befall the Greeks during the war—worse than Sicily, the chaos at Corcyra, the carnage of the Ionian War, and a variety of other catastrophes from Decelea to Melos. Perhaps the reason why we find that generalization hard to believe is that the plague broke out in the second year of a conflict that, nevertheless, went on for another quarter century.

2. *Hellenica Oxyrhynchia*, 12.3. It is surprising that Thebes experienced a growth of refugees, given the rarity of Athenian attacks across the border. There was plenty of raiding across the highlands of Mount Parnes, but most of the aggression came from the Thebans. Athenian-inspired attacks on Mycalessus and Tanagra were mere excursions. The only sizable invasion—that of Demosthenes and Hippocrates, culminating at Delium—was an abject failure.

3. For the Long Walls, see 2.13.8; cf. 1.89.3, 1.93.8, 1.107.1, 1.108.3, and Gomme, *Commentary*, 2.39–40. Although the line of twin fortifications stretched over four miles, they were completed in just a fraction of the twenty years devoted to the construction of the Parthenon. Together with earlier municipal walls, they formed a network of fortifications found almost nowhere else in fifth-century Greece.

4. See 2.51.2–5. Diodorus (12.45) has a few wrinkles in his description of the outbreak, stressing the role of overcrowding.

5. Thucydides on the social consequences of the plague: 2.53. For the contrast of accommodations before and after the evacuation, see 2.17, 2.52; cf. Diodorus 12.45.2–3. On the number of Athenians working on municipal projects, see Aristophanes, *Wasps*, 709, and Aristotle, *Constitution of the Athenians*, 24.3.

6. *Wasps*, 792–93; on two houses, see Plato, *Laws*, 5.745B, and Aristotle, *Politics*, 6.1330a14–18. On evacuation in general, see Hanson, *Warfare and Agriculture*, 112–21. Many argue that the refugees gave city folk their first real intimacy with the rustics of Attica, a rather different picture from the usual view that ancient Greek cities drew little distinction between city and country, rural and urban citizens. For the controversy, see Jones, *Rural Athens*, 204–07.

7. 2.54. In part, Thucydides gave a great deal of detail about the evacuation of 431 because it was prior to the plague and seemed the most extensive. On areas of Attica that were never evacuated during the war, see again Hanson, *Warfare and Agriculture*, 151, 161–66.

8. Plutarch, *Pericles*, 35.3. Apparently, the Greeks understood that the disease could be spread by infected carriers, even by those who had yet shown no real symptoms of the malady.

9. On Solon's purported use of chemical warfare, see Pausanias 10.37.7; cf. also Aeneas Tacticus 8.4. Mayor, *Greek Fire*, 99–118, has an interesting discussion of the classical equivalents of biological warfare, citing a number of ancient passages to show how diabolical the Greeks were in an age well before our modern notion of weapons of mass destruction.

10. For the plague and the Peloponnesians, see Pausanias 8.41.7–9 and 10.11.5; for the oracles at Athens, see Thucydides 2.54.3; cf. 2.54.4. For the general ancient consensus that population density and cramped quarters resulted in the

disease, see Diodorus 12.45.2–4; cf. Mayor, *Greek Fire*, 126–27, for ancient plagues in the context of war.

11. A good review of the history of the debate and the issues involved is found at Sallares, *Ecology*, 244–62, and Gomme, *Commentary*, 2.145–62.

12. Xenophon, *Hellenica*, 2.2.10–11. Did the fear of another outbreak influence the survivors, now crammed into Athens once again, to be terrified about a new round of pestilence and thus more ready to capitulate in a way not true three decades earlier?

13. 2.51. Two critical aspects of the infection—contagion and acquired immunity—seem to have been widely recognized very quickly. On various aspects of the plague, with close attention to Thucydides' vocabulary, see again Gomme, *Commentary*, 2.150–61.

14. Initial mention can be found in the brief summaries in Parlama et al., *City*, 272–74. Full discussions of these salvage operations await further scholarly publication.

15. John of Ephesus, fragment II E–G; Procopius, *Persian Wars*, 11.23. Constantinople, like Athens, was a great port and thus visited by traders from three continents who traversed the Mediterranean.

16. Resentment against the new arrivals: Plutarch, *Pericles*, 34.4. For the various reasons why the Spartans stayed home or left Attica early, cf. 2.71.1, 3.89.1, 4.61, and Hanson, *Warfare and Agriculture*, 135–37.

17. On the unburied dead, see Euripides, *Suppliant Women*, 16–17, 168–69, 308–11, and 531–36. For the bones of fallen Syracusans during the Carthaginian War, see Diodorus 13.75.2–3.

18. 2.48.2. In this sense, his analysis of the plague also serves as a blueprint for the narrative of the Peloponnesian War itself, which was no accident but a chronic malady that had prior clear symptoms, allowing a diagnosis and demanding a prognosis.

19. 2.52–53; cf. 2.53.4. We do not know quite how long the rampant rate of death from the disease lasted, but in Thucydides' description the resulting social pathologies seem to have followed from the outbreak almost immediately—and lasted well beyond the cessation of the mass infection.

20. 2.53.1. We sometimes forget that the Athenian assembly that voted to execute about 1,000 Mytileneans in 427 had themselves seen far more death and destruction than that which they were going to sanction on Lesbos. It may well be that in some terribly ironic fashion the plague also accounts for the destruction of Plataea, in that had it not broken out, Sparta would have gone to Attica in 428 and bypassed Plataea, which apparently could not be stormed or starved out through the Thebans' efforts alone. Had the disease broken out in the last, rather than the second, year of the war, and had

80,000 Athenians perished in 404 rather than in 430, the nature of Athenian conduct in the conflict might have been far different.

21. 3.87. After the less virulent second outbreak of 426, we are never told precisely *when* the plague left for good.

22. 3.87.3; cf. Diodorus 12.58.2. Also see Strauss, *Athens After*, 75–78; he discusses at length the effects of the plague on the manpower reserves of the Athenian military.

23. 2.49.8. Although Thucydides says that the survivors were often left maimed, we do not hear anecdotal reports in later literature about those who were disabled. Cf. Pausanias 3.9.2.

24. 3.3.1. In his funeral oration (cf. 2.35–41), Pericles had bragged about the Athenians in Kennedyesque terms, saying that they would pay any price and meet any danger to respond to the needs of their national security. But by 428 Thucydides could remark, "The Athenians, inasmuch as they were suffering both from the plague and the war that had recently broken out and was now at its height, considered it to be serious business to make an enemy out of the island of Lesbos. It had had a fleet and unimpaired power, and so at first they would not give credence to the charges [that the Lesbians were fomenting rebellion], instead attributing more weight to the desire that they might not be true" (3.3.1).

25. 6.26.2 Despite the use of the Greek adverb "just" (*arti*), a major outbreak had not hit the city for at least a decade.

26. See variously at 2.31.2, 2.61.3, and 3.13.3–4. Just five years into the war, the Mytileneans could make the public argument that Athens was ruined (*eph-tharatai*)—an odd description for a still powerful state that would soon savagely put down the rebellion on the other side of the Aegean and execute over 1,000 ringleaders.

27. Plutarch, *Pericles*, 36.4. From Plutarch we learn that Pericles perished after a drawn-out bout with disease, which slowly tapped his formidable powers of resistance, the force multiplier to a rash of miseries in his last years, which had seen the death of his legitimate sons, sister, relatives, and close friends to the disease, as well as an earlier divorce and later estrangement from his eldest son, Xanthippus. He perished before seeing his last illegitimate son executed in the hysteria following the victory at Arginusae: Plutarch, *Pericles*, 36.7.

28. Pericles: 2.65.10. We must remember that the initial Athenian strategy of withdrawal behind the Long Walls was the logical result of nearly three decades of Periclean leadership that had sought to systematize and institutionalize Themistocles' earlier ad hoc idea of abandoning the Attic countryside and avoiding pitched infantry battle. Thus, Pericles' death early on in the war

meant that some thirty years of military policy ended with him, to be re-placed by uncertain strategies that had not previously been a part of the de-cision to build fortifications, create the empire, invest in the fleet, and shy away from hoplite battle.

29. Diogenes Laertius 26; Aulus Gellius, *Attic Nights*, 15.20.6; cf. Plutarch, *Aristides*, 27. Most of the evidence comes from later derivative sources that in some cases could have confused remarrying after the death of a spouse with polygamy—or seek in gossipy fashion to suggest extramarital relationships among prominent Athenians.

30. Plutarch, *Pericles*, 37.4–5. In some sense, this exemption was all for naught: after sharing in the successful command at the climactic naval victory of Arginusae, the younger Pericles was summarily executed on the insane charge that along with the other generals he had been derelict in retrieving the corpses of Athenian sailors. His illustrious pedigree won him no leniency from the mob—some twenty-three years after his father had fallen to the plague.

31. Diodorus 12.45. Ancient observers were fascinated by the plague precisely be-cause of the relative rarity of such mass death in classical Greece.

32. Plutarch, *Pericles*, 38.2–3. Anyone who has suffered a chronic and debilitating disease will not be surprised by how quickly the confidence in rational med-icine fades and one enters the realm of faith, superstition, and speculative treatment in search of relief.

33. Diodorus 12.58.6; cf. Thucydides 3.104. We should not be surprised at the re-turn of such traditional palliatives. After the initial outbreak of 431–430, the disease waned until a second, but weaker flare-up in 426, before gradually going dormant and disappearing. And despite the crowded conditions brought on by Decelea (413–404) and the final blockade of the city by Lysander (404–403), Athens never again experienced anything like the *annus horribilis* of 429—ongoing proof enough for most surviving Athenians that such piety and cults had paid off handsomely.

34. Plutarch, *Pericles*, 37.1–2. For all the obvious pathologies of Alcibiades, our contemporary sources—Thucydides, Aristophanes, and Xenophon—agree on his remarkable unconquerable spirit. Fed by both ego and natural talent, Alcibiades quite literally never gave up: despite personal exile, treason, scan-dal, financial ruin, and military defeat, he fought to the very end amid a host of enemies.

35. For the farms of Alcibiades' family, see Davies, *Athenian Propertied Families*, 20. Everything he owned—and his real and movable property was worth per-haps 100 talents (in today's dollars about $48 million!)—was confiscated

after his exile in 415 and perhaps largely returned when his sentence was lifted in 407, before being lost again when Alcibiades left in the last years of the war.

36. Socrates did not get the plague: cf., e.g., Diogenes Laertius, 2.25, and Aulus Gellius, *Attic Nights*, 2.1.4–5, who also wrongly claims that the philosopher was the only one who did not succumb—impossible when we remember that the second outbreak of 427 was especially virulent and that prior exposure had given thousands of earlier survivors immunity from reinfection.

37. 5.41.2. The proposed treaty—never enacted—is interesting in that it suggests substituting a single pitched battle in lieu of an open-ended conflict to adjudicate potential disputes. The Spartans, hoplites par excellence, at first labeled the idea moronic (*môria*) before promising to discuss it further. The nature of the first decade of the Peloponnesian War, coupled with news of the horrific plague at Athens, had apparently prompted nostalgia for the old Hellenic idea of such simple solutions.

38. For a description of these later great plagues, see Lucretius, *On the Nature of the Gods*, 6.1138–1286; Virgil, *Georgics*, 3.478; Ovid, *Metamorphoses*, 7.523; and Procopius, *History of the Wars*, 2.23.1.

Chapter 4

1. Plutarch, *Pericles*, 34.1–2. In the first year of the war (431) Pericles personally commanded the massive expedition against Megara ("the greatest Athenian army that had ever been assembled in one body," 2.31.2). And in the next season, even before the Spartans had left Attica and while the plague raged inside the city, Pericles led a formidable force of 100 ships, 400 hoplites, and 300 cavalrymen on a punitive expedition against the Peloponnese—all this from a man sixty-four years old and with a mere year to live.

2. See P. Krentz, "Deception," 186–91; Pritchett, *Greek State*, 2.163–70. We must be careful in making such generalizations given the nature of our incomplete sources; that being said, in the fifty years following the Persian War, Krentz counts only ten instances of such unconventional tactics, which might suggest that the Peloponnesian War really was a watershed event in the history of Hellenic military practice.

3. 4.93.3 to 4.94.1. See also Rawlings, "Alternative Agonies," 234–49, for the use of hoplites in the Peloponnesian War well apart from the phalanx. After the terrible hoplite defeat at Delium in 424 (cf. the context of Thucydides' remark that Athens had no properly organized light-armed corps), Athens never again invaded Boeotia—except in 415 to dispatch the infamous Thracian

peltasts under Diitrephes, who slaughtered the poor schoolboys at Mycalessus (7.29).

4. 4.28.4, 4.111.1; Xenophon, *Hellenica*, 1.2.1. "Peltast" originally denoted a Thracian light-armed warrior who carried on the forearm the crescent-shaped hide
shield (*peltê*); but later it seems almost to have meant any light-armed soldier,
without specific reference to either Thrace or the nature of his shield.

5. 6.43.2; cf. 2.81.8, 4.100.1. See Pritchett, *Greek State*, 5.7–10, for a list of stone
throwers and slingers in the Peloponnesian War.

6. 4.55.2. Cf. Bugh, *Horsemen*, 94–95. The Spartans, remember, were not exactly
unacquainted with diverse enemies. Their hoplites had fought and defeated
Persian cavalry and archers at the battle of Plataea (479) and for some fifty
years hence put down helot insurrectionists. The inadequate nature of the
Spartan cavalry would be a chief complaint in the fourth century; cf. Xenophon, *Hellenica*, 6.4.10–11.

7. For laments about the new warfare, see the ancient citations in Hanson,
"Hoplite Battle," 204–06. Agrarian warfare prior to the Peloponnesian War
assumed that a state would not bring to bear all its potential resources to
conflict but fight in accordance with reigning cultural, political, and social
protocols. Archers were objects of universal disdain in Greek literature; see
the discussion of such passages in Hanson, *Western Way of War*, 15–16.

8. Controversy surrounds Periclean strategy: his defenders claim it was not
defeatist or passive but, in fact, entailed a variety of offensive measures, such
as these raids. Its chief supporter was Hans Delbrück (*Warfare in Antiquity*,
135–43), who, disillusioned over the carnage of World War I, saw Pericles as
the progenitor of the strategy of "exhaustion" or "attrition" (*Ermattungs-
strategie*), which was far preferable to the waste of "annihilation" (*Niederwerf-
ungsstrategie*). Thus, a wealthy empire like Athens could win by not losing,
tying the Spartans down in a variety of distant and diverse theaters while
avoiding a knockout blow from their vaunted phalanx. On Tolmides, see
Diodorus 11.84.3.

9. 2.25–32; Diodorus 12.42. For a modern catalog of these raids, see Westlake,
"Seaborne Raids," and Grundy, *Thucydides*, 346–59. For their expense, see
Zimmer, *Greek Commonwealth*, 436–37. Occasional resistance to Athenian raid-
ing could be stiff. In Elis, for example, during the second reprisal of 430, the
Athenians ravaged and besieged small towns with impunity, until the Eleans
at last came out en masse to offer hoplite battle and thus quickly drove the
Athenians back to their ships; cf. Diodorus 12.44.

10. The various elements of the Athenians' first seaborne response are found at
2.23, 2.25, 2.26–27, 2.31. For the expense of Greek temples, see Gomme, *Com-*

mentary, 2.22–25, which weighs ancient evidence that the Acropolis buildings may have cost more than 1,000 talents each, before concluding that they probably did not.

11. 3.95.2. For the attack on Thyrea, see Diodorus 12.65.8–9; on the Aetolians, cf. 3.98.2–5. There were about 300 hoplite marines committed to the campaign; so the butchery of the 120 meant losses in infantry alone of some 40 percent. There is uncertainty whether hoplites who embarked on triremes (*epibatai*) were from the hoplite (middle-class) census, or drawn from the ranks of the poorer (thetes).

12. 3.111–13. The irony of it all is that Athenians were bushwhacked in Aetolia by native light-armed troops and then a few months later themselves did the same to the Peloponnesians with the help of similar native tribes in Amphilochia. To those who were cut down in the mud and grime of these hilly backwaters, oligarchy versus democracy meant little, if anything.

13. Plato, *Laws*, 4.706 B–D. We must remember that Plato was talking mostly about Athens and drawing on the strong memories of youthful acquaintance with Socrates for the dramatic landscape of his dialogues. In Plato's middle age, there were a number of fourth-century hoplite battles—Coronea, Nemea, Leuctra, second Mantinea—that belie his pessimism that the Greeks either could not or no longer would fight a "fair fight."

14. 2.67, 2.90.5, 2.92; cf. Herodotus 7.137. Throughout the war there were Peloponnesian ships off the Megarian coast, enormous plunder taken around Pylos and Decelea, and constant Boeotian raids across the Attic border. At various times these zones of chaos were something altogether different from either war or peace—but apparently the domain of thieves, exiles, and killers; e.g., 3.51.2, 5.115.2, and *Hellenica Oxyrhynchia*, 12.4–5. The anonymous Oxyrhynchus historian reminds us that the Boeotians carted off goods from Attic farms that the Athenians themselves had plundered from others.

15. 3.32; cf. 2.67.4. In one of the great understatements voiced during the war, some Samian envoys visited Alcidas when he harbored at Ephesus and remonstrated with him that his policy of executing innocents who were probably unwilling subjects of Athens "was not a very good way of freeing Greece." For the butchery of Alcidas and other examples of murdering during the Peloponnesian War, see Pritchett, *Greek State*, 5.212–15.

16. 3.34.2–4; 3.36. Behind the butchery of the two fleets was a larger strategic question. After four invasions of the Attic countryside and the loss of a quarter of the population to the plague, was there still the material strength and willpower to retain the empire—or could local oligarchs and a few Spartan ships cause widespread revolt that would soon stop money and food from entering the Piraeus?

17. See also Thucydides 2.6.2 and Diodorus 12.65.8–9; cf. 4.57, 5.84, 6.61. While there was always an immediate logic to terrorizing local populations and taking prominent suspects into custody, it is hard to fathom how the slaughter of any of these hostages led to the strategic advantage of either Sparta or Athens.

18. Xenophon, *Hellenica*, 2.1.30–32, 2.2.3–4. At war's end in 404 there was at least some cooling of barbarous passions, in the sense that the Spartans themselves did not engage in wholesale executions of the captured populations, nor did the Athenian democrats who returned to power within the year mete out death sentences to the failed oligarchs associated with the Thirty Tyrants. Cf. Plutarch, *Lysander*, 9.5–7 and Xenophon, *Hellenica*, 2.1.31–2; we are not quite sure whether the decision was to cut off hands (to prevent rowing entirely) or merely thumbs (to guarantee no captive could ever again wield the spear). Cf. also Hamel, *Athenian Generals*, 51–52.

19. 4.80. Cf. Diodorus 12.67.3–5, which relates that the most prominent Spartans were entrusted with the grisly business of liquidating the 2,000—and apparently in their own homes, no less. The tally of corpses is no guide to what captured the attention of ancient historians. Thus, the fate of these 2,000 helots merits a fraction of the narrative of the few hundred who died at Plataea or the long account of the 1,000 Mytilean rebels who were executed by Paches. See Cawkwell, *Thucydides*, 9. The mysterious massacre of somewhere between 4,000 and 5,000 Polish officers in April 1940 by the Soviets in the Katyn Forest near Smolensk was part of a larger bloodbath that saw the Soviets eventually murder over another 20,000 Poles, whom they'd captured after dividing up the country with Hitler in autumn 1939. The Russians blamed the Nazis for the atrocity—at first a seemingly credible charge, given that they shot the officers with German bullets—and did not accept responsibility until the Gorbachev era.

20. 4.48; Although it was far more difficult to kill thousands with iron-edged weapons, we should not thereby think it taxed the ingenuity of the Greeks—after all, a less sophisticated Aztec priestly caste may have murdered over 80,000 in a mere four days with obsidian blades, exceeding the daily carnage of industrial murder at Auschwitz centuries later. The Aztec king Ahuitzotl inaugurated the Great Temple to Huitzilopochtli in Tenochtitlán by using four convex stone tables and rotations of fresh executioners to kill some fourteen victims a minute for some ninety-six hours. Cf. Hanson, *Carnage and Culture*, 194–95.

21. For a variety of statistics relating to the practice of insurrection and the use of traitors by both sides, see Losada, *Fifth Column*, 16–29.

22. Athenian subject states were prone to revolt after the Sicilian disaster, and in

turn Spartans worried about their own allies after a series of reversals such as Sphacteria, Cyzicus, and Arginusae. A cynic might conclude that most Greeks had no strong political prejudices toward either democracy or moderate oligarchy but simply preferred to live under the political system that offered the greatest hope of peace and tranquillity, and thus made the appropriate corrections to match the ebb and flow of the war. For Thucydides' famous metaphor of war as a "harsh schoolmaster" (*biaios didaskalos*), see 3.82.2.

23. On the slogans of revolutions and the role of intervening outside powers, see, in general, 3.82, and especially Lintott, *Violence*, 94–103. The nature of the *mesoi* is discussed in Hanson, *Other Greeks*, 179–218. For the class alliances of the hoplites at Athens, see Hanson, "Hoplites into Democrats," 289–93.

24. See Plato, *Seventh Letter*, 322B–C. Part of the strange attraction of Athenian conservatives for Sparta was the notion that it embodied something like Athens' prior rural past before the advent of empire. Thus, it is natural that part of the Spartan demands at war's end was to force the Athenians to accept the "ancestral constitution" (*patrios politeia*) that had existed in the sixth century before the rise of the democracy. Cf. Aristotle, *Constitution of the Athenians*, 34.3, and Diodorus 14.3.2.

25. 3.36.4. See the long, depressing account at 3.25–50. Cleon's fingerprints seem to have been on a number of both audacious and bloodthirsty Athenian actions, from success on Sphacteria to failure at Amphipolis. Indeed, he may well have been behind the Athenian proposal in 430 to execute the Peloponnesian ambassadors captured in Thrace; cf. Gomme, *Commentary*, 2.201.

26. 3.75.3–5. The idea that there was now an enemy within remained constant throughout the rest of the war. In 411 the Athenian fleet off Samos was paralyzed for a time, unsure of the loyalty of crews after the political upheaval on the island (8.63.2).

27. 3.81.5. In the end, Corcyra remained an ally of Athens, and the thousands who died had no strategic effect on the outcome of the war. See a modern discussion by Price, *Thucydides*, 34–5, 274–77. The Spartan strategy in detaching from Athens important naval allies and subjects such as Mytilene and Corcyra was aimed at reducing the numerical superiority of the imperial fleet but also reflected that, for much of the first decade of the war, the Peloponnesians simply had no real idea of how to counter the military resources of Athens.

28. For surmises about numbers of those killed, see Lintott, *Violence*, 109; later violence on Corcyra and a long account of why stasis plagued the Greek world are discussed at Diodorus 13.48.

29. For the calamities on Chios and the executions at Samos, see 8.21, 8.24, 8.38, 8.40, 8.56, and 8.73–75. Chios, Lesbos, and Samos were among the most important subject states of the Athenian empire. The calamity on Sicily (wrongly) convinced them that, unlike earlier miscalculations during the plague years, Athens now really was weakened to such a degree as to be unable to patrol the Aegean with any real force.

30. Cf. 2.27.1–2, 5.1, 5.116 and Xenophon, *Hellenica*, 2.2.9. The war, of course, had begun with the effort to take Plataea, which upon surrender was cleansed of Plataeans and the land handed over to Boeotian opportunists.

31. For Sitacles' war with Macedonia: 2.98; Messana: 4.1, 4.24; Epidaurus: 5.54.3–4, 5.55.2–4; Carthaginians and Sicily: Diodorus 13.44–115.

32. 4.2.4. "If he wished" (*ên boulêtai*). Usually the Athenian assembly exercised ironclad control over their generals in the field, who understood that failure, as Thucydides himself could attest, meant exile at best, with a death sentence not all that uncommon. Demosthenes seems not to have been an elected general at the time of Pylos.

33. 4.28.5. See Kagan, *Archidamian War*, 322–33, for a proper appraisal of Cleon's military talents, which apparently were considerable despite the character assassination so prominent in both Thucydides' history and Aristophanes' early comedies. Cleon may have been one of the prominent demagogues responsible for Thucydides' exile during the Amphipolis campaign a few years later.

34. For Thucydides' various quotes, see 4.32.4, 4.34, 4.40.1–2. Thucydides often places great weight on morale and reputation. While the Pylos campaign made sense strategically (and should have led to even more helot defections), the real importance was more intangible, involving the ability of a successful power to transmit fear and win respect.

35. See Diodorus 11.72 (Sicily); Herodotus 5.31 (Naxos); Thucydides 8.40 (Chios) and 7.27.5 (the 20,000 Attic slaves that fled to Decelea). On the fall of Pylos in 409, see Diodorus 13.64.6.

36. For a sampling of Spartan paranoia, see 4.41.3, 4.55.1, 4.80.2–3, 4.108.7, 4.117.1–2, 5.14.3, 5.15.1, and 5.34.2. For the number of slaves involved in the fighting on both sides and their strategic importance during the war, see Hunt, *Slaves*, 56–101. Cf. Thucydides 4.41. Kagan, *Archidamian War*, 248–51, has a good analysis of how the psychological trauma of the Spartan loss translated into immediate Athenian strategic advantage.

37. 4.55.3–4. To fathom the Peloponnesian War it is crucial to understand that the capture of 120 Spartiates affected the Spartans as much as the plague and the Sicilian expedition (an aggregate 120,000 or so dead) did the Athenians.

Spartans were just as resolute as Athenians, but there were simply not many of their elite left when the war broke out in 431.

38. For Thucydides' observations about the effects of the new Athenian confidence in raiding, fortifying, and plundering the Peloponnese, cf. 4.45, 4.53, 4.55.3–4, and 4.80.1.

39. On Brasidas' various successes in northern Greece, see 4.85–87; 4.105, 4.110–13, and 4.120–35; many of these events are discussed later under sieges. For his career, see Cartledge, *Spartans*, 185–97. And for his corps of former helots, see Hunt, *Slaves*, 58–60, 116–17.

40. 3.114, 4.118, 5.18, 5.23, 5.77, and 5.79; cf. 8.18. Formal treaties inscribed on stone (as reported by historians)—as state documents rather than private narratives—are good indicators that once atypical conduct in war had now become enshrined as part of contemporary Hellenic custom and practice.

41. 5.84, 6.61, 8.65.2, 8.90. On Alcibiades' more nefarious schemes in general during the war, see Ellis, *Alcibiades*, 72–97, and Henderson, *Great War*, 291–97.

Chapter 5

1. Herodotus 7.9; Plutarch, *Pericles*, 33.4. Herodotus finished his Persian War histories perhaps in the first decade of the Peloponnesian War, at a time when the general course and duration of the conflict was still unclear. True, Pericles may well have actually said what Plutarch wrote; but the biographer compiled his biography in the Roman era almost five hundred years later, with knowledge of the Athenian hoplite disaster at Delium and the alliance's failure at Mantinea.

2. Xenophon, *Hellenica*, 1.1.33; Diodorus 13.72.3 From Diodorus' account the Spartans went to absurd lengths to draw the Athenians out from their walls by setting up a victory trophy in front of the Academy and challenging the Athenians to ease their humiliation by coming out and contesting the monument in open phalanx battle. But shame as a catalyst to battle had been discredited since 431.

3. 3.91. In some ways, such small successes misled the Athenians terribly about the quality of leadership needed for the Sicilian expedition of 415–413. The general Nicias had a fine record at Solygia and Tanagra, both brief, small amphibious operations of limited scope. The problem was that these mostly inconsequential victories were sometimes equated with strategic wisdom and thus served as models for future operations—with disastrous consequences, as Delium and Sicily both showed. By the same token, Demosthenes' own setbacks in Aetolia and Boeotia might have warned the Athenians that his

impetuousness did not always lead to triumphs like Amphilochia or Pylos—
and thus that he really was a questionable figure to lead the second armada
to save the first in Sicily.

4. Diodorus 12.69.2. Perhaps due to the modern fascination with special operations (as, for example, in the various Israeli counterinsurgency and rescue
missions) or the mystique of intelligence (as in the case of the ULTRA in-
tercepts of German intentions in World War II), we tend to see Demosthenes as a visionary who sought to avoid simplistic hoplite battles or
conventional sea fights. In fact, most of his campaigns were poorly thought
out, and when they went awry led not to stalemate but to retreat, if not abject defeat. See the sober assessment of Roisman, *General Demosthenes*, 73–74.

5. 5.14.1. We must be careful here in downplaying entirely the role of hoplite
battle based on the evidence of its relative infrequency during the war. Given
the clarity and hallowed tradition of such fighting, it retained a psychological importance that went well beyond the numbers who died in any one encounter. Had the Athenians won at Delium or their allies at Mantinea, in a
few hours they could quite literally have changed the course of the war. By
the same token, the key figures that did alter late-fifth-century and fourth-
century Greek history—Brasidas, Cleon, Lysander, Cleombrotus, Pelopidas,
and Epaminondas—all died in hoplite armor on the battlefield.

6. The battle is described at 4.93–96; cf. 5.72–73 for the battle of Mantinea.
Diodorus 12.69–71 adds some valuable details on Delium omitted by Thu-
cydides, such as the postwar establishment of a Delia, a commemorative
Theban festival funded by the spoils of the battle. For a modern account of
the engagement, see Hanson, *Ripples of Battle*, 171–243. For the details of the
Athenian objectives in the campaign, see Roisman, *General Demosthenes*, 33–41.

7. 4.96.3–6. Accidental killing would occur again during the Athenian night attack on the heights above Syracuse (7.44.1), but unfamiliarity with the rough
terrain and darkness explains most of the confusion. Here we are reminded
how dust, the density of formations, and the heavy infantry helmet could
impair vision—or was it also in part not the senses per se but the sheer panic
and fright of such close fighting that instead accounts for the irrational behavior? For the passages in ancient literature attesting to the common disorientation inherent in ancient hoplite battles, see Hanson, *Western Way of War*,
185–93.

8. See Thucydides 7.44.1, remarking on the disastrous night attack above Syracuse.

9. 1.15.2. Plato, *Republic*, 2.373E. On the historical importance of hoplite ideology, and scholarly controversy as to its origins and in Greek culture and so-

ciety, see the review of the arguments in Hanson, "Hoplite Battle," 230–32; cf. 213–15, 221. Occasional exceptions and alternatives to hoplite battle, which were usually lamented as such by the Greeks, are more likely to prove rather than refute the idea that the preferred and idealized way of settling disputes until the fifth century remained decisive fighting between phalanxes.

10. Aristotle, *Politics*, 4.1297b16; Herodotus, 9.7.2; cf. 1.82; Strabo, 10.1.12; Polybius, 13.3–6; Demosthenes, *Third Philippic*, 48–50. The changing attitudes toward hoplite warfare from the sixth to fourth centuries are reviewed, with discussion of ancient passages, in Hanson, *Other Greeks*, 321–49.

11. 1.106.2, 4.133.1–2, 4.40.2. "Best" and the "flower" are often the terms used by Thucydides to suggest that a dead hoplite, especially if killed by a semibarbarian, light-armed skirmisher, or someone poorer, was a far more grievous loss than a sailor, javelin thrower, or archer. For hoplite chauvinism, see Aristophanes, *Peace*, 1208–64, 1214–17, 1260–63, and Euripides, *Phoenician Women*, 1095–96.

12. 5.75.3. Thucydides implies not so much that the victory at Mantinea proved that the Spartans were always invincible in war or that their trust in the supremacy in hoplite battle was sound. Rather, he means that through the trauma they inflicted on other Greeks in such a visible way at Mantinea, they made the rest of Greece realize that their own previous setbacks were due to bad luck rather than a fatal lapse in the old Spartan courage—and that such popular conceptions were vital in winning a war in which hundreds of Greek city-states had no real discernible ideology other than ensuring that they ended up on the winning side.

13. "A thing of fear": Pindar, fragment 120.5; cf. Thucydides 5.70. Lazenby, *Spartan Army*, 42–44, 125–34, is exhaustive in his collation of ancient sources to support his reconstruction of the battle, one prompted by his own undeniable admiration for the men of the Spartan phalanx. For a philological discussion of Thucydides' battle description of Mantinea, see Gomme et al., *Commentary*, 5.89–130. There are imaginative illustrations of Spartan hoplites in Sekunda and Hook, *Spartan Army*, 33–44. See also Thucydides 6.16.6; cf. 5.74.1.

14. 4.126. In general, the Greeks had a variety of strange ideas about what constituted a "civilized" society and what in turn relegated a people to the loose category of "barbarians." Among the diverse criteria were things such as speaking fluent Greek; living in centralized autonomous city-states; farming trees, vines, and grain rather than herding; eating familiar Mediterranean foods (i.e., neither feasting on exotic animals nor drinking milk); and fighting as hoplites in the disciplined ranks of the phalanx.

15. For various passages illustrating the nature of Greek generalship, see 4.44.2, 4.101.2, 5.60.6, 5.74.3, 7.5.2–3, and 7.8.2. Cf. also Hanson, *Western Way of War,* 107–16. Hamel has a valuable discussion of the short leash given to Athenian commanders by a mercurial Athenian assembly: *Athenian Generals,* 44–74; on fatalities, see 204–09.

16. 4.93.4; 5.71.3. Most scholars see real tactical innovations in hoplite battle emerging only with the career of Epaminondas at Leuctra. For a different view that Greeks as early as the Peloponnesian War massed in depth beyond eight shields, sometimes used cavalry and reserves with hoplites, and in various contexts put their best troops on the left, see in general the summation of arguments in Hanson, "Epaminondas," 205–07.

17. Lysias, 14.7, 14.10–15; cf. Plato, *Republic,* 8.556D. Perhaps we see the social divide best in the careers of the aristocratic and mounted estate-owning Alcibiades and his poorer stone-mason mentor, Socrates, who fought on foot at two battles and a siege. For a long list of ancient passages that privilege hoplite over cavalry service, see Spence, *Cavalry,* 168–72.

18. 4.96.3–6; 7.44.7–8. It was worse than that: not only did some armies lack distinctive letters or insignia on their shields, but inasmuch as most phalanxes used about the same type of equipment, it was nearly impossible, even without the normal dust, to distinguish friend from foe by appearance.

19. 5.11, 5.74, 6.71.1; cf. 4.97.1, 4.134.2. Lest we think hoplite battle is a sidelight of Greek culture and marginal to the more heralded legacy of Hellenic civilization, we should remember that our modern "trophy" is simply a transliteration of *trophê* ("a turning")—the ceremonial spot where the enemy phalanx gave way and victory was thus assured.

20. 5.73.4. Perhaps the Spartan disdain for pursuit reflects not merely the practical difficulties of running in full armor after the defeated or the heralded Spartan restraint regarding killing in less than a fair fight but, rather, inborn Laconian arrogance: why chase the defeated when one can easily defeat them on any occasion should they foolishly attempt to hazard their luck again? In contrast, the Boeotians, for example, at Delium chased the Athenians for miles to the Oropus and over Mount Parnes—a retreat that quickly turned into a mythic collective nightmare for the next few decades.

21. The aftershocks of Delium are discussed in Hanson, *Ripples,* 199–212. For a Greek, at least before the later years of the Peloponnesian War, a man delighted or ruined his family not so much by dying as by doing so either heroically or shamefully. For the ridicule of Cleonymus at Delium, see Aristophanes, *Peace,* 446, 672, 1295; and cf. *Birds,* 289, 1475. For the noble *aspidephoros: Birds,* 1095–96.

22. Strauss offers conjectures about the total number of Athenian hoplite and thetic dead in the war (*Athens After*, 80–81). We have few reliable figures for how many Spartans died during the war but must keep in mind Thucydides' warning about Mantinea, that when dealing with Spartan disclosures about casualties "it is difficult to know the truth" (5.74.3; cf. 5.68.2). For the percentages of those killed in hoplite battle, see the study by Krentz, "Casualties."

23. 6.17.5–6. Alcibiades also claimed that states had trouble getting hoplites—implying that they wanted such assets but found the old agrarian classes who made up the ranks of the phalanx too few and far between in a new-style war that ranged from Sicily to Asia Minor. I am not so sure he is correct; in the war's aftermath there were plenty of hoplite mercenaries to join the Ten Thousand in Asia Minor, most from Arcadia and Achaea, areas mostly untouched by the war, while hardly any came from Attica, which had been ravaged extensively; cf. Garlan, *War*, 102–03.

24. See Plato, *Laws*, 4.707C–E. For "moronic," cf. 5.41.2. George S. Patton was said to have wished to fight Rommel tank to tank, his Sherman against the panzer leader's Panther. And in the heated rhetoric leading up to the Iraq War of spring 2003, Saddam Hussein was reported to have challenged George W. Bush to a personal duel to decide the fate of his Baathist regime.

25. 1.141.5. Whereas the Athenian land army would have met defeat in any battle with the Spartan phalanx, it is still not clear whether such a significant home force of 30,000 infantrymen was all that outnumbered or outmanned by the Peloponnesian forces during the later annual invasions.

26. 4.34.1. We receive some of the idea of the psychological element central to hoplite battle when Thucydides here remarks that the Athenians "were suffering greatly" from the very thought of fighting Spartans.

27. Eighty-three battles: Paul, "Two Battles," 308. There is a plethora of evidence in Thucydides on the pivotal role of skirmishers and light-armed troops and the vulnerability of hoplites to such forces. In general, see the surprising variety of scenarios where light-armed troops were used effectively: 2.29.5, 2.31.2–3, 2.79.4, 2.100, 3.1.2, 3.98, 3.107–08, 4.34.1–2, 4.44.1, 4.123.4, 5.10.9, 6.21, 6.70.2–3, 7.4.6, 7.6.2–3, 7.81–82.

28. 4.40.2, 4.73.2–4. It is not clear whether by the time of the outbreak of the war the soldiers of the phalanx were still largely farmers, who as in the past had earned such prestigious hoplite service by owning enough land (about ten acres) to meet the requisite census rubric, or those who now had enough money to buy the arms and armor, or the poorer who were simply drafted and armed by the state.

29. Untraditional battle: 5.56.4–5; Aristophanes, *Clouds*, 987–90; cf. Plato, *Laws*,

4.706A–B. Symmetrical warfare—fighting in similar fashions and landscapes between two evenly matched powers—can, of course, lead to atrocious casualties if both sides follow the deadly protocols of Western warfare. Wars from the Roman Civil Wars to Verdun prove that well enough.

30. 4.42–44. Indeed, a symptom of the malaise of Greek society during the Peloponnesian War was the steady erosion in the treatment of the dead, brought about by the sheer frequency of killing and dying, and the growing hatred between Greeks, as we see from the rotting bodies at plague-ridden Athens, the exposure of corpses after Delium, the abandonment of those wounded and the remains of the killed amid the waves after Arginusae, and the apparently common practice of throwing captured crews overboard on the high seas. See, for example, Pritchett, *Greek State*, 4.235–41.

31. See 4.134 and 3.91. Thucydides' genius was that he saw that all of the Greeks' secondary fighting for some three decades was in some way caught up with the Spartan-Athenian death struggle, tangential though these border skirmishes might have been to the larger outcome of that war.

32. 5.10–12. On the rare *parataxis* of the Peloponnesian War, see Pritchett, *Greek State*, 4.45–51.

33. 4.55.4, 4.56.1. We are not sure whether Thucydides made these characteristically sweeping appraisals as events transpired or inserted such summations in his final draft after the war was completed and with the benefit of hindsight. That ambiguity may explain his peculiar redundancy in announcing a series of critical turning points—the plague, Mantinea, Sphacteria, Sicily—that all supposedly changed the course of the war, but then failing to distinguish which of these, in fact, were the more important of the landmark events.

34. On Agis' army, see 5.60.3. For Thucydides' various pronouncements about the importance of Argos' new independent stance and the ultimate significance of Mantinea, see 5.29.1–3, 5.66.2–3; cf. 1.141.2.

35. See, for example, 5.71–72; Xenophon, *Constitution of the Lacedaemonians*, 11; Herodotus 9.53–55; Plutarch, *Moralia*, 241F.

36. For inscriptions that may record the dead from the 418 battle, see the arguments in Pritchett, *Topography*, 2.50–52; cf. also his *War*, 4.143–44; his identification of the Mantinean dead of 418 with the inscription remains tentative.

37. Again, see 5.68.2; cf. 5.74.2. Mantinea was Thucydides' model battle, and from it we are to surmise what the fighting was probably like earlier at Delium and Solygia, or later at Syracuse as well. For an analysis of the fighting, see J. Lazenby, *Spartan Army*, 125–34, and *Peloponnesian War*, 121–29. Lazenby's careful reconstruction is augmented by Kagan, *Peace*, 107–35; Grote, *Greece*, 7.75–93; and Gomme, *Commentary*, 3.89–127.

38. Diodorus 12.79.6. There is some disagreement over this notion of "collu-

sion." Kagan, *Peace*, 131–33, has a brief discussion of Spartan motivations. For the larger question of to what degree armies predicated their tactics on the precise nature of the enemy across the battle line, see Hanson, "Hoplite Obliteration," 206–07, for instances in Greek history where hoplite armies seem to be especially cognizant of the quality of troops directly opposite them on the battlefield—and sometimes made critical political decisions in response.

39. On the Thespians' postbellum fate, cf. 4.133 and Hanson, "Hoplite Obliteration," 208–14.

40. 6.69–71. The nature of the Syracusan campaign reflects the logistical problems with hoplite warfare once it was asked to transcend the three-day-march radius of normal operations. To transport an army of some 5,100 hoplites—about the number in the first armada sent to Sicily—not only were a large number of ships needed but accommodations had to be made for some two hundred tons of bronze, iron, and wooden panoplies along with personal servants to carry such appurtenances. Thus, even if the hoplites could double as rowers—and more often they did not, but rather were auxiliary marines in numbers ranging from 10 to 30 per ship—a fleet of perhaps some 60 ships was needed to transport soldiers, servants, and equipment.

Chapter 6

1. The siege is infamous largely because of Thucydides' lengthy description of the four-year ordeal (2.3–4, 2.71–78, 3.20–24, 3.52–53, 3.68). Certainly, there were other, much larger states that were sacked or captured during the war—Potidaea, Mytilene, Melos—about whose death throes we learn little. Plataea's proximity to Athens and the assault's role in starting the conflagration gave it an importance not commensurate with its small size or strategic worth. In addition, because it was the first siege of the war, and a complex one at that, Thucydides uses it as a template of sorts that allows abbreviated mention of later assaults in his history. In general, cf. Hornblower, *Commentary*, 1.236–42; Kern, *Siege Warfare*, 97–108.

2. See Pritchett, *Greek State*, 5.218–19, for a list of such mini-holocausts, which suggests the greater frequency of sieges that explains the rise of mass killing.

3. 3.68.4. But nothing was quite "the end" when it was a matter of the internecine fighting of the Greek city-states. Plataea was resettled after the war—and renewed its time-honored hatred of the Thebans.

4. Thucydides (1.11) believed that the earlier Greeks simply lacked the capital to carry on sieges of any magnitude. In addition, before the rise of maritime

powers like Corinth, Athens, and Syracuse, most city-states were agrarian in nature, their citizens farmers who could ill afford months away from their crops to invade or besiege a foreign city.

5. 1.102.2. See Herodotus 9.70.2 and 9.102.2–4, for the idea that the Athenians' reputation for skill in taking fortifications predated the Persian War. Athenian democrats saw no problem in helping Spartans put down restive helots—an enslaved people whose liberation would have to wait for the great emancipator Epaminondas and his famous invasion of 369.

6. 5.91.1–2, 5.111.1–2. The key qualifier here was "due to the fear." In fact, the Athenians abandoned a disastrous siege in Egypt in 454, and a few months after this exchange with the Melians would suffer mayhem in Sicily—but only after sustaining horrendous losses before quitting.

7. 4.51; cf. 4.133. Walls seem to have induced a fear at Athens as much as the chimera of weapons of mass destruction did to the American government after September 11.

8. 1.29.5; 1.98.4. For a narrative of these brutal sieges, see Meiggs, *Athenian Empire*, 68–174. We sometimes forget that while Aeschylus and Sophocles presented their tragedies and Pericles began to envision a majestic Acropolis, the Athenian empire grew through the bloody subjugation of autonomous states that by their dogged resistance apparently wanted little part of such a renaissance. For most Greek communities local autonomy could be a more powerful desire than even enforced democracy.

9. Aristotle, *Politics*, 1255A; cf. Xenophon, *Cyropaedia*, 7.5.73, and Euripides, *Hecuba*, 808–12. We do not know how most were reduced to slave status in the Greek world, but other than being born to servile parents or falling victim to kidnapping, the aftermath of sieges seems to have been the most common avenue of enslavement.

10. Xenophon, *Hellenica*, 1.6.12–15. Within a decade after Athens' defeat, the Athenians began to grow more hostile to Thebes than to Sparta. Athenians and Spartans later served side by side as mercenaries in the march with Cyrus the Younger (401), and joined to fight Epaminondas at the second battle of Mantinea (362).

11. On enslavement, see Pritchett, *Greek State*, 5.227–30. Most often we are told that "all" or "not a few" were enslaved, rather than given specific figures.

12. 4.115.1–3, 4.116.1–2; cf. 5.83.2. Brasidas is clearly one of Thucydides' favorites, given the former's brilliant strategy to hit the Athenian empire far to the north, and to do so largely with land forces acting independently, far from home, and without supply lines, in a manner reminiscent of the 1864–65 long marches of William Tecumseh Sherman through Georgia and the Carolinas,

where he likewise lived off the land and sought to bring the war home behind traditional lines.

13. On the fate of the generals, see Hamel, *Athenian Generals*, 43–44. Usually, the assembly exercised almost complete control of the conduct of armies in the field, any independent-thinking generals knowing quite well that at the end of the campaign they would have to face a moody Athenian citizenry that through a simple majority vote might well exile, fine, or execute any commanders whom they felt to have been nonaggressive.

14. 5.111.1, 5.113.1; cf. Grote, *Greece*, 7.114. In one of the great ironies in Thucydides' history, the Athenians are made to mock the Melians' solace in "hope" ("hope—danger's comforter," 5.103.1)—that perhaps succor might still come yet from Sparta. Yet less than three years later Nicias would offer an almost identical Melian argument to his own trapped and about to be extinguished army of some 40,000, reminding them not to quit but to remember that "it is necessary to have hope." Cf. 7.77.1.

15. Euripides, *Hecuba*, 132–33, 454–57; *Trojan Women*, 95–98; *Phoenician Women*, 1195, 884; cf. 882. To the degree that we can detect a consistent ideology about the war, it is more likely that Euripides objected to the needless slaughter of civilians and neutrals, which, in his view, could only weaken the Athenian effort to win Hellenic "hearts and minds."

16. Xenophon, *Hellenica*, 2.2.3–4; cf. *Hellenica*, 2.1.15. What saved the Athenians from suffering the fate that they had so often meted out to others? Perhaps three considerations: Athens was an enormous city of some 100,000 urban residents with a preeminent reputation for cultural achievement; a right-wing cabal was in the process of creating a government sympathetic to Sparta; and the Spartans themselves were already growing suspicious of their onetime allies the Thebans, who had suffered and contributed relatively little during the war, argued over the booty collected from Attica, and were soon to challenge Sparta itself for the hegemony of Greece.

17. 7.29.4–5. In Thucydides' narrative the fact that the peltasts are Thracian is presented to explain their brutality and gratuitous killing of animals and children; but given the random slaughter of civilians at Corcyra, it is hard to see how the Thracians were any more callous or cowardly than the Greeks on occasion.

18. Cannibalism: 2.70.1. Centuries later, during Sulla's siege of Athens (87–86), cannibalism was reported to be widespread; when his legionaries entered the city they found preparations of human flesh in many of the kitchens (Appian, *Mithridatic War*, 38).

19. On various forms of bloodletting, see 2.5.7, 2.67.4, 3.32.1, 3.50, 3.81,2, 4.57.3–4,

4.80, 5.83.2, 5.116, 7.29.5, 8.21, 8.38.3, and Xenophon, *Hellenica*, 1.6.19–20. Compare these slaughters with the two hoplite battles of Delium and Mantinea to appreciate either how war itself had changed or that the Peloponnesian "War" was not so much an interstate conflict as a messy civil war between landed pro-Spartan oligarchs and poorer pro-Athenian democrats. For captives, see Pritchett, *War*, 1.78–79. His figures include only those instances where a specific number of prisoners is provided; the real tally was far higher.

20. Aeneas Tacticus, 1.1.2. Aeneas wrote in the mid-fourth century at a time when city-states sought to invest in fortifications as never before—perhaps in response to the carnage of the Peloponnesian War. While the technology of hoplite battle continued to remain static after 404, the arts of siegecraft—artillery, rams, masonry, and architecture—were transformed and refined following the fall of Athens.

21. Minoa: 3.51; Lecythus: 4.115.3. It is hard to know whether innovative siege techniques—the mound at Plataea, the tower at Lecythus, or the fire cannon at Delium—were ad hoc affairs or reflections of incipient breakthroughs in the art of siegecraft. For the difficulty of old-style hoplites mounting ramparts, see Ober, "Hoplites," 180–88.

22. Samos: Diodorus 12.28; Plutarch, *Pericles*, 27; cf. 7.43.1. For the elaborate preparations at Potidaea and the machines, see Diodorus 12.45. "Rams" is a vague term; it could cover anything from ad hoc timber and ropes to sophisticated metal-plated sheds on wheels that protected bronze-tipped rams.

23. 4.88.1. Why did Acanthus surrender on the arrival of enemy ravagers when, for example, Athens did not? From Thucydides' description it seems that Acanthus was entirely dependent on income from its vintage, and may well have had little grain stored, much less a protected port and superiority at sea, which could ensure a steady supply of imported food.

24. See Ducrey, *Warfare*, 166–68. The great exception, of course, was Syracuse, which was neither stormed nor handed over through negotiations—the one great failure that destroyed the supposed vaunted reputation of Athenian siege engineers.

25. Spartan claims about the need for an unwalled Greece: 1.90.2, 1.91.7.

26. Plato, *Laws*, 778D–779A. For the general philosophical sentiment against walls, see Ober, *Fortress Attica*, 50–63, which notes a difference in attitudes emerging during the post–Peloponnesian War fourth century, when the populace no longer believed that either urban fortifications or the martial prowess of their armies were sufficient to protect the entire citizenry. Cf. Thucydides 1.5.1 on the unfortified nature of the early Greek city-state; and for a history of the rise of wall building among the Greek city-states in the

aftermath of the Persian Wars, see Winter, *Greek Fortifications*, 300–08. For the Athenian promotion of fortifications at Argos and Patras cf. 5.82.

27. After the calamity of 413, about the only other city that Athens sought to besiege was Chios, where a civil war threatened to lead to mass rebellion in the empire (e.g., 8.55–56).

Chapter 7

1. The various reasons why the Athenians thought it necessary to go to Sicily —treaties, empire, pride, profit, and advantage against Sparta—are discussed by both Thucydides (6.15–18) and Plutarch (*Nicias*, 12.4). Thucydides has Alcibiades provide the Athenians with a variety of antebellum reasons to sail, and then ex post facto explain to the Spartans the true Athenian intent of the expeditions, leaving us in somewhat of a quandary as to when, where —and if—Alcibiades was telling the truth.

2. 8.2.1. The expedition of 427: 3.86.4. Opportunistic neutrals were also wrong in their predictions that Athens would shortly capitulate after the debacle on Sicily. As a general rule throughout the war, observers usually overestimated Athenian power in the wake of its successes and underrated its resiliency after abject defeats, failing to understand that Athens was by far the most powerful polis, and yet not so strong in and of itself to master or even unite the other fifteen hundred states of the Greek world.

3. For grain and the strategy to go to Sicily, see Diodorus 12.54.23. Peter Green's account of the invasion is predicated on the idea that food was the primary motive for the Athenian invasion; see *Armada*, 16–19. True, his book was written prior to more sophisticated comparative studies of the food-producing capacity of Attica, which tend to downplay the poverty of Athenian domestic grain resources. But Green pays close attention to our literary sources and is right in arguing that at least the Greeks themselves felt that Attica needed imported food and that Sicily was a good place to get it. On the idea of stopping potential Sicilian aid to the Peloponnesians, cf. 6.6.2 and 6.10.4.

4. 6.91.3–4. As in all of Alcibiades' reported speeches, the problem is not just that he distorted facts and analyses for his own personal interest but that so often his assessments were nevertheless astute, if for entirely different reasons from those he intended. After all, after Athens was defeated on Sicily, the security of the Peloponnese was remarkably enhanced and that of Athens herself almost irreparably harmed. Thucydides said that "the truest pretext" was the Athenian desire to add all of Sicily to its empire (e.g., 6.6.1).

5. Kagan, *Peace*, 159–91, reviews the various pretexts for the invasion. Thucydides' particulars of the great debate to go to Sicily are found variously at

6.8–25. Until Thucydides grasped that the Sicilian campaign and what followed was a continuum from the Archidamian War, most contemporary Greeks may well have seen them as two separate wars: an initial conflict with Sparta that ended in stalemate in 421, and then an entirely separate Sicilian War that broke out in 415 and ended in Athens' defeat by Syracuse two years later—which led to a second, distinct round of the old hostilities with Sparta that dragged on until 404–403, until the ultimate defeat and occupation of Athens. Athens' finances: Andocides 3.8; Thucydides 6.26.2.

6. 7.55.2, 8.1.4, 8.96.5. Most inhabitants of Sicily were Greek speakers from the time of the colonizing movements of centuries earlier. For the logic of Athens defending the poor abroad, see Xenophon, *Constitution of the Athenians*, 3.10–12. See also Thucydides' equally well-known encomia to the resiliency of Athens in the face of overwhelming odds at 2.65 and 7.27–28. On these inherent advantages of ancient democracies at war, cf. Hanson, "Democratic Warfare," 24–26; *Carnage and Culture*, 27–59.

7. 6.43–44. Diodorus (13.2.5) gives even higher numbers. If we think that 10,000 Athenian hoplites and perhaps as many as 600 cavalry marched out yearly (or perhaps even twice annually) to plunder and ravage Megarid (and yet could not take the nearby city), it is difficult to believe that not more than 5,000 hoplites, essentially without mounted escort, could do much against a city and its countryside with a resident population of about 250,000 and with numerous allies and subject states spanning a far distant island of some 10,000 square miles.

8. For the importance of presenting an image of strength upon arrival, see variously 6.11.4, 6.18, and 6.44.8–9. If Alcibiades thought political alliances with Sicilian states might defeat Syracuse, and Nicias counted on betrayal and treachery to deliver Syracuse, Lamachus at least grasped that only hard, prompt fighting could win the war.

9. See 2.79. There is a sort of hoplite mania in the speeches leading up to the voyage: Alcibiades claims that the Syracusan rabble are hardly the sort of people who can field an army of hoplites (6.17.4–5). In turn, Nicias, although giving passing mention to the light-armed, missile, and mounted troops that must counteract Syracusan cavalry, harps that "it seems to me that it is necessary for us to take along lots of hoplites, both our own and those of the allies, and in addition any we are able to get from the Peloponnese either through pay or persuasion" (6.21.2). Yet hoplites would play almost no role in preventing Athenian defeat or ensuring Syracusan victory—in fact, after 418 they would be irrelevant in deciding the Peloponnesian War.

10. Diodorus 13.7.5–6. Both the ease with which the Athenians had defeated the

hoplite army of Syracuse and their abject failure to follow up the victory made a profound impression on the generals, who belatedly realized that they had sorely miscalculated the type of forces necessary to take the city.

11. For the details of the campaign, see 6.64–82. Cf. Polyaenus, *Stratagems*, 1.39.2, on horse traps. Despite the rout and flight, only 260 Syracusans were killed, a fraction of the city's available forces. "The cavalrymen of the Syracusans, being numerous and undefeated in the battle, checked them—and if they spied any of the hoplites running ahead in pursuit they fell upon them and drove them away" (6.70.3).

12. Note that Alcibiades' tale of his proposed combined land and sea operations against the Peloponnesians actually offered Athens the only real hope of defeating Sparta—an irony when such an insightful strategy seems to have been aired only to enemies and under circumstances of dubious veracity. On purported Athenian imperial ambitions, see 6.90. Cf. Plutarch, *Pericles*, 20.3–4, for the idea that the Athenians wished to expand their empire to include Egypt as well.

13. 6.95–98. Diodorus claimed that they were able to assemble 800 horsemen. Because of the poor state of Greek siegecraft, both Alcibiades before his recall and Nicias more likely expected to take Syracuse through a variety of political machinations and intrigue, when the best hope was always to have sailed directly to Syracuse and either defeated a reckless enemy in a massive hoplite battle or begun immediate circumvallation by land and blockade by sea—as was more or less advanced by Lamachus on arrival in summer 415.

14. Syracusan despair: 6.103.3. The entire idea of sending thousands of precious sailors and infantrymen abroad while thousands of enemies invaded Attica underscores the irony of the Sicilian expedition. By the same token, disease played a pivotal role in the campaign, but mostly by enervating the Athenians, who had unwisely encamped in the low-lying marshes around the harbor. The relative vulnerability of Syracuse to circumvallation and maritime blockade, coupled with an unhealthy climate in much of its environs, made it susceptible to plague during a time of siege. But lethal disease struck not in 414, during the Athenian siege, but in 406, when the Carthaginians sought to cut off the city—and it had the desirable effect of sending the invaders back to North Africa with thousands dead rather than reducing the city (Diodorus 13.114).

15. One of the keys to the Spartans' successful siege of Plataea was that well before building their elaborate double wall of circumvallation, they had first constructed a rough ad hoc rampart around the city, to start the clock of famine and isolation as soon as possible. Had the Athenians upon arrival

thrown up a makeshift wall, and then gradually replaced it with a permanent double rampart, Syracuse might have been near capitulation by spring of the next year. But such audacity required a confident general and horsemen to ward off mounted counterattacks. Cf. 5.28 for Spartan depression on the eve of the peace of 421, and for the peace in general, see Lazenby, *Peloponnesian War*, 106–10.

16. 7.2.4. During the subsequent brutal tyranny of Dionysius I (405–367), the entire upper city was brought into the city's fortification to prevent just the type of siege that the Athenians had attempted in 414. For Titus' siege of Jerusalem (seventeen days spent on earthen work, three days to wall around the city), see Josephus, *Jewish War*, 5.502, 509; cf. 5.46.

17. A cynic might read the sudden desire of Greek states—on Sicily, the mainland, and among the islands—to help Syracuse as confirmation of sorts that many nations can entertain little ideology other than ending up on the winning side; cf. 7.18, 19, 21 for a list of the new diverse allies of a Syracuse on the rebound.

18. See the historian's famous remarks at 7.42, where he states that the Syracusans were "stunned" at the appearance of Demosthenes' relief forces, wondering "whether there would ever be any relief from their danger"—inasmuch as "despite the fortification of Decelea, an army, equal or almost equal to the first one, had now reinforced it, and that the power of Athens seemed to be considerable in almost every place." Earlier he concluded that despite the antebellum prognosis that Athens would not last more than three years, they had not only held their own against the Peloponnesians for seventeen but had now undertaken a distant additional conflict in no way inferior to the first. In Thucydides' judgment all this was nearly unfathomable; cf. 7.27.

19. 7.44.1. Even during the Peloponnesian War, the Greeks rarely fought at night—except to make an approach on a city's walls in hopes of finding the ramparts unguarded, as happened in the Theban assault on Plataea and a later attempt from Decelea by King Agis to catch the Athenians napping (Diodorus 13.72–73).

20. 7.69–73. Or as Diodorus reports the Athenians exclaiming, "Do you think we can return home by land?"

21. 7.87.6; cf. Diodorus, 13.19.2, 13.21.1, and 13.30.3–7, for discussion over the fate of the captives, and for the figure of 18,000 killed at the Assinarus and 7,000 captured, in total more than 40,000 lost in all who were sent to Sicily. For controversy over the number who actually perished in the last days of the campaign, see Gomme et al., *Commentary*, 4.452; Green, *Armada*, 352–53, and

340–44, for a few names of the dead. A decade later a speaker in the Athenian assembly could brag that as a cavalryman he had persisted in raids on the Syracusans from Catana, and gathered plunder to ransom prisoners from the quarries; cf. Lysias 20.24. By way of modern analogy, in 1955 there were still 2,000 German prisoners in Soviet hands—out of an original 120,000 captives—who had survived the Stalingrad disaster, and who were released twelve years after the battle through the intervention of Chancellor Konrad Adenauer's visit to Moscow. Cf. Antony Beevor, *Stalingrad*, 430–31.

22. From both vase paintings and literary evidence we know quite a lot above the nature of both ancient riders and their mounts. For the pragmatics of classical Greek cavalry and horses, see the relevant discussions in four recent standard works: I. Spence, *Cavalry*, 35–120; Gaebel, *Cavalry Operations*, 19–31; Bugh, *Horsemen*, 20–35; Worley, *Hippeis*, 83–122.

23. Perhaps the Greek disdain for horses was best exemplified by the defiant quip made by Xenophon (who wrote handbooks on the proper command of cavalry and the art of horsemanship) that unlike infantrymen, mounted troops had to fear falling as well as fighting enemy hoplites (*Anabasis*, 3.2.19). In fact, there is an entire corpus of passages in Greek literature that reflect the chauvinism of the hoplite in regards to the horseman. Cf. Hanson, *Other Greeks*, 247–48.

24. A great deal of research has emphasized the uneconomical nature of horse raising. See especially the arguments of Sallares, *Ecology*, 311: "The useless animal par excellence in ancient Greece was the horse."

25. The costs for buying and maintaining horses are known mostly from inscriptions on stone from Athens, and discussed in association with surviving literary evidence by Spence, *Cavalry*, 272–86.

26. The central theme of Hanson, *Other Greeks* (cf. especially 179–218), is the importance of this new agrarian class that created the institutions of the city-state, many of which were challenged by radical Athenian democracy of the fifth and fourth centuries. For the effect of Athenian literature, art, and rhetoric elevating the hoplite over light-armed fighters, missile troops, and horsemen, see Pritchard, "The Fractured Imagery," 44–49; Hanson, "Hoplites into Democrats," 289–310; and Lissarrague, "World of the Warrior," 39–45.

27. The wealthy Athenian Mantitheos, for example, boasted that in an early-fourth-century battle he faced danger as a hoplite rather than serve "in safety" as a horseman (Lysias 16.13). References to the disdain for horsemen are found at Plato, *Symposium*, 221b, and Aristophanes, *Knights*, 1369–71. Mantitheos knew well the general prejudice against cavalrymen—made worse by a perception that aristocratic, pro-Spartan knights had played an instrumental role in the failed revolutions of both 411 and 404, which sought to replace

the democracy with oligarchies of varying degrees. See Bugh, *Horsemen*, 116–53.

28. Much is made of the cavalry breakthroughs of Philip and Alexander, who formed corps of lancers whose long spears, along with armor for both horse and rider, made them true shock forces. But we forget that only at the battle of Chaeronea (338) did the Macedonians face a uniform hoplite enemy, and won there largely due not just to greater shock but to Athenian lack of discipline that opened gaps in the Greek line. Otherwise Alexander's horsemen battered mounted Persians or inferior infantry that lacked the Greek bronze panoply, closed ranks, and serried spears. After Alexander's death, the Hellenistic craze for elephants arose in part from a need to break apart the columns of phalangites that still were mostly invulnerable to charges of even heavy cavalry.

29. 4.68.5; cf. 4.72.3. For the extent of Athenian cavalry operations, see Bugh, *Horsemen*, 79–119; his catalog of deployments during the war demonstrates a frequency of usage unmatched by hoplites.

30. 4.42.1 to 4.44.1. The critical role of the Athenian horsemen at the battle, and the dramatic nature of their appearance by maritime transport, quickly became a source of Athenian pride. Cf., e.g., Aristophanes, *Knights*, 565–80, 595–610.

31. 5.73.1, 4.95.2; cf. 4.89. The alarmist logic of Hippocrates is puzzling, inasmuch as the year before, the Athenians had taken the Spartan captives from Sphacteria and threatened to kill them all should Sparta ever again invade. And between 425 and the construction of Decelea in 413 there was no Spartan invasion at all—despite the Spartans' ability to call on the Boeotian cavalry at almost any time they wished.

32. See the gory account in Diodorus (13.44–115), a native of Sicily, of the unsuccessful Carthaginian operations between 410 and 405 to take the island, an especially brutal conflict that may have cost more lives than were lost in the main theaters of the contemporaneous Peloponnesian War, and in part explains why the victorious Syracusans in 413 were in no position to aid Sparta in finishing off Athens.

33. For the confusing array of postbellum events, see Finley, *Sicily*, 68–73, and especially Lintott, *Violence*, 191–96. The amazing effort in creating fortifications on Syracuse is told by Diodorus 14.18.1–6.

34. For the famous assessment of Thucydides, see 2.65.11, which most scholars believe was one of his latest in the history and written in light of the end of the war. See Hornblower, *Commentary*, 1.347–48, and Gomme, *Commentary*, I.194–96.

35. Cf. Gaebel, *Cavalry Operations*, 100–09. The cardinal rule of Greek warfare—

cavalry could never charge the unbroken spears of the hoplite phalanx—remained unchallenged. But the Peloponnesian War proved that Greek fighting need not any longer be decided solely in small enclosed plains, between neighbors no more than a two- or three-day march away.

Chapter 8

1. See Diodorus 13.37–8, and the famous description in Thucydides (8.2) of the city-states of the entire Greek world stirring at the news, preparing to shed their neutrality and actively support the Spartan cause, with the subjects of the Athenian empire ready to revolt "beyond their ability" to do so.

2. Aristophanes, *Frogs*, 1074. Comedy and literature in general attest to blistered hands and rumps, exhausted crews, dire thirst and cold, all suggesting that trireme service was as unpleasant as it was dangerous. See Morrison, *Oared Warships*, 324–40, for the difficulties of the crew and the calculus of trireme oarage.

3. For crews, see Xenophon, *Hellenica*, 1.6.16. Given the apparent uniformity of the ranks of the phalanx and rowers in a trireme, it is hard to tell whether ancient commanders went through their call-up rosters to find hoplites or oarsmen with exceptional records of excellence. In preparation for Sicily, Thucydides says that the trierarchs gave bounties to the thranite rowers, and the generals tried to cull through the hoplite rosters to find the best oarsmen (6.31.3).

4. There is a fine description, replete with ancient references, to a trireme's striking appearance in Amit, *Athens and the Sea*, 12–13; cf. Toor, *Ancient Ships*, 66–69. On the magnificent return of the Athenian fleet in 408, see Diodorus 13.68.2–5.

5. On the sights, sounds, and impressions of contemporary triremes, see ancient observations at Xenophon, *Oeconomicus*, 8.8; Aristophanes, *Knights*, 546; Aristotle, *History of Animals*, 4.8.533B6; and Thucydides 4.10.5.

6. In theory, sailors could hear as well as infantrymen; apparently the roar of oars hitting the water would have been no more noisy than the clattering of hoplite bronze and wood as thousands marched forward. For the war cry and other songs, see Aristophanes, *Frogs*, 1073; cf. *Wasps*, 909. Cf. Thucydides 1.50.5; Diodorus 13.15.31 and 99.1; and Pritchett, *Greek States*, 1.105–08.

7. 2.89.9. Far more important than numbers per se was seamanship. In most battles victory hinged on the ability of triremes to launch quickly, get into close formation and stay there in the face of variable winds, and ram enemies heading their way.

8. Ships getting rammed: Diodorus 13.16.1–5; one hit sinking a trireme: Diodorus 13.98.3; importance of formation: Thucydides 4.13.4; stone throwing in sea battles: Diodorus 13.10.4–6; cf. Thucydides 2.92.3–4. In general, we have more graphic accounts of sea fighting than hoplite warfare. But then the former was far more common than the latter in the Peloponnesian War. And perhaps there was something about the added danger of drowning and the more frequent horror of unrecovered bodies that incited a morbid curiosity among observers.

9. 2.92.3–4. The most notable military figures in the war—Pericles, Thucydides, Demosthenes, Nicias, Lysander—at one time or another found themselves at sea in command of a fleet. Ostensibly, there was not much divide between land and naval service: Pericles both organized a seaborne attack on the coast of the Peloponnese and invaded Megara with hoplites. Lysander, the architect of the final successful Spartan naval strategy, died at Haliartus in a hoplite skirmish nine years after the war's close.

10. 1.49. Thucydides' full description of the sea fight goes on to chronicle the familiar confusion and killing of sailors in the water.

11. For various accounts of trireme fighting, see the descriptions in Thucydides at 7.23.3, 7.40.5, and 7.67.2. For problems with the current, see Diodorus 13.39–40. We should remember that the historian was both a sailor and, as an admiral, a firsthand observer of trireme warfare.

12. Xenophon, *Hellenica*, 1.6.19–20. The ships could be propelled in some fashion by half the crew. In fact, it is uncertain to what degree all 170 rowers always manned a trireme, or the tactical calculus involved in preferring fewer fully manned triremes to more numerous (and slower, less maneuverable) ships with partial crews.

13. The desperate fighting in the harbor at Syracuse is the *locus classicus* of naval warfare, inasmuch as Thucydides' account captures the desperation of the Athenians and emphasizes the enormous aggregate size of the two fleets, cf. 7.25, 7.41.3–4.

14. See 7.41.2; Aristophanes, *Knights*, 764; Diodorus 13.78.4. The tactics are the maritime equivalent of the besieged Plataeans' efforts to drop weights on the battering rams of the Peloponnesians.

15. For various aspects of trireme fighting, see 2.90.6 and 8.105.1; cf. 1.50.2 and 7.23.4. On the numbers of crewmen who went down with their ships, see the rare details of the Spartan losses at Mount Athos provided by Diodorus 13.41.2–3. On Notium, see Diodorus 13.71.3–5, and for the massive losses at Arginusae, 13.100.3–5. Reinforcements: Diodorus 13.46.

16. Aristotle, *Constitution of the Athenians*, 34.1; cf. Xenophon, *Hellenica*, 1.7.35. The

Thebans' refusal to give back the 1,000 dead hoplites after Delium—they lay exposed for days in the autumn sun—similarly sparked outrage and may have prompted Euripides to produce his *Suppliant Women*, a tragedy in which Athens under the mythological Theseus defeats the Thebans for their outrageous treatment of the corpses of the Seven Against Thebes. See Hanson, *Ripples*, 187–88.

17. Xenophon, *Hellenica*, 2.1.31–2. Plutarch (*Alcibiades*, 37.3) says that 3,000 were executed, while Pausanias (9.32.9) records 4,000. Well before 404 Lysander was one of the more brutal Spartan generals. Earlier at Miletus he was indirectly responsible for the murder of 340 Milesians in efforts to undermine the democracy there (Xenophon, *Hellenica*, 1.6.12; Plutarch, *Lysander*, 8). For the execution of prisoners shown on vase painters, see Van Wees, *Greek Warfare*, 216–17.

18. On Lysander's action after Aegospotami, see Plutarch, *Lysander*, 14. By 404 the Spartans were convinced of their victory and saw no reason not to give in to vengeance, given the utter destruction of the Athenian fleet and a litany of past wrongs committed by the Athenians.

19. 1.50.1, 2.90.5–6. Trireme warfare was often not so much a naval encounter as a land and sea operation, with infantry fighting over the proximate shores in expectation that there would be plenty of ships floundering in the surf—the crews almost defenseless and easy to harvest by waiting hoplites.

20. See Strauss, "Perspectives," 275–76, for a fascinating account about why Athenian dead sailors were not usually accorded the same degree of honorific civic attention as fallen hoplites, the causes involving not just the difficulties involving in retrieving bodies and of accurate fatality accounts at sea but a general prejudice against the lower classes who more often made up the crews of the imperial fleet. On an example of a sea fight where most on deck died under a hail of stones, see Diodorus 13.78.3–5.

21. Cf. 2.24.2. The paranoia that followed the breakout of the German battleship *Bismarck* in 1941 and the fear of Japanese capital ships in the aftermath of Pearl Harbor in 1941 were logical following such initial one-sided victories at sea: once a fleet established its credentials in sinking easily enemy ships, the mobility on the seas and the lack of credible deterrence guaranteed that it could do pretty much what it pleased until stopped.

22. For Phormio's success, cf. 2.87.3–4; for Hermocrates: 4.63.1. Athenian superiority was developed over the half century between Salamis and the outbreak of the war, when the Athenian fleet had been in near nonstop service acquiring and enlarging the empire in the Aegean and off Ionia.

23. For Thucydides' remarks about Phormio and the change of perception toward the Athenian fleet, see variously at 2.88.3 and 2.89.5–11; cf. 8.106.1–4.

24. Strauss, *Athens After*, 78–81. He goes on to suggest that the oligarchic revolu-

tion of 403, and the relative impotence of the *dêmos* in the postwar years, might well be a result of the staggering losses of poorer Athenian sailors, who were actually outnumbered by hoplites by war's end.

25. 6.31. Cf. 3.17 (the fleet on active duty in 428 of 250 ships). Thucydides has a good description of the rivalry among trierarchs as the Athenian fleet assembled to depart for Sicily (cf. especially 6.31.2–3). In general, the complex nature of the strange workings of the trierarchy is discussed in detail by Gabrielsen, *Athenian Fleet,* 105–45, and Jordan, *Athenian Navy,* 61–111—a system that was nearly ruined by the horrendous costs and losses of the Peloponnesian War and thus radically restructured in the fourth century.

26. Morrison, Coates, and Rankov (*Athenian Trireme,* 179–230, 115–17) discuss a number of passages in ancient texts that reveal just how difficult trireme service was—and how navies took extraordinary steps to ensure that their crews were experienced and in shape.

27. Aeschylus, *Persians,* 396. For passages in Thucydides attesting to the value of expertise and the Athenian prewar monopoly on such skill, see, e.g., 1.31.1, 1.35.3, 1.80.4, 1.142.6–9, and 3.115.4. On Athenian excellence, see [Xenophon], *Constitution of the Athenians,* 1.19–20.

28. "Mills": Aristotle, *Rhetoric,* 1411A24. Naming of triremes: Jordan, *Athenian Navy,* 277; Strauss, "Trireme," 318–19. Many scholars have seen the close synchronization among the oarsmen, themselves mostly landless and poor, as a valuable civic experience that lent unity and political cohesiveness to the underclass at Athens. The discipline of rowing together may well have empowered the solidarity of the "naval mob" in the assembly—or vice versa. On the ideological nature of naval service, see, for example, Strauss, "Trireme," 319–22. One wonders whether solidarity of trireme service had any empowering effect at all on the poor in oligarchic Corinth or in the Peloponnesian fleet. For sedition in the Peloponnesian fleet, cf. 8.78–80.

29. See the famous speech of the Athenian admiral Phormio, who outlined the basics of trireme tactics: 2.89.8–9. Often fighting between scores of marines on deck is referred to as battle in the "ancient fashion" (e.g., 1.49.1), which suggests that real maritime expertise was a relatively recent and largely Athenian phenomenon, one that stressed ramming and mobility and sought to evolve beyond ships merely pulling up alongside one another to board. Athenian superiority in ramming: Diodorus 13.40.

30. On breaking oars, see Diodorus 13.78; 13.99.3–4, and on the physics involved in such an intricate tactic, see Morrison, *Oared Warships,* 368–69.

31. Grappling irons were often known as "iron hands," and are ubiquitous in descriptions of fighting. For their use at some naval fights, see Diodorus 13.67.2–3 and 13.78.1. On close-in fighting on triremes, see Diodorus 13.45–6.

32. For the graphic fighting on Sicily, see 7.70–2 and especially Diodorus 13.9.3. "Amazing": Diodorus 13.45.8. The fact that such a large Athenian fleet— heretofore mostly undefeated—fought so close to shore in view of tens of thousands, and for the salvation of 40,000 men some 800 miles from home, made it a favorite topic for historians and perhaps the most famous and detailed sea battle recorded in all of ancient literature. The aftermath of battle: Diodorus 13.100.

33. "Good triremes" (which apparently meant both crews and construction): Aristophanes, *Birds*, 108. [Xenophon], *Constitution of the Athenians*, 1.19, grudgingly offers respect for Athenian seamanship. For various passages in Thucydides, including Brasidas' remarks, that reflect differences between Spartan and Athenian naval strategy, and the parameters under which both fleets operated, see 2.87.5–7; cf. 2.83.3, 2.94, 3.13.73; and 3.32.3; cf. 4.25.2–6.

34. 7.34.4–8 and 7.36.5. This same notion of a tie as victory was also true in land battles involving the Spartans. At Sphacteria they were outnumbered by many thousands, but still the surrender of a mere few hundred Spartiates shocked the Greek world and was a blow not remedied until the victory at Mantinea over six years later.

35. Xenophon, *Hellenica*, 1.6.33. There seems to be no major land battle of the classical age recorded in which a general survived when his army was defeated. Yet there were numerous occasions in the Peloponnesian War of defeated admirals sailing away despite the wreckage of their fleet. Demosthenes, Nicias, and Conon at times all survived catastrophic naval losses. Cf. Diodorus 13.77 for Conon's preparations.

36. For information on crews and the quality of rowers, see various quotes in Thucydides at 7.14.1–2 and 7.31.5; cf. 7.18.3 and 7.19.3.

37. Calm waters: Vitruvius 4.43; Thucydides' description of the Gulf of Corinth fighting: 2.84.3–4. See Diodorus 13.46.4–6 for rough waters at the Hellespont. The great Athenian victory at Salamis (480) was probably a result of ramming Persian ships more quickly and efficiently than Xerxes' crews in turn could grapple and board Greek triremes. Thus, the victory lent a sense of confidence in the efficacy of mobility and ramming to the Athenian fleet that was not always salutary during the Peloponnesian War.

38. On modern calculations concerning factors that eroded trireme performance, see Morrison, *Oared Warships*, 326–27.

39. Fatigue: 7.40.4–5; provisioning: 7.4.6; Aegospotami: Xenophon, *Hellenica*, 2.1.15–28. In sum, given the context of modern naval warfare, it is difficult for us moderns to appreciate fully how ancient fighting at sea was so closely integrated with land warfare—from the need to find water and beach ships at

night to the reliance on infantrymen on board and friendly troops on nearby shores. For the need for bases, see the evidence cited in Amit, *Athens and the Sea*, 53–54.

40. See Casson, *Ships and Seafaring*, 70–73, on the problems of provisioning a fleet of triremes in transit. For the fate of Lamachus' fleet in the river Cales, see Diodorus, 12.72.5.

41. The hulls themselves were also in constant need of repair and thus scraped and patched; e.g., Xenophon, *Hellenica*, 1.5.10–11.

42. E.g., 7.1.1 and 7.39.2. It was precisely this age-old fear of dependence upon friendly markets and harbors that explains the ultimate evolution in the fighting ship: the nuclear-powered carrier or submarine, which in theory rarely needs to come to shore, given that its fuel is nearly inextinguishable, its drinking and bathing water are by-products of its propulsion, and food can be ferried out to sea by auxiliary cargo ships.

43. On the look about the Piraeus, see Plutarch, *Themistocles*, 2.6. Nicias' lament: 7.12.5. For the move to build a 300-ship navy, see Andocides, *Peace*, 7; Aeschines, *Embassy*, 174. Amit, *Athens and the Sea*, 27–28, discusses the Athenian law decreeing construction of 20 triremes per year and also the wear and tear of the hulls.

44. On the famous voyage of the "second" trireme, which rowed without a break to overturn the death sentence carried by the first, see 3.49; cf., too, 8.101. For exhausted crews, see Diodorus 13.77.3–5.

45. See the famous passage in Plutarch's *Themistocles* (4.3) with reference to Plato (*Laws* 4.706B–C). Cf. Jordan, *Athenian Navy*, 18–20.

46. On maintenance, see 2.94.3–4. See Morrison, Coates, and Rankov, *Athenian Trireme*, 179–230, for acknowledgment of the intricacies and fragility of a modern trireme replica, and 102–06 for a good discussion of potential trireme speeds.

47. For an ancient conservative's grudging acknowledgment of the advantages that accrued to maritime states, see [Xenophon], *Constitution of the Athenians*, 2.2–4. In general, the shipping of goods by sea in the ancient world entailed about a tenth of the cost of land transport.

48. 2.94.1. Apparently the idea that a relatively small Peloponnesian raiding force might steal into the Piraeus, destroy triremes, and stay long enough to block the entry of merchant vessels scared the Athenians as much as the approach of 60,000 Peloponnesians into Attica.

49. Aristophanes *Acharnians*, 544–54; [Xenophon], *Constitution of the Athenians*, 1.2–3. This anonymous curmudgeon systematically lists the ways in which maritime states of the "worse" people enjoy advantages: sea powers can gov-

ern the importation of products of other states; they can raid and then leave far more easily than infantry forces and have considerable more range in operations; their fleets guarantee more commerce; and they are familiar with a far greater diversity of peoples. For the complex nature of the revolution of 411 at Athens, start with Lintott, *Violence*, 135–55.

50. Xenophon, *Hellenica*, 2.2.14–15. After the war, the walls, once leveled, were not only resurrected, but auxiliary efforts were made at border fortification, perhaps to enhance the idea of refusing hoplite battle without necessarily sacrificing all the cropland to enemy invaders. See Ober, *Fortress Attica*, 551–66, for the general idea of a fourth-century defensive mentality born out of the Athenian disappointments of the Peloponnesian War.

51. See Thucydides on naval costs and the remarks of Pericles 2.62.2–2. Perhaps it was no surprise that throughout the Cold War, the United States, with its superior fleet, found it far easier to project power and intervene along the borders of the Soviet Union, whether in Korea, Vietnam, or the Middle East, than the Russians could carve out client states in Latin America and expand their outpost in Cuba.

52. Meiggs, *Athenian Empire*, 104–08, reviews the low figure of 50 ships and the high of 200, concluding that Thucydides' inference that 200 triremes were lost in Egypt may be correct—if we understand that perhaps only 10,000 of the 40,000 lost imperial crewmen were Athenian citizens.

53. For a sampling of the litany of this antinaval sentiment, see 6.24.3; [Xenophon], *Constitution of the Athenians*, 1.2 and 1.10–12; Plato, *Laws*, 704D, 705A, 706B, 707A; Aristotle, *Politics*, 1327A10–1327B6. One of the few classical authors who can express heartfelt empathy for the later-fifth-century rowers at Athens is Aristophanes (e.g., *Knights*, 545–610; *Frogs*, 687–705; *Acharnians*, 677–78).

54. On the financial squeeze at Athens, see Meiggs, *Athenian Empire*, 320–39. As was always true of the genius of Athenian democracy, there was a paradox at the heart of the system: rich people at Athens who hated the poor gained prestige by outfitting ships to employ them, while the wealthier abroad were taxed in tribute to man a fleet that would usually prevent them from ever gaining control of their respective local city-states.

Chapter 9

1. Sometimes the increase of a mere obol paid per crewman, from the normal three to four in daily wages, might make a vast difference in the size of the respective Athenian and Spartan fleets. The Athenians purportedly kept the

wages of rowers rather low at three obols, rather than the optimum one drachma, in the odd belief that prosperity among the rowing classes might make it impossible for them to continue to work under such demanding conditions. On naval pay in general, see Morrison, Coates, and Rankov, *Athenian Trireme*, 118–22.

2. No money: 8.1.2. Diodorus (13.37.1) claims the war did not end in 413 because of the recall of Alcibiades and his efforts at tampering with Persian aid to the Spartans. Thucydides believed that the Athenians were fearful that the Syracusans might have sailed directly from their success in the Great Harbor into the Piraeus. But nothing in the Syracusans' recent naval past suggested that they were up for an eight-hundred-mile voyage in force—on the chances of suffering the disaster in the harbor of Athens that they had recently inflicted in their own. In fact, the Sicilians were soon wracked by civil dissension at home and fearful of Carthaginian attack and in no mood to send precious resources half a world away.

3. 2.65.11–12. During the Archidamian War, the Athenian fleet operated mostly in enemy waters around the Peloponnese and the Corinthian Gulf, where setbacks endangered only further offensive operations. The Ionian War was an altogether different theater, where a single major defeat threatened Attica's grain, commerce, and imperial income.

4. Xenophon, *Hellenica*, 1.1.25–26. Xenophon presents the stereotypical view of Persians as believing that wars are won only through material advantages, which was as unrealistic a position as the old Spartan canard that courage and discipline alone would provide victory.

5. 7.39.2. Diodorus (13.10.1–3) assumes that Ariston realized that in the relatively confined waters of the harbor the disadvantage that stubby, lower rams might impair speed and mobility was more than offset by the chance that they could sink enemy ships with a single hit and often head-on.

6. Xenophon, *Hellenica*, 1.6.3–4. The inept Peloponnesian response after Sicily and the failure to capitalize on the setback, juxtaposed with the amazing Athenian recovery, was proof to Thucydides that democratic governments could get themselves into and out of disasters in a way unthinkable among oligarchies. 8.1.3–4; cf. 7.28 and 8.96.4–5.

7. Xenophon, *Anabasis*, 1.2.9. The flotsam and jetsam of this last dirty decade of the long war washed up as mercenaries in the huge bought army of Cyrus the Younger, himself an active participant in the Ionian War. The Panhellenic nature of the Ten Thousand, and their expectation of high wages, reflected the nature of the last few years of the Peloponnesian War, in which thousands of Greeks sailed east to garner rich Persian wages in service to the Spartan fleet.

8. On these various sea battles, see 8.10, 8.41–42, 8.61, and 8.95. Once more, as after the loss at Sicily, the Athenians were paranoid that the Peloponnesians would head straight for the Piraeus—a constant fear never realized until the final disaster after Aegospotami. Cf. 8.96.2–3.

9. 8.104–6; Diodorus 13.39–40. For a description of the battle, see the discussion in Morrison, Coates, and Rankov, *Athenian Trireme*, 81–84. It was likely that in these far distant last battles of the Ionian War, the number of fatalities at sea rose (e.g., Thucydides 8.95), inasmuch as both sides were now less likely to take prisoners, the nearby shores were often without friendly troops, and the finite pool of skilled Athenian rowers became a matter of real concern: killing captured or wounded sailors was now seen as part of the larger strategy of the Peloponnesian War.

10. 8.106.2. There were some general truisms about the aftermath of major Athenian battles: sudden optimism or dejection not always commensurate with the actual situation on the battlefield; abrupt change of government (the so-called Four Hundred, the Five Thousand, and the Thirty all emerged in the wake of Athenian setbacks); and sudden fury or praise unleashed at generals, as the checkered careers of Cleon, Demosthenes, Alcibiades, and Thrasybulus attest.

11. Xenophon, *Hellenica*, 1.1.14. For Thrasybulus, see Cornelius Nepos, *Thrasybulus*, 1.3. In theory, a land power without money could still fight for a while, given the fact that hoplites owned their own armor, might forage off the countryside, and perhaps would serve without pay given their selfish interest in protecting local croplands. But triremes were state property; and if expensive to build, they were far more costly to man and maintain.

12. Xenophon, *Hellenica*, 1.5.5–9. Soon Athenian subjects began to revolt in earnest throughout the Aegean, for example at Andros; cf. Xenophon, *Hellenica*, 1.4.21.

13. Hippocrates' brief dispatch is a far cry from Nicias' long letter explaining the Athenian plight on Sicily. Unlike Nicias, the Spartan offers no real assessment and gives no advice. Cf. Xenophon, *Hellenica*, 1.1.24. The message is supposed to reflect the "Laconic" style: in this case, even under the most traumatic circumstances, emotion and elaboration do not creep into the official communication home. In general, see Diodorus 13.50–3 for the battle and the Spartan peace offers following the defeat of the Peloponnesian fleet; and for the circumstances surrounding Cyzicus, cf. Lazenby, *Peloponnesian War*, 198–204.

14. Xenophon, *Hellenica*, 1.5.11–14; Diodorus 13.71; Plutarch, *Alcibiades*, 35. A great deal of the problem was that the Spartans now had a general every bit as wily

as Alcibiades and far more skilled in playing the Persian card for all it was worth. And once Alcibiades had triangulated with both Sparta and Persia, there was no real place to go other than exile—and such a lack of options was never a good position to be in with the Athenian assembly. It is no accident that ambitious Spartans like Lysander, Callicratidas, and Gylippus were not really Spartiates but probably *mothakes*, or born to non-Spartiate mothers and raised by wealthy benefactors—their talent in war spurring them on, with no expectation that their commonplace background during peace would bring them anything special.

15. On the manpower crisis at Athens, the defeat of Conon at Mytilene, and the rise of the Spartan fleet, see Xenophon, *Hellenica*, 1.6.15–18 and 1.6.24–25; cf. Diodorus 13.77–79. For the problems of Arginusae, see Lazenby, *Peloponnesian War*, 229–34.

16. Xenophon, *Hellenica*, 1.6.26–34; Diodorus 13.97–99.

17. See Aristotle, *Constitution of the Athenians*, 34.1, for the Spartan offer of peace after Arginusae. Presumably, once more Cleophon spurned the peace feelers, demanding a return of all the cities that Athens had once held.

18. Xenophon, *Hellenica*, 2.1.28. If Spartan triremes were improving at sea, their infantry was still unquestioned. Thus, if it was unwise for the Athenians to drag their ships onto an unprotected shore and without fortifications encamp so far distant from provisions at Aegospotami, it was suicidal to find themselves pitting sailors against Spartans in a land battle beside beached and idle triremes.

19. For the executions, see Xenophon, *Hellenica*, 2.1.28; Diodorus 13.106.6–8; Plutarch, *Lysander*, 10–11. Because the triremes captured from the Athenian imperial fleet may have numbered 160, there should have been over 30,000 prisoners. How many slaves and allies were let go, or how many simply were Athenians executed before surrendering, is unknown.

20. For the battle, see Xenophon, *Hellenica*, 2.1.18–28, and Diodorus 13.105–6. In the most critical naval fight since Salamis, the seafaring Athenians essentially lost it on land and before the engagement had even started.

21. Xenophon, *Hellenica*, 1.2.13. Thus, one cousin proved traitor once and perished, and the other was a traitor three times, to Athens, Sparta, and Persia, respectively—and yet survived the war.

22. See Plutarch, *Alcibiades*, 38.1–2. After the war, the second exile of Alcibiades was acknowledged by the Athenians as "the greatest folly of all their blunders and stupidity."

23. For the detail of the last years of his life, see Ellis, *Alcibiades*, 93–98; Plutarch, *Alcibiades*, 38.

24. Xenophon, *Hellenica*, 2.2.3. What was the exact state of the Athenian fleet after Aegospotami? There were probably less than 20 triremes scattered around the Aegean or rotting in the ship sheds at the Piraeus. And the absence of both money and raw materials meant that the Athenians this time were in no shape to build yet a fourth fleet *ex nihilo*.

25. Xenophon, *Hellenica*, 2.2.19; Plutarch, *Lysander*, 15.2; Pausanias 10.9.9. Turning a land into a *mêloboton* ("sheep walk") was a proverbial rhetorical threat of ultimate retribution; cf. Hanson, *Warfare and Agriculture*, 10. For a brief discussion of the Morgenthau plan, which is often caricatured and not properly understood, see Weinberg, *World at Arms*, 794–98. Churchill also proposed that postwar Germany "be primarily agricultural and pastoral in its character."

Chapter 10

1. See Henderson, *Great War*, 489–90; Zimmern, *Greek Commonwealth*, 432.

2. See Ober, *Fortress Attica*, 209–13, for discussion of changed strategic thinking at Athens, and cf. Hanson, *Warfare and Agriculture*, 174–84, for the mostly prosperous nature of Attic agriculture in the postbellum years. In general, Cartledge, "Effects," 114–17, summarizes well the consensus that the war's effects were more subtle and enervating than catastrophic and immediate.

3. The argument not only for the positive role of the Athenian empire but also for its popularity among the grass roots of its subject peoples became the life work of G.E.M. de Ste. Croix, whose spirited and often wildly wrong invective is as engaging as his prodigious scholarship is impressive. Brief summations of his journal articles can be found in his *Origins of the Peloponnesian War*, 289–93, and *Class Struggle*, 1–49.

4. 1.23. Cities like Colophon, Mycalessus, Plataea, and Thyrea were the scenes of abject slaughter, while Sollium, Potidaea, Anactorium, Scione, and Melos were ethnically cleansed and resettled by new populations.

5. Isocrates, *On the Peace*, 86–87. Isocrates' numbers are perhaps suspect, inasmuch as Diodorus (13.21) says 200 ships were lost in Sicily and 180 at Aegospotami. But in the general Athenian collective memory, there must have been some notion that around 400 imperial triremes were lost in those two terrible defeats, a number that was pretty much within a reasonable margin of error. For Isocrates' claim about the loss of the great families of Athens, see too Diodorus 13.4, 13.88.

6. Cf. the astute observations of Cartledge, "Effects," 106–09, and Strauss, "Problem," 170–75.

7. For 22 generals, see Paul, "Two Battles," 308, and Strauss, *Athens After*, 70–86

and 172–74. It is Strauss' argument, in addition, that disproportionate losses to the thetic class during the war explain somewhat the rise of oligarchic governments in 411 and 404, as if for a while the attenuated ranks of the poorer and more radical lost influence in the democratic politics of the time.

8. Almost immediately after the war, Thebes provided sanctuary for exiled Athenian democrats. The Peloponnesian War thus ended with Athenian democrats seeking asylum in a state that had started the war by sending oligarchic radicals against democratic Plataea, emphasizing once again that ideology was so often trumped by realpolitik and the desire to balance power among the squabbling city-states. For the maze of postwar interests, see Buckler, *Aegean Greece*, 3–6.

9. *Hellenica Oxyrhynchia* 12.3, and the sources cited in Hanson, *Warfare and Agriculture*, 153–73.

10. See, for example, Davies, *Propertied Families:* e.g., 44 (Archedamos lost his property after being taken prisoner); 61 (Kritodemos killed at Aegospotami, leaving three orphans); 93 (Amytheon killed at Sicily, leaving three sons); 152 (Diodotus killed at Ephesus, leaving three children); 347 (Lykomedes killed in 424, leaving behind a son, Kleomedes, one of the generals at Melos); 404 (Eukrates killed by the Thirty Tyrants, leaving behind two sons); 467 (Polystratos lost land after Decelea, was wounded, and had three sons in the Athenian military).

11. For postwar problems in Sparta, see the ancient evidence discussed in Cartledge, *Agesilaos*, 34–54 and, especially, Lewis, *Cambridge*, 16–32. "Eat raw": Xenophon, *Hellenica*, 3.3.7.

12. Laws of war: Ober, "Classical Greek Times," 24–26. It seems methodologically unsound to question the antebellum protocols surrounding Greek warfare by pointing out occasional exceptions, such as attacks on civilian centers or desecration of shrines—as if contemporary historians might doubt the very existence of both speed laws and the public's tendency to obey them, by evidence of law enforcement's common ticketing of speeders. But for a different view, see, for example, again Krentz, "Strategic Culture," 65–72, and "Fighting," 36–37.

13. Demosthenes, *Third Philippic*, 48–52. For this and other reactionary nostalgia about the old simple war, see the ancient literature cited in Hanson, "Hoplite Battle," 202–06.

14. 5.41.3; cf. Herodotus 7.9.2. It is a general law that an escalation of violence and an erosion of restraint are in direct proportion to the length of a struggle. Andersonville or the March to the Sea was in no one's mind in early 1861. Nor did anyone envision in 1914 that in a mere three years either side in the

Great War would or could blanket the other with poisonous gas; in the same fashion, the invasion of Poland by conventional German troops did not presage Hiroshima.

15. There is an enormous bibliography of the earlier "rules of war" and their violation during the Peloponnesian War, with importance for subsequent conflicts—with ample documentation from contemporary sources. See, for example, Hanson, *Other Greeks*, 317–49; Ober, *Fortress Attica*, 32–50; and, especially, Krentz, "Invention," 25–35, for a review of the ancient and modern sources.

16. For the ramifications of eroding the census class in detail, see Hanson, "Democratic Warfare," 16–17. By the end of the war many "hoplites" probably did not even own property (Lysias, 34.4; cf. Thucydides 6.43.1); wealthy horsemen bragged that they had served on foot (Lysias, 16.13); and some rowers were hoplite farmers (Xenophon, *Hellenica*, 1.6.24–25).

17. To the modern reader, Plato's numerous blasts against the new warfare appear not only strident but nearly treasonous. See especially *Laws*, 4.707C; cf. 706B. In some sense, his criticism is analogous to the stereotypical agrarian conservatives in Roman, British, and American times who see the acquisition of empire as a destabilizing influence on existing norms—too many foreigners, too much new money, and too many obligations ruining the old landed hierarchies of the past.

18. See the famous passage on the rise of the polis in Aristotle's *Politics*, 4.1297B16–24. We should remember that the city-state—the embodiment of the beginning of Western civilization—did not start out so much to guarantee personal freedom for all residents as to ensure the protection of property for a new meritocratic middling class of landowners.

19. See Xenophon, *Hellenica*, 1.6.31, for the purportedly better Peloponnesian crews. Hunt (*Slaves*, 83–101) presents a good argument about why the mass use of slaves at Arginusae may not have been all that unusual but, rather, the culmination of a long practice of using servile rowers in the navies on all sides during the Peloponnesian War. By the end of the war there may well have been 500 Athenian, allied, Peloponnesian, and Sicilian triremes on the Aegean at any one time—requiring a pool of some 100,000 oarsmen who could not have all been free citizens, given infantry requirements and the need to produce food.

20. For the paradox of increased military efficacy at the price of the old agrarian exclusivity of the city-state, see the long discussion, with a list of citations to classical sources, in Hanson, *Other Greeks*, 351–96.

21. 1.83.2; cf. 1.80.3–4 and 2.24.1.2. A good rhetorical lamentation about the role of money in war is found at Isocrates, *On the Peace*, 8.48.

22. The fury of Athenian philosophers at the new war is best captured at Plato, *Laws*, 4.706B–C, and Aristotle, *Politics*, 8.1326A. In general, see Kallet-Marx, *Money and Naval Power*, 201–06, and Kallet, *Money and Corrosion*, 227–84, for the role of money and capital in the Peloponnesian War and the break that such financial sophistication marked with warfare of the past.

23. 4.40.2. There is an entire corpus of reactionary thought in Greek literature that protests loudly against missiles, archery, and artillery as somehow unfair or immoral. See a discussion in Hanson, *Other Greeks*, 338–49.

24. On the military revolution in the various arts of siegecraft immediately following the Peloponnesian War, see Winter, *Greek Fortifications*, 310–24; Kern, *Ancient Siege Warfare*, 163–93; and the debate between Ober, *Fortress Attica*, 197–207 (arguing for a postbellum new defensive policy of rural fortification in the fourth century) and Munn, *Defense of Attica*, 15–25 (maintaining that there was no attempt to ensure real border defense by new bases and forts in the Attic countryside).

25. Archilochus, fragment 114. For the idea in Greek literature of the general as a common man, see Hanson, "Greek Warrior," 112–13. For a different view, cf. Wheeler, "General," 140–49.

26. For ancient encomia about the two men, see 4.81.1–3 and 4.108.2–3; and cf. Plutarch, *Lysander*, 30.

27. There is a new notion in literature of the post–Peloponnesian War era concerning the proper tactical role—intellectual or moral?—of the general in the early fourth century. For a discussion of the ancient sources, see Hanson, *Other Greeks*, 258–61, 308–10, and Wheeler, "General," 145–53.

28. Xenophon, *Memorabilia*, 3.1.1; Xenophon, *Anabasis*, 2.1.7; cf. Plato, *Laws*, 828E–834A. For the new type of military commanders who appeared after the Peloponnesian War and engaged in plundering and raiding to pay the cost of their operations, see Pritchett, *Greek State*, 2.59–117.

29. In similar fashion, most in 1861 felt that the Confederacy, given the region's reputation for chivalry and excellence in arms, would produce superior military leadership in the American Civil War. But for all the tactical excellence of a Lee or Jackson, the South simply did not produce many military minds quite like Grant, Sherman, or Sheridan, who grasped the rare interplay of tactics, strategy, morale, and economic power in choosing where and how to fight.

30. Powell, *Athens and Sparta*, 200–01, is quite good in collating passages from Thucydides that reflect the historian's belief that Athens lost rather than Sparta won.

31. For these examples of fear and panic adjudicating state policy, see 2.21 (Athenian empty hopes that the Spartans might turn back and not really rav-

age Attica as they had threatened) and 4.40–42 (the Spartans worry that after their defeat at Sphacteria, enemies would sense their weakness); cf. 5.102–03 (the Melian reliance on empty hopes that the danger might be still averted). For a list of examples of opportunism during the war and the dangers of perceived weakness, see Powell, *Athens and Sparta*, 144–47.

32. Pindar on war: fragment 120.5. On the attitudes of old and young about war, see, for example, 1.72.1, 2.8, and 6.24. See also Astymachus and Lacon (3.52–53); Saugenês (see his grave stele in R. Higgins, *Tanagra and the Figurines* [Princeton, 1986], 52–53); Scriphondas (7.30.3); and Xenares (5.51.2).

WORKS CITED

Amit, M. *Athens and the Sea: A Study in Athenian Sea-Power.* Brussels, 1965.

Anderson, J. K. *Military Theory and Practice in the Age of Xenophon.* Berkeley, 1970.

Anglim, S., et al. *Fighting Techniques of the Ancient World: 3000 B.C.–500 A.D.* New York, 2002.

Badian, E. *From Plataea to Potidaea.* Baltimore, 1993.

Beevor, A. *Stalingrad.* New York, 1998.

Buckler, J. *Aegean Greece in the Fourth Century B.C.* Leiden, 2003.

Bugh, G. *The Horsemen of Athens.* Princeton, 1988.

Cartledge, P. *Agesilaos and the Crisis of Sparta.* Baltimore, 1987.

———. "The Effects of the Peloponnesian (Athenian) War on Athenian and Spartan Societies." In D. McCann and B. Strauss, *War and Democracy,* 104–23.

———. *The Spartans.* New York, 2003.

Casson, L. *Ships and Seafaring in Ancient Times.* Austin, 1994.

Cawkwell, G. *Thucydides and the Peloponnesian War.* London, 1997.

Davies, J. K. *Athenian Propertied Families.* Oxford, 1971.

Delbrück, H. *Warfare in Antiquity: History of the Art of War.* Vol. I, translated by W. Renfroe. Lincoln, Neb., 1975.

De Souza, P. *The Peloponnesian War, 431–404 B.C.* Oxford, 2002.

Ducrey, P. *Warfare in Ancient Greece.* New York, 1985.

Ellis, W. M. *Alcibiades.* London, 1989.

Finley, M. I. *A History of Sicily: Ancient Sicily to the Arab Conquest.* New York, 1968.

Fisher, N. "*Hybris,* Revenge and Stasis in the Greek City-States." In *War and Violence in Ancient Greece,* edited by H. van Wees, 83–123.

Foxhall, L. "Farming and Fighting in Ancient Greece." In *Warfare and Society in the Greek World,* edited by G. Shipley and J. Rich. London, 1993, 134–45.

Gabriel, R., and K. Metz. *From Sumer to Rome: The Military Capabilities of Ancient Armies.* New York, 1991.

Gabrielsen, V. *Financing the Athenian Fleet: Public Taxation and Social Relations.* Baltimore, 1994.

Gaebel, R. *Cavalry Operations in the Ancient Greek World.* Norman, Okla., 2002.

Garlan, Y. *War in the Ancient World.* London, 1975.

Garnsey, Peter. *Famine and Food Supply in the Graeco-Roman World.* Cambridge, 1988.

Gomme, A. W. *A Historical Commentary on Thucydides.* Vols. 1–4. (Vols. 4–5 with A. Andrewes and K. Dover.) Oxford, 1945–70.

Green, P. *Armada from Athens.* New York, 1970.

Grimsley, M., and C. J. Rogers, eds. *Civilians in the Path of War.* Lincoln, Neb., 2002.

Grote, G. *A History of Greece.* 4th ed. London, 1872.

Grundy, G. *Thucydides and the History of His Age.* Oxford, 1948.

Hackett, J., ed. *Warfare in the Ancient World.* New York, 1989.

Hamel, D. *Athenian Generals: Military Authority in the Classical Period.* Leiden, 1998.

Hanson, V. D. "Epaminondas, the Battle of Leuktra, and the 'Revolution' in Greek Battle Tactics." *Classical Antiquity* 7.2 (1988): 190–207.

———, ed. *Hoplites: The Ancient Greek Battle Experience.* London, 1991.

———. "Thucydides and the Desertion of Attic Slaves During the Decelean War." *Classical Antiquity* 11.2 (1992): 210–28.

———. "Delium." *Quarterly Journal of Military History* 8.1 (1995): 28–35.

———. "Hoplites into Democrats: The Changing Ideology of Athenian Infantry." In *Dêmokratia: A Conversation on Democracies, Ancient and Modern,* edited by J. Ober and C. Hedrick, 189–312, Princeton, 1996.

———. *Warfare and Agriculture in Classical Greece.* 2nd ed. Berkeley, 1998.

———. *The Western Way of War: Infantry Battle in Classical Greece.* 2nd ed. Berkeley, 1998.

———. "Hoplite Obliteration: The Case of the Town of Thespiai." In *Ancient Warfare, Archaeological Perspectives,* edited by J. Carman and A. Harding, 203–18, Gloucestershire, 1999.

———. *The Soul of Battle: From Ancient Times to the Present Day—How Three Great Liberators Vanquished Tyranny.* New York, 1999.

———. *The Wars of the Ancient Greeks.* London, 1999.

———. *The Other Greeks.* 2nd ed. Berkeley, 1999.

———. "Hoplite Battle as Ancient Greek Warfare: When, Where, and Why." In *War and Violence in Ancient Greece,* edited by H. van Wees, 201–32.

———. "The Classical Greek Warrior and the Egalitarian Military Ethos." *Ancient World* 31.2 (2000): 111–26.

———. "Democratic Warfare, Ancient and Modern." In *War and Democracy,* edited by D. McCann and B. Strauss, 3–33.

————. *Carnage and Culture: Landmark Battles in the Rise of Western Power.* New York, 2001.

————. *Ripples of Battle: How Wars of the Past Still Determine How We Fight, How We Live, and How We Think.* New York, 2003.

Henderson, B. W. *The Great War Between Athens and Sparta.* London, 1927.

Herman, A. *The Idea of Decline in Western History.* New York, 1997.

Hornblower, S. *A Commentary on Thucydides.* Vols. 1–2. Oxford, 1990–96.

Hunt, P. *Slaves, Warfare, and Ideology in the Greek Historians.* Cambridge, 1998.

Jones, N. F. *Rural Athens Under the Democracy.* Philadelphia, 2004.

Jordan, B. *The Athenian Navy in the Classical Period.* Berkeley, 1975.

Kagan, D. *The Outbreak of the Peloponnesian War.* Ithaca, N.Y., 1969.

————. *The Archidamian War.* Ithaca, N.Y., 1974.

————. *The Peace of Nicias and the Sicilian Expedition.* Ithaca, N.Y., 1981.

————. *The Fall of the Athenian Empire.* Ithaca, N.Y., 1987.

————. *On the Origins of War and the Preservation of Peace.* New York, 1995.

————. *The Peloponnesian War.* New York, 2003.

Kallet, L. *Money and the Corrosion of Power in Thucydides: The Sicilian Expedition and Its Aftermath.* Berkeley, 2001.

Kallet-Marx, L. *Money, Expense, and Naval Power in Thucydides' History 1–5.24.* Berkeley, 1993.

Keegan, J. *A History of Warfare.* New York, 1993.

Kern, P. *Ancient Siege Warfare.* Bloomington, Ind., 1999.

Krentz, P. "Casualties in Hoplite Battles." *Greek, Roman and Byzantine Studies* 26.1 (1985): 13–20.

————. "The Strategic Culture of Periclean Athens." In *Polis and Polemos,* edited by C. Hamilton and P. Krentz, 55–72, Claremont, Calif., 1997.

————. "Deception in Archaic and Classical Greek Warfare." In *War and Violence in Ancient Greece,* edited by H. van Wees, 167–200.

————. "Fighting by the Rules: The Invention of the Hoplite Agôn." *Hesperia* 71.1 (2002): 23–39.

Lawrence, A. W. *Greek Aims in Fortification.* Oxford, 1979.

Lazenby, J. *The Spartan Army.* Warminster, 1985.

————. *The Peloponnesian War: A Military History.* London, 2004.

Lebow, N., and B. Strauss, eds. *Hegemonic Rivalry: From Thucydides to the Nuclear Age.* Boulder, 1991.

Lewis, D. M., et al. *The Cambridge Ancient History.* Volume 6, *The Fourth Century* B.C. Cambridge, 1994.

Lintott, A. *Violence, Civil Strife and Revolution in the Classical City.* Baltimore, 1982.

Lissarrague, F. "The World of the Warrior." In *A City of Images: Iconography and Society in Ancient Greece,* edited by C. Bérard et al., 39–52. Princeton, 1989.

Lloyd, A. B., ed. *Battle in Antiquity.* London, 1996.

Longrigg, J. "The Great Plague at Athens." *History of Science* 18 (1980): 209–25.

Losada, L. *The Fifth Column in the Peloponnesian War.* Leiden, 1972.

Luginbill, R. "*Othismos:* The Importance of the Mass-Shove in Hoplite Warfare." *Phoenix* 48 (1994): 51–61.

Mayor, A. *Greek Fire, Poison Arrows, and Scorpion Bombs: Biological and Chemical Warfare in the Ancient World.* New York, 2003.

McCann, D., and B. Strauss, eds. *War and Democracy: A Comparative Study of the Korean War and the Peloponnesian War.* New York, 2001.

Meiggs, R. *The Athenian Empire.* Oxford, 1971.

Mitchell, S. "Hoplite Warfare in Ancient Greece." In *Battle in Antiquity,* edited by A. F. Lloyd, 87–106.

Montagu, J. *Battles of the Greek and Roman Worlds.* London, 2000.

Morrison, J. S. *Greek and Roman Oared Warships.* Oxford, 1996.

Morrison, J. S., J. E. Coates, and N. B. Rankov. *The Athenian Trireme.* Cambridge, 2000.

Munn, M. *The Defense of Attica: The Dema Wall and the Boitian War of 378–375 B.C.* Berkeley, 1993.

Ober, J. *Fortress Attica: Defense of the Athenian Land Frontier, 404–322 B.C.* Leiden, 1985.

———. "Hoplites and Obstacles." In *Hoplites: The Ancient Greek Battle Experience,* edited by V. Hanson, 173–96.

———. "Classical Greek Times." In *The Laws of War: Constraints of Warfare in the Western World,* edited by M. Howard, G. Andreopoulos, and M. Shulman, 12–26. New Haven, 1995.

———. "Thucydides, Pericles, and the Strategy of Defense." In *The Athenian Revolution,* edited by J. Ober, 72–85. Princeton, 1996.

Parlama, L., et al. *The City Beneath the City: Antiquities from the Metropolitan Railway Excavations.* Athens, 2000.

Paul, G. M. "Two Battles in Thucydides." *Classical Views* 31.6 (1987): 307–12.

Powell, A. *Athens and Sparta.* London, 1988.

Price, J. J. *Thucydides and the Internal War.* Cambridge, 2001.

Pritchard, D. M. " 'The Fractured Imagery': Popular Thinking on Military Matters in Fifth Century Athens." *Ancient History* 28.1 (1998): 38–58.

Pritchett, W. K. *Studies in Ancient Greek Topography, Parts I–VII.* Berkeley, 1965–93.

———. *The Greek State at War, Parts I–V.* Berkeley, 1971–91.

Raaflaub, K., and N. Rosenstein. *War and Society in the Ancient and Medieval Worlds.* Cambridge, Mass., 1999.

Rawlings, L. "Alternative Agonies: Hoplite Martial and Combat Experience Beyond the Phalanx." In *War and Violence in Ancient Greece*, edited by H. van Wees, 233–59. London, 2000.

Rich, J., and G. Shipley, eds. *War and Society in the Greek World*. London, 1993.

Rodgers, W. L. *Greek and Roman Naval Warfare: A Study of Strategy, Tactics, and Ship Design from Salamis (480 B.C.) to Actium (31 B.C.)*. Annapolis, 1964.

Roisman, J. *The General Demosthenes and His Use of Military Surprise*. Stuttgart, 1993.

Sabin, P. "Athens, the United States, and Democratic 'Characteristics' in Foreign Policy." In *Hegemonic Rivalry: From Thucydides to the Nuclear Age*, edited by R. N. Lebow and B. Strauss, 235–50.

Ste. Croix, G.E.M. de. *The Origins of the Peloponnesian War*. Ithaca, 1972.

————. *The Class Struggle in the Ancient Greek World: From the Archaic Age to the Arab Conquests*. Ithaca, 1989.

Sallares, R. *The Ecology of the Ancient Greek World*. Ithaca, 1991.

Santosuosso, A. *Soldiers, Citizens, and the Symbols of War*. Boulder, 1997.

Sekunda, N., and R. Hook. *The Spartan Army*. London, 1998.

Spence, I. "Perikles and the Defense of Attika During the Peloponnesian War." *Journal of Hellenic Studies* 101 (1990): 91–109.

————. *The Cavalry of Classical Greece: A Social and Military History with Particular Reference to Athens*. Oxford, 1993.

Strauss, B. *Athens After the Peloponnesian War: Class, Faction and Policy, 403–386 B.C.* Ithaca, N.Y., 1986.

————. "The Athenian Trireme: School of Democracy." In *Dêmokratia: A Conversation on Democracies, Ancient and Modern*, edited by J. Ober and C. Hedrick, 313–25. Princeton, 1996.

————. "The Problem of Periodization: The Case of the Peloponnesian War." In *Inventing Ancient Culture: Historicism, Periodization, and the Ancient World*, edited by M. Golden and P. Toohey, 165–75. London, 1997.

————. "Perspectives on the Death of Fifth-Century Athenian Seamen." In *War and Violence in Ancient Greece*, edited by H. van Wees, 261–84.

Thorne, J. A. "Warfare and Agriculture: The Economic Impact of Devastation in Classical Greece." *Greek, Roman, and Byzantine Studies* 42 (2001): 225–53.

Toor, C. *Ancient Ships*. Chicago, 1964.

Van Wees, H., ed. *War and Violence in Ancient Greece*. London, 2000.

————. *Greek Warfare: Myths and Realities*. London, 2004.

Wallinga, H. T. *Ships and Sea-Power Before the Great Persian War: The Ancestry of the Ancient Trireme*. Leiden, 1993.

Weinberg, G. L. *A World at Arms: A Global History of World War II*. Cambridge, 1994.

Westlake, H. D. "Seaborne Raids in Periclean Strategy." *Classical Quarterly* 39 (1945): 75–84.

Wheeler, E. "The General as Hoplite." In *Hoplites: The Ancient Greek Battle Experience*, edited by V. Hanson, 121–71.

Winter, F. E. *Greek Fortifications*. Toronto, 1974.

Worley, L. *Hippeis: The Cavalry of Ancient Greece*. Boulder, 1994.

Zimmern, A. E. *The Greek Commonwealth*. Oxford, 1924.

Abydos, 102, 276, 279, 280

Acanthus, 59, 119, *181*, 194

Acarnania, *28*, 94, 96, 98, *181*

Acharnae, 50, *51*, 52, 53

Acropolis, 9, 17, 66, 85, 102, 285, 315

Aegean Sea: map of naval battles, 279

Aegina: Athenian fort at, 117; casualties, 101, 110, 191; grievances against Athens, 14, 19, 20, 101; maps, *28, 51, 69, 181*; as target of Athenian raiding and killing operations, 94, 96, 101

Aegospotami: aftermath, 72–73, 189, 248, 284; Alcibiades at, 18, 285; Athenian fleet at, 72, 116, 249, 264, 283–85; casualties, 103, 191, 248, 264, 275; cost, 264; map, *279*; as one of most decisive naval engagements in European history, 283–85; role of leadership superiority, 307; Spartan victory, 34, 189, 283–85

Aeneas Tacticus, 192, 195

Aeschylus, 6, 10, 294

Aetolia, 32, 94, 97–98, 112, *181*

Africa: as origin of plague outbreak, 73

Agis (Spartan king): after Athenian loss at Aegospotami, 286; and Decelea, 43, 60, 103, 235, 267; leads fifth invasion of Attica, 58; and Mantinea, 150, 151, 155, 156, 157, 158; orders building of Peloponnesian fleet, 235

agriculture: attacks on, 35–37, 39, 41, 44–45, 53–57, 62; significance in Greek life, 38; significance in Peloponnesian War, 38

Alcamenes, 295

Alcibiades: about, 6, 18, 62–63, 86, 88, 120–21, 199, 232–33, 284–85, 319; and Aegospotami, 18, 285; convinces Athens to attack Syracuse, 46, 208,

233; at Cyzicus, 277, 284; death of, 18, 199, 285, 295; at Delium, 124, 129, 131, 135, 145; dismissed after Notium, 34, 280, 284; kidnaps Argive conservatives, 101, 121; as leader, 11, 48, 277, 278, 280, 293, 306, 307; and Mantinea, 135, 152, 155, 233; at Notium, 278, 280; as one commander of Sicilian expedition, 33, 205, 206–7, 208, 211, 232; at Potidaea, 62, 63, 86; recalled from Sicily, 33, 207, 208, 233; rehabilitation of, 34, 276; rivalry with Nicias, 152, 201, 203; role in Melian siege, 199; on Sicily, 232–33; switches sides in Sicilian War, 203, 207, 208, 233; Thucydides' view, 83; treachery of, 16, 64, 120–21, 231, 232–33; urges anti-Spartan alliance of Athens, Argos, and Mantinea, 33, 152, 155, 233; view of Sicilian invasion, 203; view of Sicily's hoplites, 146–47; as ward of Pericles, 63, 86

Alcidas, 100, 107, 108, 123, 191

Alcmaeonid family, 5, 63

Alexander the Great, 5, 141, 248, 265, 268, 292, 307, 308

Ambracia, *21*, 96, 98–99, 112, *181*

Amphilochia, 32, 94, 96, 98–99

Amphipolis: aftermath of Peloponnesian War, 298; Brasidas captures, 32, 119, 140; Cleon and Brasidas killed at, 32, 83, 119, 150, 151, 228, 295; and exile of Thucydides, 119, 140; hoplite battle at, 127, 150–51; map, *181*; and Peace of Nicias, 83, 150, 151; role of Athenian cavalry, 228; Socrates at, 17; Thucydides fails to save, 114

Anactorium, *21*, 94, *95*, *181*

ancestral oaths, 109, 168

ancient medicine, *see* plague

Androcles, 121, 295

Andros, 97, 279

Antiochus, 278, 280, 284

Antiphon, 8, 294, 295

Arcadia, *21, 95, 181*, 273

Archidamian War: chronology, 31–32; vs. Ionian War, 272

Archidamus (Spartan king): about, 319; leads Attic invasions, 25, 50, 57, 220; at outbreak of Peloponnesian War, 14, 24–25, 293; at Plataea, 167, 168, 169, 170–72; Thucydides' view, 53–54; warns about war's cost, 41, 283, 303

Archilochus, 306

Arginusae: aftermath of battle, 76, 282; Athenian fleet size, 264; Athenian victory, 34, 114, 140, 249, 281–82, 303; casualties, 247; as a major battle of Ionian War, 283; map, *279*

Argolid, *see* Argos

Argos: about, 315; Alcibiades at, 101, 120, 121; Alcibiades urges anti-Spartan alliance with Athens and Mantinea, 33, 152, 155, 233; Athenian interest in, 109, 259; casualties, 109; civil strife, 33, 104, 297; contribution to Peloponnesian fleet, 273; and long wall concept, 26; maps, *21, 28*; renews border war with Epidaurus, 33, 110; as Spartan target, 97, 186

Aristides, 15, 140

Aristocrates, 286

Aristogenes, 286

Ariston, 274

Aristophanes: about, 6, 319; aftermath of Peloponnesian War, 298; describes Athenian sea power, 266; describes trireme rowers, 240; as fifth-century Greek, 294; plays, 56, 102, 294, 308; remarks on conditions in wartime Athens, 68; view of Athenian naval superiority, 255; view of Cleon, 116; view of Cleonymus, 145; views on agriculture, 37, 38–39, 56; views on hoplites, 15, 37, 149; and war, 134, 308

Aristotle, 182, 247, 302, 304

Asclepius, 85, 87

Asia Minor, *see* Ionia

Asopius, 295

asymmetrical war, 89–123

Athenian War, 6; *see also* Peloponnesian War

Athenianism: defined, 14

Athens: Aegospotami defeat, 72, 283–87; aftermath of Peloponnesian War, 290–93, 298; Alcibiades urges anti-Spartan alliance with Argos and Mantinea, 33, 152, 155, 233; vs. America today, 8–9; antipathy toward, 8–9, 13,

15; Arginusae victory, 34, 114, 140, 249, 281–83, 303; attacks Syracuse, *215*; Attic agricultural land ravaged, 35–37, 39, 41, 44–45, 53–57, 62; bases established around Peloponnese, 92, 94, 111, 118, 123, 259–60, 304; citizen behavior at Lysander's approach, 101, 189, 286; constructs new fleet after Sicilian loss, 34, 275, 281; Cynossema victory, 34, 102, 241, 250, 264, 275, 276, 280, 283; Cyzicus victory, 34, 102, 277, 278, 280; Delium defeat, 32, 76, 115, 127–32, 135, 176, 189, 193, 201; desire to avoid pitched battles, 43, 45, 61, 124, 147; early fleet activities, 31, 43, 89, 93–97, 104, 105, 266–69; Epipolae defeat, 34, 212, 213, 214, 216; exacts forced contributions from wealthy citizens, 251–52, 262, 263; financial issues, 41, 251–52, 262–63, 271, 273, 303, 304; fleet destroyed at Aegospotami, 72, 283; fleet strength, 23, 249–51; fourth-century vs. fifth-century, 290–94; government, 17, 27, 102, 104, 105, 290, 311; Great Harbor defeat, 34, 214, 218, 219, 241, 242, 254, 271–72, 273; grievances against Peloponnesians, 19–20; impact of Peloponnesian War, 5, 272, 294–95, 296, 297; initial military strategy, 26–30; lawlessness of Athenians, 101–2; and Long Walls, 8, 26, *51*, 69, 266, 267, 287, 290, 291; maps, *21, 28, 51, 69, 95*; military manpower, 81, 115, 201, 301–3; military strength, 16, 27, 29, 105, 116–17, 147, 148, 205–6, 217; occupies Pylos, 32, 102, 112, 113, 116, 117, 118, 125, 151; oligarchic revolution, 34, 226, 263; during Peace of Nicias, 203–4; Peloponnesian grievances against, 19–20; Peloponnesian War summary, 16, 18–20; population growth, 27; problems accommodating Attican refugees, 45–46, 48, 65, 66–68, 70–71; receives peace feelers from Sparta, 277, 282; reconciles with Sparta after Peloponnesian War, 291; role of assembly, 47, 102, 140, 185, 190, 202, 214, 216, 217, 241, 277, 307, 311; role of cavalry, 208, 209, 210–12, 225–26, 228, 231–32; and root causes of Peloponnesian War, 13–14, 15–16; scope of Sicilian loss, 202, 219–21, 222, 223, 250, 271; sea battles against Peloponnesians after Sicily, 275–78, *279*, 280–85; siege against Melos, 33, 94, 97, 102, 121, 176, 185, 186–88, 189, 199, 204, 272; siege against Mytilene, 32, 105–6, 173, 176, 185, 186, 189, 254; vs. Sparta (characteristics), 6, 9, 14, 15, 18, 19, 26, 27, 29, 83, 243–44, 267, 307; Sphacteria victory, 32, 91, 113, 114, 116, 117, 125, 147, 149, 151, 152, 301; and spread of democracy, 13–14; surrenders, 34, 286–87; terror against innocents,

186–89; two-front war, 52, 125, 201; urban dwellers vs. Attic farmers, 42; war readiness, 40; at war's end, 72–73, 189; wealth of, 16–17, 25–26, 27; why it lost the war, 292–94; why Sparta triumphed, 309–12

Attica: about, 53–54, 315; after Peloponnesian War, 290, 297; maps, 21, 28, 51, 69, 181; olive trees, vineyards, and grain fields, 35–37, 39, 41, 53–57, 62; Peloponnesian invasions, 15, 19–20, 25, 31, 32, 35, 36, 40, 48–52, 57, 58, 62, 70, 75, 89, 123, 124, 147, 152, 217

Bacchus, 85
Beloch, Julius, 30
Bengston, Hermann, 30
betrayals, 103–5
Black Death, 71, 79; see also plague
Boeotia: about, 315; after Peloponnesian War, 291; and battle of Coronea, 41, 63, 125, 126, 148, 165; and battle of Oinophyta, 38; called "dancing floor of war," 275; contribution to Peloponnesian fleet, 273; defeats Athenians at Delium, 32, 125–31; in First Peloponnesian War, 19, 41; maps, 21, 51, 69, 95, 181; military strength, 22; and Mycalessus, 189–90; razes walls of Thespiae, 32, 160; role in Attic plundering, 42, 48, 236; role of cavalry, 22, 42, 225, 228; role of Demosthenes, 112; as Spartan ally and Athenian enemy, 20, 52, 127, 165, 194; see also Chaeronea; Delium; Leuctra; Thebes

Boeotian vs. Theban: defined, 127
Brasidas: about, 118–20, 319; and Acanthus, 194; captures Amphipolis, 32, 119, 140; and close-order ranks, 138; death at Amphipolis, 32, 83, 119, 150, 151, 228, 295; vs. Demosthenes, 118, 120; as leader, 11, 96, 113, 140, 278, 306, 307; reflects on earlier Spartan naïveté, 40; and sieges, 185; slaughter at Lecythus, 191; Thucydides' view, 8, 83; unconventional tactics, 111, 118–19, 184, 201; use of helots, 118–19, 302; view of Peloponnesian vs. Athenian naval strategies, 255

bubonic plague, 71, 75; see also plague
Busolt, Georg, 30
Byzantium: Athenians seek to regain, 34, 199, 284; map, 28

Caesar, Julius, 7, 171, 216, 265
Callicratidas, 34, 256, 281, 286, 295
Caria, 28, 97
Carthage, 139, 222, 229–30, 273

Catana, Sicily, 208, 209, 210, 211, 222, 231
cavalry: cost issues, 224–27; description, 223–24; Greek deference for horse, 224; vs. hoplites, 224, 225, 226, 301; issue of horse pasturage, 224, 225; in Peloponnesian War, 227–29; role in Sicilian expedition, 208, 209, 210–12, 225–26, 228, 231–32

Cedreae, 177, 189
centuries: and system of dating, 293–94
Cephallenia, 28, 117, 181, 267
Chabrias, 307
Chaeronea, 164, 182, 292
Chalcedon, 177, 199, 284, 295
Chalcidaeus, 295
Chalcidice, 91, 104, 110, 181, 184
Chares, 307
Charoeades, 295
chattel, see slaves and slavery
Cheonymus, 48
Chios, 28, 109–10, 191, 235, 275, 279, 297
Churchill, Winston, 83, 135
Cinadon, 299
city-states: antipathy toward Athens, 15; birth of, 105; on eve of Peloponnesian War, 49; losses in Peloponnesian War, 297; as targets in Peloponnesian War, 94, 97; traditional battle protocol, 133; see also Athens; Sparta

civil war: Peloponnesian War as, 10–12
class: in Greek warfare, 75, 91, 92–93, 107, 143, 205
Cleinias, 63, 125, 145
Cleomedes, 186
Cleomenes, 58
Cleon: about, 320; death at Amphipolis, 32, 83, 135, 137, 150, 151, 228, 295; joins Demosthenes at Sphacteria, 114; as leader, 11, 48, 52, 116–17, 118, 140, 306, 307; and Mytilene, 106, 179; vs. Pericles and Nicias, 116; Thucydides' view, 83, 116

Cleonymus, 48, 131, 135, 145
Cleophon, 48, 277, 295
close-order ranks, 90, 137–40, 159, 223; see also pitched battles

Cnidus, 31, 291
coalition warfare, 159–60
Conon, 254, 280, 281, 286
Constantinople, 75, 87, 180
Corcyra: Athenian role, 19, 20, 94, 103, 118, 259, 267; casualties, 109, 191, 248; civil strife, 104, 109, 201, 297; fleet strength, 20, 23, 106; maps, 28, 181; sea battle with Corinth, 218, 245, 248, 255; siege of Epidamnus, 175, 182; Thucydides' interest, 106–9

Corfu, *see* Corcyra

Corinth: about, 315; aftermath of Peloponnesian War, 298; in First Peloponnesian War, 19; fleet strength, 23, 273; grievances against Athens, 12, 13, 15, 19; maps, *21, 28, 95, 181*; sea battle with Corcyra, 218, 245, 248, 255; as Spartan ally, 109; at Syracuse, 214, 273–74

Coronea, 41, 63, 125, 126, 148, 165

Cratippus, 31, 291

crops, agricultural: attacks on, 35–37, 39, 41, 44–45, 53–57, 62

Cunaxa, 83, 146

Cynossema: Athenian fleet size, 264; Athenian victory, 34, 102, 241, 250, 264, 275, 276, 280, 283; casualties, 275; as a major battle of Ionian War, 241, 283; map, *279*

Cyrus the Younger, 34, 83, 146, 273, 303, 320

Cythera, 94, *95*, 96, 117, 151, *181*, 267

Cyzicus: aftermath, 273, 278; Athenian victory, 34, 102, 277, 278, 280; casualties, 275; death of Mindarus, 242, 277, 284, 286, 295; as a major battle of Ionian War, 241, 283; map, *279*

Darius (Persian king), 11; *see also* Persian Wars

Decelea: about, 16, 315; Isocrates' view, 292; King Agis at, 43, 60, 103, 235, 267; maps, *51, 181*; role of Athenian cavalry, 228; Spartan garrison, 33, 60, 64, 72, 103, 121, 124, 236, 275

Delbrück, Hans, 60, 61

Delian League, 290

Delium: battle aftermath, 131–32, 300; Boeotian coalition problems, 159–60; Boeotians defeat Athenians, 32, 76, 115, 127–32, 135, 176, 189, 193, 201; casualties, 115, 135, 145; civil strife, 104; death of Hippocrates, 5, 135, 140, 295; hoplites vs. light-armed auxiliary fighters at, 142–43; as large set-piece pitched battle, 90, 124–32, 134, 141, 144, 153; map, *181*; role of Athenian cavalry, 228; role of Demosthenes, 112; role of Pagondas, 306; Socrates at, 17, 124, 129, 131, 145; Theban farmers at, 126; Thespian hoplites at, 149, 160

Delos, *28*, 85, 110

democracies, 13–14, 102, 104, 105, 290, 311

democracy: defined, 316

Demosthenes (Athenian general): about, 320; vs. Brasidas, 118, 120; conducts campaigns in Aetolia and Amphilochia, 32, 97–98; death of, 34, 112, 220, 300; fortifies Athenian base at Pylos, 112, 113, 306; joined by Cleon at Sphacteria, 114; as leader, 112, 118, 306, 307; role in

Delium campaign, 125, 126; sent to Sicily, 33, 112, 217–18, 219, 232; unconventional tactics, 111, 112–13, 116–17

Demosthenes (orator), 292, 300

destruction of crops, 35–37, 39, 41, 44–45, 53–57, 62

Diitrephes, 189–90

Diodorus: about, 320; and battle of Delium, 129; on cause of Athens plague, 84; death accounts, 296; description of Great Harbor battle, 241; description of trireme battles, 254; view of Arginusae battle, 281; view of Athenian defeat on Sicily, 220, 236

Diodotus, 179

Diomedon, 286

Dionysius, 230

Dionysodoros, 307

Dionysus, 85

disease, *see* plague

drachmas: defined, 316

Egypt, 268

Eion, 140, 175, *181*

Elis, *21*, 24, 33, 94, *95*, 96, 152, *181*

Epaminondas, 134, 140, 141, 154, 159, 199, 275, 298, 307

Ephesus, 226, *279*, 280

ephors, 24, 118

Epidamnus, 175, 182

Epidaurus: Athenian naval attack, 70, 94, 251; and gods of medical cures, 85; maps, *95, 181*; renews border war with Argos, 33, 110

Epipolae: Athenian defeat, 34, 212, 213, 214, 216

Epitadas, 295

Erasinides, 286

Eretria, *181*, 275, *279*, 280

Erianthos, 287

Euboea, *21, 28*, 69, 235, 236, *279*

Euripides: about, 6; as antiwar poet, 220; death of, 294; as fifth-century Greek, 294; plays, 44, 76, 102, 132, 182–83, 188–89, 294, 308; purported polygamy, 84; view of farmers, 39; view of Peloponnesian War, 17–18

Eurylochus, 295

Eurymedon, 108, 109, 112, 126, 242, 295

Euthydemus, 295

farmland: attacks on, 35–37, 39, 41, 44–45, 53–57, 62

fire: as siege tactic, 193

First Peloponnesian War, 15, 19, 30, 40, 93

fortifications: postwar, 305–6; *see also* siegecraft; walls

friendly-fire casualties, 129–30

Golden Age of Greece: Peloponnesian War as form of sabotage, 10–11; Peloponnesian War ends, 5–6

Gongylus, 213, 233

Gorgias, 294

Grant, Ulysses, 11, 61, 265

Great Harbor, Syracuse: Athenian defeat, 34, 214, 218, 219, 241, 242, 254, 271–72, 273; map, *215*

Greece: lawlessness in, 99–103; Peloponnesian War as form of sabotage, 10–11; Peloponnesian War ends Golden Age, 5–6

Grote, George, 30, 188

gunpowder, 137, 139

Gylippus: about, 320; as leader, 11, 140, 306, 307; role in bringing Peloponnesian relief forces to Sicily, 33, 213, 214, 216, 217, 230, 232, 233, 244; Thucydides' view, 83

Gythium, 23, 93, 177

Hagnon, 79

Haliartus, 126, 148

Hannibal, 18, 265

Hellespont, 241, 244, 275, 276, 316; maps, *28, 279*

helots: Brasidas' use of, 118–19, 183, 302; casualties, 102, 191; defined, 316; Demosthenes' use of, 116–17; as dispossessed people, 25; as former slaves, 116, 183; unrest among, 23, 24, 43–44, 111, 302

Henderson, Bernard, 289

Heraclitus, 307

Hermione, 94

Hermocrates, 229, 249

Herodotus, 115, 124

Hesiod, 66

Himera, 232

Hippias, 100

Hippocrates (Athenian general): death of, 5, 135, 140, 295; at Delium, 5, 125–26, 127, 128, 129, 130, 228; as leader, 307

Hippocrates (father of medicine), 84

Hippocrates (Spartan general), 277, 286, 295

Hipponicus, 126

Histiaeans, 101

Hitler, Adolf, 4, 83, 265, 311

Homer, 93, 308

hoplites: Athenian, 15–16, 27, 79, 80–81, 145, 147; Athens vs. Boeotia at Delium, 127–31; body armor and weaponry, 136–37, 138, 139–40, 141–42; vs. cavalry, 224, 225, 226, 301; characteristics, 3, 37, 38–39, 105, 145, 147, 148; and coalition warfare, 159–60; defined, 90, 316; depth versus width of phalanxes, 141–42; description, 141–46; large set-piece encounters, 90, 124, 135, 141–42, 153–60; at Mantinea, 153–60; as military ideal, 133–35; need for change, 141–42, 146–48, 301; vs. nonhoplite, nontraditional warfare, 90, 91, 124, 141, 147; number lost to plague, 79, 80–81; number who took part in Peloponnesian War, 115; in Persian Wars, 146; Pindar's view, 136; pitched battles vs. siegecraft, 161, 174, 176; rules of battle, 144–45, 300; vs. sea power, 240, 243–44, 250, 262, 264, 265–66; on Sicilian expedition, 160–61, 208, 209–10; Spartan reliance on, 14, 22; *see also* pitched battles

horsemen, *see* cavalry

Hyperbolus, 48, 295

Hysiae, 97, 185, 186, 187, 189, 191

Iliad, 93, 308

infantry, *see* hoplites

infectious disease, *see* plague

Ionia: Cyrus arrives as satrap and aids Sparta, 34, 273; defined, 316; map, *28*

Ionian War: Aegospotami as end, 283–84, 286; casualties, 275; chronology, 34; defined, 275; losses on both sides in early years, 280–81; map of Aegean naval battles, *279*

Iosos, 97

Iphicrates, 307

Isocrates, 292–93, 294

isthmus: defined, 317

Josephus, 87

Kagan, Donald, 30

Kitchener, Lord, 61

Kos, 97

Krentz, Peter, 90

Labdalum, *215*, 218

Labotas, 286, 295

Lacedaemonians, 15, 16

Laches: death of, 137, 158, 295; and Delium, 129, 131, 135; as leader, 307; and Mantinea, 158

Laconia, 21, 24, 181, 298

Lamachus: about, 320; death of, 33, 83, 137, 207, 213, 232, 295; loss at Epipolae, 223; as one commander of Sicilian expedition, 33, 205, 207, 209

Laurium, 53, 57, 58, 70, 271, 273

"law of the Greeks," 180, 299–301

leaders: Athenian vs. Spartan, 83, 307; attitude of Athenian assembly toward, 311–12; frequent fate, 140, 294–95; postwar, 307; responsibility for Greeks killing Greeks, 11; Thucydides' views, 53–54, 83, 114, 116, 120; as valuable military asset, 306–7

Lecythus, 165, 176, 185, 186, 189, 191, 193

LeMay, Curtis, 61

Leontini, Sicily, 202, 204, 222

Lesbos, 97, 109, 235, 279, 297; see also Mytilene

Leucas, 94, 181

Leuctra, 126, 128, 148, 159, 164, 299

light-armed troops, 91–93, 124, 141, 147

Locris, 21, 96, 273

Long Walls (Athens): after Athenian loss at Aegospotami, 286–87; destroyed, 8, 287; as important strategic development, 26, 267; maps, 51, 69; rebuilt, 290, 291; value to Athens, 266; see also walls

Lucretius, 87

Lycophron, 140, 150

Lysander: about, 320; after Peloponnesian War, 290; and Athenian defeat at Aegospotami, 72, 73, 191, 249, 283–84, 285; at Cedreae, 189; and King Agis' move against Athens, 267, 286–87; as leader, 83, 140, 278, 283, 293, 306, 307, 312; at Notium, 280, 284; orders execution of Philocles, 248; partnership with Cyrus, 34, 273; sails into Piraeus, 34, 41; Thucydides' view, 83

Lysias, 136, 286

Macarius, 295

Mantinea: after Peloponnesian War, 148, 199, 305; Alcibiades urges anti-Spartan alliance with Athens and Argos, 33, 152, 155, 233; Athenian manpower at battle, 81, 201; as Athenian missed opportunity, 201; battle description, 151–61; casualties, 140, 146; description of hoplite armies, 158, 159; government, 24, 152; as greatest one-day Spartan victory of Peloponnesian War, 158; as large set-piece pitched battle, 90, 134, 141, 144, 153–54; maps, 21, 95,

181; and rivalry between Nicias and Alcibiades, 152, 203; role of Athenian cavalry, 228; size and description of hoplite armies, 155–56; Spartan victory, 33, 135, 158; Theban farmers at, 126; today, 154–55

maps: Aegean naval battles, 279; Athenian attack on Syracuse, 215; Athenian subject states and allies, 28; Athens and environs, 69; coast of Peloponnese, 95; final Sicilian military operations, 222; invading Attica, 51; Peloponnesian League and other Spartan allies, 21; Peloponnesian War battles and sieges, 181

Marathon, 11, 15, 16, 38, 40, 131, 146, 292

medicine, see plague

Megalopolis, 199, 305

Megara: casualties, 191; civil strife, 104; contribution to Peloponnesian fleet, 273; farmland invasions by Athenians, 31, 59, 82, 298; in First Peloponnesian War, 19; grievances against Athens, 12, 13, 14, 19, 20; maps, 21, 95; role of Athenian cavalry, 228; as Spartan ally, 109

Melesander, 295

Melian Dialogue, 179, 187

Melos: aftermath of siege, 197, 297; Athenian siege against, 33, 94, 97, 102, 121, 176, 185, 186–88, 189, 199, 204, 272; casualties, 110, 176, 191, 248, 300; Euripides' view, 17; impact of plague-related Athenian chaos, 85; maps, 28, 181, 279

Mende: Athenian siege against, 32, 176, 184, 186; casualties, 191; civil strife, 104; map, 181

Messana, 109, 110

Messene, 199, 305

Messenia: casualties, 191; fomenting helot rebellion, 152; as garrison state, 24; maps, 21, 181; slavery in, 111, 116, 302; Spartan occupation, 24, 25, 114

Methana, 117

Methone, 94, 96, 118

metics, 27, 80, 82, 302, 317

Miletus, 97, 279

Miltiades, 15, 140

Mindarus: about, 321; death of, 242, 277, 284, 286, 295; sends Spartan fleet into Aegean, 34

mining: as siege tactic, 193–94

Minos, King, 99

missiles, see light-armed troops

Mycalessus: casualties, 176, 190, 191, 300; civilian slaughter, 176, 179, 191, 300; Thracian mercenaries attack, 34, 179, 189–90; walls breached, 165

Mycenae, 182

Myonnesus, 100, 107

Mytilene: aftermath of siege, 197; Athenian loss under Conon, 280, 281; Athenian siege against, 32, 105–6, 173, 176, 185, 186, 189, 254; casualties, 106, 109, 110, 191, 247, 248; Euripides' view, 17; impact of plague-related Athenian chaos, 85; Paches at, 101; role of Alcidas, 100; seeks Spartan help to revolt against Athens, 44, 82; and Spartan lawlessness, 102–3; Thucydides' description, 105–6, 109

Napoleon, 3, 7, 46, 133, 142, 202, 221, 252, 265, 274

Naupaktos, 96, 110, 118, 244, 248, 255

Naxos, 182, 222

Nemea, 126, 148, 160

neoconservatives, 4

Nicias: about, 321; after Solygia, 150; betrayal of Syracuse, 103; vs. Cleon, 116; death of, 18, 34, 220, 295, 300; as leader, 85, 307, 312; negotiates peace treaty, 151; as one commander of Sicilian expedition, 33, 141, 205, 206, 208, 210–11, 212, 213–14, 216, 217–18, 219, 232; opposes Athenian expedition to Sicily, 204; prequel to Delium, 126; rivalry with Alcibiades, 152, 201, 203; view of trireme fleet, 261; see also Peace of Nicias

Nisaea, 117, 176, 213

nontraditional battles, 90; see also asymmetrical war

Notium, 100, 246, 278, 279, 280

Oeniadae, 94, 181

Oenoë, 50, 69, 176

Oinophyta, 38, 125

oligarchies, 14, 104, 105, 317

olive trees, vines, and grain fields: attacks on, 35–37, 39, 41, 44–45, 53–57, 62

Olympic Games, 33, 152, 293

Oropus, 69, 85, 126, 131, 236, 279

Ovid, 87

Paches (Athenian general), 100–101

Pagondas: at Delium, 127–28, 130–31, 160; as leader, 83, 125, 142, 306, 307; speech, 83

Paine, Thomas, 8

Paralus (son of Pericles), 5, 83

Patras, 26, 120

Patton, George S., 207

Pausanias, 81, 140, 286

Peace of Nicias: broken, 43, 213, 300; chronology, 33; defined, 151; discussions, 32, 147; prompted by loss of generals at Amphipolis, 83, 150, 151; situation during, 82, 97, 149, 201–4; as stalemate, 309–10; as time-out, 47

peace treaties, 120; see also Peace of Nicias

Peithias, 107

Peloponnese: defined, 317; maps, 21, 28, 95

Peloponnesian War: aftermath, 289–99; antithetical characteristics of Athens and Sparta, 6; vs. Athenian War, 6; casualties, 11, 109, 191, 275, 294–97; chronology, 31–34; as civil war, 10–12; damage to Greek world, 294–98; description of cavalry, 223–24; end of, 34, 189, 283–84, 286; as form of sabotage, 10–11; friendly-fire casualties, 129–30; lack of planning for, 20; land battles and naval showdowns vs. nonconventional war, 90, 91, 97–99, 116, 121, 148; lawlessness across Greece, 99–103; leadership, 11, 53–54, 83, 114, 116, 120, 140, 294–95, 306–7, 311–12; length of, 5, 148, 199, 250–51, 262; map of battles and sieges, 181; material losses, 297–98; military lessons, 299–309; as modern scholarly pursuit, 4, 7–8; monetary issues, 303–4; and nature of war, 307–9; number and targets of raiding and killing operations, 94; number of specific naval engagements, land battles, and sieges, 94, 148; official start, 19–20, 25, 35, 48–52, 293; role of cavalry, 227–29; root causes, 12–16; study of major betrayals, 103–5; summary, 16–20, 175, 251; and Thucydides' Peloponnesian War, 4, 7–8, 312–14; as two-front war for Athens, 52, 125, 201; two types of warfare, 97, 107; types of battles and combatants, 89–93; vs. war in modern times, 3–4, 8, 10, 12, 61; ways to relate story, 30–31; weaponry, 3, 90–93, 136–37, 138, 139–40, 141–42

Peloponnesian War (Thucydides), 4, 7–8, 312–14

Peloponnesians: Athenian grievances against, 19–20; Attic invasions, 15, 19–20, 25, 31, 32, 35, 36–40, 48–52, 57, 58, 62, 70, 75, 89, 123, 124, 147, 152, 217; defeat at Arginusae, 281–83, 303; financial aid from Persians, 271, 273, 276, 278, 281, 304, 308, 311; fleet strength, 23, 271, 272, 273–74; military strength, 22, 23, 29, 48, 49, 115–16, 148; role in Spartan triumph over Athens, 310; sea battles against Athens after Sicily, 275–78, 279, 280–85; at Syracuse, 214, 217, 273–74; see also Sparta

peltasts: defined, 91, 317

Pericles: about, 321; Acropolis temples, 17, 66, 102; belief in sea power, 20, 94, 252, 267; children of, 5, 83, 84, 140; vs. Cleon, 116; death of, 5, 18, 32, 78, 83, 135, 295; flaws in strategy of attrition and forced evacuation from Attica, 45–48, 61; funeral oration, 67; as guardian of Alcibiades, 63, 86; as leader, 11, 140, 307, 312; opposition to pitched battle, 20, 30, 43, 61, 124; strategy of attrition, stalemate, and Attic evacuation, 20, 29–30, 42, 43, 44, 45–48, 117, 309; view of pending war as "inevitable," 19; view of plague's impact, 82

Pericles the Younger, 5, 84, 286

Persia: aids Peloponnesians, 34, 236, 271, 273, 276, 278, 281, 304, 308, 311; role in Spartan triumph over Athens, 311; as threat after Peloponnesian War, 291, 309; view of Peloponnesian War, 11

Persian Empire, 5, 279

Persian Wars, 5, 11, 19, 40, 46, 146, 167–68, 197; see also Marathon; Salamis

phalanxes, 317; and close-order ranks, 90, 137–40, 159, 223; depth versus width, 142; see also pitched battles

Pharnabazus, 273, 284, 321

Philip of Macedon, 125, 134, 141, 198–99, 290, 301, 305, 308

Philocles, 248, 295

Phocis, 21, 96, 181, 273

Phormio, 32, 240, 244, 249, 250, 255, 271, 295, 307

Phrynichus, 121, 295

Pindar, 136

Piraeus: about, 317; maps, 51, 69

pitched battles: Athenian desire to avoid, 43, 45, 61, 124, 147; body armor and weaponry, 136–37, 138, 139–40, 141–42; economy of action, 145; as military ideal, 133–35; occasions when phalanxes collided, 149–50; one day vs. multi-day, 144; vs. siegecraft, 161, 174, 176; views, 148; see also hoplites

plague: in ancient world, 80; description of symptoms, 73–76; dread of recurrence, 86–87; explanations for, 70–71, 84; impact on Athenian war-making potential, tactics, and methods, 67, 70, 71, 78–82; and loss of civilizing influences, 77–78; mass burials, 75–76; nature of epidemic, 71–73; problems accommodating Attic refugees, 45–46, 48, 65, 66–68, 70–71; as public health issue, 46, 72, 73, 76, 86; Thucydides' account, 66–68, 73, 74, 76–77, 78, 82

Plataea: besieged, 32, 126, 163–75, 176; breakout of some, 172–73; casualties, 191, 195, 300; city ceases to exist, 186, 297; fire as siege tactic, 193;

Greek victory over Persians, 148; initial assault by Thebans, 19, 20, 31, 35, 48, 89, 164–67, 194; life under siege, 190; and Persian Wars, 41, 126, 167–68; retribution for resistance, 174–75; second assault by Spartans, 71, 167–72, 186; slow starvation, 172, 173–74, 175; Spartan aftermath, 197; stalemate, 172; stone walls, 164–65; surrender, 173–74; today, 163–64

Plato: about, 6; argues for both urban and rural residences, 68; on Athenian success, 105; stepfather, 125, 129, 145; on war, 98, 99, 150, 268, 294, 302, 304, 307; works, 18, 133, 298, 307

Plemmyrium, 218, 232

Plutarch, 52, 85, 86, 89, 321

polis (poleis): defined, 317

Potidaea: aftermath of siege, 172, 197; Alcibiades at, 62, 63, 86; Athenian siege against, 14, 70, 71, 79, 97, 175, 176, 185, 186, 190, 251; casualties, 191; impact of plague, 70, 71, 195; map, 181; reasons for siege, 19–20, 259; Socrates at, 17; surrenders to Athens, 31, 172

Prasiae, 94, 96

Pritchett, W. K., 90

Procles, 295

Procopius, 87

Propontis, 275, 276

Protagoras, 85

Protomachus, 286

Pylos: Athenian base at, 32, 102, 112, 113, 116, 117, 118, 125, 151; civil strife, 104; maps, 95, 181; role of Demosthenes, 112, 113, 306

Pyrilampes, 129, 131, 145

ravaging of agricultural land, 35–37, 39, 41, 44–45, 53–57, 62

Rhegium, Sicily, 110, 208

Rhodes, 91, 193

rowers, trireme: as Athenian citizens, 253; casualties, 246–49; doubling as infantrymen, 257–58; inability to see, 240–41; loss at Sicily, 272; as manpower issue, 252, 264; vs. phalanx hoplites, 240; provisioning, 258–60; during sea battles, 242–44; system of oarage, 237–39, 240

Saladin, 221, 265

Salaethus, 101, 173, 295

Salamis: map, 51, 69; Persian War battle, 11, 15, 140, 268, 281, 283, 284, 292; as Spartan target, 97

Samos, 13, 28, 109, 175, 182, 191, 279, 281, 297

satrapies: defined, 318

Scione: Athenian siege against, 32, 101, 176,

184–85, 186, 188, 189, 272; Brasidas at, 119; casualties, 110, 191, 248, 300; city ceases to exist, 297; impact of plague-related Athenian chaos, 85; map, *181*

Scirtae, 155, 156

sea battles: catastrophic Athenian loss in Sicily, 34, 214, 218, 219, 241, 242, 254, 271–72, 273; in eastern Aegean, 272, 274–78, 279, 280–85; vs. hoplite battles, 240, 243–44, 250, 262, 264, 265–66; reasons for fighting close to shore, 241, 258; role of merchant ships, 245

sea power: achieving, 252; advantages, 266–68; as Athenian burden, 268–69; cost issues, 268–69; reasons for, 265–68; social effects, 268–69

Segesta, Sicily, 202, 204

September 11 attacks, 3–4

Sestos, 175, 241, 283

Sicilian War: aftermath, 229–30, 235–36, 255, 273, 275; Athenian fleet size, 264; Athenian naval course from Greece to Sicily, 261; battle preparations, 82; casualties, 81, 191; chronology, 33–34; first Athenian expedition, 32; impact of plague-related Athenian chaos, 85; lessons, 230–33; maps, *215*, *222*; Punic attack on Sicily, 111; reasons for, 97, 202–6; reignites struggle between Athens and Sparta, 235; role in ultimate Spartan triumph over Athens, 311; role of Demosthenes, 33, 112, 217–18, 219, 232; role of Peloponnesian leadership superiority, 307; Sicily's contribution to Peloponnesian fleet, 273; size of expeditionary force, 205–6, 251; tripartite command, 205, 206–8; *see also* Syracuse

siegecraft: about, 179–82; after Peloponnesian War, 198–99, 304–6; ancient, 175–76, 179; as Athenian specialty, 184–86; casualties, 176–77, 190–91; cost to attackers, 195; description by Aeneas Tacitus, 192–94; fire as tactic, 193; and Greek city-states, 196–98, 305–6; Lecythus, 165, 176, 185, 186, 189, 191, 193; map, *181*; Melos, 33, 94, 97, 102, 121, 176, 185, 186–88, 189, 199, 204, 272; mining as tactic, 193–94; Mytilene, 32, 105–6, 173, 176, 185, 186, 189, 254; near-term aftermath, 197–98; options for defenders, 175, 180, 182, 185; during Peloponnesian War, 175–79, 198; vs. pitched battles, 161, 174, 176; role of Alcibiades, 199; treachery as tactic, 194–96; tunneling as tactic, 170, 193–94; *see also* Delium; Plataea; Syracuse

Sitacles (Thracian king), 110, 228–29

slaves and slavery: as critical to fleets, 300, 302–3; as fate of besieged, 182–84; in military strategy, 111–12; role in warfare, 115–16; *see also* helots

Socrates: about, 6; at Amphipolis, 17; at Delium,

17, 124, 129, 131, 145; as mentor of Alcibiades, 63; at Potidaea, 17; purported polygamy, 84; as teacher, 294; trial and execution, 5, 99, 102, 247, 293; view of Peloponnesian War, 17, 18; view of Salamis victory, 147; as warrior, 17

soldiers, *see* hoplites

Sollium, 94, 95, 96

Solygia, 32, 90, 140, 144, 150, 161, 228

Sophocles: about, 6; after Sicilian expedition, 236; as Athenian fleet commander, 112; death of, 294; as fifth-century Greek, 294; impact of plague, 87; plays, 56–57, 87, 102; view of agricultural ravaging, 39, 56–57; view of Greek hoplite battle, 129; view of war, 6, 308

Sparta: about, 318; Aegospotami victory, 34, 189, 283–85; aftermath of Peloponnesian War, 9, 11, 290, 291, 295, 298–99; vs. Athens (characteristics), 6, 9, 14, 15, 18, 19, 26, 27, 29, 83, 243–44, 267, 307; Attic invasions, 15, 19–20, 25, 31, 32, 35, 36, 40, 48–52, 57, 58, 62, 70, 75, 89, 123, 124, 147, 152, 217; Euripides' view, 18; evolution of maritime strategy, 23, 44, 235; financial issues, 22, 271, 273, 276, 278, 281, 304, 308, 311; garrison at Decelea, 33, 60, 64, 72, 103, 121, 124, 236, 275; government, 14, 17, 22, 23–24, 27; initial losses in Ionian War, 277; initial military strategy, 23–26; and Mantinea, 33, 135, 151–60, 158; maps, *21, 28, 95, 181*; military assembly votes for war, 15; military strength, 22, 23–25, 147; mystique of invincibility, 113, 115, 138, 148; Peloponnesian War summary, 16, 18–20; postwar relationship with Syracuse, 229, 230; reconciles with Athens after Peloponnesian War, 291; and root causes of Peloponnesian War, 12–13, 14–15, 16; sends peace feelers to Athens, 277, 282; and Thebes, 109, 134, 291, 297; why it triumphed over Athens, 309–12; *see also* Peloponnesians

Spartan Similars, 155, 156, 226

Sphacteria: Athenian victory, 32, 91, 113, 114, 116, 117, 125, 147, 149, 151, 152, 301; maps, *95, 181*; role of Cleon and Demosthenes, 114, 306

Spiraeum, 275, 280

Sthenelaidas, 15

Strauss, Barry, 250, 296

Sybota, 218, 243, 245, 248, 264

Syme, 275, 280

Syracuse: aftermath of Athens' Sicilian invasion, 229–30; Athens attacks, 90, 144, 176, 212, 213, 218–19, 220–21, 222, 223; before Athens' Sicilian invasion, 204–5; casualties, 191; death of Eurymedon, 108, 242; death of Lamachus, 83; Great Harbor sea battle, 214, 218, 219, 241,

Syracuse (*cont'd*):
242, 254; as greatest Peloponnesian War siege, 199; maps, *215, 222*; reasons for Athenian attack, 202–6; role in ultimate Spartan triumph over Athens, 311; role of Alcibiades, 146–47, 203

Tegyra, 126, 148
terror: as method, 90; *see also* asymmetrical war
Thasos, 182
Thebes: after Peloponnesian War, 291, 297; antipathy toward Athens, 15; attacks Plataea, 19, 20, 31, 35, 48, 89, 164–67, 194; Boeotian refugees in, 65–66; Delium victory, 76, 160; farmers as warriors, 126; losses from war and its effects, 296–97; maps, *21, 69*; mythical assault on, 175; as setting for Athenian stage plays, 165; and Sparta, 109, 134, 291, 297
Themistocles, 15, 26, 45, 140, 278, 281, 307
Theopompus, 31, 291
Theramenes, 277, 278
Thermopylae, 16, 140, 160, 301
Thespiae, 32, 128–29, 149, 160
Thessaly: civil strife, 104; in First Peloponnesian War, 19; maps, *28, 181*; role of cavalry, 225
thetes, 42, 80, 250, 264, 296, 318
Thirty Tyrants, 34, 248, 285, 290
Thorikos, 17
Thrace: Chersonese peninsula, 276; maps, *28, 279*; mercenaries attack Mycalessus, 34, 179, 189–90; pelast mercenaries, 91
Thrasybulus, 276, 277, 278, 286, 306
Thrasyllus, 284, 286, 295
Thronion, 94, 96
Thucydides: about, 6–8, 10, 321; after Peloponnesian War, 291; on Attic invasions, 25, 36, 40, 54–55, 56, 57; battle views and descriptions, 103, 105–9, 114, 128, 129–30, 139, 141, 150, 151, 156, 157–58, 160, 163, 171, 173, 174, 190, 204–5, 214, 217, 219, 220–21, 223, 231, 240, 243, 245, 255, 258, 276; casualty figures, 110, 249, 295–96; describes Athenian loss at Syracuse, 220–21, 223; describes bloodletting on Mytilene and Corcyra, 105–9; exile of, 116, 119, 140; on human nature, 109; justifies length of his narrative, 292; on military manpower, equipment, and operations, 22, 49, 94, 97–98, 134, 138, 147, 149, 228, 251, 261, 265; narration of events, 30, 31; and nature of war, 312–14; notable passages, 40, 78, 179, 187, 220–21, 313; number of land engagements in his text, 148; as philosopher, 7;

as plague survivor, 67, 72; reading today, 4, 7–8; report on Melian Dialogue, 179, 187; on root causes of Peloponnesian War, 12–14; on siegecraft, 187–88, 190, 195; treatment of Peloponnesian War, 7, 8; on use of slaves, 115, 116, 303; on value of sea power, 265; view of democracies, 311; view of Pericles, 47, 48, 83, 303; view of plague, 65, 66–68, 73, 74, 76–77, 78, 82, 83; view of Spartans, 117, 151; views of leaders, 53–54, 83, 114, 116, 120; as warrior, 4, 7, 8, 17, 114, 294; on war's impact, 104; on why Sparta triumphed, 309
Timocrates, 242, 295
Timotheos, 307
Tisias, 186
Tissaphernes, 236, 321
Tolmides, 93
Torone: Athenian siege against, 32, 165, 176, 184, 189, 272, 297; Brasidas at, 119; casualties, 101, 191
trees, vines, and grain fields: attacks on, 35–37, 39, 41, 44–45, 53–57, 62
trierarchs, 251–52, 257, 262
triremes: about, 236–37, 318; in action, 242–44; Athenian loss at Sicily, 271–72; boarding, 254; building, maintenance, and repair, 260–62, 263, 264; casualties, 246–49; commanders, 251–52; cost of building and maintaining, 262–63, 268, 269; defined, 90; design innovations, 244, 255; fast vs. slow, 256–60; fragility, 244; in Hellespont sea battles, 241; limitations, 257, 258–59, 260–62; manpower issues, 246–49, 257–58, 264; naming, 253; as naval strategy, 252–60; officers, 257; provisioning, 258–60; role in war effort, 147; role of grappling hooks, 254; salvaging, 245–46; system of oarage, 237–39; as transport vessels, 257; typical speeds and distances, 261–62; use of sails, 261–62; visual spectacle, 239–40; vulnerability in storms, 258; ways to defeat, 241–42, 245, 252–53, 255
Troezen, 45, 94
Troy, 175
tunneling: as siege tactic, 170, 193–94

U.S. Army War College, 4
U.S. Civil War, 10, 11, 302

Venizélos, Eleuthérios, 4
vines, trees, and grain fields: attacks on, 35–37, 39, 41, 44–45, 53–57, 62
Virgil, 87

walls: cities where breached, 165; description of breaching, 192–93; disrepair at Mycalessus, 165, 190; and Greek city-states, 196–98, 305–6; Plataean, 164–65; as strategic concept, 26; strength as important, 174–75; weapons and tactics against, 165, 169–72, 304–5; *see also* Long Walls (Athens)

weaponry, 3, 90–93, 136–37, 138, 139–40, 141–42

weapons of mass destruction, 66; *see also* plague

Wilson, Woodrow, 4

Wingate, Gen. Orde, 112

Xanthippus, 5, 83

Xenares, 295

Xenophon: about, 38, 322; aftermath of Peloponnesian War, 8, 298, 309; on agriculture, 38; casualty figures, 296; death of, 295; description of triremes, 239–40; *Memorabilia*, 307; notable passages, 277, 286; quotes Spartan vice admiral Hippocrates, 277; reports on Athenian reaction to final defeat, 101, 189, 286; vs. Thucydides, 30, 291

Xerxes (Persian king), 5, 11, 26, 140, 187, 202, 284

Zacynthus, 28, 95, 118, *181*, 267

Zimmern, Alfred, 289

ABOUT THE AUTHOR

VICTOR DAVIS HANSON has written extensively about various aspects of classical warfare in *The Western Way of War*, *The Other Greeks*, and *The Wars of the Ancient Greeks*. He has also published the military histories *The Soul of Battle* and *Ripples of Battle*, as well as two bestselling collections of essays: *An Autumn of War* and *Between War and Peace*. He is a professor of classics emeritus at the California State University and he has been a National Endowment for the Humanities Fellow, a fellow at the Center for Advanced Study in Behavioral Sciences at Stanford, an Onassis Fellow in Greece, a visiting professor of military history at the U.S. Naval Academy, and a recipient of the Eric Breindel Memorial Award for journalism. He lives and works with his wife and three children on their forty-acre tree and vine farm near Selma, California, where he was born in 1953. Hanson is also currently a classicist, military historian, and senior fellow at the Hoover Institution, Stanford University.